P9-AZW-444

By George Plimpton

The Rabbit's Umbrella (juvenile)
Out of My League
Writers at Work, Vols. I–IV (ed.)
Paper Lion
The Bogey Man
American Literary Anthology, Vols. I–IV (ed.)
American Journey: The Times of Robert F. Kennedy (with Jean Stein)
Mad Ducks and Bears

Mad Ducks and Bears

Mad Ducks

and Bears

GEORGE PLIMPTON

RANDOM HOUSE   NEW YORK

Copyright © 1973 by George Plimpton

All rights reserved under International and Pan-American Copyright Conventions. Published in the United States by Random House, Inc., New York, and simultaneously in Canada by Random House of Canada Limited, Toronto.

Library of Congress Cataloging in Publication Data
Plimpton, George.
  Mad ducks and bears.
  Based on the contributions of the author, J. Gordy, and A. Karras.
  1. Plimpton, George. 2. Gordy, John. 3. Karras, Alex. 4. Football—Biography.
I. Gordy, John. II. Karras, Alex. III. Title.
GV939.A1P55   796.33'2'0922   73–85563
ISBN 0–394–48847–4

Manufactured in the United States of America
9 8 7 6 5 4 3 2
First Edition

Besides the principals of this book, Alex Karras and John Gordy, to whom I am thankful simply for the pleasure of their friendship as well as for their hours of commitment to this effort, I am grateful to the following: Commissioner Pete Rozelle of the National Football League, who allowed me to participate in the Colts-Lions pre-season game in Ann Arbor, Michigan; Coach Joe Schmidt and the Lions, even Jim Mitchell who thumped me, and especially the veterans still with them who were on hand in 1963, the time of *Paper Lion;* Carroll Rosenbloom, the owner of the Baltimore Colts, his coaches, especially head coach Don McCafferty, and in particular the Colt players themselves who took me into their camp and were gracious with their time and contributions.

I am also thankful to the editors of *Harper's Magazine* for permission to reprint two sections of the book that appeared in a slightly different form, and to Andre Laguerre, the managing editor of *Sports Illustrated,* and his features editor, Pat Ryan, who published some of this book, and who continue to sanction these frenetic adventures of mine for their magazine.

I am grateful to others: Christopher Cerf, who was involved with the book at its conception; David Wolper of Wolper Productions, and the DuPont Company, who produced a television special on my stay with the Baltimore Colts entitled "The Great Quarterback Sneak," and all of those who worked on the production, especially its director, William Kronick.

I am also indebted to those who were encouraging about the book as it progressed, and put it together: Barbara Shalvey, who did the transcriptions, and Molly McKaughan, who worked on the book in its final stages.

For Freddy

"... rage, rage against the dying of the light"
—Dylan Thomas

Mad Ducks and Bears

1

This book was not my idea. I had happened to be in Detroit watching the Lions prepare themselves for a Sunday game against the Chicago Bears. I had been invited to watch the practices, then the game, and to stay over the next night for the annual team hayride—a mid-season ritual initiated in 1960 by Darris McCord, the defensive end.

After one of the midweek practices John Gordy came up to where I was standing on the sidelines and started talking about his idea for a book. He was one of the offensive guards on the Detroit Lions, about the best in the league at that difficult position. During the time I had spent with the team, he had been a sympathetic friend and a lively source of information. He was called The Bear because his body was covered with a thick pelt-like thatch of hair, and on his way to the shower, a towel around his middle, one of his teammates would invariably lean out of his locker room stall and call out, "Hey John, don't forget to take off your overcoat!"

Gordy's notion for the book was simple and practical. It was to be about linemen. He had figured out that of the twenty-two different positions on a football team (counting both offense and defense) there are fourteen players who can be described as linemen. He was including linebackers, who do indeed often play head-to-head on the line of scrimmage. It was his conservative reckoning that at one time or another fifty million Americans had played on the line of scrimmage, and that well over one and a quarter million active players (if one counted the nine- and ten-year-olds in the Pony Leagues) were colliding against each other every autumn weekend.

"That's a whole mess of people," he said. "Now my point is this: they're all potential readers. The people who are doing it now, those one and a quarter million, will want to know how to do it *better*. They'll have to get the book in order to survive against these linemen who *have* read it and put its theories in practice. As for the other fifty million, the retired linemen—well, they played in the line at some point in their lives, and it was the best thing they ever did, and maybe they've gone a bit to flab and they'll want to read the book to be refreshed by what it was they once went through. We'll cash in on the nostalgia kick."

I interrupted. "Maybe it *wasn't* the best thing they ever did in their lives. Maybe they hated it."

"Well, then they'll buy the book to try to figure what the hell they did it for," Gordy said. "They'll buy the book in droves —all those puzzled people."

"It all sounds very carefully thought out," I said.

I asked Gordy what he felt I could do to help. I could "put it together," he said. It wouldn't take much time. There would be some diagrams; it would be a sort of "manual." He would devote himself to the text on offensive line play, and for the defense he felt that his training camp roommate, Alex Karras . . .

I blinked. "Karras!"

In truth, Karras was an excellent choice. He was an All-

4

Pro defensive tackle, relatively short for that position—being a massive hydrant-like figure of 245 pounds—but possessed of tremendous strength in the upper part of his body and a startling quickness of foot which carried him into opposing backfields in a savage bustling style of attack which caused some observers to refer to him as The Mad Duck. Since he was not overpowering, but relied on deftness and guile to get to the opposition, his theories on defensive lineman technique would be valuable; furthermore, his mind was freewheeling, full of fancy, and he loved to drift into extemporized skits and monologues, which would help brighten the instructional text of the manual.

I told Gordy I'd think about it overnight, and the next day I went up to him during practice and said I would do what I could to help. The thought of working with those two friends was irresistible. Gordy grinned and said that was fine.

After the team practice I spoke to Karras. The locker room was almost deserted when he appeared; he had been sitting in the training room treating a bone bruise in the whirlpool. He liked the idea of the book. He said that he was very eager to get on with it. "It's important," he said, "that right off we instruct our readers that they should never be intimidated by the opposition." His voice rose in the empty room, and I knew that an impersonation was imminent. Reaching into his locker, he produced a golf hat with a decal which read JEWISH OPEN; he set it on his large pumpkin-shaped head and peered out through the black horn-rimmed spectacles he wore off the field.

"All right, men, listen up! As your head coach, with the Big Game coming up tomorrow, I'm telling you that I want this game. Why should we be scared? We're going out there tomorrow and we're gonna crack heads. They're gonna know they've been in a ball game, right? And the team I'm talking about is the Kansas City Chiefs, just in case some of you people didn't know. Now I understand that a lot of you guys are scared of the Chiefs. I understand there's been a lot of whimpering and players going and getting sick in the back of their lockers thinking about playing the Chiefs. Well, I don't think that's the proper spirit, men, and that sort of attitude is not in my book. There's no need to be scared. Their front four is big, but they can be

5

dominated if we go out there and want to crack heads. Now let me diagram a play that'll show you how I want you to dominate these people."

Karras turned to the locker room blackboard and with a piece of chalk drew the traditional symbols for the offensive line.

He stepped back. "Okay. That's our offensive line. Now here's the Kansas City front four." He stepped forward again with the chalk.

As Karras was halfway through drawing the absurdly outsized circles designating the Chief's front four, Friday Macklem, the Lion's equipment manager, came out of his office and said, "Hey, Alex, what are you fooling around with that blackboard for?"

"We're writing a book," Karras said.

Friday looked at the strange diagram. "Why not?" he

asked. "The big question," he said after a while, "is whether the country is ready for it. What's the book about?"

"Well, largely about linemen," I said. "About their life, how they perform their skills . . ."

"You going on the hayride Monday night?" he interrupted.

I nodded.

"That's the best possible introduction to the behavior patterns of linemen you could ever ask for." He whistled and shook his head. "If you survive, you may want to take on another assignment."

I watched the Sunday game, in which the Lions beat the Bears, but I had an engagement that kept me in Detroit on the evening of the hayride. I told Darris McCord that when I was done, I'd drive out and try to find his party. He gave me directions to Howell, a small town twenty miles northwest of Detroit, to the Kaiser farm there. When I got to the farm I was to step out of the car and listen, and off in some direction I'd be able to hear the general hubbub from the hay wagons; even if the party was a couple of miles across the fields. I could strike out cross-country to meet up with them.

It was after eleven o'clock when I arrived at the Kaiser farm and got out of my car. It was cold and I could see my breath. A full Halloween moon was up, and underfoot a thin ice crust cracked as I walked across the farmyard. Sure enough, in the distance, beyond a dark line of trees at the end of the pasture, I could hear the hollering and the carrying-on—first a sharp scream or two, then a maniacal warbling laugh, as if someone, far across those frozen fields, was being tickled to death.

I started across the fields toward the tree line. The first Lion I met was Mike Lucci, the team's middle linebacker; he jumped when he saw me looming up. "Christ!" His wife was with him, a young girl, pale-faced in the moon and looking dazed, as if she could not rid herself of a disturbing mental image. Wisps of straw stuck to their clothing.

"You'll come to a road," Lucci said. "Turn down it toward the noise. They're on their way back to the farm. We couldn't take it any longer."

"The big ones are crazy," the girl said succinctly. "It's very scary."

It was easy to find the party. There were two wagons— one drawn by tractor, the other by a pair of horses—moving side by side to allow the players to leap, vast hurtling shapes in the darkness, from one to the other with great bellowing cries. The straw in the wagons was alive with motion.

A number of people were walking alongside. I joined Nick Pietrosante, the big running back.

"Who's up there?" I asked.

"Mostly the linemen," Pietrosante said. "Everyone else has got down and is walking."

Gordy's head appeared above the side of the wagon, his hair askew with straw. He asked me up; I declined. A pumpkin flew out of the wagon in a high arc and landed with a dull thud beside me in the darkness.

"We had a pumpkin fight down the road a piece," Pietrosante said. "There must have been twenty pumpkins in the air at the same time."

"Where's Karras?"

"He's probably up there in the straw. The Mad Duck's in his nest."

"The what? The mad duck?"

"They're *all* mad ducks, absolutely certifiable," Pietrosante said.

"Are there any girls still up there?" I asked.

"Maybe one or two have sifted down to the bottom."

Even when we got back to the Kaiser farm, the merry-making continued in the wagons, standing huge in the center of the farmyard, rocking and squeaking on their axles. The horses were led away, moving swiftly from the traces, so that the farm-hand had to trot hard to keep in front of them. A girl got down from one of the wagons, her dress bulging grotesquely where the players had stuffed her with hay. A beer can arched out after her and clattered tinnily at my feet, crushed in on itself by a hand of such enormous strength that the can was almost as flat as a shingle. In the farmhouse a vacuum cleaner started up; revelers were getting the straw cleaned off their clothes.

Darris McCord appeared at my side. "Well, what did you think?" he asked.

"It's a great party," I said.

"It's finishing earlier this year. Usually it goes on until dawn. We don't hardly ever lose a game after the hayride. Of course, maybe it's because everything seems easier after it's over. Most anybody who survives feels he can beat up on the world."

"I never actually got up in the wagons," I admitted. "I walked alongside. But the linemen certainly like it."

"Yes," said McCord. "For us, it's the normal way we live—in heaps."

I never saw Alex Karras at all that night. Somebody told me that he had fallen asleep in his hay wagon, tucked under a heavy blanket of straw like a huge mouse.

Afterwards I kept in touch with both Karras and Gordy, but the manual never progressed the way I imagined it might. My original notion was that the two players would write, or perhaps dictate into a tape machine, various short essays on such topics as "The Pass Rush," "How to Brush-Block," "The Proper Three-Point Stance and Common Mistakes," and so forth. We would get someone to draw the X's and O's of the necessary diagrams, and I would put it all together, perhaps in a month or so. It would be called *The Pit*, or *In the Trenches*, or perhaps *High Numbers* in reference to the 50s–80s category of numerals that linemen wear on their jerseys. We would add a catchy subtitle such as "Or How to Bite Through a Helmet." Then we would sit back and see if John Gordy's prognosis about the tens of thousands of potential readers had any validity.

But slowly the book became something else. Neither Gordy or Karras did their obligatory essays. When I saw them in Detroit, or they came to the apartment in New York, there was very little discussion about the *technical* aspects of football. Sometimes Gordy rearranged the furniture, set up standing lamps, and rushed around indicating the various routes of the offensive guard. The apartment seemed very small at such times.

Karras and I watched nervously. But he did this rarely, and I don't think Karras ever did any such demonstrations. Perhaps it did not really interest them.

What did begin to emerge when we got together to "work on the book" was an irreverent, roguish account of their lives as football players, full of anecdote, reminiscence and story, often tempered by grievance, but always with an underlying attitude of humor—as if their occupations were only acceptable in that light. It was good that the emphasis swung away from the original concept, because I worked slowly with what they gave me, having other things to do, and finally Gordy quit football and Karras got into his twelfth year, which would have made our lineman's manual, if we had kept to that idea, as outdated as a book by Bronco Nagurski on how to play fullback.

Then something else contributed to the shift in direction of the book. Following my stint with the Lions in 1963—joining them to write a book about an amateur amongst great professionals—I thought I was done with such participation forever. But in the summer of 1971 I was coaxed "out of retirement" (as my friends put it) to do a television special—once again playing last-string quarterback, this time not with the Detroit Lions, who felt that television crews would disrupt their training season, but with the Baltimore Colts, who were the world champions and did not feel that my presence, and the television entourage, would unhinge them.

I trained with the Colts for almost a month—preparing to quarterback four plays against my old teammates, the Lions, in a pre-season game at Ann Arbor. Right up through that confrontation I kept a diary and filled up an extraordinary number of notebooks, not because I had so much to say but because I dislocated the thumb on my throwing hand during practice, which necessitated holding the pen in my fist and writing the daily notations in an enormous scrawl which filled a page after a word or so.

Selections from the diary have been included in this book. It seems appropriate; Gordy and Karras were very much a part of the experience. Gordy (in his first year out of football) was my technical adviser at training camp, tutoring me endlessly in the plays the Baltimore coaches had devised, and also helping the television crew. Karras, of course, was still active, the first-string Detroit tackle, and he would be waiting for me at Ann Arbor. Someone asked him how he was going to react to my presence on the field. He thought for a while. He said finally, "I am primarily a very docile person . . . easy-going . . . very happy. The only time I am really violent is on the football field. I'm going to catch him and I'm going to knock his block off. It's as simple as that."

When Karras and Gordy turned up in my New York apartment, shucking their coats, and coming down the steps into the living room, it seemed to me that a proper starting place for their book was to get them both to talk about that moment when they knew they were going to become football players. Whatever their professions, most people can recall such a moment, one special instant when they suddenly know what to make their mark in, as if someone had suddenly opened a door for them and said, "Well, there it is. It's in there." Perhaps a number of people slide into their professions without being aware of such a moment, but it turned out that for both Karras and Gordy there *had* been an occasion they could look back on and say that was the pivotal point.

    For Karras it was a shot he made on a basketball court when he was in high school in Gary. He was sent into a game against a team running third in the state. Karras had no particular wish to go into the game. He was a reserve; because of the athletic proficiency of his older brothers, he lacked confidence; furthermore, the pressure on him was inordinate, the game being extremely close and in its final minute.

"I went down the court," he said, "and they threw me the ball. I don't know what made me do it, but I said to myself that for once in my life I was not going to pass the ball off. That's what I generally did—I'd get the ball and throw it to someone else quick, like a bomb was ticking in it. But this time I took a shot, pushed it up with one hand, and it went in, and we won the game."

Gordy was laughing. He sat on the living room sofa, Karras opposite him. "Oh God," he said.

"I'm serious," Karras said. He seemed hurt that this private divulgence was not being accepted solemnly.

"*Basket*ball!" Gordy was finding it hard to contain himself thinking of someone of Karras' physique on a basketball court.

"No, I'm serious," Karras said. "That's when I found my confidence."

"Okay, okay."

"And if the shot hadn't gone in?" I asked.

"I probably would have ended up as an elegant fop," Karras said expansively. "Maybe I would have learned the harpsichord. At this very moment I might be the Secretary of the Interior, lolling on a sofa in Washington with an ecology student, reaching out from time to time with a long arm and hitting a sad chord on the harpsichord, instead of sitting around with you bums. Of course, *I* could have turned out to be a bum too."

"That's for sure," Gordy said.

"You want to know something?" Karras crossed his knees and put his fingertips together. "I don't think I would have been much of a football player if I didn't have a name like Karras. That hard *K* sound is the key. If my name was Harris, an *H* instead of a *K*, and they'd baptized me Alexander . . . with *that* name, 'Alexander Harris,' I'd never have made it as a football player—at least not as a defensive tackle. It's not a football player's name. Maybe I could have been a flanker with a name like that . . . but more likely I would have turned out to be the Secretary of the Interior."

"Would you say this theory was true of other football players?" I asked.

"Absolutely," he said. "John Unitas. Think of that name. It suggests authority and teamwork. Twenty percent of a football player's genius is the name he was born with. Leo Nomellini—what does that name bring to mind but power and an afternoon of terror for the guy going in against him? Sam Huff? A guy that's going to blow you over. Csonka? It sounds like a blow to the gut. Dick Butkus? Look at the collection of consonants—*that*'s why he's a great linebacker. If his name was Robin Jenkins, he couldn't have made it in the *Ivy* League."

"I see," I said. I was trying to think of a name in football that did not necessarily conjure up such associations.

"Or take the other side of the coin," Karras said. "Milt Plum. That's why Plum was never a great quarterback with the Lions, however gifted he was with natural ability. He was destroyed by his name. His parents probably wanted him to play the cello and take them for picnics up on the hill when they were eighty years old, so they called him Milt. You played bridge with him when you were at Detroit, right?"

"That's right," I said. "He was very good."

Karras nodded. "Of course, there's not much his parents could have done, given that name Plum, but suppose they took out the Milt and called him Jack and spruced him up with a good middle name. Suppose they called him Jack *Kong* Plum."

"Jack *Kong*?"

"Sure. Some of his aunts might have objected—on the grounds that there weren't any Kongs they could recall in the Plum family tree, but someone called Jack Kong Plum would have been a helluva quarterback. He'd talk different, and he wouldn't have played bridge, and he'd walk different with a name like that. He would have started out *right* in football."

"What about you, John?" I asked.

14

"My freshman year in high school," Gordy told us, "I was five feet two and weighed one hundred and nineteen, and I played trumpet in the band. We marched at the games. I didn't care at all about football. I ate hot dogs and looked at the girls. Then I changed high schools. I didn't have any friends in the new place, Isaac Litton High School in Tennessee, and I was lonely. Then one day a girl walked up to me in the corridor and told me that if I went and got a crew cut—this shows you how long ago it was—maybe some of them would start talking to me. A red-haired girl. Well, I hightailed it down to the barbershop and came back with a crew cut that apparently made me acceptable enough so that I was invited to the weekend high school dance.

"Well, that night I got into a fight. I was leaving the place with a girl who was a cheerleader. A guy by the name of Joe Henderson came running out and wanted to know what I was doing taking his girl home. He was a *huge* guy, about six foot eight—"

"Did he have hair under his arms?" Karras asked.

"He did," Gordy said. "He had a *lot* of hair under his arms. He grabbed me. Out of fright I swung a punch at him, and down he went, right there on the street under the arc light. I reached down and grabbed his jacket, and he busted out crying and carrying on and asking me to leave him alone. This big guy, and all of a sudden there he was on the ground.

"Well, I got this tremendous surge of confidence. After that, I didn't play the trumpet anymore. I didn't even know that professional football existed then, but I would guess that knocking down that guy put me on the road to it."

"To think," Karras said, "that you drove that poor nice Tennessee boy to an early grave."

"What are you talking about?"

"Probably a nice big gentle boy who kept canaries at home and took care of an elderly aunt who coughed a lot, and he went out every morning on his bicycle at six A.M. on the newspaper route, throwing *The Nashville Hillbilly* up onto front porches, and he only had one thing in life he truly loved, which

15

was this pretty cheerleader, Margie, whom he dreamed about every night as he lay there hoping his aunt wasn't going to have a coughing fit, and you went and *popped* this guy."

"What do you mean," Gordy said in anguish. "He was a big *thug*. Margie? What are you *talking* about?"

". . . was forced to run away to sea," Karras was rambling on. "Completely driven out of that town. People kept coming up to him and yah-yahing at him for being beaten up by a hundred-pound trumpet player. His canaries wasted away. His aunt got so weak from worry that she died from the effects of lifting a cupcake off the shelf. He had nothing left. Shipped out of New Orleans, and the dope fiends got him in Hong Kong."

"Hong Kong?"

". . . and his last words, just barely overheard, through the smoke of that dope den: 'Save the last dance for me, Marge.' "

"That's horrible," said Gordy. "Ridiculous."

"Hey, Alex," I asked, tapping a pencil. "What about childhood idols? Was there anyone in football you kept a picture of—something like that?"

"Hell, yes. On my bureau top when I was a kid I kept a picture of Bronco Nagurski. It was a sort of formal picture. He was dressed in a team blazer, wearing a big tie with a wavy design of flowers. It was the biggest picture in the room; you would have thought it was my dad. I wanted to be a fullback. In the dark his eyes followed me everywhere. He was the biggest idol I ever had."

"Did you ever meet him?" Gordy asked.

"Well, years later, the season I was suspended and went into professional wrestling, this one time I went up to Minneapolis for a match. I was late, and I came running into the place and the promoter said, 'You're on the tag team tonight.' 'Wonderful,' I said. He didn't mention my partner on the tag team. So I went down to the locker room. Locker rooms that wrestlers use are different from any other—dingy and small and dirty, and always with this very distinctive smell, a body smell that's worse than anything you find in places where football and baseball players have been. I don't know why. Maybe it's because a lot of wrestlers are big, haystack guys that sweat a lot and maybe take a bath once a month. The smell of wrestlers lies in these little rooms in layers.

"Well, I went down there to change my clothes, and in the shadows I saw this older man practicing with a pair of dumbbells, pumping his arms. I kept looking at him. A much older man. Suddenly it came to me that it was Bronco Nagurski, my childhood idol, standing over in the shadows and pumping these barbells towards the ceiling. I could hardly believe it. I went over and introduced myself; sure enough, it *was* Nagurski. He was my tag-team partner. I stared at him, bug-eyed. Hell, I knew more about him than *he* did."

"Was he that down and out that he had to wrestle for a living?" Gordy asked.

"I don't know why he did it," Karras answered. "I always heard he had a fortune salted away somewhere. Certainly he was the cheapest man who ever walked the earth. It's the God's truth that he was wearing the *same tie* he wore when he played with the Chicago Bears."

"Come *on!*" Gordy said.

"I swear. I saw it! It was hanging on a hook right there in the locker room, a big tie with a flower design—the exact same one that was in the picture on the top of my bureau."

"Go on," Gordy objected. "Nobody wears the same tie for twenty years."

"Nagurski does," Karras insisted.

"It would have rotted off his neck," Gordy said.

"Well, maybe this one was made of some special material—asbestos, or something—but sure as I'm sitting here it was the same one." He glared at Gordy.

"That's crap," Gordy said.

The tension in the room was eerie. I always remembered that while the two of them were roommates, and good friends, invariably they had a fight in training camp, exploding at each other on a hot August day—an annual event . . .

"Hold on," I said. I cast around for something to say. "Would anyone like a drink before lunch?" They grumbled out some orders and I went to the kitchen to fill them.

When I came back the two of them had calmed down and Gordy was just finishing a dissertation on the benefits of a beef and bourbon diet. Karras began talking about jockeys' diets. "You know what jockeys do?" he was saying. "They eat so much that they stuff themselves, and then they throw up. I've seen them do it. 'Give me some more broccoli . . . excuse me for a minute. I'll be right back.'"

"You've *seen* this?" Gordy asked.

"Well, there's not much to see," Karras said. "I mean, it's not like watching a five-hundred-pound Jap wrestler get sick." He shifted in his chair. "I'll tell you who *did* turn the stomach. That was Bob St. Clair of the 49ers. He used to eat uncooked steak. When I went out for the Pro Bowl some years ago, I sat with him for the pre-game meal. He said to the waitress, 'Bring me a cold steak.' She asked, 'What do you mean by cold?' He said, 'Cold and raw.' She looked surprised, but she went and got him a raw steak and he ate the whole thing."

"Yes, I've heard that about him," Gordy said.

"I'll tell you something else about St. Clair," Karras said. "He shot a deer one time—Leo Nomellini of the 49ers told me this—and when the deer went down, he ran for it. He dove at that deer and cut it open and grabbed at the heart and *ate* it. Ate it right out of the deer."

Gordy said, "Get out of here!"

"God's truth," Karras said. "Leo Nomellini told me. Ask him. Actually, St. Clair got sick that time. Not because of the deer's heart. Something else. He had the grippe or something. He really believes the raw food idea. Even his *kids* eat their meat raw. He takes the steak and cuts it in very thin pieces for them. It takes him a long time to eat, because there's so much chewing to do—maybe twenty minutes for each piece . . .

"The *biggest* eater I ever heard of," he went on, "was Mack Lewis of the St. Louis Cardinals. He was about six foot thirteen inches tall and he weighed about four tons. He was gigantic. He played at Iowa. He was a great, jolly giant. He laughed all the time. Everything amused him. Someone would say, 'Hey, it's three o'clock in the afternoon,' and that would just about double up Mack Lewis—he'd laugh for six minutes.

"Well, the coaches at St. Louis tried to pare some of that weight off him, so they put him at the Fat Man's table. He'd sit there, roaring with laughter, and they'd put a little thin sliver of steak on his plate. That's it. That's all he had—that, and a little glass of water. But the weight never seemed to come off him; he still weighed four tons. So the coaches followed him, and they discovered that fifteen minutes after his meal at the Fat Man's table, he was at the frozen custard stand down the road from the training camp eating these *pails* of ice cream. He couldn't help himself. The coaches kicked him out. I'm not sure he minded much. He was the best-humored man there ever was. He didn't care if he was in football or not, as long as he had something to laugh at."

"I don't suppose that laissez-faire attitude is at all typical?" I asked.

"It's better to be more positive," Gordy said. "And lay off the ice cream."

"But I always had doubts," Karras said. "Obviously I'm grateful for what football's done for me, but I wasn't so sure at the beginning. I hated high school and college football, mainly because I was constantly being pushed around and forced into it. I hated the whistles that are always shrilling in the background when you're being goaded. I assumed that in the pro leagues whistles weren't needed, so when I finished college football, that was what I hoped I'd heard the end of: whistles.

"But when I graduated I was picked for the All-Stars. I got to training camp, and Otto Graham, the coach of the All-Star team, called us together for a big pep talk. He had a whistle around his neck and he said we were going to beat the hell out of the Detroit Lions, who were the champions the year before, in the All-Star game. He said, 'We'll be the first All-Star team to win against the National League champions since . . . since eighteen oh three.' I wish coaches would all shut their mouths, so we don't have to run our asses off trying to keep them looking good because they've made statements like that. We had a hard day of scrimmaging. Charley Krueger was on the team, and he had come from Alabama where Bear Bryant is the coach and the whistles go from dawn to night. He kept saying, 'Man, this is easy. This is apple pie.' Meanwhile, I was dead. I'd been smoking three packs of cigarettes a day. But Charley, he was in top form and he kept saying, 'Man, this is a breeze.'

"When the scrimmage was over, I started walking to the gym. But Otto Graham yelled, 'All right now, let's all line up at the goal line.' So I turned back and lined up on the goal line with the others. Then Graham said, 'Now when I blow this whistle—'

"Well, that was it, man. I knew what was coming next: grass drills. Sure enough. '—I want you guys to fall down and get up and fall down and get up, fast, real *fast*, until I blow the whistle. Then stop. When I blow the whistle again, I want you to run three steps forward, three back, then three forward until . . .'

"Well, that was it for me. I started walking out across the playing field for the locker room. Otto Graham saw me, and he blew his whistle—which was not good judgment—and shouted, 'Where are you going?' I said, 'I'm leaving. I've had enough.' He said, 'Where are you *going*?' His eyes were bugged. He looked like someone had hit him very hard in the throat. I said, 'I'm going to the Detroit Lions' camp.' He said, 'You can't go there. You're supposed to stay here. You can't go to the Lions' camp.' I said, 'Oh yes I can.' He said, 'Oh no you can't.' I said, 'Oh yes I can.' "

"Man, that was some dialogue," Gordy said.

"Everybody was standing on the goal line ready to do these grass drills and they couldn't believe their ears. So I said to Graham, 'I don't want to play in the All-Star game.' He said 'What?' I said, 'I'm not playing.' He said, 'Well, what's the problem?' I said, 'I don't want to do any of this stuff—these drills.' He said, 'Wh—, wh—, didn't you do this in college?' 'Yes,' I said. 'But I'm not going to do it here.' That really threw him. He said, 'You've got a real bad attitude.' So I said, 'Yeah? How much are you paying me here in this camp? A hundred and fifty dollars to fall down. And stand up. And fall down again. I'm twenty-three years old. I'm going to the locker room.' I began to walk in, and one of the coaches came running after me to get ahold of me. I said, 'Don't, fellow.'

"Well, they finally got me to hang around. The rest of the time in camp I had this bad shoulder. 'Oooh, my shoulder hurts.' Graham wrote the Detroit coach, George Wilson, a letter in which he said that I had the worst attitude he'd ever seen in a football player. He had no idea how I'd ever gone as far as I had in football. I would be of no help to the Detroit Lions.

"Well, after the All-Star game I got to Detroit. Wilson told me, 'There's this letter,' and he showed it to me. So I said, 'Well, that's *his* opinion.' Wilson said, 'You're right.' I thought, this guy's got to be halfway decent. I got along famously with George. He was the only coach I ever got along good with . . . He didn't carry a whistle."

"So from that point on, there were never any doubts?" I asked.

Karras shook his head and sucked in his breath. "I'm telling you, I began wondering about the game again—the first time I ever started in a pro game. It was against the Chicago Bears in an exhibition game in Norman, Oklahoma. What a way to break in! What happened was that Jim David was playing cornerback for us, and he was the roughest who ever played that position. If a *line judge* wandered into his area he was looking for trouble. Well, Harlan Hill, who was playing flanker for Chicago, came into Jim David's territory on a little look-out pattern. The Chicago quarterback threw the ball to someone else, but that didn't make any difference to Jim David, no *sir*. Someone was in his area, so David took a few steps and *whack!* he broke Harlan Hill's jaw. Hill got to bleeding pretty bad, so George Halas, the Chicago coach, took him out and sent in some guy whose only function was to get revenge on Jim David. And he did, too. He hit Jim David and busted his teeth. All his teeth just fell out. I couldn't believe what I was seeing. David stayed in the game, wobbling around, his jersey just red with blood, and it was a horrible sight, especially to a rookie like me. Then Gil Mains, our big tackle, kicked somebody and somebody kicked Gil Mains, who fell over and dislocated his arm. He had to be taken out. Then someone from the Bears got hurt. They brought out a stretcher. By the time they got him off the field he was covered with these sweat bugs that live in the ground in Norman, Oklahoma. Then Rick Caseras of the Bears fumbled the ball and their center picked it up and started to run. One of our people hit him with a flying tackle and completely compounded his ankle, just tore his foot all around. He was sick as hell. He was going *y-a-a-a-a!* The guy's name was Damone. I'd played against him in college; he used to play with Northwestern. I stood around and watched this with my jaw down to my knees. I mean, what was I getting into? It was the fiercest thing I'd ever seen. About eleven guys were hurt in that game in Norman, and on the way home in the airplane the public relations man for Chicago keeled over and dropped dead. Right out of his seat. So I said, Well, maybe I'll give this sport a year. Then I'll quit."

"Jeezus! What about you, John?" I asked. "Did you ever think of quitting?"

"Well, I *did* quit," Gordy said. "In nineteen fifty-seven, my first year, and I was playing first string, the Lions won the championship—the top of the world. But it wasn't for me. I had a horrible time. The pressures were so considerable. And the hassles! Bobby Layne was on my back all the time. I never felt a part of the team. I remember before the championship game we had a meeting in the locker room in Tiger Stadium to vote on the disposition of the championship shares. The lockers are wire mesh, and I was sitting in the back of mine, peering out and watching what was going on. Layne was running the meeting, and he began to yell at somebody. Hell, he was yelling at *me!* 'God damn it,' he said, 'are you going to vote or not?' I didn't think I could! I was the first-string guard, but hell—I was a *rookie.*"

Karras was clucking sympathetically.

"It wasn't only that," Gordy went on. "Every Sunday I had to play against these monsters. Twice a season I had to come up against Leo Nomellini and Art Donovan and get myself thrashed. It wasn't any fun at all. Well, after that first championship season, I went home to Tennessee and everyone I knew from my team was coaching, and they all seemed so happy. They walked around with big half-moon grins. They seemed so happy that I looked at myself, all smashed up and nervous, and thought, What the hell am I doing?"

22

"You couldn't come up with much of an answer, could you?" Karras said.

"Just visions of a future involving Leo Nomellini and Art Donovan," Gordy replied. "So then Leroy Pearce, who was a young end coach at Tennessee, asked me if I'd like to take a job coaching the offensive line at the University of Nebraska. I was offered exactly what I was getting playing with the Lions: seven thousand. Well, how could I turn it down? It meant I wouldn't have to think of Nomellini or Donovan anymore. Of course, I had no crystal ball to see how big and lucrative professional football was going to become. In the back of my mind was always the notion that playing pro ball was just an interim before getting into coaching. So that when that job was offered, I jumped at it.

"Well, I discovered that the pressures are exactly the same in coaching. It was no fun at all. Every Sunday I sat in front of the television set and watched the fellow playing in my position with the Lions, and I felt sick that I wasn't out there. I was being eaten alive by nostalgia."

"What was it you were nostalgic for?" I asked. "The physical aspects?"

"That was a big part of it," he said. "A couple of times at Nebraska I actually *hit* the kids I was coaching. I got so mad that I'd line up opposite them and go at them to show them what it was like. I did it without any pads. It made me feel great."

He noticed me staring at him. "Oh Christ!" he said. "The best thing in football was to really *pop* someone. One of the great joys of my life was to get a bead on a guy and really put him out. Absolutely! To lift him up right under his chin, or under his throat with the top of your helmet and put him on his back on the grass. You've done your job, you've gotten your good grade. The movie's going to show it. That's it. Yes, that's why I came back to the Lions the next year."

"What about the pleasure of winning?"

Gordy thought for a minute, looking at his big hands, and then said a curious thing: "The great pleasure of winning was sitting next to Alex after the game on the stool outside the lockers and realizing that you were free the next day, and that you didn't have to spend twenty-four hours going through the nightmare of rehashing what you did wrong, or worrying why you lost, and that you didn't have anything to fear when it came time to watch the game films on Tuesday. What I'm saying is that part of the joy of winning was that you could just *forget* about it. That's odd, isn't it—that you would go through all that pressure and pain just to forget about it. And, of course, the horror of losing is just the opposite—that you're not going to be *allowed* to forget it. The nightmare. You're stuck with it. You're going to see it in the game films. It's only after the films and being made to run grass drills by the coaches—almost like doing a type of penance—that the nightmare begins to fade. That was the best part of football: not to have nightmares . . ."

Karras said, "That's right. It made winning awfully sweet. Of course, there were the obvious pleasures—the associations you made."

"That was the best part?" I asked.

He thought awhile. "I guess the best part for me was the thrill I got seeing what great football players can do physically— to see what they *really* can do. It's breath-taking to see Jim Brown do things that the normal player can't. That's why the Pro Bowl game means so much to football players: we get to see the sort of company we keep. I guess the greatest thrill I can remember happened to me in a Pro Bowl game, and hell, it was a play where I didn't do what I was supposed to do. I was the *goat*, really, and yet I'm not sorry . . .

"In their game plan," Karras went on, "the other team decided that they'd run take-offs on me every once in a while— that is, influence me by pulling the guard opposite on a sucker play and hoping I'd pursue, which being an aggressive tackle I was likely to do, and then slipping the ball carrier, who was likely to be Jim Brown, into the hole I'd vacated. It's called the 'Oh, shit' play, because that's what the tackle says when he realizes he's been suckered and pulled out of position and the fullback's ripping through his spot.

"Well, I'd been out late the night before—when it's Pro Bowl time in Los Angeles the players aren't much tempted to be in bed at eight—and I'd had a few drinks and I didn't feel good. Consequently, I wasn't as aggressive as I would have been normally; I didn't feel like pursuing that pulling guard. Well, the other team didn't know that, so they called the 'Oh, shit' play, with Jim Brown carrying the ball.

"Next to me in the defensive line, I should add, was Gino Marchetti. Greatest, roughest end there ever was. Brutal. He'd been out with me the night before. *He* had a headache, and *he* wasn't going to be influenced either. So the two of us stayed, and they ran Jimmy Brown right at us. His guards were gone. He had no interference. It's the worst thing that can happen in the sucker play, that the tackle is not influenced. Not only did I have a straight, unimpeded shot at Brown, but so did Marchetti. My greatest desire was to *really* put Brown down—the greatest running back ever—and I was going to *kill* him. So I uncorked as hard as I possibly could. Marchetti must have had the same thought in mind, because he went at Brown like he'd come out of a cannon. Both of us, and we hit him *pow!* You could tell he was hurt. He was knocked back about ten yards, his head snapped, and he was like a buffalo going down; he still had the ball but he was shaking his head. The defensive backs, they saw it too, and they began to swoop down on him, like scavengers, to pick at him. They moved for him, but Marchetti and I, we were savoring what we'd done; we just stood there and gloated.

"Well, something happened. As Brown was going down, he caught himself. He shook his head a couple of times, and as the scavengers were barreling in on him, he regained consciousness and went eighty-six yards for a touchdown! The most fantastic, brilliant run I've ever seen in my life! I stood there, next to Marchetti, and we watched it like spectators. I suppose we should have finished him off when we had the chance. But I don't regret it. It was probably the greatest thrill I've ever had in football."

"I can understand that," Gordy said. "In professional ball, and especially in something like the Pro Bowl, you often ask yourself, What am I doing out here on the field with these great athletes?"

"When I was in the steel mills," Karras said, "the open

hearths . . . well, I can *see* myself there, you know, with a shovel, and talking to Stashakowski. 'How ya doin', Stash?' He says, 'Okay, boy.' I can *see* that; it doesn't surprise me. But to see myself doing the same things those great football players are doing—none of us can really understand or believe that. I've never met a football player who could."

"Absolutely right," said Gordy.

3

Karras was staying in town the next day. Gordy was off some-where, but Alex said he would turn up anyway. He might find some things to say.

When I had been at the Detroit Lions training camp in 1963, it was the year of Karras' banishment from football, for charges of placing small bets on other NFL games. This was substantiated by Karras himself on a radio broadcast, and he was suspended for a season. That summer his teammates did so much reminiscing about Karras that on occasion the training camp took on the aspect of a prolonged wake. Like an uninvited guest at such a ceremony I knew nothing of Karras except by reputation, but because of the endless stories about him he began to solidify in my mind so much that soon I felt a proper mourner at his absence.

The first story about his undergraduate days at Iowa I heard from Dick LeBeau, the cornerback and archivist who collected vivid portraits of his teammates. He would divulge them when he was of a mind—often at such unexpected moments as during a poker game in one of the dormitory rooms where everyone's attention was on the cards—LeBeau's story in his Ohio twang as much a background music to the football players hunched around the card table as the Muzak is to a factory worker.

"When Alex was at Iowa," he would announce abruptly as he sat with his back up against the wall, his guitar across his legs, "Forrest Evashevski, the Iowa coach, took him under his wing and tried to make him more comfortable socially."

"Gimme two cards."

"This big homecoming weekend comes along, and Evashevski decides to take Alex to a big sorority dance. Big deal there at Iowa."

"Two dollars."

"He tells Alex to find something complimentary to say about everyone—*that* was the key to social behavior. So Alex arrives at the dance with a paper bag full of sandwiches. That was what *he* was worried about—going hungry . . ."

"Amos, you son of a bitch, I'm raising you two."

"Alex sits in the back of the dance hall looking out at the girls who all look like drum majorettes, and occasionally he dips a big hand into his paper bag and breaks off a bit of sandwich. All of a sudden—"

"I'll see you."

"—this big girl comes across the dance floor heading straight for him. She has a face that looks like it's blocked a punt. Maybe three or *four* punts. She's damn near bigger than Alex. He doesn't know what to do; he's trapped. So he gets up to dance with her. All the time they move around the floor he's thinking about what Evashevski told him—to find something complimentary to say. But he can't *think* of anything. The music stops, and the two of them stand there just looking at each other. So Alex finally says, 'You know something? You *sweat* less than any fat girl I've ever seen.'"

"Hey, LeBeau, pass me over that can of beer, willya, man?"

I had never asked Karras about that story. I knew it was suspect because Evashevski and Alex did not get along at all, certainly not enough for the Iowa coach to volunteer as social adviser. But it was too nice a line to lose ("You sweat less than any fat girl I've ever seen"), and it would have been a big wrench to have Karras say, "What's LeBeau *talking* about. I don't dance with fat girls—not unless they come up and grab me from behind. The only true part of that story is the paper bag and the sandwiches."

There were others who remembered him at Iowa. Jim Gibbons, who afterwards became his teammate at Detroit, remembered Karras' arrival as a freshman. About a hundred of the freshman athletes were gathered for an indoctrination in Hillcrest dormitory when Karras blundered in, looking for his room.

"He'd just arrived," Gibbons told me. "He was overweight then, about two hundred and fifty pounds, but what I remember is that he was carrying his clothes in his arms. The guy had no suitcase. He was carrying his entire wardrobe the way you carry a tray. I didn't know him at all in those years. He was very quiet. You'd look around and he was there, but he was silent.

"The other thing I remember about him was when we filled in the questionnaire giving our background as athletes. Most of us had a line or two to write—State Honorable Mention, that kind of thing. When the rest of us were done, Karras was still slaving on his. He handed in *two pages*. Hell, he was the greatest athlete at any number of sports who ever came out of Indiana."

When Karras arrived at the apartment, we started talking about his early days, and I mentioned what Gibbons had said about him.

"That's right about the other sports," he said. "Wrestling, basketball, baseball. I was good at them." He'd enjoyed baseball and basketball more than football, he said, because his older brothers played very little of either sport, which left the field to him without the anguish of sibling rivalry. Football, on the other hand, threw him into direct confrontation with his brothers, both of whom were not only older but larger. Louis, seven years his senior, was six-four and two hundred fifty pounds, and Alex recalled him as "mammoth" almost from his first memories. He had an awesome reputation on the east side of Gary, which was the roughest part of town. "When Louis came around the corner," Karras said, "it was like a whole street gang had turned up. People backed into doorways." Louis went on to play football at Purdue, and then with the Washington Redskins.

The second brother, Teddy, was just sixteen months older than Alex, but also bigger, and tough on his younger brother. He was good enough to go on to play at Indiana, where he was captain, and then professionally with the Chicago Bears.

"I learned to run from Teddy," Alex said. "I hung around with his crowd, and when Louie played we'd go down to the football field to watch. It cost money to get in, so we sneaked in over a tall barbed-wire fence in the back of the stadium. Teddy and his friends would boost me up first, and I'd drop down, ripped by those barbs, and stand on the inside of the fence, waiting for the cops to spot me. Then my job was to run long enough and fast enough, staying ahead of them like the rabbit at the greyhound races, so that Teddy and his friends could get over the fence while the cops were occupied chasing me. Maybe it was the ham in me, but I really liked it—the dodging, the speed, the excitement of it, the crowd yelling and carrying on. It got to be quite a show. The crowd used to wait for me every game, because they knew I'd be dropping down over the fence, and I guess maybe the cops knew, too. They never caught me, but looking back, I guess they enjoyed being part of the show. They ran hard, but some of them wore these big grins . . ."

He winced. "But football itself—that was another matter. Teddy was real rough on me. I guess *he* was why I didn't like football then. Because though I was never worried about getting hurt, I *was* scared of doing something wrong which would mean that Teddy would sit on me. He was the disciplinarian. Perhaps he didn't want me embarrassing him in front of his friends. He was tough. In fact, Louie stood around and watched to make sure that Teddy didn't kill me."

Karras leaned forward out of his chair and put his hands on his knees. "I remember once years later when the Lions were playing the Chicago Bears, George Halas of the Bears substituted the guard playing in front of me. I was really taking off and popping this new guy, just murdering him. As you know, I don't see well; I just knew he was a guy in a Chicago uniform wearing a black helmet. But then after this real vicious pop I gave him, I heard this voice say, 'Hey Al, it's me. It's your brother. It's Teddy.'

"I've often wondered if subconsciously I didn't somehow know that it *was* Teddy, and that I was making up for all those horrors and that punishment, all those times he'd sat on my head back in those high school days. And maybe it wasn't only Teddy, but all the discipline guys, the guys who blow whistles . . . That was the man in front of me who I was beating up."

Despite his doubts about football, Karras admitted that he was wondrously good at it during those early years. His father, very weak then, dying of cancer and bundled up in blankets, used to sit out on the upstairs porch and watch his three sons playing in the parking lot, and once he told his youngest that he was going to be the best of them.

"I never could understand why he said that," Karras said. "I couldn't see myself doing as well as Louie and Teddy. I hardly remember my father—I was thirteen when he died—but I remember what he told me as something private we had between us."

By the time he graduated from high school Karras had been selected All-State *four* times—the only instance of this in Indiana—and what is more remarkable, he was selected in successive years at three different positions: guard, offensive end, and fullback in his senior year.

By his senior year over a hundred offers from colleges across the country had come in. "Favors" began to be bestowed. The people at Indiana University sent a crew of professional painters around to spruce up the Karras house; they put up ladders and painted the house from top to bottom. The most persistent offers kept coming in from Florida State, where a new coach had been installed and a crash football-building program was being initiated; letters arrived every week or so urging Karras to come down and see what they had to offer.

"It was very tempting," Karras said. "I'd never been out of Gary—except to Hammond, Indiana, which is eight miles away. I thought, Well, I'll go. I got off the plane in Jacksonville wearing Levis and an Indiana Athletic Department T-shirt. I had my toothbrush in my back pocket. I don't believe I had any baggage. My idea was that if they saw my Indiana T-shirt they might think I was awful close to going *there*, like being rushed by a fraternity, and then they'd really put on a show to get me to change my mind—a big Cadillac to drive down the beach, pompom girls whisking their pompoms outside my door at night, and a lot of Florida State Athletic T-shirts to wear, along with maybe some nice Mister Jax slacks to go with them. So I got off the plane with no baggage and a big pop-eyed look of expectancy.

"Down at the foot of the ramp I could see the Florida State coach. There was no mistaking him; he was an enormous man, about six-eight, and he was close to three hundred pounds. He was looking eagerly at the door of the plane. At that time I weighed two hundred pounds and was about six feet tall. I thought I was pretty hot stuff, but when I stepped down the ramp, ready to greet this guy, I noticed that *he was looking intently over my shoulder*. He was still looking up at the entrance waiting for some mammoth guy to step into view, some guy who had to bend double to get off the plane and would then straighten up seven feet at the top of the ramp, his eyes blinking in the sunlight—*that* was the guy he expected. Well, I was terribly embarrassed. I didn't know whether to turn around and get back on the plane or pretend I was a porter. I decided I had to introduce myself, and when I reached the bottom of the ramp I walked up and stuck out my hand. His eyes dropped. I could see the tremendous disappointment in them when he realized that I was not the Karras that he had imagined. He drove me to the Florida State campus without saying a word. I stayed there for five days *alone*—nobody even looked in my direction. I never saw the coach again until I went out to the airport to fly home. He was there with some of the other kids from around the country who'd come to look the place over. I thanked him for the five days. 'Gee,' I said to him, 'you never did ask me if I could play football.' He looked puzzled. I think he'd forgotten who I was—somebody's fat cousin, perhaps."

"What finally tipped the scales in favor of Iowa?"

He stirred in his chair. "My brother, Louie, said it would be best for the family if I went to Iowa. That was all there was to it. There was no malarkey of following family tradition—going to Indiana because Teddy was there, or Purdue because Louie had gone there. It was a question of expediency. I never asked about it because I didn't want to stir up any mess. The family hadn't had any money since my father's death—he was only forty-eight then—and it was decided that if I went to Iowa things would be easier for them. There was never any question."

"Alex, what would you have done if you'd stayed in Gary?"

"I'd probably be a first helper in the open hearth. I'd have three stripes on my Levis. I worked in the steel mills every summer when I was a kid. I was a cinder snapper—which means that you bank the furnaces so they won't overflow. Also, you throw in minerals. After it's tested, you're told, 'It needs three teaspoons of zinc.' So you throw the zinc in with a shovel.

"I've had easier jobs. Just before I went to the University of Iowa I was filling doughnuts with jelly at Mister Donut's doughnut shop at two sixty-eight an hour. The owner of the place was a big Indiana booster, and he thought he was doing me a favor by giving me the job."

"How many could you do in an hour?"

"I got up to pretty good," Karras replied. "There was a little machine with a nozzle . . . I wasn't the manager's best doughnut filler, but I was coming along. Of course, that sort of job was rare. At that time everyone was interested in seeing me play football in college. Naturally they wanted me to be strong as an ox, so I had a lot of hard jobs. I worked for the city late that summer, and they gave me a big jackhammer to operate. I did that for three months. When I'd gone to see the Mayor, he'd said, 'No soft job for you, Karras. What's this I hear about you filling doughnuts? Christ Almighty! Hey, Felix! Bring in that jackhammer for Karras. No, the *big* model. You can't lift it? Well, get Harry to help you. Bring that thing on in here. Look out for the coffee table! Now Karras, I want you to take this jackhammer home with you and carry it to work every morning, because we want you to be big and strong so we can be proud of you when you go off to college."

"Jim Gibbons told me that you arrived at Iowa carrying your wardrobe in your hands."

"I didn't have any clothes," Karras said. "I arrived there with two pairs of Levis, three T-shirts, and my brother's black double-breasted suit I'd graduated in from high school. The kids would ride me, but what could I do? So I went down to the gym and stole seven T-shirts to improve my wardrobe. They had IOWA ATHLETIC DEPARTMENT stenciled on them, and they were brown-colored. The department thought maybe people wouldn't steal their shirts if they had these real shit-brown models. The shirts *didn't* look good, but they were better than what I had. Still, I felt real backward—and I *was* backward. I hated college. I was never part of the system at Iowa. Since I'd come there from a fairly poor family, I always had a chip on my shoulder about people who did have money. When I got there, I went into a shell and just rebelled against everyone. I skipped classes and sat in my room and talked to nobody. I was alone in the world and as glum as a loner can possibly be. The other Iowa players called me 'The Blue Boy.' "

"Didn't you have a roommate?"

"Eventually," Karras said, smiling. "Mike Nahod. 'Big Mesho' we called him. He looks like me, a lot of people think. He was my roommate one year. Big, heavy-set guy. Big Mesho. Yes, he got me out of my shell. But it wasn't very constructive. The 'Tons of Fun' they used to call the two of us. We got kicked out of the dormitory because we tore the place up. We had this big feud with these guys who lived two rooms down the corridor. In between the two rooms was a pre-med student from Hawaii. A wonderful guy. Every night he was in his room trying to study. We drove him crazy. We were always having these water fights with the guys down the hall, and this pre-med student would hear something and think there was someone at his door who wanted to see him, maybe a chemistry professor who wanted to compliment him on a paper, and he'd step out . . .

34

'Yes?' And *boom!* he'd get hit with a bucket of water, first from one side and then from the other. He was always stepping out into a heavy crossfire. I warned him all the time. He was a terrific guy, but his luck didn't run good. Every time he came out of his room he got hit. I mean, he'd open the door of his room just to sneak a look, just peering down the corridor to see if the coast was clear, and *boom!*—first from one side and then from the other. He was always wet, this guy.

"Finally we got into trouble with the authorities. They said, 'That's enough. There's too much water in the halls. The floors are getting warped. We'll give you one more chance. No more of this or you'll get yourselves kicked out of the dormitory.'

"Well, about a day after we got this ultimatum, Big Mesho and I came in very late, maybe three-thirty in the morning, and we didn't feel much like sleeping, so we dropped in on a friend called Sharman—a gigantic guy, mammoth, about six feet eleven in height—and we borrowed an overcoat of his. Then I got up on Big Mesho's shoulders and I put on this coat so that it hung down over the two of us, and made me about twelve feet tall. It was the damnedest sight you ever saw in your life! We lurched down the corridor and Big Mesho reached out of the overcoat and pounded on the door of the dormitory proctor. He was a sort of Mister Peepers character, about five feet one and he weighed thirty-three pounds. It took quite a while for him to answer the door, and we waited there, rocking back and forth. Finally, he opened the door. He had this little kimono on, and from Big Mesho's shoulders I could look down and see the top of his head. Then he looked up the long length of this overcoat, and when he saw me looking down at him, his mouth opened and out came this little high scream. 'Waaaaa!' It scared Big Mesho. He turned and began running. I hollered, 'Big Mesho, look out!' But he couldn't see where he was going, or maybe he forgot that with me on his shoulders the two of us were ten or twelve feet tall, and he ran me right into a gigantic light fixture hanging from the ceiling. I hit it with my head, and the whole damn thing came down—a beautiful thing, about five hundred dollars' worth of light fixture. Well, that was it. They gave us the thumb.

"I finally found a place to live over an Italian restaurant where I set the all-time record for eating submarine sandwiches. Ten, I think it was. That's when my weight began to balloon up. The college authorities began to worry. They could see that I was getting so huge that I'd be useless as a football player. So they set these conditions. My place was about six miles from the campus. So the authorities made me run to class. Then I ran to the stadium for practice. Then back to class, then back to the stadium for more practice, and then finally home. The authorities were very pleased. The trouble was that when I got home I went down to the back of the Italian restaurant where I hoped nobody would see me and ordered up ten submarine sandwiches."

"What sort of campus jobs did the authorities have you doing for your scholarship?" I asked.

"I was very much into the arts," Karras said.

"The arts?"

"That's right. I was an usher at an art-film theater. I spent twelve hours a day watching foreign movies. In fact, I got my foreign language credits—French and German—out of that experience. It was a lonely time, a real lonely scholarship. I spent all that time in the movie house with six people with long hair and thick glasses staring at films where these very sad men and women wandered around in large gardens among the statues. Sometimes they actually spoke, and that was when you had to really pay attention, though it was all right if you missed it because they were almost sure to say the same thing again.

"But I was also into the other arts at Iowa—especially painting. One of the scholarship jobs I had during the summer when I came back to the college to make up the courses I'd flunked during the winter was to paint the football stadium. The authorities gave me a bucket and a brush—a long green brush. I went out to the fifty yard line and looked up at all those seats —fifty thousand of them—and it was there that I coined the phrase that all stadium painters use to this day: 'My God, where do I begin?' "

"Where *did* you begin?"

"I painted the base of the goal posts. I painted a few

seats. I wasn't in any big rush. My idea was to paint one seat with a lot of care, six or seven coats, so that the son of a bitch really *glowed,* rather than do a half-ass job on a lot of seats. That summer I only worked on one or two seats."

"I see."

"I was also into sculpture. In fact, I was enrolled in a sculpture course. The authorities gave me a job in that class. There was a big wooden box with water and clay in it, where the clay was kept moist overnight, and my job was to dig out a big lump of clay for each student as he came by on his way in. I wore a little bib. That was my job; it was all I had to do in the course. The instructor said, 'Come in every day, Karras, and pass out the clay. That's all you have to do to get through the course satisfactorily. You'll get a good passing mark.' He didn't think I had any talent for sculpture. He didn't try me out or anything; he just figured that I was a football player and couldn't do anything else. Well, that was all right with me. So the students would disappear with their lumps of clay behind a partition, and when they were all in there with the instructor I would take off my bib and have a couple of Cokes down at the local drugstore. I'd check my watch from time to time, and when the class was over I'd be back at my wooden box with my bib on to get the clay back from the students. I did okay, and one day the instructor said, 'Karras, you're doing fine. The way you're coming along you'll be getting a better grade than just passing. Keep it up.'

"For five weeks I never went behind the partition. Then one day this girl came hurrying in. She was late. I'd noticed her before, though she'd never come by my box and asked for a lump of clay. She was very strange-looking and beautiful, and she wore a long housecoat that came down below the knees. Well, as she rushed into the room behind the partition she shucked off this coat; it just fell away from her shoulders to a heap on the floor behind her, and she was *bare-naked.* I mean, there was her ass twinkling into the other room.

"Well, I went rushing in there behind her, with my bib on and all, to see what was going on—the first time I was ever in the classroom—and she was in the middle of this huge circle of little tables, with a student sitting at each one with his lump of clay in front of him, and they were *sculpturing* her. They had been doing that for five weeks and I didn't know it!

"I rushed out and got myself a lump of clay and I took over one of those little tables right up close and started working. No more cokes down at the corner drugstore, nossir! I didn't know what I was doing, but I had a good time. That's the truth. I got a B in that course. It was called Anatomical Sculpture."

"Did you ever turn out a sculpture?"

"Of course I did," Karras said. "I did a frog."

"A frog?"

"The lump of clay looked a little like a frog when I set it down on the table. So I punched at it a bit and painted it green and sent it to my mother in Gary. She still has it. It sits in the house somewhere. It's huge—about ten inches across and quite flat. It weighs seven or eight pounds. People ask my mother, 'What's that thing over there?' 'That's Al's frog,' she says. She's very proud of it."

"What other courses did you take?"

"It always seemed like I was in the basic courses. I was in basic English for three years. I was in general math for three years, too. I flunked the final exam so badly that they kicked me out and made me come back to summer school. What happened about that final math exam was that I was in a fraternity with this math whiz named Phil Lawson. He was a real tall guy, with big thick glasses, and he was a typical fraternity brother—I mean he just loved it. He was a real *good* guy; he got straight A's and B's, and he came from a fine family and all that. Well, I was having such trouble with math that on the final test I had to get a B to pass the course. There was just no way I could get a B in that exam on my own. In fact, on my own I would have been pushed to get a D minus. I was horrible at math. So I went to Phil and said, 'Phil, if I don't get a B in this final, I'm going to flunk the course. And if I flunk the course, then I won't be eligible for football, which will be bad for the fraternity.' He said, 'Oh my.' He was one gigantic dope. So I said, 'Here's what we're going to do. We'll go to the examination together. You get an exam and I'll get an exam. I won't put anything down on my exam paper. You put my name down and *you* do my test paper. Make sure you don't get an A. Just get a solid C for me, and then I'll talk my way into a B for the course.' He said, 'Oh my!' I kept conning him, and finally he said, 'All right.' He was a real fidgety guy, but I kept calming him down. I said, 'Don't worry, Phil. You'll be all right. All you got to do is get a C.' He said, 'That isn't what's bothering me. It's the *principle*.' I said, 'Think how bad it will be for the university, and for the *fraternity*, for Chrissakes, if I can't play football. *There's* your principle for you.' For a week I kept talking to him in order to build up his confidence.

"Finally the day came for the examination, and we went in together and got our exam papers. I whispered to Phil to sit way in the back and I'd go sit in the front row. So the exam started, and all these students started scribbling away in their books. I scribbled away too—playing tic-tac-toe, and drawing some rabbits, and thinking of the girl in Anatomical Sculpture, and just smearing up the paper because what I was going to do when the exam was over was hide mine and hand in Phil Lawson's with my name on it.

"So we're all slaving away, me with my rabbits and tic-tac-toes, and Phil up there behind me working on my solid C, when all of a sudden I heard this *proctor,* some assistant instructor who'd been prowling up and down the aisle making sure that students weren't cheating—I heard him say in this terrible loud voice, 'Phil Lawson, what are *you* doing here?' It was a good question, because Phil was an advanced mathematics major and was into calculus and crap like that, so it was a big surprise to find him taking an exam not much more advanced than long division. My heart just about stopped. I heard Phil say, 'Oh my. I'm sorry, I'm sorry. I'm in the wrong place,' and I turned around in time to see him bolting from the room. He just ripped out of there like a big dog was after him. So what was I to do? I had to hand in the paper that was covered with rabbits and tic-tac-toes. I used to wonder what they made of it— the professors—sitting correcting the papers and mine coming up. 'Hey Charles, I wonder if you'd take a look at this.' So I flunked that test and they kicked me out and made me come back to summer school. Poor Phil was scared half to death."

"What was it about the football program at Iowa that was so dismaying to you?" I asked.

"The coaches," he said. "Forrest Evashevski was the head coach, and Bob Flora was the line coach, a big bald-headed man who always rubbed his neck with his hand as he talked to you. He'd run it right around his shirt collar like it was strangling him. We didn't get along from the start. Maybe he resented Iowa paying so much to get me to go there—I don't know. Anyway, the first time he saw me he called me 'Greaseball' because he knew I was Greek. The next time he saw me he called me 'Poolroom Johnny' because he found out that I was from Gary. There wasn't any humor in this; he was trying to make me feel low. That was a characteristic of his, and I think what he liked best in life was being Evashevski's hatchet man and being asked to tell a player that he was being cut or losing his scholarship money. He always did this with a tremendous smile on his face."

"What about Evashevski?"

"A big tall egotistical blond," Karras said, "who had this enormously low voice that used to scare the hell out of people. He always told you first thing that he was the blocking back in the Michigan backfield who'd made Tom Harmon great. That always got into the first or second minute of conversation, whether he was talking to a thirteen-year-old kid or a grandmother in her nineties. You'd see these people getting puzzled as they listened to him, like he was talking in some weird code. They probably didn't know who Harmon was—or what a blocking back was, for that matter. His ego came on especially strong on the day of the games, when he dressed up in a long tan coat with a fur collar. The team would spend its last hours before a game lying on mattresses in a sort of ballroom at the local motel, looking up at the ceiling and getting psyched up for the game, and then Evashevski would make this tremendous entrance, striding through the double doors with his tan coat and fur collar and that voice that sounded like the bottom notes on an organ. He and I didn't get along. He started siding with Flora and began calling me 'Greaseball.' He called me that once in the locker room, and I threw a shoe at him and got up to go after

40

him. But everybody grabbed me. I don't know why he thought he had so much social status that he could look down on me like that. He comes from Detroit, and I called up a friend from there once when I was at college and found out that he was Polish. So I said to him, 'Why do you call me Greaseball. Hell, you're a Polack!' 'The hell I am,' he said. 'I'm *Russian*.' "

"Russian!"

"Correct," Karras said.

"When did you begin to have trouble with Evashevski?"

"In my sophomore year," Karras said. "When I got back to school I was fifteen pounds overweight, and he and Flora began blowing whistles at me—making me run in place, stopping and starting, stopping and starting, for half an hour after practice to try to get that weight off. They seemed to enjoy doing it—Flora especially, who had this big wide grin on his face like he'd stepped out of a Nazi horror film. You know my hatred of whistles, how when anybody blows a whistle—even a little girl with pigtails—I'm like as not to rear up and *stomp!* All that first month they blew the whistles. Then in a scrimmage I cracked my ankle. It never got better and for weeks I limped like crazy on it. They kept me going. I played the entire opening game against Wisconsin on that ankle. Bobby Knovsky was opposite me—we teamed up later when I got into wrestling—and he beat the hell out of me, the worst physical beating I ever got in my life. I don't know why they didn't take me out. I was embarrassing, pathetically bad. Flora had to be nuts."

"What did Evashevski do?"

"He benched me. He came around to my locker after the game and said that he had never seen anyone play so bad. So I asked him why he didn't substitute me. That was the end for me that year. He benched me, and the team began to slide downhill."

Sitting in his chair, Karras looked distraught. "Those were the blue times," he said. "I spent those long times lying on the bed in my room and looking at the ceiling and thinking those bad thoughts about Evashevski and Flora."

"What happened the following year—your junior year?"

"Well, I came in at two hundred and ten pounds and a

thirty-two-inch waist, and no one on the team recognized me. That wasn't surprising, because no one knew who I was anyway. They said, 'Who's that flanker standing over there? Who's the thin bird?' They started me out on the fourth string. I was eager for it. I wanted to show Evy and Flora what a pair of clowns they were. I tore up a guy's knee and went to the third string, then to the second, and in the final scrimmage I played such a great game that those two dummies told me I was going to start against Indiana.

"It was one of the first times I ever felt good about anything at Iowa, especially since my brother Teddy was the captain at Indiana. The newspapers were full of it—how the two brothers would be playing against each other in the line. My mom came down for the game, and so did Louie, and I knew they were watching me, and then just before kickoff Evy hollers out 'Burroughs!' and they start Burroughs at my tackle spot.

"I died—I absolutely just died. I sat there in this cold rage on the bench. Then after about two minutes Evy walked over and sent me in and I played for fifty-eight minutes. I played both ways, offense and defense, and I just slaughtered the people opposite. I played a little opposite Teddy, but not as much as I would have liked because I owed him a few whacks. We won the game, thirty-five to nothing.

"Afterwards Evy came around to my locker. I was still in a rage about his sending in Burroughs, and I told him so. He grinned and he said that he had done it for psychological reasons. Well, I came off my stool and I told him that he could take his psychological crap and shove it back where it came from— real *pissed* I was, and damned if I didn't leave the campus and take off for Gary. I was real screwed up, and thinking back on it I must have been close to a nervous breakdown."

"How do you make any sort of accommodation with someone who drives you to a condition like that?"

"I told Evy that I would only come back to Iowa and play football on the condition that he and Flora laid off me. In fact, the condition was that they could not say *one word to me.* So they promised. And they kept to it, too; they left me alone. It worked fine. I made All-American and we won the Big Ten title and the Rose Bowl. As a coach Evy was fine. That team, and the one he put together the next year, in fifty-seven, were as good as any in the history of football."

"And he never said a word?"

"Finally after my last game Evy came up as we were walking off the field, and he talked to me for the first time in a year. He said, 'I want you to know that when you first came up to the varsity as a sophomore I wouldn't have taken ten cents for you; now I wouldn't take a hundred thousand dollars.' I looked at him and said, 'Evy, as far as I'm concerned, you're still a dumb Polack.'"

Not long after that conversation, I found out where Forrest Evashevski was living—now out of football, he had settled down in Petoskey, Michigan, where he was in the real-estate business—and one morning I could not resist calling him up on the phone. I had mixed feelings about doing so, because he was so definitively established as a thorn in Karras' attitude about football that I did not relish having it blunted by whatever his old coach might say.

When Evashevski came on the phone his voice was deep, and I jotted down "organ-like." I told him I wanted to ask him some questions about Karras and he said he'd answer them, though he seemed slightly reserved at the start. Karras had published some reminiscences about his Iowa days in a Detroit newspaper, in which he had publically criticized Evashevski. The silences at the other end were long and cool. I wondered vaguely how long it would be before he warmed up enough to tell me that he had been Tom Harmon's blocking back.

I began by asking him about Dick LeBeau's story— whether he had indeed taken Karras under his wing at Iowa and tried to help him socially. But I wasn't more than halfway into the story about the big sorority dance and the fat girl when Evashevski interrupted. "Is that the story with the line, 'You sweat less than any fat girl I've ever met'?"

"Why, yes," I said, surprised. "That's right. Then it's true?"

"No," he said. "That's a real old chestnut. That's a story

that's been around for years. I'd be very surprised if it originated with Karras."

"Oh? Well, I'd never heard it," I said lamely.

I could hear him breathing easily on the other end of the phone.

"What about the relationship between you and Alex?" I asked after a pause. "I understand that it was . . . well, *strained.*"

"I've heard and read all those things in the Detroit paper Alex has said about me and about Flora. There's not much truth to them. Sometimes I think he went to a different school and played under different coaches."

"Oh?"

"I can't pretend that I was easy on him that sophomore year. I never lettered him. That hurt. Perhaps I invited his antipathy," Evashevski went on somewhat formally, "by riding him into greatness. He could have remained fat and sassy and coasted through life if someone hadn't come along to goad him. Perhaps his reaction is based on resentment that he ever *had* to be goaded."

"What happened in his sophomore year?"

"I think someone did Alex a terrible disservice," Evashevski said. "After his freshmen year he must have been told that if he wanted to go on into professional football he was going to have to put on more weight—that to be a defensive lineman you had to be real big and weigh two hundred and seventy pounds. That was crazy advice because Alex's God-given natural ability was based entirely on quickness and agility, not on strength or weight. Whether someone actually *did* advise him to put on weight or not, I don't know; I *do* know that in his sophomore year a football player that I expected to come in to school at maybe two hundred and twenty pounds turned up a fatty at over *two sixty.* His ankles gave out; they couldn't hold up all that weight. We were rough on him. Once I put a hunting jacket on him with fifteen pounds of lead weight in the pockets and made him wear it through practice, just to show him what *fifteen* pounds of extra weight felt like. He resented all that—

44

who wouldn't? But I don't apologize for how I handle football players, much less Karras."

"What about the time you started Burroughs against Indiana?" I asked. "The psychological move that got Karras so angry he went back to Gary after the game."

"I don't remember that," Evashevski replied. "I certainly wouldn't have done it for psychological reasons. I suspect that we must have received the kickoff and our offensive team went out on the field first. Alex played both ways, but he really wasn't very good as an offensive tackle. His great true gift was to move and pursue. Burroughs was probably a better equipped offensive player."

"What about the conditions that Karras laid down in his junior and senior year? That he'd only play if you laid off him, and that no words—"

"That's not true," Evashevski interrupted. "No player who ever played for me laid down conditions. He played only under my terms."

"Oh?"

"No coach could operate under such conditions—players telling him what to do. It never happened."

"What about calling him Greaseball, and a shoe being thrown and all that?"

"Never happened. Perhaps Flora called him one, but I doubt it. After all, Flora's Italian . . ."

"Well, I really don't understand," I said after a long silence.

Evashevski could sense my distraction. "I'm sorry I have to discredit what he's been telling you. I should say that I have complete respect for Karras as a football player. He was a *fine* player. That part of him I understood."

"I wonder if some players to be truly great need to do this sort of thing—construct a collection of fall guys, some sort of imaginary nemesis they can challenge and overcome."

"I don't know," said Evashevski. "The psychological aspects of football are invariably puzzling. I've misread players and teams so many times. There are some players who can sing songs in the shower before a game. All I say is, 'Bless 'em!' —for whatever it is they have to do to prepare for a game as long as they can execute for you."

"One last question," I said. "What is the extraction of the name Evashevski?"

"You mean what nationality?"

"Yes."

"It's Polish," Evashevski said.

"What?"

"That's right. Polish. My mother's side of the family was Scottish, and my father's Bohemian and Polish. You sound surprised."

"No," I said. "Not really."

Gordy was saying, "The first time I ever saw Karras at the Detroit Lions, I remember thinking that he should have been wearing a beanie with a propeller on it."

Karras stirred in his chair. "What the hell are you talking about?"

"That's right. You came in and sat down on the team bus. Your hair was real short and your face was round as a pumpkin, and I remember thinking how round and big it was and that it needed a beanie and propeller on top. You also looked scared."

"All the new people were scared," said Karras. "We were scared of the veterans, and especially Bobby Layne."

Bobby Layne was the team leader then, a veteran Texas-gamecock quarterback whose imprimatur on the team, a type of roustabout devil-may-care attitude, lasted long after his departure. He was a supreme individualist, even to his equipment on the field—delicate little pasteboard shoulder pads and an old-fashioned helmet that looked as if it had been plucked off the head of Red Grange.

"Know something?" Karras said. "The coaches never liked Layne much. He trampled on their authority. When he was on the field, it was his field, not their's. The coaches would work these plays out on the blackboard, precise diagrams which they'd copy into the playbooks for the players to study and learn, and then down on the practice field Layne would give a little yawn and say, 'Hey, George, tell that boy over theah when he makes that outside cut, to take it about fahv more feet deep. Heah?' The coaches didn't like that sort of thing. It made them look like fools. But they went along with it, because they knew that nobody knew quarterbacking like Layne."

"He knew that," Gordy said. "*That's* for sure. But what he especially knew was how to make life miserable for the rookies. Jesus!"

Karras nodded. "My rookie year in training camp Layne got ahold of me and he said, 'Rookie, from now on you just follow me around like a puppy.' In fact, that's what he called me for a while: 'Puppy.' Then he changed it to 'Tippy.'

"I was his personal chauffeur. He'd come out of the team meeting and holler for me down the dormitory corridors. I tried to hide from him. Under the bed—anywhere. But he'd find me and I'd have to pick his car up and bring it around front. We'd start off at nine o'clock and go downtown and hit about thirteen bars. He'd drink nothing but Cutty Sark whiskey and water ('Jes' pass me along a Cutty and water') and he'd make me drink with him. I never drank like that before in my life."

"Did you have to pay for all that booze?" Gordy asked.

"I never paid for a thing; I just had to chauffeur. Sometimes he'd drive—mostly when I was too sick from drinking to be the chauffeur. One night he was driving and I was sitting beside him holding my head in my hands. He was happy. He was singing 'Ida Red.' That was his favorite song, though he only knew two or three phrases from it, which he'd sing over and over. I looked across at him and when my head cleared I could see that he had his right foot up on the dashboard, and his left leg *out the window*. He had something jammed in the accelerator which held it right to the floor, because we were doing about one hundred miles per hour, the car just shaking itself to pieces, down the expressway, and there he was, leaning back in his seat, his legs straddled out in front of him, singing 'Ida Red' to beat the band, and I'm telling you I got down off the seat on my knees and *begged* him to stop the car. But he wouldn't.

"We survived that trip, how I don't know. I woke up for a few nights screaming at the ceiling. So after that I tried to chauffeur no matter how much Cutty and water I had in me. Sometimes I rested my chin on the steering wheel and drove four miles an hour. He didn't seem to mind. He used to sit in the back seat alone sometimes, and sometimes up in the front with me. There'd be maybe two or three guys he used to run with, but most of the time we were by ourselves. He always liked me for some reason. I guess I showed him a lot of respect. I just stayed drunk. For six weeks of training camp I was drunk all the time—drunk and *sick*. We never got any sleep. We'd come back at six in the morning and climb in the goddamn window. I'd get an hour's sleep. Breakfast at seven-thirty. Morning practice. Then I'd get a few hours of sleep before afternoon practice. I used to reek, just *reek* of booze. People thought I liked it. I hated it, but I had to: Cutty and water, hour after hour. The crazy thing was that *he'd* turn up at practice and it was, 'Let's go, men. Let's go here. Snap. Snap. Let's get *going* here.' He'd work his ass off, just cool and rough, while I was reeling around and breathing hard and throwing up all the time.

"He never could go to bed. He told me a number of times, 'I don't like the dark. I'm scared to go to sleep.' Someone told me once that when he was a kid, about seven years old, a car he was riding in with his father turned over out in the Texas back-country, and his father was killed. Layne spent two days and two nights sitting by that upside-down car with his father inside, until they found him. I don't know if that story's true, but if it is, I can imagine why the dark scared him and he didn't want to sleep."

"Where'd you used to go with him?" Gordy asked.

"After afternoon practice I'd drive him—he had this old Pontiac—to a place called the Bar-B-Que, which later burned down, and he'd drink six or seven Cutty and waters. Then I'd drive him back to camp and we'd eat the evening meal. After that, we'd set off again and drink until it was time for the team meeting. Then after the team meeting we'd go out into the night and hit any number of places. One of them was this wild place called The Flame, and when we walked in, the crowds would stand up and yell 'Mr. Layne's here!' and they'd go crazy. Nobody took any note of me. I was just a flunky. That's what you had to go through as a rookie."

"Remember Birmingham, Alabama?" Gordy asked. "First pro football game I ever started in. Layne was the quarterback. They had no facilities at the ball park, so we got into our uniforms in the hotel and rode out to the stadium in a bus. An exhibition game against the Washington Redskins. I had to play against Gene Brideaux, the great end. He was on my back that whole game. I couldn't pass-block worth a damn. He just killed me. Layne kept yelling at me in the huddle, 'Hey, keep that guy *off* me!' Well, I'd been in the Lions' camp two weeks and I didn't know anything. I was just being humiliated. I never wanted to kill anyone so much in my life.

"After the game we got on the bus to go back to the hotel. I sat there, blood all over me, and sweat, with my mouth hanging open, and thinking how bad I'd been humiliated. Then, as we're getting off the bus in front of the hotel, Layne says to me, 'Gordy, you're going downtown and buy us a case of beer.' I wanted to punch him right in the mouth."

Karras laughed. "Yeah, I'll bet that's just what you did—belted him one."

"So I said 'Yessir,'" Gordy continued easily. " 'I'll go up-stairs in the hotel and change out of this uniform—'

" 'No,' Layne said. 'To hell with changing. Go out and get me a case of beer. I want it *now*.'

"Well, I had to walk the streets of Birmingham, or Mont-gomery, or Mobile, some damn place like that . . ."

"One of those 'I hate everything' towns," Karras said.

". . . looking for a case of beer in my football outfit. Carrying my helmet by the strap, the cleats of my football shoes making this big clopping sound against the pavement, covered with blood, everyone on the street staring at me, you know, and when I turned into this store the guy in there almost fainted dead away. I still had my teeth out—they were back in the hotel room—and when I asked the guy 'Could I have a case of beer?' he must have thought it was a robbery or whatever. He said, 'Here, take it.' I said I'd come back and pay as soon as I got to the hotel and changed into street clothes. It didn't seem to make any difference to him. 'Here, take it,' he kept saying.

"So I took the case back to the hotel. I delivered it to Layne, and then I went upstairs to my room, lay down on the bed, picked up the phone, called my wife in Nashville, and said 'I'll be home next weekend.' Swear to God! And I started crying. I did! I thought I'd let my father down. I'd let my mother down. I'd let my wife down. I'd let everybody down. I'd been chewed out by Bobby Layne. And now I was supposed to go back to Detroit to training camp and sleep on the third floor of a boy's school on a mattress shaped like a hayloft and get up the next morning and stand on a chair in the dining room and sing 'Oh Tennessee,' the veterans all yelling at me, and go to practice and try to learn how to pass-block when I knew damn well that I could *never* learn such a thing. I'm telling you, sometimes football is the toughest thing in the world to make yourself continue to do."

Karras stirred. "One time we were in Norman, Oklahoma —you remember that game against Chicago I told you about when all those guys got hurt. Well, I have a real phobia about bugs and mice and stuff like that."

"About what?" I asked, startled.

"Bugs especially." Karras said. "I just go crazy with that stuff. Well, there we were—in Norman, Oklahoma, in August. It must have been a hundred and ninety-five thousand degrees hot. I started sweating my ass off as soon as we arrived there. I was wearing a heavy pair of pants—my old woollies. I had on a sports coat about an inch thick. I was really living.

"Well, we got to the hotel, which had a screen door in

front which was covered with these giant green grasshoppers—
it looked like an army of praying mantises! They were all going
z-z-z-z-z-z-z. Jesus Christ! So I got by them into the hotel, and I
said, 'That's it for me. I'm not going anywhere. I can't stand
those bugs.' So I went up to my room, and I decided to stay
there all night. I had a hamburger sent up. To show you how
cheap the hotel was, the hamburger only cost twenty-three cents.
I got undressed. There wasn't even a TV set in the room. I
turned on the radio. 'Howdy folks. This is your ol' pardnuh . . .'
I lay on the bed just sweating my ass off. There was no air
conditioning in that place, and the sweat just poured off. I was
thinking about the Chicago Bears. About two-thirty in the morning I was just getting ready to go to sleep when the telephone by
the bed rang and it was Bobby Layne's ol' gravel voice at the
other end. 'Tippy,' he said, 'get up here.'

"I said, 'Yes, sir. Where are you, sir?'

"He said, 'I'm up on the sixth floor.'

"So I said, 'Okay, sir. I'll be right up there.'

"So I put on my old woollies and the sports coat that
was one inch thick, and my big tie, and I gave myself a quick
glance in the mirror. My! I had a flat-top haircut. I really looked
terrible—though at the time, of course, I thought I looked real
flashy."

Gordy laughed. "You with a round face and a flat-top!"

"And this huge wide tie," Karras went on. "Which wasn't
'in' at that time. It was Teddy's old tie. I scampered up the stairs
about four flights and knocked on the door. Harley Sewell answered it. Offensive guard. He just hated me—always detested
me. I don't know why, but he did. They were drinking beer.
Cans all over the place. How they could drink that beer! Jesus!
They were all sitting around, all that clique. I walked in with
my head down, and Layne said, 'Tippy, we want hamburgers.'

" 'Yes, sir,' I said. 'The hotel has them. They cost twenty-
three cents.'

" 'The hotel kitchen's closed down,' he said. 'You'll have
to go out for them.'

" 'Yes, sir,' I said. 'How many hamburgers would you
like?'

"Well, they ordered up about fifteen of them, all different, some with pickles on the side, relish, cheeseburgers, every variety they could think up. Layne gave me some money. I said, 'Sir, do you know where in Norman there are any hamburger places open?'

"He said, 'No, goddamn it, find one.'

"They closed the door on me. I thought, 'Well, here I go.' I had to walk out where those bugs were. It was about three in the morning by then. I gave myself a little running start and got out through the door with the praying mantises waiting on the screen. But outside these other bugs started hitting me. They started pounding off my glasses. They got into my sports coat that was one inch thick. They landed on my brother's old tie. I tried brushing them off as I walked. I said, 'Oh man. Where am I going?' There was nothing. I looked around and all I could see was darkness, maybe a streetlight shining way off in the distance. A quiet Southern town, except for a freight train miles away and the humming of the bugs. Boy, was I hot! Finally I took my coat off. I began to trot along. I thought of those guys waiting back in the hotel, drinking out of the beer cans and getting hungry and looking at the door, waiting for it to open with me there, holding a big paper bag with their hamburgers. After I'd covered about two miles, I saw this little beat-up place that said EAT on it. Now it was three-thirty or four. So I went in—there wasn't a soul in the place, just this thin guy with glasses behind the counter—and I ordered up fifteen different kinds of hamburgers. The guy really looked scared. He knew I hadn't come in by car or anything; he'd have heard the motor. I'd just come in out of the night. What did he think, seeing this big guy standing there with these wool pants? Maybe he thought I was going to sit right down there at the counter and eat my way through all those crazy sandwiches, all fifteen of them. He cooked them up, though, and then he handed me this big paper bag, with the grease beginning to stain the bottom. Man, that was a bad place. I said to myself, 'I'm late. I'd better run back.' So I started running. Hot as a bitch. Bugs all over me. I'm just dying. I got to the hotel and through the screen door with all the praying mantises on it and ran up to the sixth floor.

I knocked on the door for about five minutes, and Harley Sewell finally opened it.

" 'What do you want?' he asked.

" 'I've got all these hamburgers,' I said.

" 'We all went to bed,' Sewell said. 'Goddamn it.' And he slammed the door on me.

"So there I was with this big bag of burgers at four-thirty in the morning, standing in the hotel corridor, looking at a closed door. I went down to my room, threw the paper bag in the corner and went to bed. I suppose the cleaning woman must have found them the next day when I was out playing the Chicago Bears. I wonder what she thought. Jesus! Maybe she thought the guy who'd been in that room was a real big eater, some guy who weighed about five hundred pounds, and in this paper bag was a sort of snack he'd left behind by mistake."

"Maybe the bugs got to the sandwiches," Gordy suggested. "Maybe there wasn't anything left in the paper bag."

"Wouldn't surprise me," said Karras.

"I'll never forget the bugs in Norman, Oklahoma," Gordy said. "We played the Philadelphia Eagles there. Remember? The playing field in Norman looks nice and fresh and green, but when you hit the ground on a tackle or a block, it comes alive— z-z-z-z-z—these bugs coming out of there. Sweat bugs, I think they are. You get terribly tired playing in that awful heat in Norman, but you don't relax lying around on the ground, nossir! The bugs will get you. If you get hit to the ground, you jump up as fast as you can. God's truth! You hardly ever see anyone lying on the ground in Norman, Oklahoma."

"We got beat horrible in that Eagle game," Karras said. "I recall it."

"It was the biggest Chinese fire drill I've ever been in," Gordy said. "We got beat so bad it was funny. Earl Morrall and I, the only veterans, and *nine* rookies started the game. Nineteen fifty-nine. I was playing left tackle and the defensive end opposite me kept spinning in one place, and then hitting me again. I never did figure that out. He'd hit, spin in a circle, and then hit again. We were all horrible. The defense had to come in every two or three downs. And most of *them* were rookies, too."

"Yeah, I remember," Karras said. "I did a lot of laughing behind my hand."

"And it was hot," Gordy continued. "But the place was packed with people. Big occasion in Norman. Right behind our bench was a box with the governor in it, and the lieutenant governor, and Bud Wilkinson, who was the Oklahoma coach then, and Gomer Jones, who became the head coach later on, and all their wives. These dignitaries were practically on the bench with us, watching us getting beat, and Joe Schmidt, sitting right in front of them, was getting more and more embarrassed. He and the other regulars hadn't played. He kept shouting at Coach Wilson, 'Haven't you seen enough of those goddamn rookies?'

"Finally, along in the fourth quarter, Wilson says, 'Okay, Joe, get your group in there.'

"Joe jumps up. 'About time!' he shouts. He's really ready to go. He's going to show everybody, especially those dignitaries. He looks around. 'Where's my helmet?' He looks under the bench. 'Who's got my helmet?' The players are all looking at him—*they* don't have his helmet. What do they want his helmet for? They've got their helmets on. They're ready to go out on the field. Joe's looking everywhere."

"He must have thought the bugs ate it," Karras said.

Gordy could hardly tell the story he was laughing so hard. "Oh Christ!" he said. "Oh my. 'Where's my helmet?' Joe kept shouting. Oh Jesus! What the dignitaries had to be thinking! Schmidt began looking in their *box*, which was right there. He was frantic. 'Where's my motherfucking helmet?' he shouted. 'Who's got it?' The wives all shrank back. They didn't want to have anything to do with him."

"Yeah, that was funny," said Karras. "Norman was some town—something crazy always happened when we went there, especially if Bobby Layne was along."

"What about today?" I asked. "Do the rookies defer to you like you did to Bobby Layne in those days—I mean 'Yes, sir' and all of that?"

"No respect," said Gordy. "They come equipped with these huge egos, big money and reputations, and they're not going to take any nonsense." He got up and began pacing around the apartment. "What they're chiefly rebelling against is that first restrictive year we all went through—under the rule of those authority figures like Bobby Layne who made us get up in the dining room and sing our school songs and generally treated us like dirt. The rookies today refuse to do that, and it's a shame because it made you feel a much stronger part of the team after you'd gone through it. The greatest thrill of my life was coming back my second year and suddenly being patted on the back and *accepted*, even by Layne."

"Didn't *anyone* rebel in your day?" I asked.

The two looked at each other. "Remember Carl Smith?" Gordy asked. "He played fullback at the University of Tennessee. He came to training camp in nineteen fifty-four. The singing was going on in the dining room, but Carl was never there. So a group of us looked in on him in his room and he was sitting at a desk, without a plate or anything, eating out of a brown paper bag! In it were mashed potatoes."

"And gravy!" Karras added.

"Yes, and gravy, and meat—all jumbled up in this brown bag, and he had a spoon in his drawer. It still had food on it. He would eat his food there simply because he didn't want to get up and sing in the dining room. The only time he ever wanted to face a veteran was on the football field. There, at least, he was confident of what he was doing. Of course that's a mild sort of rebellion compared to today."

"Did he ever make the team?"

"Never made it," said Karras. "Probably ate too much paper."

"Were the veterans ever helpful in your first year?" I asked. "Gil Mains was your predecessor, wasn't he?"

"Yes, 'The Horse' we called him," Karras said. "I remember the first league game I was going to start as defensive tackle was against the Cleveland Browns. At that time they had an offensive guard named Harold Bradley. I knew about him. He'd played at Iowa—it seemed like at least twenty-five years before *I* got there. A big black guy. Just huge! I remember he used to come back to Iowa every once in a while, and I'd hang around and just *stare* at him.

"Well, I went into consultation with The Horse. I was embarrassed to ask him because he was hurt, and he was probably figuring I was trying to take his job, but I reckoned it was a question of survival. So I asked him, 'What can I expect?' He started talking about Bradley. 'Alex, he's probably the strongest guard I've ever seen in my life. He's going to kill you. You're not going to get past him. He's going to make you look foolish.' Well, *that* wasn't the sort of stuff I wanted to hear. I began thinking of leaving camp!"

"Didn't he give you any advice?"

"Yes. He said that the only thing I was never going to have to worry about playing against Bradley and the Browns was traps. 'Never worry about traps,' he said. 'They never trap.' Well, when I got in that game, they trapped me forty-three times, I swear."

"That's typical," Gordy said. "Those guys really made you work things out for yourself. It wasn't easy, but maybe you were the better for it."

The two of them sat quietly, thinking back on those days. Finally Karras said, "You know something crazy? Bobby Layne was traded away by Detroit to the Pittsburgh Steelers. He ended up his career there. We played them one Sunday, and this play came up where he was chased out of the pocket and ran out of bounds. I was chasing him, really reaching for him, and when we got out of bounds I still went for him. I racked his ass. Back behind the bench somewhere. Knocked a water bucket over, I remember. I don't know why I did it. It was crazy. We got a big penalty and I was chewed out plenty."

"What about Layne?" I asked.

"I can remember him looking at me out of that crazy helmet he wore. 'Hey, what did you do that for?' he says.

"I couldn't have told him. No way."

5

A year or so after Karras and Gordy had talked about him I met Bobby Layne. I was giving a lecture at Texas Tech, which is in Lubbock, where Layne had settled down in somewhat restive retirement from football, working in real estate, oil wells, and one thing or another, and every once in a while collecting himself a big night or so on the town in Austin, Houston or Dallas which got into the news. I heard stories about him from my Texas friends. Certainly in Lubbock he was an institution that ranked with the college itself, or the empty skyscraper downtown that had been nearly destroyed by a tornado, or the big cotton silos. "Mr. Layne?" the cabdriver said on the way in from the airport. "He's the biggest baddest thing there is around here. When he dies, they should stuff him and set him up out on Route 70, just outside town, with a sign hanging from him. People would come for miles around to look. Some sharp boy could make a heck of a lot of cash running a concession like that. 'Course I'll tell you something else, which is that Bobby Layne ain't never going to die off. He's one tough sumbitch."

Just before I went off for the lecture, I looked in the Lubbock telephone directory and found two numbers for a Robert Layne. It seemed too formal a listing for a man known so universally as "Bobby," but it turned out to be the right one. When he came on the phone we made an appointment to meet at my motel after I had finished with the students, and he'd show me Lubbock.

He picked me up at ten o'clock in the evening. We shook hands. He seemed very fit, just as I had remembered him from photographs: the large strong face, the sandy hair close-cropped. He was holding a glass in his left hand, and his voice was high, slightly nasal and querulous as he urged me to get a "leg up"; we had a big evening ahead and no time to lose.

"We're going down to Neal's Barbeque in the colored section," he said. "I'll tell you who's going to be there—Wyatt Ward, that's who. Everybody calls him 'W.W.' I knowed him ever since he was a shineboy at the country club. I like him because he *acts* dumb, but he's smart. He was a tremendous football player, a great running back when he was in high school, but he never went further because he was no good when the quarterback called 'automans'—which is his word for automatics. He says, 'Those automans, they mess up my mind.'"

We drove into the east part of town, with its blocks of one-story white windowless buildings with narrow doors that open directly onto the dirt street, each place identified by a neon sign with a fancy design blinking swiftly on and off, and a grandiose name—The Thunderbird, The Top Hat, The Tuxedo Club. We parked the car and walked into one called The Glass Hat. Part of the building was set aside for Neal's Barbeque. The proprietor, a diminutive black named Shorty, came forward to greet us. He had a single tooth in the front of his mouth. He showed it in an enormous grin. He was delighted to see Layne. Layne pummeled him, which unleashed a short fit of coughing. Layne pummeled him some more. "Shorty, you goin' to put the hurt on my stomach with some ribs?" Shorty showed us the ovens where the spareribs glistened in the heat. "He started out bootlegging," Layne told me. "His stuff costs you two forty-five a pint. *Good* stuff. Right, Shorty?" He pummeled him again.

The sound of a jukebox drifted through a door at the far end of the room. I wandered around while the two of them chatted and laughed. Layne ate some ribs, and also a pie, and then some more ribs, picking the ribs off the oven grill, smacking his lips and mopping his hands on a paper napkin. We walked into the night club, our eyes adjusted to the soft pink jukebox glow, and we could see a couple moving on the little dance floor and one or two people sitting on the bar stools. Layne found a table, reaching for it with pale hands that shone, along with the white of his shirt cuffs, in the darkness.

"Where's W.W.?" he called.

A man slid off a barstool and joined us at the table. "Goddamn it, W.W., you're so black I can't scarcely see you," said Layne. He slapped him delightedly across the shoulders and introduced us. Ward sat down next to me.

"Hey, W.W.," said Layne. "Tell George why you never stayed in football."

Dutifully, it seemed to me, Ward said, "Aw, those automans messed me up real bad."

Layne yelled with laughter. " 'Automans'! Oh, goddamn it, Wyatt, you are something else. What'd I tell you?" he said to me happily. "W.W.'s something, right?"

Drinks arrived. Layne took a gulp of his. "Hey, W.W., listen to this. When we come in here, Shorty was out in front, standing by his ovens, and he was standing there coughing and wheezing. So I ask him, 'Hey, Shorty, you got the whooping cough?' You know what Shorty says? He says, 'No, man, I got the *measles!*' God Almighty. Ain't that grand? I ate one of Shorty's pies when he said that about the measles. That was the greatest pie I ever ate. Look at my stomach." He leaned back in his chair and pushed his stomach out at us. "Shorty put the hurt on me real good with that pie."

People began to collect around the table, and when the chairs were gone they stood on the perimeter like ranchers around a campfire. Layne would squint in the darkness to see who they were, and then would give a whoop of recognition and ask how their babies were doing, or Aunt Sue, or what was going on in their lives. The voices rose, and it was hard to hear.

To my left W.W. said in my ear "The word's around the East Side. There'll be people comin' on in heah through the night to see Mister Bobby. That man is a whizzer. I don' think he know that a man is supposed to sleep."

Layne was telling a story. "I was standing out in front of the hotel and this guy stepped up in front of me and took my cab. Well, I didn't like that nohow. I got into a big ruckus about that. So the next cab that came around had a colored light circling on the roof, and for generally disturbing the peace they took me off to a li'l bitty ol' jail no bigger than that dance floor . . ."

At this point a man wearing a white hat leaned over the table. His hat floated eerily above his dark face, barely distinguishable in the gloom of the night club. I could see the pale white of a toothpick working in the corner of his mouth. He started to tell a story, interrupting Layne's—he just *began*, with no prompting, his voice suddenly cutting in on the table conversation as if a connection had fused in an old radio and somehow the instrument had turned on. We all looked up.

"I want W.W. to hear this," he was saying. "It's a true story. I'm telling you no lies about this."

"Who's this guy," someone at the table asked.

"The man came out of that saloon with a *wheelbarrow*. Now that's no lie," the man said. He shook his head solemnly. "Right into the main street of Yuma. That's the point. There was an old man wearing a bathing suit in that wheelbarrow. He had a beard. What was going on? Now *where* was they going with that wheelbarrow . . .?"

Layne was twisted around in his chair. "My earbones hurt. You talk too much."

The man with the hat lowered his voice, but he leaned in on the man standing alongside and pressed the story on him. The toothpick worked busily. I would have liked to hear about the wheelbarrow in the streets of Yuma, but to my left W.W. leaned in and began talking about Layne again. "He has no patience with someone like that. He don't mind strangers, but

61

he's happiest with friends. We don't talk about football. I mean, he don't take to it at *all* when folks come up and says, 'You was the greatest *this* and you was the greatest *that*.' There is two things that he don't like. One of them is being annoyed by people like that, and the other is not having something to do. He is some lively man. When he takes a trip outside of Lubbock, this town curls up and is daid. Nobody moves. Everybody's resting up. You can tell when he comes back—it's a *feeling*. 'Course now he's slowing down some. He's much more of a family man. Why, the other night he went to bed at one in the morning, and he was still sleeping at four the next afternoon, and I thought he was plumb daid, but he was just getting himself ready and revvying up because for the next few nights he didn't go to bed at all.

"What do we do? Oh, we sit around in clubs like this. Sometimes we disconnect the jukebox and the speakers and just sit and talk. It's real quiet. We talk about his oil wells— he's drilling over there in Oklahoma—and he draws these diagrams on the tablecloth which I don't understand nothing about. What do I know about oil wells? He gets real mad when I tell him I don't understand."

It was getting difficult to hear Wyatt, for the noise around the table, now ringed two deep, was cacophonous. Layne was trying to press some money on a bystander. He literally pulled the person's trouser pocket ajar and stuffed in some bills. "Now you go and buy yourself six hogs, heah?"

"Oh, Mister Layne, I dunno."

W.W. said in my ear, "He and I had a big discussion about carrying too much money around. If he had as much money as Mister Howard Hughes, why there wouldn't be a po' person in the Southwest. He always had a big roll of bills at the beginning of an evening. I kind of broke him of the habit. He was going to get himself robbed; he's so generous a man that the word'd get around. We got an underworld here in Lubbock, sure enough—some characters'll entertain you real good and smart."

Layne caught the end of W.W.'s remarks. "You tellin' him about the Lubbock underworld? Oh my!" He slapped the table with the palm of his hand. He leaned across, and when everyone had quieted down he told how when his son, Robert Jr., had got married, W.W.'s pals had broken into the biggest clothing store in Lubbock and fetched out a fancy pink oxford suit, very lively threads, which they thought W.W. should wear to the wedding. But W.W. turned out to be very particular. The pink suit didn't please him. There was a green suit in that very same store which he'd seen; why hadn't they picked *that* one? So his friends got in there a second time, a risky business since they had removed not only the pink suit the night before, but some more stuff too, so that the store management knew the place had been ripped off severely enough to arrange for more security, such as perhaps a pair of trained guard dogs. But W.W.'s pals got in there successfully again, and there were no dogs, and they found the green suit, though being a particular man W.W. had grumbled that it didn't fit properly along the shoulders.

The circle of onlookers laughed, and in the darkness I could hear the slapping of hands against knees. It was a story they must have heard many times, but it was a classic, and it was being told by Mister Bobby, and W.W. hung his head modestly. As the chuckling died away, the man in the white hat suddenly started off again: "When the man got into the rowboat, why the water come flooding right in over the back and down she went, right there in the Municipal Boat Basin three miles outside of town . . . that's the point—"

Layne spun in his chair. "Who is that talking? Man, you are *messing* with people's earbones."

A chorus of agreement arose. The man in the white hat raised his hands in protest. "That's the point," he said mysteriously.

Another round of drinks turned up. I began to worry about the time; I had not had much sleep the night before. Layne saw me glancing at my watch. "I never wear a watch," he said. "When you look at a watch you see that time is going by, and what's the use of that? Besides, I know what time it is, anyway—just by the *feel* of things. It's eleven-twenty right now. Right?"

He was about twenty minutes off. "Just about right," I said.

Layne nodded and began telling me about his ranch near a town called Jayton—how time didn't make no difference there, the one place he loved to go to get away from it all, where he and his pals had these great cookouts, and every season a big shoot, gunning at quail over bird dogs brought down from Oklahoma.

"Hey, what are you doing tomorrow?" he asked.

I told him that I had a one o'clock conference with some students at the University, and then an afternoon plane to catch back to the East.

"Why, we'll fly out to the ranch in the morning. It's just an hour out. I'll be pounding on your door at eight in the morning. You ain't leavin' Lubbock without seeing the ranch."

"Don't go shooting out there," W.W. warned me. "The gunfire can be goddamn heavy. I got a pellet here in my knee from an over-and-under shotgun some friend of Mister Layne's was waving around."

"Hell, I remember that guy," Layne said. "You're talking about that weak-stomached sumbitch who got sick when a bourbon bottle was passed under his nose."

"You recall when McCade shot the hell out of John Murphy?" W.W. said. "Why, with all that buckshot in him, Murphy real quick weighed two pounds more than when he arrived at the ranch."

Layne roared with laughter and pounded the table.

"It sounds pretty dangerous out there," I said to W.W.

"Aw, you'll have a good time," he said. "He loves that place. You'll have a *good* time out there."

Layne turned up at the motel room just when he said he would, knocking loudly on the door. It was very bright outside, especially after the dark of the room with its thick curtains drawn against the dawn, and I squinted for a while. On the way out to the airport Layne talked about the Lubbock tornado—still the big topic in town, though it had happened two years before—

and how it had ducked into the community one rain-swept night with quick massive devastation. He pointed out the tallest building in town, a fifteen-story insurance building, which he said had been "bent crazy" by the force of the wind, and was now inhabited only by pigeons. We drove out past the country club, where the funnel had touched down in the darkness and killed twenty-six people. "Out by the airport the planes were blown right up on roofs," he said. "Why, out there the wind was so strong that it blew a straw right plumb through a windshield so it stuck there."

"No kidding."

"Damn right. That's true."

We drove in silence for a stretch. I noticed a rushing liquid sound when we rounded curves, and Layne told me it was a large Thermos jug on the back seat filled with ice and cans of beer. "Pearl," he said. "I cut my teeth on Pearl when I was sixteen and weighed a hundred and sixty pounds and ran like a deer."

I asked, "Bobby, what do you remember about Gordy and Karras from those days when you were with the Lions?"

"Oh hell, man, I don't remember them worth a *damn*. Why, they were *rookies*. Nobody remembers rookies. Gordy? 'Gorday,' we called him, giving him the French accent. Don't ask me why. 'John Gorday from Tennessee.' We thought that was very funny. Broke us up. That's the only thing I remember about Gordy—that it was funny to think of him as a Frenchman. But, you see, it was important not to get to know rookies, so we didn't pay them much attention."

"Why was it a bad idea?"

"Well, hell, they were trying to take jobs away from the people that you knew for a long time and sat around and played cards with and bullshitted with—and the rookies, hell, they were trying to break up the family. When Dick Flanigan, out of Ohio State, who played middle linebacker for us, why when he got beat out of his position by Joe Schmidt, well, we thought Joe Schmidt was some sort of sumbitch. He'd done in our friend. So it was the rule that you never spoke to a rookie, 'cept to tell him to get you something, like a pizza or a beer.

65

That went on until the first exhibition game of his second year, when it looked like the boy was going to stick around. Then, if you felt like it, you could say 'howdy' to him."

"Was it the same when you broke in as a rookie?"

"The treatment's always been the same." He pounded the steering wheel with his fist. "I broke into the League with the Chicago Bears. The guy I recall was Bulldog Turner. He was the Main Man. That year he came in overweight and the Bear coaches—George Halas was some sumbitch strict man—they put him at the Fat Man's table to get the pounds off him. Hell, they fed him *lettuce*. Well, at night he and Ed Sprinkle and J.R. Boone, a li'l bitty back from Tulsa, they'd play hearts up in their room. It was my job as a rookie to stuff food into Bulldog Turner, who had an appetite that a couple of *heads* of lettuce wasn't going to do nothing to solve. He'd sit there looking at his cards and bawl for food. They made me break into the commissary to get him stuff."

"Do you suppose Bulldog Turner would remember you?" I asked.

"I'll tell you that if you went and found yourself Bulldog Turner to talk to—why, he wouldn't remember me at *all* when I was a rookie. Hell no. And if you went further and asked him about *his* rookie year—why, he'd remember some guy who horsed him around when *he* was a rookie, Christ, some ol' Indian chief who wore no helmet. And if you could find *him*, sitting in front of some damn teepee, and asked him if he could remember anyone called Bulldog Turner—why, he'd look at you and say, 'Boy, what sort of a grab-assing question is that?' He wouldn't know. What I'm saying is that you pay a rookie no attention at *all*. Why for?"

We arrived at the Lubbock airport. Layne's pilot was waiting by a single-wing Cessna and rushed forward to help him with the green Thermos.

"I know you?" Layne asked.

"Nossir," the pilot said. "The regular guy you use is sick—flu or something." He was a young man, just barely out of high school, and obviously pleased to have Layne in his care.

"You want me to stow this job in the back?" he asked about the Thermos.

"Hell," Layne said. "We're not delivering it to nobody. Set it alongside me in the seat."

We took off. The flight was over flat country to start, the huge cotton fields laid out in regular rectangles and squares below, but then the land gave way to arroyos and gulches, and the cultivated areas became smaller and irregular in shape. An occasional turkey vulture, almost at our level and turning slowly in a thermal current, streamed past below the wing tips. The roar of the engine and the rush of air was soothing, and I half dozed in the back seat while the pilot and Layne chatted in the front.

I heard the quick hiss of a beer can being clicked open.

I heard the pilot ask, "Hey, Bobby, are you a Leo?"

"A what?"

"A Leo?"

"What the hell are you talking about?"

"It's an astrological sign. When were you born?"

"Oh yeah," said Layne. "You're one of those guys. I was born in December."

"A Sagittarius," said the pilot. "That's very interesting. Very."

"I'm sure it is," Layne said. "Very big deal." He looked back over his shoulder at me. "See that mountain off there? Sammy Baugh's got his spread in the foothills."

This was how they ended up, I thought drowsily: the famous Texas quarterbacks, sitting out on their front porches gazing at their acreage, their jaws moving on chaws, their spurred boots up on the rail, and their gnarled hands, which had made them such fortunes spiraling footballs, resting now on the noble brow of a bird dog. I remembered Baugh at the Detroit Lion camp where he was an assistant to Harry Gilmer, also from Texas. They wore white cowboy hats on the sidelines, and Baugh, who chewed tobacco, carried a Dixie cup with him to spit into when he went indoors, and when it was full he left it on a coffee table, or on the piano, or in a corner by the grandfather's clock, and went off to find another. The plane was wobbling now as the pilot turned it for the landing at the Jayton strip. Feeling queasy from that quick recall of the detritus of Baugh's chewing habit, I was relieved when the wheels touched down.

"Hey, d'ja see that?" the pilot called out. "Damn near got ourselves a rattlesnake with the right wheel. D'ja see him? Right out there sunning himself."

Layne's jeep was parked off to one side of the field. My ears buzzed in the abrupt silence after the pilot cut the engine. Back up the strip there was no sign of the rattlesnake. The heat rose in waves off the tarmac. The pilot put the Thermos in the jeep and Layne drove. The pilot came with us, sitting in the back seat with the beer. We came around a bend, past a water tower standing at the edge of the cotton fields, and drove into Jayton. A sign announced its population: 703. The next town down the line was Spur, forty miles across the flatlands. The speed-limit signs brought us down to thirty miles per hour. The shop fronts were one story high with signs tacked above the door: CHUCK'S SWAP SHOP, PETE'S. The cars out front had their side and back windows soaped with various slogans; GO TOUGH, one of them read.

"Look there," Layne said. "This town is all fired up about the Jayton Jayhawks, the high school team. They got a big game tonight against Rule."

"Rule?"

"Town of about two hundred folks. What'd that sign back there say 'bout Jayton's population? Seven-oh-three? Well, that means nine hundred and three folks'll be seeing that game tonight over on the high school field."

The pep signs were everywhere along the main street. The town barber had soaped the front window of his shop (which was called Sleepy's Barber Shop) with the exhortation, SLEEP SAYS SHAVE'M!

Layne said, "Texas football, let me tell *you*. This town is riled up fierce." He slowed the jeep down and shouted at a group of men lounging by the gas pump of a filling station. They all wore pale blue coveralls—the old-fashioned switchman's model with the big back pockets, and the suspenders crossed over their shoulders. "You go git 'em, heah?" Layne shouted, his voice high and reedy.

The men waved at him.

Layne turned back to his driving. "Best doggone li'l ol' town in Texas," he said.

"How many of your friends come out here during the shooting season?" I asked.

He replied that the group hired out the bungalows in the little motor court ("The Jayton Hilton," they called it) and at the peak of the festivities perhaps twenty or thirty men were on hand out at the ranch. Of course, they didn't all shoot. Many of them sat out in the front yard, and smoked and talked.

"What's the general talk about?"

"Oh, football," Layne said. "We tell about the funny things that happen. Don Meredith ever tell you 'bout the time he quarterbacked for the Cowboys against that great Giant team that had Katcavage and Robustelli and Huff and all those people?"

"Not that I can remember."

Layne pounded the wheel. "Sam Huff damn near fell over on his back he was laughing so hard. What happened was that Meredith called this play in the huddle and when he got onto the line he took a gander out over the defense and he saw Huff and another linebacker move into the gaps and hell, man, he knew those cats were *coming*. So he decided to call an automatic at the line—a quick trap, which is the best thing you can call against the blitz, and he opened up his mouth and shouted, '*Red! Green! Blue! Shit! Time!*' and he stepped back and made the signal for a time-out. Christ, he couldn't remember how to call the automatic, but what he did say came out in the right sequence, like it was a signal: *bam, bam, shit, time!*"

The pilot in the back seat was laughing hard.

"Some story, eh, Jim? Damn right that's some sumbitching story. True, too.

"Hey, you know what Meredith once said on the Jack Parr television show?" Layne went on. "Parr asked him if he came back in afterlife what he would come back as, and

Meredith thought for a spell and then he said that he'd like to come back as Bobby Layne's *cabdriver*. That's something, eh? So Parr asks, 'Why do you want to come back as Bobby Layne's cabdriver?' and Meredith says, 'Well, he tips good, and boy, you sure go to some interesting places!' "

"That's quite a compliment," I said.

We passed a sign that read SPUR 35 MILES.

The pilot leaned over the back of the front seat. "Hey, Bobby, you ever say anything to Huff and people like that on the other side of the line?"

"Naw," Layne said. "I'm not saying it don't happen though. Norm Van Brocklin, when he was quarterback, had this trick he played on Art Donovan of the Colts, who was maybe the best defensive player in the league and it was worth trying stuff on that boy—*any*thing. His father was the famous boxing referee, and Brocklin's trick was to come up to the line of scrimmage and call down to where Donovan was waiting, all poised to wrastle some poor sumbitch: 'Hey Al, how's your daddy?' And then in the next beat set loose the play right *at* Donovan. What he was hoping was that Donovan was going to hear the question 'bout his pappy and maybe turn it over in his mind and say to himself, 'Well now, how sweet of ol' Norm to ask about Daddy,' or even better, that maybe he'd come up out of his stance and look up into the sky to ponder the question, and then *boom!*"

The pilot in the back seat was captivated. "Hell, what an idea. Did it work?"

"Naw," said Layne. "Hell, I don't know. I wouldn't think so. Not on Donovan. Oh no. But that was all right. You had to try things. I'll tell you 'bout a play we had when I was with the Pittsburgh Steelers. It was called 'What's the matter' play. What happened was that a situation came up against those same damn Giants—Huff, Robustelli, Katcavage, Roosevelt Brown— and we had fifteen yards to go for a touchdown. Those cats were real poison when you got down close, so in the huddle I called the 'What's the matter' play. What happens is this. I walk up behind the center but I keep my hands tucked in my crotch. I call out 'Red!' which begins the signal count, but all of a sudden

John Henry, the fullback, calls out of the backfield behind me, 'Hey, wait a minute.' So I stop the count and rear up and I turn toward him and I sing out, 'What's the matter?' Across the line the Giants begin to relax and they think, 'Oh man, what a bum team *this* is,' and they stand up to enjoy the confusion, when suddenly, two beats after the word 'matter' the ball is hiked right past my hip to John Henry and he takes off—I mean like he just tears!"

The pilot pounded the back of the front seat. "Well, what about *that* one?" he cried. "Did it work?"

"Damn sumbitching *right*," Layne said. "Sam Huff was laughing so hard he could hardly run after John Henry. He run like he was crazy drunk in some cabbage patch, just stumbling along holding his sides."

After our own laughter had died down, we drove along in silence for a while.

"Hey, Jim, you say there was a rattlesnake back on the strip."

"Yes*sir*," the pilot said. "Almost got him with the right wheel."

"*God*damn."

Layne asked for a beer, and I reached back into the bucket, where the ice was sluicing back and forth, and opened a can for him.

"What was the point of keeping your hands in?" I asked.

"How's that?"

"On that 'What's the matter' play."

"Hell, man, if you put your hands under the center, you're not allowed to bring them out again, less you want to have a time-out called against you." He looked at me aggrieved, as if not knowing about that rule was a reflection on the quarterback fraternity, however limited my own involvement in it.

"Oh yes," I said.

"Here's the turnoff," he said. He whipped the wheel around and the jeep turned onto a dirt road. "We're just about getting there. I'm telling you, this is the best damn place in the world." The jeep swayed between the high red-dirt banks, over which the cotton fields had given way to a lumpy expanse dotted with mesquite bushes. We turned off on a track that rose up precipitously and the jeep's tires spun and threw back stones.

"Let's walk up," Layne said.

The camp stood on the brow of the hill—a low cabin, with a fenced yard at one end in which bird feathers, the residue of countless pluckings, stirred slightly in the soft air. Back of the cabin, sitting in the backyard, was a large gold and black school bus, its wheels gone, resting on its undercarriage amongst the weeds. HILES BAPTIST CHURCH read the letters along its side, with the additional legend above the windows: LUBBOCK'S FASTEST GROWING SUNDAY SCHOOL. Most of the windows were gone, or the glass shattered into white sunbursts by the impact of rocks or gunfire.

"Guns," said Layne. "Bought that sumbitch from the Baptists and fixed it up nice, four bunks in there for the hunting folk, and then the kids came up and shot the hell out of it . . . my *own* kids," he added ruefully.

Around the front, the land fell away steeply into a canyon. On the edge was a skeet trap, with boxes of clay pigeons set alongside. Layne cocked the arm back, loaded it and pulled the lever: the clay pigeon sailed out over the gulch, black and gold, spinning prettily until its momentum failed and it dropped from sight and we heard it tinkle faintly on the rocks below.

The slight wind, hot and sweet, stirred the feathers in the yard. We looked across the canyons at a distant curve of brown barren hills. "Isn't that some country?" Layne asked.

"Yessirree," the pilot said.

Layne strode into the house and we could hear him puttering around inside. The pilot and I stayed in the yard and talked about astrology.

"I've been studying the occult for three years," the pilot said.

"What do you make of Layne?"

"Oh hell, he's sure your basic Sagittarius, all right. He's either jovial or he's against you. There's nothing halfway about him. He's great, isn't he?" He peered at Layne's cabin with a delighted smile, as if he had a prime specimen trapped in there.

"What made you think he was a Leo?" I could not resist asking.

The pilot glanced over. "Well, he has some of the characteristics of the Leo. I mean, I've been observing him. But it's better that he's a Sagittarius, much better. He takes nothing at face value. That's Sagittarius. I'll tell you something else: Sagittarius rules the legs, anything that's outside in the open air—dogs, horses, football . . . Of course, it depends on where the planets are in his chart. Neptune has to do with high spirituality. He might have a bad hookup with that. But if Neptune is in a good position, he could be tuned in to being a great artist—a Picasso or a Leonard Bernstein."

Layne began yelling from inside the house. "Hey, where the crap are you guys?"

We went inside to join him. The place was musty, long closed against the air; the furniture had bottoms that sagged; the beds were double-deckers; some bird feathers had drifted in and one of them floated between us, stirred up by the draft from the door. "Can't get this place too cleaned up," Layne said. "Or the women'd get to like coming out here, and it wouldn't be the same."

"Man, not much chance of that," the pilot said. He poked at a beer can with his foot. Layne looked at him sharply.

I shuffled my feet uncomfortably and said that I was worried about getting back to Lubbock in time for my conference with the Texas Tech students.

Layne looked out the window. "It's getting along about eleven o'clock."

I glanced at my watch. This time he was about a half-hour off. "I can't be late for them," I said.

"You'll come back here to Jayton when we have a shoot," Layne said.

"Damn right," I said.

We walked down the road towards the car, the pilot behind us humming a country-western tune.

"Bobby," I asked, "do you remember a game when you were playing for Pittsburgh in which you were run out of bounds, and Alex Karras came out of nowhere and really belted you one? They damn near threw him out of the game for it? A water bucket went over. It was way out of bounds. Do you remember that?"

Layne was silent for such a long time that I thought he had his mind on something else and had not heard the question.

"Naw," he said finally. He reached for the door handle of the jeep. "Naw, now what would I want to remember a thing like that for?"

6

John Gordy and I were sitting in the apartment waiting for Karras. I was still trying to return to the original concept of the book, and my plan was to spend the morning talking to the two of them about the technical aspects of line play. I had a clipboard ready with some questions on it.

"Where do you suppose he is?" I asked.

"He was sleeping in the hotel when I left," Gordy said. "He sleeps late sometimes. He has his own time clock."

"You were roommates right from the start, weren't you?"

"I'd have taken any sort of roommate," Gordy said, "because before Alex joined the team I roomed with Gil Mains, a wild horse, the weirdest, wildest man in the world. Just crazy. He'd come in late sometimes, and I'd be sleeping, and he'd turn on the lights and whistle and stamp around and sing, just to aggravate me. He'd pick the most solemn moment of the day, like when I was sitting and writing an old aunt who was dying of something, and he'd throw a firecracker under my chair."

I got Gordy a soft drink and we looked out the windows and watched the boats work the currents of the East River.

"Hell," I said finally. "Let's get started. He'll be along." I sat down and looked at the questions on the clipboard. "What about some general questions—what sort of player is the toughest for an offensive lineman to play against?"

Gordy settled himself in the chair opposite. "The quick ones," he said. "Like that Alex sleeping back there in the hotel. Or Art Donovan of the Colts. Leo Nomellini of the 49ers. *He* was a horror. One time in San Francisco, Earl Morrall, who was quarterbacking for us then, came out in the papers the day before the game and said that Leo Nomellini was over the hill. I gave this big yell when I read it, and I said, 'If you think he's over the hill, *you* go and play against him.' Nomellini was a raving maniac trying to get to Earl that afternoon. Of course, to get to him he had to get through *me*, and oh *Christ!*"

"What could you do?"

"You could just hope for the best," he said. "If you had to play against Leo or Donovan, one of those great cats, it meant that for five days before the game, from Tuesday on, it was very hard to sleep nights."

He grimaced. "The worst thing about playing Leo Nomellini was that he had these eyes that crossed. He had no teeth either, and his mouth was always open, so that behind the bars of his helmet he looked like a death's-head. But it was the eyes that were the worst—those awful crossed eyes. Sometimes you can pick up from a guy's eyes where he's going to make his move; he'll flick a look, and you can read him. But Nomellini's! One one way, one the other. Hell, if you ever looked at those eyes, you could feel the strength drain out of your kneecaps—like a sparrow facing up to a cobra. It was not a heartwarming sight."

"Jesus! Well, what *do* you look at?"

"The best thing to watch is the number on his jersey. Never the hips or the head, which can fake and throw you off."

"What do you see in your mind's eye as you start to pull and run interference?"

Gordy answered obliquely. "Once I asked John Brodie, the San Francisco quarterback, about what he pictures as he swings at a golf ball. He's a helluva golfer and I'm a horrible one. I'm always picturing my grip, or the stance, or bringing the hips around. But for him, it wasn't that at all; it was the ball leaving the club and its flight to the green. That makes sense—though it's never helped *my* golf any—because I realize that I do the same thing in football. Leading interference on a running play I have three routes as a pulling guard—a short pull, a long pull, and a deep pull—and in each case I can picture in my mind a sort of quick flash, what's probably going to happen. I've watched the movies, so I have a preconception as to how the defensive players are going to attack the play. Of course I can't be sure. I may have to hook the linebacker in, or the cornerback out, or vice versa. My moves depend on them. But you get to learn their methods of attack; they'll come at you a certain way. In some cases they'll look like they're really going to hit you, then they'll try to dodge around you. In that instance, you've always got to take an inside-out angle and pop the guy, and the runner behind you is a schmuck if he doesn't get out and away. Here, let me show you how it works." He stood up and motioned me out of my chair. I demurred.

On occasion, when Gordy wanted to make a point, rather than use words or draw a diagram on a piece of paper, he would stand me up, moving chairs and standing lamps around to represent tackles and defensive ends, and then with quick darting hops and feints would simulate the moves on the line of scrimmage. Occasionally, an end table would go over or a lamp would sway alarmingly. He was always very intense when he demonstrated his skills, and a sort of wayward look came into his eye which made me wonder nervously, on those occasions when I stood in front of him representing a defensive tackle, if it wasn't the turf of Kezar Stadium that he imagined underfoot and someone like Leo Nomellini opposite him.

"I got to keep notes," I said. "Truly."

He looked miffed.

"How many options," I asked, sitting back, "does a defensive man have?"

"They can do one of three things," Gordy said, settling down again. "They can meet you head-on, in which case it depends on who gets in the best licks. Or they can try to rip you out by hitting low; then you've got to keep your knees together and try to bowl *them* over. Or finally, they can try to dodge around you. We call those people *olés*. Like the *olé* the crowd gives when the bull goes by the guy, they'll give you an *olé*."

"Which are the most difficult to deal with?" I asked. "The *olé* people?"

"They're not harder, but it's frustrating. You want to hit someone, and you can never get a good lick in on an *olé*. But actually there's not too many of them. An *olé* is usually a guy who doesn't want to hit. He'll never strip the interference, which means he can put the defense in a lot of trouble. If he gets around me and then misses the tackle, his people are in a jam: I'm still on my feet, still in the play, and looking for someone to pile into and create a lane for my runner. We called Lem Barney, our cornerback, an *olé* for his first year. He understood what we were getting at and he changed his ways. Of course, sometimes the *olé* gets away with it. There's nothing more embarrassing than one of those guys getting around you, making his tackle on the runner, and there you are thundering along, assuming your guy is still on his feet behind you, looking for people to knock down, really eating up ground—like a locomotive barreling along without any cars attached. You run a long way in a play like that before you pull up, and when you get back in the huddle, you're the last man there, and some guy looks up, real cynical, and says, 'Give John the ball; he's really *eating* up ground.' "

"What about the guy behind you, running with the ball—can he help you?"

"Oh my, yes," Gordy replied. "A good halfback can fake the defensive man right onto your shoulder. Mel Farr, who's as good a runner as Detroit or anybody ever had, would stay long after practice, and we'd run the routes so he knew my moves and

I knew his—the two of us working together so that the defensive man *would* end up on my shoulder. I never worked with anybody as good, as fast as Mel. That year he gained almost a thousand yards, and he was out of two games. God, that was fun!"

"Did you ever touch the football?" I asked. "In all those years?"

"Very rarely. On fumbles. When I was at Tennessee I caught a fumble in the air and ran eight yards for a touchdown. Don't laugh! We won, twenty–fourteen. We were undefeated that year. In the pros I only ran with a fumble once. I got killed. The only thing to do if you see a football rolling around is just to fall on it. It saves a lot of wear and tear on the head."

"Is what you're talking about typical of all offensive line play?"

"Well, all of them except the center, who has it easier," Gordy said. "On pass protection he doesn't usually have a man playing on his nose. His job is to take two steps back and help the guard if he's in trouble, or a tackle, or to cut down a linebacker's charge if he sees it coming. There are a lot of possibilities. Centers get kidded a lot because they don't have any specific opponent on pass protection. But a good center can really help you out."

"What about snapping the ball?"

"That's not hard. But I don't want to demean what centers do. I've never done it when it's twenty below zero and the wind is coming across Lake Erie into Cleveland's Municipal Stadium, and I've never had to do it consistently sixty times a game for twenty games a year. I wouldn't want to degrade a center because one or two bad snaps a year at the wrong time can cost you the whole season. The pressure can get awful rough on a center. But they practice, over and over again, a relatively simple act, until it gets grooved and they can do it whatever the pressure."

"Why is it that centers seem to last so much longer in the leagues?"

"They don't take that physical beating—that pounding, play after play. I've only seen one play in which the center was required to pull and run interference. The Chicago Bears had it in their repertoire."

"Tell me about your own rituals and procedures and thoughts with a game coming up," I said.

Gordy reflected. "I follow a very set and thought-out plan. I go to the stadium very early, and never in the team bus, which takes so damn long and has all those players sitting in rows staring straight ahead looking as though they'd all just lost their mothers. So I go alone, or with Alex, by car, and when I get to the locker room I take off my clothes and leave my shorts and T-shirt on. Next, I get my ankles taped, one of the first people up on the training table, and then I sit in the locker cubicle and read the game program. There's one in each cubicle. All game programs are exactly the same. For years I haven't been surprised by anything in a game program. But reading them passes the time."

"Not much conversation?"

"A certain amount. There are only a few players there at that hour—just the early arrivals, the guys who don't like the bus. They kid the trainers and everybody laughs."

"Is the humor rich?"

"Rich? I don't think that would be my word for it," he said. "Let's see. A typical crack that would get everyone laughing might be to work a couple of pieces of the tape on your ankle loose, and then you go up to the trainer and say, 'Real good job on the tape. My little boy could have done better.' "

"Is that it?"

"Well, it's not one of your great funnies. But it's typical. The situation in the locker room before a game is so tense that almost anything will produce a sort of nervous laugh."

"I guess so," I said. It seemed such an odd scene—the guffaws starting up over "My little boy could have done better." A football player hearing the laughter from up by the training table would look up from reading the game program in his cubicle and call out, "Hey, what's so funny?" One of the tackles comes towards him, his shoulders still heaving with laughter, and draws up a stool to sit down and tell him. "It's a real beaut,"

he says. "Gordy comes up to the . . . the . . . training table."
The tackle can hardly control himself. "Oh, Jesus."

"Yes? He comes to the training table. And?"

"Haw haw haw."

"Then what happens?"

"So Gordy hops up on the table. Right?" The tackle
buckles over again. "I can't *bear* it."

"You want some water?"

"No . . . no . . . So Gordy . . . he says to the trainer . . .
haw haw haw."

"Yes?"

"I forgot . . . I forgot a part. Gordy has . . . oh, Jesus! . . .
worked some tape . . . loose on his foot . . . so it's . . . oh, Christ
. . . *hanging* there . . ."

"Yeah, yeah."

"And . . . Gordy puts his foot . . ."

"Yes?"

". . . up in the trainer's . . . face . . . and . . . oh, Christ
. . . he says . . . he says . . ."

"For Chrissake, *what* does he say?"

"He says . . . 'My . . .' "

"Come *on*."

". . . 'little boy . . .' "

"Yes."

". . . 'could have done better.' Haw haw haw haw . . ."
The tackle wipes the tears from his eyes.

"Is that it?" The player in the cubicle looks down at his
football shoes. "I don't get it," he says. "Tell me again."

But the tackle has gone down the line to tell someone
else, so the player in the cubicle shakes his head and picks up
his football game program to begin to read it for the third time.

I looked across at Gordy. "That sort of funny mood
doesn't keep up for very long, does it?" I asked. "I mean all the
laughing and carrying on?"

"Christ no," he said. "In fact, the mood really begins to
change when the bus pulls up outside and those guys start to file
in with that look on their faces—that grimace, that pre-game

look. Then I know it's time. But I have a strange psychological edge, which is that I've been in the locker room for a while. These newcomers are the recruits and I've been there, in military training, for a week—that's what it's like. It gives me a sense of power and responsibility. So I walk around like a sergeant and tell everybody 'Let's go . . .' because I've already been there. Does that make sense?

"Then I go back to my cubicle and I put my jock on," he continued. "And my T-shirt, if it's not too hot in there. I put my hip guards on. I slide the pads into the pockets built into the pants for them, sliding each one in with care to get it just in place. Then I belt the hip guard tight. After a while I slip on my football pants, but I don't pull them up; I just keep them around my knees. I sit there. Then the pre-game nerves start."

"Alex is sitting next to you?"

"He has the next cubicle. Sometimes he'd wait for the bus because he didn't want to leave the hotel room. He probably felt more secure in there. I always had to get the hell out of our room. I'd been there all night, and to stay around the next morning was like sitting at the dinner table with dirty dishes after you've eaten a meal. But it was always an effort for Karras to get out of there and to the ball park. You remember how nervous he was before a game? Sometimes, sitting next to each other in the cubicles, we'd find something to say, but when you're getting down to it . . . that time coming up . . . it's real quiet in there. You remember it," he said.

"Oh man, do I," I replied, thinking back on that sepulchral silence in those big locker rooms crowded with men sitting in front of their cubicles, the only sound the water dripping in a shower at the far end.

"Then at the last moment I put on my jersey," Gordy continued. "It's a very special one, the last one at Detroit after Joe Schmidt, who used one before he retired from the game. It has a long tail in the back that comes around between the legs and buttons up in front."

"Why that sort of jersey?"

"I never like my shirttail coming out, which always hap-

pened when I wore the usual model. If you have a shirttail floating out behind you, someone's likely to grab it."

"Big Daddy Lipscomb's tail used to come out," I recalled.

"True," said Gordy. "But there weren't many people
around who wanted to grab ahold of *that* one. The kind of jersey
I wore not only kept the shirttail from coming out, but it kept
the material fitting very snug and tight on the body so that no
one could get ahold of it. Then I put the vaseline on—rubbing it
over the shoulders and down the arms, clear, for a white jersey,
dark for the dark-colored jersey—so that when a defensive guy
grabs you, his fingers slip and there's nothing to catch on to. Then
I took my teeth out and wrapped them in a Kleenex to give to
Friday Macklem for safekeeping."

"Vaseline's illegal, isn't it?" I asked.

"Oh, I imagine it is," said Gordy decorously.

"Are there other tricks like that? For instance, do running backs put vaseline around their hips?"

"Yeah, but it doesn't help them much, because no tackler
is ever going to hang on to a running back's hips with his fingers.
A running back's not going to go down unless he's arm-tackled.
So it's not much use. But for me it's important, because defen-
sive players can legally grab at me to try to throw me away.
When they get a fistful of vaseline they bitch like hell."

"Do the nerves really get bad just before the game?"

"I had a really bad time," Gordy said. "You see, the only
way I can ever work up enough confidence to get on the football
field at *all* is to watch the films of the guy I'm going to be playing against. Starting Tuesday I watch those films over and over
until I know every move he's going to make. I watch the films
so often that after a while I'm physically *on* that film and match-
ing and beating him. Then for a night or so before the game I
don't need the film anymore. It's all there in my mind, and I can
lie in bed and mentally see myself through a game against him.
Sometimes I catch myself moving my body so hard that the bed
thrashes across the floor, and I've always got him beat. But you
know something weird? Just before the game starts, I don't
think I've got a *chance* against him. I feel I'm going to get licked
to pieces and humiliated."

"Why is that? Do you forget everything?"

"No, fortunately that stays there. But what's happened is that I've goaded myself into being tough, and yet I still haven't performed. Talk is cheap; now I've got to go out there and actually *do* it. Can I? I get absolutely scared to death. The most scared I ever got was the Pro Bowl game. Then I didn't even have the security of a game film to help prepare myself. I had no idea what I was going to face."

"Do you ever think how *big* the guy opposite is?" I asked, moved to ask because it was the first thing *I* would worry about, and secondly because Chuck Walton, an offensive lineman on the Lions, had once told me that he *preferred* playing against the bigger man. "He's just not going to move as fast," he'd said. "At least you can find him and hit him a lick. The nightmare people are the quick fast ones like Karras. Look at Henry Jordan, the Dallas linebacker. Two hundred and fifty pounds. Well, I could never *find* that guy to hit, which was what I was supposed to do. I knew he was on the field somewhere because I'd keep hearing his name over the public-address system."

I told Gordy this. "Oh yes," he said. "The big tough guys who rely on their strength are by far the easiest. The play that you hope for is from the guy who *thinks* he can bowl you over because he's so much stronger and bigger than you are. That's what Merlin Olsen of the Rams used to do when he started. He came into the league at six foot six, two hundred and ninety pounds, and he spent the first year trying to run over me because I'm only six foot four and two hundred and fifty pounds. But I *love* that situation. I'll be bruised and beaten up for sure, but a player with that one single obsession will never get to the quarterback. He's easy to deal with. Every year when I start against a new player, whatever his reputation, that's how he behaves: he bulls straight ahead. The next year I watch the films of his early games to see if he's starting to make any moves yet. After about five plays I can tell if he's developing his technique. If not, then I'm pretty safe for another year."

"Why don't the coaches try to teach those first-year players?"

"They just don't, for some reason," Gordy said. "Maybe

there are some that try, but I've never seen them. They make you learn by yourself, by experience. It's ridiculous. Of course, many of the great moves can't be taught; they're close to instinctive. I mean you couldn't lead a grandmother out to the line of scrimmage and expect her to learn to get through into the secondary, not if you spent a year teaching her fundamentals. You have to have the essentials. But I've never known why coaches don't go to work on rookies, especially the great ones. You should have seen Olsen his first year. He just stumbled around."

"Couldn't their mistakes be corrected?"

"Maybe," he said, "with defensive people. But I know that for offensive linemen it's hard. The mistakes and bad habits seem so insignificant—a slight dip of the shoulder or the head, or even the blink of an eye—that they're hard to spot and correct."

"The blink of an eye?"

"A *flinch*. If you blink or flinch when the tackle makes his move, if he's a quick one like Karras or Donovan, he's gone. You never saw him, or even touched him."

"What about the drills? Do they help?"

"Almost all the drills in football are a waste of time," Gordy said. "For years, a lineman had this drill where he hit the tackling dummy and bounced back and dug his feet in and then hit the bag again. That's fine for getting the legs in shape, but no lineman ever *blocks* that way. The proper position for an offensive lineman is to have his knees crouched, rear end low, back straight, his neck arched back because he mustn't ever duck his head or flinch, and his fists right in front of his jersey numbers so he can balance himself and is ready to punch away . . ."

"What do you mean by 'punch away'?"

"Stand up." This time Gordy wouldn't listen to my excuses. "To hell with your notes," he said. "You'll remember."

He pulled me out of my chair.

"Okay," he said. "I'm an offensive lineman set up properly. You're coming at me. Now put your hands on me. Try to throw me one way or the other. No, no, really work on me. Pull me *this* way."

I grunted and wrenched at him.

"Now watch how I counter." A fist flew out and thumped against my chest. I staggered up against a wall.

"See that?" Gordy shouted.

"Yeah, sure," I said.

"That's the move," he went on, brimming with enthusiasm. "Did you catch how I kept my balance and threw you off yours?"

"Yeah, that certainly was something," I said.

"Okay, now you try it. You be me, you be the offensive lineman. I'm Karras or Nomellini, trying to get through you. Right. Now move around this way."

"Look out!"

"What's that?"

"That's an ashtray. It's all right, it was just a small ashtray."

He put the pieces on the table. "Okay," he said, "now let's get in the proper position."

"Right," I said with no enthusiasm. I dropped into an approximation of the crouch he had demonstrated, fists cocked at my chest ready to shoot out at him.

At that moment Maria, the woman who comes in to clean the apartment a couple of times a week, materialized at the door, stared briefly at the two of us poised like wrestlers, and cleared her throat to announce that there was someone at the door downstairs. It was Karras. In the nick of time, I thought. He was wearing knit wool slacks and a stylishly cut jacket—one of the first of a number of mod outfits that he had begun to cultivate, none of which seemed to suit his big squat frame, or the round pale face with big spectacles that floated above the ensemble like a moon.

"Sharp," said Gordy in admiration.

Karras sat down in the armchair. "Has he been telling you lies?" he asked. "All linemen tell lies—especially offensive linemen."

"We were talking about linemen's techniques," I said. "But now that you're here, perhaps we could get into something else—perhaps the *psychological* aspects." I was eager to protect the furniture and lamps from the *two* af them demonstrating the physical particulars of their crafts.

"He's not a collision man," Gordy said, looking at me with mock despair.

"He's going to be the Assistant Secretary of Commerce," Karras said.

"Alex, what about your position?" I asked. "Do most defensive tackles play the same way?"

"We all play a little differently," he said. "I'm very aggressive, and I try to move forward all the time, to go as fast as I can through the head of the guard opposite so I can get on the other side of the line and start feeling for who has the ball. Many linemen tend to lay on the line of scrimmage and move along it laterally, like fingers on a piano, to work an opening."

"Can the opposition take advantage of your type of play?" I asked.

"What I have to look out for is the quick trap. This means that the lineman opposite, usually the offensive guard, releases me and lets me move into the trap where I can be cut down from the side, usually by the offensive tackle. I can't ignore the possibilities of the trap play, but I can't get so leery of it that it affects the aggressive type of football that I like to play. Actually, what makes a trap play work is the running back. The best one I ever saw at it was Gale Sayers of the Bears, because there wasn't anyone could hit a hole as fast as he could. He could have had the worst blockers in the league, executing the sloppiest of trap plays, but all they had to do was breathe some bad breath on you for two seconds, and he was by you and gone."

"Do you have any mental exercises you go through before a game to stir yourself up?"

"Well, I'm not normally an aggressive person, so I compensate by working up antagonisms, like against good-looking quarterbacks. A lot of it is psychological. I tell myself before a game that I'm Paul Bunyan. I wake up in the hotel room in the morning and say to myself, 'Paul, we're going to have ourselves a game this afternoon. We are going to remove the stuffings from people.' I can feel myself inflate. When I leave the hotel bedroom I crouch down so my head won't hit the top of the bedroom door. Down in the lobby the players say, 'Hey, Alex, what are you bent over like that for? You got a stomach cramp or something?' 'The name's Paul,' I say."

He picked up a glass and turned it in his hand. "That's 'compensation,' " he said. "I do it a lot."

"Do you think the mental preparation required is different for different positions?"

The two of them looked puzzled.

Somewhere in my notes, I explained, Merlin Olsen of the Rams had told me about the different temperaments of football players. For example, linemen, "our people," were more "self-motivated" than backs and receivers. His point was that linemen do not perform their skills under the sort of public scrutiny received by a back, who runs the ball in an open field and, say, fumbles it. "Our work is done in close quarters," Olsen had said. "You can make a serious mistake, but it won't be noticed. Linemen are motivated by a more complicated, self-determining series of factors than the simple fear of humiliation in the public gaze which is the emotion that galvanizes the backs and receivers."

The two of them nodded and agreed that it was an interesting speculation.

"Are there differences between the basic temperaments of offensive and defensive linemen?" I went on.

Both Karras and Gordy considered this and seemed to think there were.

"First of all," Karras said, "our jobs are so different. An offensive player like John has to concentrate much more. He has a certain assignment to perform, and he must do it on a certain signal. So in a sense he's confined; he's geared to a type of machine; he must function and mesh with others. Whereas defensive linemen like myself, we can express ourselves more fully. Our moves, our attack, is more freewheeling and extemporaneous."

"That's right," Gordy said. "Most of the time—and always on pass-blocking—the offensive guard's job is passive. If the guy trying to get to the quarterback goes to the left, we go the same way. If he goes the other way, so do we. If he loafs, we can loaf. Everything is dictated by what the guy opposite does. Most of the time, of course, shielding the quarterback means that you've got to take a beating—it's like being a dog cowering in a corner. The only time we can get in our true licks is when the quarterback calls a running play which requires that the guards pull to run interference. Then you can go out and smack down a little cornerback and have some *fun*." He made a rumbling, keening sound in his throat.

"Why wouldn't Alex's job be more complicated?" I asked. "After all, he has to make the first move."

Karras explained. "It's natural to knock over a guy. It isn't natural to have to stand there and let the other guy deliver blows to your head."

"As well as kicking and gouging and kneeing," Gordy added.

"And do you think these two postures affect the players involved?" I asked.

"The defensive linemen are more temperamental, more sadistic than the offensive people," Karras said, "and uncontrollable. It's because of the nature of what each does. The poor offensive lineman can't get violent and kick and bite and scratch; if he does, he gets a penalty for it. A defensive lineman can do just about anything. He can damn near haul an ax out of his jock and slash around with it before he'll be called for anything."

Gordy nodded his head. "I think of the defensive lineman as an aggressor," he said. "The two terms 'offensive' and 'defensive' are really inaccurate as regards what actually happens during a play. I'm called an offensive linesman because our team's on offense, but what I'm trying to do is keep an aggressor from knocking me down and getting at my home and family. I'm defending."

"Does that image actually exist in your mind out on the playing field?" I asked. "The home?"

"When I was at college," Gordy explained, "I imagined that my mother and father were in the backfield behind me sitting on little stools, and that I was protecting them from someone trying to do them harm. When I got into the pro leagues, what I imagined back there was my baby son, lying in a little cradle. You can imagine to what heights of protectiveness *that* image pushed me."

"I should say," I agreed, impressed.

"But, you see," said Karras, "that's all defensive and frantic. The defensive lineman, the guy John calls the aggressor, has for *his* impulse something quite different. I would guess that if you looked through their backgrounds, you'd find that the majority of defensive linemen have been rejected somewhere along the line, even if they're hardly aware of it. They make a vendetta out of it; most of them have chips on their shoulders. There's somebody they're trying to get back at by taking it out on the quarterback. I'm not the only one."

"And the image that kicks off this aggression?"

"For me, my simple hatred of quarterbacks," Karras said, "is because I see them as 'goodies,' people who've had music lessons and a barber who calls them 'Master Harry,' and they go on to Eastern colleges and talk snuffy, and their hair is groomed flat against their heads, and they have these thin, delicate noses, and they take their girls on picnics with big straw hampers to hold the dishes, for Chrissakes, and *napkins*, and they're so polite, they kiss on the cheek in public, and hell, I don't think they *piss* or anything. Of course I know where this all comes from; it's because I grew up in Gary, with all its horrible roughness, and there had to be someone you took it out on, some glamour cat with all the luck. It burns in you if you're brought up in a neighborhood like that, like a fever, and so its opposite becomes the target.

"I've *never* liked quarterbacks. Sometimes I can't bear to watch them play because they're so bad, especially the ones we had on the Lions. If I were a coach and saw some of the things that quarterbacks do, I'd call a time-out and motion the quarterback over to the sidelines. He'd come over, ambling the way they do, very cocky and slowly because he knows that sixty thousand people are watching him, and the television cameras too, and everyone is admiring him—this general, this goddamn *field* marshal, this big deal *cat*. Everybody in the stadium knows that the coach is going to put an arm around this kid's shoulders and whisper in his ear, and everybody's looking and thinking, 'Oh, that's great—the Old Man and the Whiz Kid, look at the two of them.' Well, that's not what *I'd* like to see. If I were the coach, I'd motion him over and wait for him with my head down, and he'd shuck his helmet off just as he got to the sidelines so everybody could see he had this terrific crop of golden hair down to his neck, and he'd lean forward so that I could get my arm up around his shoulder and whisper to him—and right then, when he was in range, I'd rear back and let him have it with a left cross—pow!—right in the kisser." Karras thumped a fist into his other palm with concussive force. "Damn right. And then when he was lying on the ground I'd stand on him for a while and look out on the field with my arms crossed."

"But suppose the quarterback you're trying to get to out there on field also comes out of an environment like Gary? I mean, most of them *do*—John Unitas, say, out of the sandlots of a Pennsylvania steel town. So many of them are products of the same background."

"It's curious," Karras said. "I have my worst games against Unitas. Something happens. I can almost feel myself stop reaching for him because I can't make that proper adjustment in my mind."

"What do you see out there, Alex?" I remembered how bad his eyes were. "I mean, can you actually see the guy about whom you've worked up all this venom?"

"I can distinguish color. And movement, of course. I mean, I really do have bad eyesight. My vision is zero-thirteen. I mostly see shadows and fuzzy masses unless I'm wearing glasses. I can't see the stadium. But I've never felt sight was very important, since the main thing I have to do is get past the man in front of me and that's a question of reacting to pressure— *reading* him, so that it's not unlike types of Oriental wrestling. Sight isn't as important as touch."

"But once you're past that man, don't you have to see who you're going to tackle?"

"Well, you can sense that from the flow of the play, and what other people are doing. Being half blind is actually *helpful*, because all the faking and spinning around back there and cleverly executed handoffs are supposed to fool someone who can *see*. They don't fool someone who's *feeling* his way into the backfield. I used to call my technique a Braille system, and everybody would laugh. But it's really true. A blind man is incredibly sensitive because he's so attuned to what's around him. He's all nerve ends, and quick, like the way a person's perceptions are very sharp moving around a dark room. The slightest touch or shape makes you jump; you're like a cat."

"Did anyone ever try contact lenses on you?"

"I wore them for part of the nineteen fifty-nine season. Coach Wilson called me up and said, 'You're having so much trouble following the ball that I've arranged for you to see an eye doctor and get a set of contacts.' I got them, and I was just horrible. I saw so well that it destroyed the whole way I'd learned to play the game. I wandered around in the backfield looking at things. I relied too much on what I saw, and I lost those good instinctive moves—I wasn't so *sensitive* any more.

"Besides, one of the advantages of bad eyesight is that everything seems a little smaller. With the contacts, I didn't like what I saw out there—I mean those big guys. I didn't like that much at all. You can't be too scared of what you can't see."

"What about when you're on the bench? Can you tell what's going on?"

"I don't see very much of what's going on out there. On the bench I try to sit next to someone with good eyesight. Once I sat next to Bill Swain, who played linebacker, and he'd lost his contact lenses. He sees worse than I do, and we sat there and joked about it. Swain said to me, 'Hey, do you think we're facing in the right direction?'

"You know, I'm an entirely different person with my glasses off," Karras said, abruptly shifting tack.

"In what way?"

"My voice gets much lower, for one thing." He took off his glasses. "Like *this*," he rumbled. "My whole character changes. I become a football player. I turn mean. I can feel the hair growing in my armpits."

"Suppose your glasses fall off by mistake?"

"It's happened. At a birthday party right in Bloomfield Hills. I was leaning over the birthday cake trying to read what was on it, and my glasses fell off. They bounded on the cake and fell to the floor somewhere. Right away I felt different. I looked around, squinting, trying to see. There had to be a football game going on. I could hear the cheering from the stands. It sounded like they were singing 'Happy Birthday' to someone—probably the rival coach. Apparently there was a time-out—the players across the line were just standing around waiting for time to be called back in. Who were they? I strained to see. The Green Bay Packers, probably. Sons of *bitches*. I could feel myself puffing up with meanness. Then the referee—who seemed to be wearing a black and white striped dress, very odd—lifted his hand to his mouth to blow the whistle and I knew that with time back in I was really going to knock the stuffing out of someone."

"Well, what happened?"

"My wife caught sight of me without my glasses and knew instantly what was going on. She came running over and found the glasses and slapped them on just as I was beginning to breathe heavily and reach for someone."

"That's pretty frightening," I said.

"Damn right," he said.

"You wouldn't be invited anywhere anymore," I said.

"It's rare enough as it is," he said.

"Alex, what are you thinking about at the moment that the quarterback begins to call the signals?" I asked.

"Well, if it's fairly sure to be a pass play, *he's* the one I'm thinking about. The quarterback. He's the guy I've got to get to. I can't think about the man in front of me; I've got to get around him as quickly as I can. If John's the guy opposite, and he's dropping back on pass protection, for me he's just kind of a little peg I've got to get past. One could say that the offensive lineman has no more significance than the fence you climb over to get an apple off the neighbor's tree. The apple is what has all your attention. Anytime I begin to think about killing the man in front of me, then I'm not going to be able to rush the passer."

"And that's what *I* have to do," Gordy said. "Make him

look at me; make him fight *me*. I remember the first time I played Alan Page of the Vikings. The game started and he's like I'm not there. *Whack-whack.* But I remember thinking at the time that he was *going* to be a great tackle. He wasn't yet; there were still a few things that he had to learn. So I went to work on him. Pretty soon, like a bite that a person starts scratching, this damn peg that he was trying to get around began to get on his nerves. He looked at me, and then all of a sudden I had him. He took a full bull inside charge, and I ran him across the line. He stopped and started to go the other way. Look, like this . . ."

He got up. Again he made me stand opposite him and began shoving me around the room. "Look, look . . . like *this!*" A lamp tottered. Karras watched solemnly. "See? See how it works? He went here; I was there. Suddenly he realized I was the jerk who'd been keeping him from what he wanted to do, and from down by his shoe tops he began to swing a stiff-arm, like a big club, to pop me in the head, and I ducked. I had him. I was in good shape. He might hit me and maybe I'd get stitched up now and then, but he wasn't going to get to the quarterback. He was near berserk. He was staring at me. He shouted to the line judge, 'He's holding me! He's holding me!' Well, I *wasn't* holding him. He just had to assume that, because he wasn't getting in to smack that quarterback down and there had to be some reason."

"He wasn't getting into that house of yours," I said.

Gordy was grinning. "No, he wasn't. I was slamming the door on him and he was feeling the pain in his fingers."

"Does the offensive guard, this guy who's supposed to be passive, ever lose his cool? I mean, go berserk the way Page did?"

"Obviously he shouldn't," Gordy said. "But I've done it. Les Richter, the Ram linebacker, blind-sided me once—that is, he blocked me damn close to a clip when I was moving away from him, and when I pulled up he swung around and hit me in the face with a *cast*. He had this cast on from his wrist to his elbow, and it drove my teeth right through my lip and blood just went all over the place. Well, I busted the next two plays trying to get to him. It must have looked crazy—some idiot running amok on every play. I mean, I just moved from my stance at the quarterback's signal, and my head came up, looking for Richter, and I went for him. If he'd been sitting in Section E, forty rows up, I'd have gone for him, I swear."

"Did Richter know you were after him?"

"Sure he did. We kept it up for seven years. To block Les I would do anything. There were no holds barred. He runs a race track at Riverside now. I've done some things socially with him, and we enjoy each other's company. But on the field, ever since that particular time when he hit me with the cast, I've always gone over the side after him."

"So there are personal duels?"

"Absolutely."

"You had a pretty good one with Mike Pyle, the Chicago Bear center," I remarked to Karras, remembering a number of incidents between them.

Karras stirred. "Yeah. He's one of the goodies. He's the kind of guy that gets along with the coaching staff. I never heard a coach say a bad word about him. He's that kind of guy."

"I met him once in Chicago," I said. "He seemed a very agreeable cat. He's from Yale," I added, grinning.

"He gets along with everybody. I'm always leery of guys like that," Karras said. "But my feuds were mostly professional rather than emotional. For years I had one against Alex Sandusky of the Colts, who's the best guard I ever played against. We had great respect for one another. We never said a word to each other all those years, except at the very end. I'll never forget. It was a real bang-up affair. I was trying with anything I had to kill him, and so was he from his side. I got my nose broken. After that game was the only time we ever talked. We came off the field together and he said, 'Boy, am I ever tired.' I said, 'Me too.' He said, 'This is it for me. I can't take this beating anymore.' And that was the last. He retired."

Evening had come, and the river flowed fast and dark beyond the windows. Gordy began chewing noisily on some crackers. "Chow time?" he asked. "Shall we go out and get a bite somewhere?"

"Sure," Karras said.

"Do you ever see him socially, Alex?" I asked.

"Who?"

"Sandusky."

"No. He wrote me a letter after he saw the movie of *Paper Lion*. He said he thought I was good in it. He wrote, 'When I come to Detroit, we'll go out and have a drink.' He never came. I never said a word to Sandusky all those years, except for the last. All those years and he never said a word to me, one way or the other. And I did some bad things to him, and he did some bad things to me. But we had great respect for each other."

One spring day, Alex Karras called me up and invited me to
come out to Flint, Michigan, to play in a golf tournament bearing his name—The Alex Karras Golf Classic.

"It's *your* tournament, Alex?" I asked. "A *golf* tournament?"

"That's right. It's been put together in three weeks. It's
to benefit victims of cystic fibrosis. I don't know what it's going
to do to my bad-guy image. Maybe I can run away with the pro-
ceeds," he said. "Well, are you coming?"

"But you know my golf," I said. "It's awful. It's about as
bad as yours."

I had played golf with both Karras and Gordy. I doubt
that among athletes there is any group as inept at golf as football linemen. That generalization may be as unsteady as the one
which states that there are no pianos in Japan, but I have never
seen a tackle or a guard on the golf course whose caddy for

safety's sake didn't tend to keep the golf bag between him and ball when the lineman was sashaying back and forth getting ready to hit.

Gordy used to speculate that linemen were poor golfers because they spent so much of their time down in a three-point stance. Their backs were bad. But they kept at the game because every once in a while all that strength would flow properly into a golf swing, everything just right, and a titanic shot would result. Still, even Gordy's best remembered shots had a mournful duffer's quality to them. Eight or nine times he had told me about a 280-yard drive to the green, his best ever, that he had made on an Air Force course outside Nashville, but when it landed it had hit a colonel on the ankle. "Got him on the first bounce," Gordy said proudly.

Karras was as undistinguished a golfer as his friend. His actions on a football field were as confident and quick as the motions of a dragonfly above a pond, but on the golf course an earthbound quality and something of the hermit crab seemed to take over. His golf swing was a heavy swooping snatch at the ball, and from a distance it looked as if he were flailing at something that had got inside his shoe; invariably at the conclusion of his swing a large piece of turf was dislodged from the fairway and sailed into the air with his ball perched on it like a decoration.

It always surprised me that a man possessed of such satanic, if controlled, fury on a football field could keep himself contained playing such awful golf. But on the few occasions we played together, the sole impression Karras gave was of enjoying himself hugely, even when he disappeared into the deepest rough to flail away at an errant shot.

Still, I could not have been more surprised by his phone call asking me to play in his tournament. "You'll have a great time," he said. "My tournament is going to be different. No one's going to play good golf. The whole tournament has been set up as a duffer's revenge on the game.

"We've got these gags," he explained, "that are going to bring good golfers right damn down to their knees. We've hidden these tape machines around the golf course. There'll be these terrible noises coming out of the woods—cars crashing, elephants screaming, things like that, all on tape and amplified to really make the golfers jump. We thought of mining the greens so they'd blow up. Tiny Tim is going to rush out and carry on, and strum his ukulele, and we've got parachutists . . ."

"Tiny Tim!"

"He's been asked to the tournament. No kidding. He agreed."

"And you put all this together?"

"Pete Buterakos and me," said Karras.

"Holy smoke," I said. "Pete Buterakos? Well, I guess I'd better arrange to come."

I had never met Buterakos, though I had heard members of the Detroit Lions talk about him. Football was his passion, and he was around them often. He was a salesman who had made a fortune selling cemetery plots. His sales pitch combined quantities of zest and lunacy, coupled with self-confidence; his lectures on motivation were famous throughout the Midwest. I had once heard the tape of a speech he had given at the Lions' training camp—a wild burst of inspirational cajolery delivered with evangelical fervor and punctuated with the crash of the various props which were his particular trademark and were used to illustrate his points. To show that life is an "obstacle course," he would hoist up a track hurdle. Or he'd turn on an air hammer to illustrate that life is "full of windbags," or set off a smoke bomb to indicate "a clogged mind." On the tape of the inspirational talk I heard, there was a sudden deafening crash which I was told was a cherry bomb ("life is full of abrupt changes" had been the cue for it) which he had rolled out behind him and which had blown a big chunk of plaster out of the wall. The Detroit coaches had him around annually for these talks in the hope of perking up the team, and as Joe Schmidt, then the head coach, once said, "Buterakos keeps you not only on the edge of your seat, but usually two or three feet above it."

"What a salesman," Karras once said reverently. "He'll do anything." He described a speech on business administration he had heard Buterakos deliver before forty-five hundred people in Flint, during which he had talked for over an hour and tossed a variety of props into the audience, including live pigs ("There are pigs in the business world"), rubber snakes ("Competition can turn good men into snakes"), and blood-soaked rubber daggers ("At the top there are people waiting to stab you in the back"). He climaxed his talk by bursting through a mock brick wall that had been set up on the stage.

"What did he do that for?" I asked.

"To show that you can overcome anything," Karras said. "For him there's no such thing as an obstacle. When he went through the wall he was wearing a Superman outfit."

Buterakos turned out to be the proprietor of a small golf course near Flint named Shady Acres where the tournament would be held, utilizing the pro-am format of having one local athlete (most of them from the Lions, but a few representatives from the Tigers, the Piston basketball organization, and the Detroit Red Wings hockey team) playing in a foursome with Flint businessmen who would cough up fifty dollars (to benefit cystic fibrosis) for the privilege. A number of outside celebrities were going to come in to play—"A whole mess of astronauts," Karras told me. "And of course Tiny Tim."

"Is Tiny Tim going to play golf?" I asked.

"I'm going to parachute into the middle of the tournament," Karras said, "and Tiny Tim is going to rush out and present me with a bouquet. In the background the Ortonville band is going to play 'Tiptoe Through the Tulips.' That's what's organized for Tiny Tim at the moment. We may have something else for him to do."

There had been a number of meetings in Flint at which details of this sort were planned. Buterakos was very much in evidence. At one meeting he gave a roar and threw a dead fish onto the table—a big red snapper he had bought from the local fish market. "These proceedings are *dead!*" he shouted. "You've got to swim against the current to get anywhere. You've got to have more zest, more pep. Now let's get down to business." Various duties had been assigned. Carl Brettschneider, the former Lion linebacker, was supposed to turn up at the tournament with a large selection of balloons to be passed out to the crowds by a local Flint clown named Upsie-Daisy. "That's all you're expected to do," Brettschneider was told. "Can you pull it off?"

"Sure," he said. "I'm going to devote two nights to blowing them up."

When Brettschneider turned up early on tournament day, Buterakos ran up and asked, "Where the hell are the balloons?"

"Well," said Brettschneider, "I've got some good news for you and some bad news. The good news is that I've decided I'm going to play in the tournament. The bad news is that I haven't got the balloons."

"No balloons!" Buterakos was furious. "What the hell's Upsie-Daisy going to do without balloons to pass out?"

"I've thought about that," said Brettschneider. "Upsie-Daisy can *shake hands* with people. It's more personal. What can you do with a balloon? But to have your hand grabbed and get the big hello from Upsie-Daisy—well, that's something."

Buterakos was not mollified. He took a hard look at Brettschneider and blew a piercing blast on his whistle. "Let's move it," he said. "Let's goddamn move it."

Buterakos' whistle was his personal trademark; he wore it on a white cord around his neck. I heard it for the first time at five-thirty the morning of the tournament. Arriving in Flint late the previous night, I'd had only three hours' sleep in the motel before the whistle shrilled out in the corridor and a sharp rap sounded on the door. He was waiting for me—a big-chested elf, my first impression was, the whistle tucked in a corner of his mouth as he stared at me with peaceful brown eyes that seemed to belie what I'd heard of his energy. I told him that I wasn't expected to tee off until nine o'clock or so, and that I was awfully tired. No, he said, I had to come out to the golf course and see the "whole damn thing unfold—right from the beginning."

I gave in, and we drove out to the golf course. I stood and stomped my feet in the cold. There was no end of activity. Buterakos said it was worth having a tournament just to see so many of his friends up at six A.M. He pointed out a man struggling with a wheelbarrow full of soft drinks. "That's Dave Doherty. He's got an undescended testicle—one ball. Hey, Dave," he shouted. "You're really working your ball off."

Doherty shook his head wearily.

"He takes a lot of kidding," Buterakos said.

He took me over to a table crowded with tape recorders. The man tinkering with them looked up and said, "Hey, Pete. You want to hear the lions?" He flicked a switch which turned on a weird jangle of sound. "The tape's on backwards," the man said, "but that's a fantastic sound—right, Pete?"

Buterakos beamed at me. "The sound effects are going to be something else." We watched a man going by carrying a small cannon. Buterakos explained that it was to be hidden behind the first tee and shot off from time to time, just at the height of a competitor's backswing. "Wait till you hear that thing," he said. "It'll make the golfers jump into the next county."

Karras arrived. He wore his heavy horn-rimmed glasses and was dressed in a white mesh shirt and yellow golfing trousers. His golf hat bore the JEWISH OPEN decal. "Have the horses gotten here yet?" he asked.

He was assured that they had. At that moment a small cart appeared around the corner of the clubhouse with two ponies in the traces. A man with a guitar walked alongside.

"You know what that guy's going to do?" Karras said to me. "He's going to travel around the golf course in that little cart, with those ponies dragging him, and he's going to stand up with this big Mexican grin and sing 'The Mexican Hat Dance.' He's going to belt out that song all day long, just that *one* song. He said to me, 'But I know a *lot* of songs.' I said, 'No, "The Mexican Hat Dance" is the one we want. It's a big golfing song because it inspires golfers when they're putting. He didn't know what putting was. So I told him, 'That's when the guys are bending over the ball, trying to put it in the hole, and that's when you should get in real close with those ponies and your cart so you can belt "The Mexican Hat Dance" right at them.'"

Out in the parking lot, the competitors began arriving, getting their golf bags out of car trunks and toting them to the lawn in front of the clubhouse. I recognized some of the Lion players—Nick Eddy and Mel Farr, who played in the offensive backfield, and Mike Lucci and Wayne Walker, two of the starting linebackers. The rest were primarily Flint residents, mostly businessmen, two hundred of whom in the course of three weeks had bought fifty-dollar tickets. Many of them went down to the practice putting green and began working on their putting strokes. They seemed very serious. They wore the latest style in golfing attire, fancy golf shoes with flaps over the laces, and golfing hats with the decal of their home course. Almost all of them had the hunched shoulders and locked knees of the Arnold Palmer putting stance. Their impressions of the tournament must have been reasonably favorable; there were at least some concessions to tradition. A scoreboard. And the caddies had the name of each foursome's leader on the back of their shirts—a fine professional touch, except the letters were stuck on with adhesive that wouldn't hold, and one or two of the letters dropped off and left startling variations of the original name. In no time at all Nick Eddy's name was reduced to ICK EDD. Mel Farr's took on Mideastern simplicity: EL FA.

The first indication of the tournament's special quality was the Mexican guitarist's serenade at the practice putting green. As Karras said later, he must have gone wild seeing all those golfers putting at once. "De *da*, de *da*, de *da*, de da-da-da-da-de-*dah*," he sang with an enormous grin, his foot tapping, his fingers strumming hard.

The golfers looked up. "Hey, can it, man," I heard one of them say. The foot kept tapping, the guitarist imparting an odd beseeching quality to the song, straining for a therapeutic effect.

If there was any remaining doubt about the tournament's character, it was settled at eight-thirty A.M. when the first foursome went off. Bill Munson, the Detroit Lion quarterback, was the first golfer off the tee. The amplifiers were suddenly turned on full tilt—the sudden scream of tires, the rattle of gunfire—and just at the top of his backswing someone pulled the lanyard of the cannon. The report was deafening. Munson leapt straight up in the air with his legs a-twangle, like a puppet gone awry. A cloud of white smoke drifted down the fairway and Buterakos' whistle began shrilling. "All right, Munson, let's not just stand around. Move it out."

Visibly shaken, Munson addressed the ball and knocked out a drive, then stood by as the three Flint businessmen in his foursome teed off, their faces grim in concentration as around them there blared trumpet calls, cymbal clashings, and the amplified sounds of toilets flushing.

It was difficult to gauge the reaction of the players. When the cannon went off, they started up from their Arnold Palmer stances down on the putting green and looked at each other; they stood around somewhat nervously, resplendent in their togs, like egrets about to take flight, but I didn't see anyone pack up and go home. When their time to drive off came, it was extraordinary to see them in that hurricane of sound on the first tee—Buterakos intoning a windy biography about each of them into a microphone ("That sweet, sweet guy on the first tee is Clint Jones of Flint, out on ten thousand dollars' bail his niece scraped together . . ."), the amplifiers bellowing their startling variety of sounds, and the golfer himself, poised over the ball, murmuring to himself to let his "left side come through" or whatever mental tip had priority, and actually worrying not about a slice but about the cannon going off. Those who hit straight drives moved off down the fairway with alacrity.

"Look out for the swamps!" Buterakos shouted after them. "Look out for what's going to be coming out of the swamps!"

"What's going to be coming out of the swamps?" I asked him.

"What swamps?" he asked. "No swamps on this course."

My own foursome moved off an hour or so later without incident, but behind us Errol Mann, the Lion place-kicker, mishit three drives in a row, one of which went four feet. I heard later that he pleaded with Buterakos to turn off the noise so that he could concentrate, and Buterakos had agreed and then palmed him a trick golf ball that smoked and popped sharply into two pieces when Mann lashed at it.

Storm clouds had been gathering most of the morning,

and the first drops began to come down about one o'clock—a heavy abrupt spatter in the trees off the fairway. My own foursome had reached the far corner of the course, and we were out of shot of the tape recorders. The "Mexican Hat Dance" man had materialized on two greens as we were putting out. With the rain, golf umbrellas were hastily put up, and under them nervous discussions went on about the lightning which was ripping around, making us start nervously. No one could agree on the safest place to be. The rain began to come down so hard that the landscape went gray and the raindrops flickered off the fairways like hailstones. One of our group went out and stood in the middle of the fairway under an umbrella. His caddy stayed with us. We were under trees, such a large patch of them that we felt ourselves safe, but the golfer was insistent and said we were wrong and all damn fools. We watched him through the hissing sheets of rain and wondered if there was enough metal in our umbrellas to conduct electricity. The lightning was awesome. Someone muttered that Karras and Buterakos had let their special-effects department get out of hand.

After a half-hour of constant downpour we trudged back to the clubhouse. The golf course lay under stretches of water, still being pocked by rain as the thunderheads moved on. Both competitors and onlookers had pushed inside the clubhouse, and the noise was fierce. I could hear Buterakos' whistle going as he desperately tried to keep things stirred up. I saw him trying to lead a group in some squat-kicks that I assumed were variations of a Greek dance. "Faster, faster!" he kept shouting at the band.

"It's a disaster," someone said in my ear. "The band ought to be playing 'Nearer My God to Thee.'"

Across the way a heavy-set man was shouting, "Tiny Tim's not coming. He's got halitosis."

"It's laryngitis," I was told. "The weather. He's got to protect his vocal cords. That's what his manager said."

Karras came by carrying a bouquet of blue flowers.

"I hear Tiny Tim's not coming," I said.

"Things were going too smooth. I knew something like this was going to happen. It was so well planned, too."

The rain stopped, and after a while the tournament

started up again. We heard the "Mexican Hat Dance" man off in the distance and could see the ponies straining to pull the cart through the mud. There were distant explosions.

My own golf was atrocious. The rain had soaked my golf pants and they had split completely down the seam in the rear without my being aware. A girl had come up and said, "Hey, are those good-luck pants or something?" and I had reached back to find the back of the pants gone. My golf style changed abruptly; I developed a tendency to keep my back to the trees and away from the crowds, and on the putting surface I changed my Arnold Palmer putting crouch to an upright telephone-pole stance, so straight that I could barely reach the ball with the putter.

When we got in from the round, I went back to the motel to change. I returned for the post-tournament golf dinner, which was held under a vast moldy tent, somewhat low-slung and inadequately lit so that one had the sense of eating in a brewery cellar illuminated by lanterns. The noise was deafening. A bagpipe band entered under the flaps at one end of the tent and skirted around for a while, marching up and down between the long wooden tables until someone gave a signal and they sat down at a table for dinner, the instruments propped up on the benches beside them.

Karras had urged me to come to the golf dinner because it would be "different"; the prizes were not what I would expect. In fact, I would not recognize the usual pro-am dinner—with its familiar climax of applause and the day's low-ball team sauntering up to the awards table to receive silver bowls and sets of matched irons—"No, *sir*," said Karras.

Preceding the awards was an auction which Karras presided over, shouting above the noise. The Flint merchants had donated a number of items, any one of which would have tested the mettle of the most expert of auctioneers. Among other things, there were ten Big Boy flashlights to be got rid of; ten stencil kits; five domino sets; and quite a lot of men's wear. "What do I hear for these socks?" Karras would shout, holding them aloft. "Do I hear a dollar for these socks? They run from size ten to thirty-three. Size thirty-three will cover your entire body!" The last item was a small desk globe. Karras tried to sell it to the man with one testicle. "Dave, you'll want this thing around the house," he called out tenderly.

For the awards ceremony Karras was relieved by Sonny Eliot, the Detroit TV weather-caster. Eliot is an extraordinary phenomenon in the area—a small lively man with a quicksilver approach who has added such a dimension of entertainment to reporting the weather that he is a considerable hometown celebrity, right up there with Gordie Howe, the hockey player, and Al Kaline of the Tigers, and six blocks ahead of the mayor. Detroit people set alarm clocks to be sure they don't miss Sonny Eliot's program, which concludes the eleven P.M. evening news —waking up to see what comic ingenuity he can bring to a weather front bearing down on the Peninsula area.

But even Eliot seemed somewhat shaken by his duties. Taking over the microphone, he held it as if he expected it to explode. Karras and Buterakos stood behind him and prompted him from time to time. The chief awards were for the winning foursome. All day long there had been rumors that each member of the low-ball team was going to win a car. Flint is a big automobile town with many General Motors divisions, particularly Chevrolet, and a number of people lining up birdie putts doubtless sparked their concentration by reminding themselves that a car could be riding on the stroke.

"And now the grand moment!" Sonny Eliot shouted. A silence descended. A group near the "Mexican Hat Dance" man turned around and tried to get him quieted down. "Each member of the winning foursome . . ." Eliot shouted, and he read off their names ". . . receives an auto-mo-*bile*"—incredulous cries— "and we got these cars right outside waiting for their new owners!"

One of the winners was sitting down the table from me, and his eyes were bright with excitement. He had bought a Big Boy flashlight set during the auction and he began banging it on the table. "Holy Christ!" he shouted.

Eliot was calling directions to a group of people down at one end of the tent. The flaps were hauled back and we stood up from our benches and craned to see in the semi-darkness what turned out to be four wrecks hauled in from a junkyard, victims of head-on collisions, wheelless, jumbles of blue metal, and Sonny Eliot began shouting, "All right, you winners, you'll find the keys above the sun visor. Gentlemen, start your engines and let's get those damn things out of there."

The winner with the Big Boy flashlight began shaking his head. I felt a twinge of sympathy. There must have been some part of him which felt that he really *was* going to get a car, with its new-leather smell, and he was going to slide into the front seat and reach for the keys . . .

After the ceremony I wandered over and spoke to Karras, who had a cigar stuck dead center in his mouth. He removed it and said that he and Buterakos were already jotting down ideas for next year's Karras Classic. "It's going to be bigger and louder," he said.

Buterakos came by. "We're talking about next year's Karras Classic," I said.

"We're going to shoot Alex out of a cannon," Buterakos said. "Did he tell you about the trumpeters in the trees?"

"Oh yeah," said Karras. "There're going to be these trumpeters in the trees. A lot of them. You'll see them sitting up there, and they'll blow a lot of cavalry charges."

"What about the animals?" Buterakos said. "Tell him about the animals."

"Yeah," said Karras. "These animals are going to rush out onto the fairway from the forest—whole herds of them. We'll ship them in secretly at night and get these kids to drive them out during the tournament. Strange animals, too, like llamas; these Flint golfers' will look up from their shot and say, 'What the hell's *that?*' "

"And yaks," Buterakos said. "The bushes part and these yaks stream out."

"Is there an animal called a ginook?" Karras asked abruptly.

"A ginook? I don't think so," I said.

"Well, there ought to be," Karras said. His eyes were fixed. "The bushes part and these ginooks rush out, a whole mess of them.

"Then we're going to have these mysterious professionals playing with some of the foursomes. We'll tell these Flint businessmen that boy, are they lucky. 'You may not have drawn Al Kaline for your celebrity,' we'll tell them, 'but you've got an honest-to-God professional playing with you. You've drawn Bill *Tank*. You're going to break the course record.'

" 'Bill who?' they'll ask.

" 'Why, Bill Tank. The pro. He's out of San Fernando Country Club. Came in third in the Western Open one year.'

"So these Flint guys get all excited," Karras continued, "and they get out early on the course to practice their putting. They bet on themselves. Then, to meet them on the first tee, we get this seedy cat in old britches and he says, 'Tank's the name. I'm your pro partner,' and he steps up and hits the ball about thirty-two feet. He drinks a lot, this guy, out of a stone jug, and on the fourth hole he topples into a sand trap and they can't get him out of there. He's out cold."

"How is the rest of Bill Tank's foursome going to take this?" I asked.

"Take it? Well, the thing is, you keep them off balance so they don't know if they're being taken for a ride or maybe just unlucky. You ride out to see them in a golf cart, somewhere on the back nine, all excited, and you say, 'Gee, for God's sake, where's Bill Tank? You guys must be ripping the course apart.'

"They give you one of these—the cold look—and say that Tank's back in some goddamn sand trap, out colder than ice. 'What a damn shame,' you say, 'what a real damn shame you got him on one of his bad days.' "

"Alex," said Buterakos. "I'm going to stir up the natives." He gave a blast on his whistle. "Get the drinking under way!" he shouted. As he walked off he called back, "You tell him about the midget?"

"Yeah, the midget," said Alex. "Well, we tell this one foursome that they've got a great pro playing with them, this guy called Jim 'Dynamite' Grogan, and they get to the first tee all excited and say, 'Well, where's Grogan?' and the midget steps up and says, '*I'm* Grogan.' He's real nattily dressed in a golf outfit, very correct, and he's got this great hulking caddy, a real monster of a guy, who carries the midget's golf bag tucked under one arm, the way you carry a telescope.

"The midget steps up to tee off. He's got this British ball he's playing with, which is a little smaller than the American, and after he's put it down on the tee, he squints out from under his tiny little golf hat and says in that little helium voice that midgets have, 'Hey, how *long* is this course?' They tell him it's about six thousand yards. 'Six thousand *yards?*' the midget says.

"Well, it turns out that the midget regularly plays these par-three courses, with the more difficult holes marked up to fours and fives, and he gets around in what scratch players do around a regular course—maybe seventy, seventy-two. He's never played a regular course. So he tells these Flint businessmen, 'Gee, you guys, this is quite an experience for me. This is some privilege, playing a regular course.'

"He steps up to the ball and he's got this real perfect grooved swing, sweet as anything, except the arc of it isn't more than three feet. The ball goes out, *click*, real straight for fifty yards down the center of the fairway. The midget watches it, real proud, and the Flint businessmen hear him say to himself, 'Oh, you sweetheart. You really sweethearted *that* one.' "

"How do the Flint businessmen go for this, Alex?" I asked.

"You blame the PGA," Karras said blithely. "You tell the Flint businessmen that the PGA recommended this guy, and how are you going to tell from the guy's name, Jim 'Dynamite' Grogan, that he measures in at a shade over three feet tall?"

"And the caddies?" I asked. "I suppose you'll have a number of them planted to do mischief."

"The caddies!" Karras began to laugh, his hand flying up to his mouth. "Oh my," he said. "The caddies. Oh Christ. We'll get these real wise-guy caddies, these old Scottish people, old and wrinkled, and with these thin mean voices, so that you think they're terribly old *women*, one hundred and fifty years old, but they 'know the course.' And they give these Flint guys this weird advice—like they show the guy an angle off the tee facing a forest that goes all the way to the Canadian border, and they say, 'Clear that tree and you're home-free on the dog-leg.'

" 'Hell, man . . .'

" 'It's the shot, I'm telling you. Hit it right and you drop right down for a wee easy chip. I've been working this course for sixty years.'

"So the guy faces around in this absurd position, just as crazy a shot as hitting off the stern of a boat, and he hits a tremendous drive, probably the best drive of his life, and after a while they can hear the ball rattling around in the tree trunks. So the caddy says, 'What did you hit it in there for? That's a bloody forest.'

" 'You *told* me to,' the guy says.

" 'You were supposed to *fade* the shot,' the caddy says, 'not hit it into the bloody forest,' and he gets all disgusted and stomps around, this furious wizened little man, and the guy from Flint feels all *guilty*."

Buterakos' whistle was shrilling in the distance. "His mind is turning," Karras said. "Hey, you want some golf tomorrow?"

"You must be kidding, Alex."

"I know a good course a hitch down the road," he said. "We'll play early tomorrow morning."

"Will there be trumpeters in the trees?" I asked.

He looked at me. "What are you talking about?"

"Or llamas? The bushes parting and these llamas rushing out?"

"You gone loco?" he asked. "A friendly game of golf—that's all I had in mind."

"I wasn't sure," I said. "I just thought I'd ask."

8

They came in the morning. Both seemed in good spirits, though the night before we had been on the town with a group of people and everybody had got home, Karras and Gordy to their hotel, about three in the morning. One of the girls out with us that evening was Wendy Vanderbilt, the daughter of Alfred Gwynne Vanderbilt, who owns a great stable of race horses—a very pretty girl whose date, a young man wearing a black suit of expensive cut, sat brooding at the little night club table around which we were crushed. He kept looking across at her, half listening to the rest of us.

Karras was talking about him that morning. He referred to him as Vanderbilt's "sidekick." "Hey, do you know what the sidekick said to me last night?"

"What?"

"He said to me that he enjoyed boxing. I said, 'That's wonderful.' He said, 'I think I could knock you out.' I said, 'Well, you might be able to knock me out, but before you did, I would probably beat the crap out of you!' He looked at me, and then he said, 'You might have a point there.' Isn't that great? 'You might have a point there.' " He leaned back and roared with laughter.

An evening out with Karras and Gordy always seemed to attract its dramas, as if some quality in them courted a punchinello mood. I remember having dinner with Karras one night in a small uptown Italian restaurant, years back, when I first knew him, and he was carrying a little case which he opened up on the table and showed me. Inside was an electric vibrator machine, a hand model, with a long electric cord, and various interchangeable implements that could be attached to it. These accessories lay in shaped indentations in the box, like instruments in a surgical kit, and Karras picked out a few of them to demonstrate. "These fit on the vibrator itself, which is called the Picomaster," he told me. "I'm into big, big business with the Picomasters. I'm the Midwest distributor. I should tell you that these vibrators are the best of their kind—known in the trade as the 'Cadillac' of vibrators."

"Very grand," I said.

"Right. Now here are some of the accessory attachments for the Picomaster. This rubber suction cup is for the female pectoral region," he said in a voice heavy with sincerity. "This attachment," he said, taking another accessory out and clicking it onto the vibrator, "is for general massage purposes."

He looked around.

"Ah."

Behind him, at a neighboring table with her back to us, was a woman in a dress cut just below the shoulder blades. She was bending over her soup. Karras leaned down, found a socket in the wall next to our table and plugged the cord in. A low hum rose from the vibrator. "The Picomaster lives," he said.

He turned in his chair and applied the "general massage" unit to the woman's back. She stiffened abruptly, and her escort, sitting across from her, looked up in alarm. "Hey, what the hell?"

"Don't worry," said Karras. "It's the Picomaster! Hold steady there, ma'am."

She had half turned and was staring into Karras' big pale face; her spoon remained poised an inch above the soup.

"That's better," Karras said soothingly. "The brushes on this massage unit are *sisal*—the very best sisal and just the thing to soothe jangled nerve ends."

The woman's back was beginning to glow a vaguely mottled red under the vibrator brushes. I kept watching her escort, expecting a violent reaction. He had a tentative, somewhat worried expression; perhaps he recognized Karras, or had been intimidated by his size.

"Helen?" he asked, as if her reaction would determine what he was going to do. There was no answer.

"I wonder if you would tell me how it feels, ma'am," Karras said solemnly.

"Well, it feels sort of *rubbery*," she said after a while.

"Exactly," said Karras. He removed the vibrator from the woman's back and turned in his chair. He looked directly at me, but his eyes were not focused; he was fantasizing again, this time speaking a commercial into the lens of a television camera. He intoned: "And *that's* the Picomaster, the Cadillac of hand vibrators, the only sure-fire cure for what ails you, and you've seen it *live*—a Picomaster at work on the back of this lovely young woman picked at random. Now watch how this woman, newly massaged by the Picomaster, digs into her soup with renewed vigor."

His eyes focusing again, he said, "What I need is a long extension cord. I could give a demonstration to everyone in the restaurant."

The woman tapped him on the shoulder. "Are you *taping* this, or something? Is there a camera somewhere? Don't I have to sign a release or something?"

"No, ma'am," said Karras. "It's a personal survey. We're just spreading the word."

I had asked Karras and Gordy to my apartment that morning in the hope that they would talk about football players

114

and their business ventures, such as the involvement with the Picomaster vibrator. Business was always a constant topic with players. Invariably, there was a frantic, naïve quality to such discussions—wild-eyed excitement as they described oil fields, mutual funds, land values, food franchises, speculations in timber, duck farms, fortunes to be made by investing in locomotives, boxcars or penny stocks. One could scarcely get through a day at training camp without hearing a big tackle clear his throat and remark, "Nice yield on that Caroline-Sidney preferred." There was only one Lion player who ever admitted to me that business matters were beyond his ken. "Hell," Dick LeBeau, the cornerback, told me, "I couldn't sell ass on a troopship."

I began by asking Karras about the Picomaster. Had that been a success? Both he and Gordy groaned. From the first, I was informed, the Picomaster venture had been a painful business. It was a distribution deal, arranged with a German manufacturer's representative, and they found themselves overwhelmed with enormous stocks of vibrators they could not seem to unload.

"They arrived in enormous cartons higher than a man's head," Gordy said.

"Remember the time we took the Picomasters out to the race track?" Karras said. "We were desperate, trying to sell them. Pete Larco and I went out. Larco," he explained to me, "was a partner in the Picomaster deal. He runs a restaurant, Larco's, where all the Lions go after a home game. Well, we went out to the race track at six o'clock in the morning, just after the horses had been exercised. We went in and talked to this guy, one of the top trainers in the country, who said, 'You know, I don't think anyone in the horse business has ever *thought* of rubbing horses down with a vibrator. But why not? Let's try it on the most temperamental horse we have.'

"Well, we were all real excited. We went down to the stables where there was this one horse, absolutely mammoth, a real Thoroughbred, you could tell, who was just *tense*, man. The trainer said, 'Calm, baby. Calm, baby.' He turned the vibrator on, *b-z-z-z-z*, and put it on the horse's neck. God's truth,

I'm not lying. The horse went *b-b-l-l-a-a-h-h-h* . . . just completely relaxed. Like a lamb. Damn near went to sleep on us right there in the stall. The trainer really flipped. 'It's the first time this horse has ever relaxed,' he said. 'This vibrator of yours will revolutionize horse racing!' We thought we were saved. A Picomaster for every Thoroughbred."

"Of course that horse never ran a good race again," said Gordy.

"That's right," Karras said. "Larco and I went out to the track the next time he ran. We put a fin on him, a 'sure thing' we thought, because of the Picomaster, but I don't recall that he ever came out of the starting gate. At least, that's what we decided—that the horse had put his head out of the gate at the starting bell to see what all the commotion was about and then had gone back in there to *sleep*. But at the time the trainer thought the vibrator had great therapeutic value. He bought his for cash right there in the stall."

"John," I asked Gordy, "How were you involved in the Picomaster project?"

He clasped his head. "Oh my," he said. "I was one of the pitchmen. I worked in Montgomery Wards. I was there from eight o'clock in the morning to six o'clock at night. I never talked so much in my life. I stood up on a little platform. 'All right, all right. Gather round. We're going to have a demonstration of the amazing new revolutionary Picomaster.' "

"We had these plants in the audience," Karras explained. "We'd pay them to stand out there—crumpled over, with one arm twitching like the guy had the palsy—and John would call out, 'You, sir. You with the arm! Come up! You look like you need . . .' And this guy would *crawl* up on the stage, all bent over like a hunchback, and John would say, 'All right, sir, we'll just kind of rub you down with this vibrator, we'll just kind of rub this thing here, this *hump* . . .' and the guy would straighten up like an arrow. 'It does feel better. Yessir, it does.' Oh, it was terrible."

"All day long I did it," Gordy said. " 'Gather round, gather round!' " He was laughing so hard he could barely stay in his chair.

"Remember the *arthritis*?" Karras shouted.

"Oh Christ!"

"John would run the vibrator over this guy's *fingers*. 'Can you feel it, sir? Can you feel any change?' 'Why, I do believe I can! My fingers are better! My fingers are better!' 'That's right, sir, your fingers *are* better.' "

Gordy shouted, "Then I'd say to the crowd, 'Did everybody hear this amazing statement, right from the lips of a man who's had arthritis since he was nineteen? Speak right up, sir.' 'My fingers are better. My fingers are better.' "

"It's a wonder the Food and Drug authorities didn't lock us up for a hundred and ten years," Karras said.

It took a while for the two of them to calm down and I was able to ask them if they could generalize about business and football. "*Can* a player become involved in another profession?" I asked.

"It's impossible," said Gordy. "The frightening thing about playing professional football is that it gives you a false sense of security. The trouble is that a player enters football when he's about twenty-one. Barring an injury which obviously will put him out earlier, he has a career of ten to fifteen years during which he advances his education only in football. He has time for little else. But the guy up in the stands who comes to watch him play, who envies him, who daydreams of doing great things out there on the field—well, all that time *he's* pecking along in his own profession, day by day, learning, until finally at thirty-five he's a vice-president or a manager, and he's got all that practical experience behind him. On the other hand, the football player, when he leaves his profession to try another —hell, he's just *starting*."

"He's been dormant for fifteen years," Karras said. "So he goes in there for his first job interview and says, 'My name is Alex Karras. I played football for the Detroit Lions.' And these cats look up from their big wide desks, and they rattle some papers, and they say, 'Hey, Al, how's the team going to do on Sunday?' "

"Does this make you feel sorry for yourselves?" I asked. "I mean that you picked football?"

"No, no," Karras said. "I've accepted it. There's a good pension plan."

"It's just being realistic," said Gordy.

"Besides," Karras went on, "what I've done since I've started pro ball is to scrimp and save, so that when I finally leave football I'll have enough to invest in something that will give me a comfortable annual income."

"And how much money do you think you'll have to invest, Mister Karras?" asked Gordy, playing the straight man.

"I feel," said Karras, "that twenty-seven dollars and fifty cents will take me to great heights."

"Christ, that's the truth, man," Gordy said.

I asked if it wasn't possible to apprentice at a job while playing football, but both Karras and Gordy said that playing professional football and being in business at the same time was an impossible combination, and that a player's ability at both suffered if he tried them simultaneously. "It's like someone being a doctor," Karras said, "and turning around early in the morning and being a milkman. I mean, you've either got to be one or the other. A guy can't honestly concentrate on the game of football and be in business at the same time."

"What about during the off-season?"

"The off-season isn't that long," Karras said. "By the time you're wrapped up in some business arrangement, you get that call again, you put the jockstrap back on and out you go."

"Besides," Gordy said, "if you've got to be in training camp by July tenth, you should be working out in June, and if you're an older player, you probably should start getting ready in April. And in the off-season many of us should be in the training room lifting weights. That sounds like a dumb thing for a man to be doing on a winter morning, but I'm worried about a pinched nerve, and my shoulder problem, and the tendonitis in my arm, and the operation on my knee, and the twisted Achilles tendon—all that *junk*. I have to do it. If I can build up a certain muscle tone around the nerves of my neck by lifting weights, then I'm less likely to have that pinched nerve in training camp, and I'm likely to have a better year as a result.

"And hell, in the evening, when maybe I could be working at another job, it's better if I watch football movies every now and then to keep myself thinking about my stance, about pulling, about my footwork, about watching my opponents, about—well, how the hell can you think about putting together conglomerates when you've got all *that* tugging at you? You've got a very limited time left to think about other things."

"That's true," Karras said. "Besides, most employers don't want to hire a guy for five or six months who's got his mind half on something else. Consequently, about the only job a football player can get is selling things door to door, and the simpler the object—like a screwdriver—the better. It's important to get your foot in the door, and that's the one advantage the football player has. He knocks on the door and he says, 'Hello, my name is Alex Karras. I play with the Detroit Lions.' 'Oh yes,' the guy says, and if he's a football fan he lets you in. That's it—just an entrée. Beyond that, it's tough, especially if what you're trying to sell him is anything complicated. No one has the time to teach you the business properly. So this guy asks, 'How does the three-inch channel distributor compare to this *five*-inch baby?' What am I to do? I look at my shoes and I repeat, like a robot, 'My name is Alex Karras. I play with the Detroit Lions.' "

Actually, Karras was demeaning his abilities as a door-to-door salesman. Joe Schmidt once gave me a description of Karras selling Bibles door to door—one of his jobs, along with professional wrestling, during the year of his banishment from the NFL for gambling. Karras had met a Bible distributor, a very sharp cat, who had said, "Karras, the Bible is the only item in the world that people are ashamed *not* to buy. There can only be one hitch." "What's that?" Karras had asked. "That's if the people say, 'Sorry, we're Jewish.' Well, we have an *answer* to that," the distributor said, rummaging in his suitcase. "We have these Bibles made in Germany by Jewish craftsmen. Right? So if they come up with 'I'm Jewish,' you just throw the Bible at them and tell them it was made by Jews. Karras was naturally skeptical, but he felt he could make at least one sale—to Joe Schmidt, who, besides being a close friend back then, was a

God-fearing man and a regular churchgoer, to say nothing of being of German heritage. So Karras tucked a couple of Bibles under his arm and went to call on Schmidt.

The exchange was difficult from the beginning. When he opened the door, Schmidt was delighted to see Karras, but when he discovered the purpose of the visit, he said firmly, "No, Al, I've already got a good family Bible in the parlor. I don't need another."

"Well, you'll need a reserve," Karras said crisply.

"What would I want a reserve Bible for?"

"In case something happens to the one you've got now," Karras said impatiently. "Christ Almighty. Suppose the mice got at it."

"The mice?"

"Right, man. The mice. Or maybe termites, Joe. I mean, suppose you open up the big family Bible at some great occasion, the christening of a baby, with everyone standing around all *pious*, and it turns out that Revelations has been eaten away."

"What the hell are you talking about?"

"That's when you can wheel out the reserve, Joe. You look at all the worried people standing around there in your parlor, the baby beginning to whimper, and you give them the quiet, superior smile and say, 'Fear not, folks, I've got a reserve Bible for just this sort of emergency.'"

Schmidt grunted sourly, and Karras, sensing umbrage being taken at the suggestion that the Schmidt house harbored enough mice and termites to threaten the family Bible, shifted his tactics abruptly. "Joe?"

"What?"

"Joe, this Bible I'm trying to sell you, it's different—it's a *German* Bible, for one thing. Joe, wasn't your pappy a kraut?"

"For Chrissakes, Al, what the hell difference does it make if it's a German Bible?"

"It's been made by Jewish craftsman."

"Listen, Al, I've got things to do. I'm not really in the market for a Bible," Schmidt said, not unkindly. "Why don't you try someone else? What about Night Train Lane? Try him."

"Joe," said Karras, groping desperately. "There's one big difference in the German edition."

"What's that?"

"They've . . . they've changed it. They've fooled around with the ending."

"They've *what*?"

"That's right," Karras said. "The whole ending's different. It *comes out* different."

"What are you *talking* about?"

"You remember all that business about the Resurrection and Christ rising up from the dead and sitting on the right hand of God?"

"Yeah?"

"And how they rolled away the stone from the front of the cave and He wasn't there?"

"Yeah?"

"Well, that's not the way this German Bible has it. They roll away the stone and guess who's sitting in there looking out, smart as brass."

"Oh, damn, Al. I don't know."

"Guess."

"What?"

"Take a guess."

"Oh, I don't know. Was it Christ?"

"Christ? Hell, no. Much more interesting than that. Try again."

"Mary Magdalene? Pontius Pilate? Damnit, Al, I don't know *who* was sitting in the cave. Why don't you just tell me and let's get it over with."

"Joe," Karras said, holding up a Bible seductively, "it'll cost you exactly fifteen dollars and six cents, which includes the sales tax, to find out . . ."

That was enough for Schmidt. He closed the door, and went down to the basement of his house so he wouldn't hear the knocking and the doorknob rattling.

That morning I asked Karras and Gordy if the Lions had ever got together on a *joint* business venture. Wouldn't a cooperative attempt . . . ? Gordy interrupted with a burst of laughter. "Al," he said, "do you remember the phonograph record we thought was going to make us all billionaires?"

Karras doubled up in his chair.

Gordy could hardly speak. "I got this idea that some of the Lion players would get together as a singing group and cut a record. Everyone in town would buy it. Dick LeBeau and Joe Schmidt were the vocalists. Bruce Maher would play the guitar. I was the producer. So I got the players together and we rehearsed. Then I hired a band, and we actually physically cut a record and had ten thousand copies made. One side was 'The Grapes of Wrath' featuring Dick LeBeau; the other was 'Cry Out, Freedom' by John Philip Sousa. The day we finished was the day John F. Kennedy was assassinated. Can you imagine coming out with a record called 'Cry Out, Freedom' right after that?"

"The timing was bad," Karras agreed, "but that's not the reason you only sold ten records. I bought one of those records, put it on the jukebox at the Lindell A.C. bar and played it every three minutes. 'The Grapes of Wrath.' The guys would be leaning along the bar, a whole line of them, drunk, barely able to stand, and when that song 'The Grapes of Wrath' came on they'd get *sober*. They'd say, 'What the hell was *that*?' "

"You're right," Gordy said. "It was the *worst* song. Once we had a disc jockey party to introduce them all to the record. We gave them each a copy and sent them back to their turntables. We never heard it played. We called around: 'I'll send you another copy if you've lost the one we gave you.' I felt like telling them that if they really liked it I knew where I could get my hands on ninety-five hundred copies."

"Do you remember The Four Coins?" Karras asked. "A singing group. They sang 'Shangri-La'—Greek kids from Pittsburgh. One day the Coins were in Detroit and they came down to the bar. I thought maybe I could convince them to do something about 'The Grapes of Wrath,' so I gave them free drinks. I never gave *anyone* free drinks. I asked these guys, 'When was the last time you had a real hit record?' They said, 'Nineteen thirty-three,' or whenever the hell it was. I said, 'Well, I've got something for you; it's going to be your *next* hit. We'll fix up a royalty deal, but you got to give five percent to the guys who did it originally.' They said, 'Sure, why not?'

"You know something? I really thought they'd like it. I was beginning to think 'The Grapes of Wrath' was pretty good, maybe because I'd heard it five thousand times on the jukebox and it had got to me. So I turned it on. The Four Coins sat there without any expression. When it was over, I was real excited. 'How did you like it?' One of the Coins looked like he was going to vomit on himself. He said, 'That's the worst song I've ever heard.' "

"Who sang the 'Cry Out, Freedom' song?" I asked.

"Joe Schmidt," Karras answered. "Joe's got a bathroom voice; sounds good in bathrooms."

"He's very embarrassed about that record," Gordy said. "When he was made head coach of the Lions, some guy called up and said they were going to hawk 'Cry Out, Freedom' outside the stadium on opening day. Joe called the mayor and got him to refuse to issue these guys a peddler's permit."

"I think that's why he traded away Bruce Maher to the Giants," Karras said. "I told Joe, 'Now there's only LeBeau left to remind you.' "

"I suppose in these fly-by-night schemes—well, you can take a helluva bath," I said.

"In my case," said Gordy, "it was a chain of hamburger joints. 'Gordy's Lionburgers.' " He shook his head and Karras snickered.

"These business guys came to me and said that since I was a football player with a name, they would agree to accept me—and my money—in the restaurant business. It all seemed very glamorous—my name up in lights on this big sign: GORDY'S LIONBURGERS. And easy: they would keep the books and records and run the place. No problem at all!

"Two years later, I couldn't find those people. Or the books or the records. Or the money. I was ruined—literally— and I had to declare bankruptcy. The whole thing was a disaster. We did have two Gordy's Lionburgers stands physically up and running, but they were failing badly. My name wasn't as big as I thought it was. I should have known that offensive guards haven't got selling names. Besides, people didn't associate 'Lionburger' with the Detroit football team. Maybe they thought we were offering them exotic cuts from big cats. I don't know. I do know that a lot of people came in and ordered *loin*burgers. I'm telling you, I got a good business degree out of that experience—the Lionburger Hard Knocks School."

"Is that typical? Do a lot of football players go through experiences like that?"

"They certainly get the opportunity," Gordy said.

"That's right," Karras said, shifting in his chair. "Like oil strikes. Always! Ever since I've been in the league there have been oil strikes. A football player runs into the room and shouts, 'Man, I've got a deal on oil. The gusher's coming in! The oil is one *inch* under the ground. All they've got to do is put a little finger in there and the oil just pops up.' "

"That's right," Gordy said. "The oil is just offshore, and as soon as the tide goes out all they've got to do is walk out and fetch it in."

"What sort of person gets players involved in propositions of that sort?"

"Almost everyone," said Gordy.

"It's usually a guy from New York," Karras added, "with a slick, shiny suit, and a nice tie, and a gigantic jeweled diamond for a tie clasp. Now someone like that, you *know* he's got to be making money, right? See, I'm sitting there in the bar with my hand around a small beer, and I've got my T-shirt and Levis on, and this guy, all shiny, steps up and says he needs five hundred dollars of *my* money and he'll make me a rich man."

"Why do players fall for this sort of thing?" I asked.

"One of the reasons," Karras replied, "is that football players are gullible because they've been surrounded and protected by such nice people. In high school, the coaches are nice because they want you to do the job. So are the teachers, because being on the football team you represent the school. It's the same at college. So you've hung around with nice people all the time, and you tend to think that *all* people are nice, including the guys in the shiny suits."

Gordy nodded. "Then you find that they have the ax out."

Karras said, "They're sharks. Most of the time you find them in the bars. They always begin by coming up and saying, 'How ya doing?' One time we were just getting ready to close the old Lindell A.C. bar and move into the new place. It was the year I was suspended. I was in the new place, polishing the bar and looking out at the empty barstools, when all of a sudden in comes this guy from New York with a shiny suit and a gigantic stickpin and a ring on his finger so big that he had difficulty lifting his hand, which had in its fingers a glossy calling card that read: MAX EINSTEIN. 'How ya doing?' he said. He sat down on one of the barstools. 'I've got a real jewel for you.'

" 'Okay,' I said. 'What is it?'

" 'You know how much salmon comes out of Alaska per month?'

"I'm always being asked goddamn questions like that—those real impossible questions which are used to start a long boring speech. I'd give anything to know the answer. Like if one of those guys asked me, 'Hey, buddy, you know how much orange juice the American public drinks per day?' and I was able to answer real quick, 'Sure, four thousand three hundred and seventy-two tons. What of it?' Well, that would throw him. Something would go wrong in his eye.

"Anyway, I always try to answer questions like that in the hope that just once I'll stumble on the right answer. So when he asked how much salmon came out of Alaska, I said, after thinking awhile, 'Thirty-five tons.'

"He didn't even answer me. He asked, 'You know how many salmon canneries there are in Alaska?'

" 'Two?'

" 'Five,' he says. 'There's a cannery in Alaska that's going under. You can get it for a song—twenty-five thousand dollars.'

" 'What's the deal?' I asked.

" 'I've got these fishing vessels,' he said—Max Einstein from New York with his big stickpin and he's got *fishing* vessels.

Fifteen of them. 'Not only have I got fifteen boats,' he went on, 'but I've found virgin waters. I'm telling you, no one has ever taken salmon out of these waters. They are *virgin*.'

"I said, 'That sounds pretty good. What's the picture?'

"He said, 'I need twenty-five thousand to get the cannery started properly.'

"I asked him if he had a lawyer in Detroit.

" 'No,' he said, 'but we can fix up the papers between ourselves.'

"I told him that I thought I could get a lot of the other Lion players involved.

" 'That's great,' he said. He was getting very excited. 'We want you to get as many of the guys as possible. If you can get enough other guys, you won't have to pay your share. We'll *waive* it.'

" 'What are we going to call this cannery?' I asked.

" 'Virgin Waters Cannery!'

"Man, I'll never forget that: Virgin Waters Cannery. But by that time I was experienced enough not to bite on such proposals. Two years before, he'd have caught me, *easy*. I'd have been in for five big ones, and I probably would have persuaded some of the other players to come in with me. At training camp I would have gone into their rooms. 'Hey, do you know how much salmon comes out of Alaska?' And I'd start my pitch."

"You would have gotten me," said Gordy.

"You know how I would have ended up?" asked Karras. "I'd have had fifty thousand cans of salmon in the basement of my house! My kids would have been eating salmon until it came out their ears. Virgin Waters Cannery!"

"What else have you got down there in the cellar?" Gordy asked.

"Are those phonograph records down there?" Karras wondered in alarm. "Are the 'Grapes of Wrath' and 'Cry Out, Freedom' in my cellar? Jesus Christ, they could be! It's awful crowded down there. I know there are some Picomasters down there—four or five big crates."

"My cellar's pretty crowded, too," Gordy admitted.

126

"You got a lot of old Lionburgers down there?" Karras asked. "I always thought you were lucky because at least your stuff was *perishable*."

The two of them sat quietly, considering the state of their respective cellars.

Karras stirred. "Sometimes it's a guy with an invention who traps the football player. Inventions are big. One time a guy called me and said over the phone, 'How ya doing?' He told me that he had a real jewel for me—an inventor who'd come up with a great new health machine. So I said, 'That sounds great.'"

"What's so great about a health machine?" Gordy asked.

"Well, I was *curious*," Karras said. "The inventor might have been a guy with a billion-dollar idea. You never can be sure. So I asked the guy to tell me more."

"'This thing is sensational,' the guy said, 'but I can't explain it to you over the phone.'"

"'It must be quite something,' I said.

"He said, 'Come on down and you can look at it and see whether or not you would care to invest in it. Why don't you bring a business partner with you—maybe another football player?'

"So I called up Pete Larco, who had been partners with me in the Picomaster venture. I said, 'Hey, Pete, how ya doing?' I told him we might have another venture, with almost as much potential as the vibrators. This was when we were just starting with vibrators and before the crash. He said, 'You're kidding! But I'm not through with the vibrators yet.' Even *then* he was sick of vibrators. He was up to his ass in them. He had to move vibrators to get to his telephone."

"I remember that," said Gordy. "He had this nice little apartment downstairs in his restaurant, and it was *stocked* with vibrators. They were coming out of the wall."

"There was about this much space left," Karras said, indicating with his hands, "where you could walk in between to get to the bathroom. A wall of Picomasters."

"Yeah," Gordy said. "'Where's the toilet paper, Pete?' 'Under the vibrators.'"

"But Pete's like me," Karras said. "When I told him about the inventor and his health machine, he got curious. 'It sounds sensational,' he said. 'I'll be right down.'

"So this guy who had telephoned me took us into the old part of Detroit where this inventor had his workshop. It was actually a little auto repair shop, and the workshop was up these wooden stairs in an attic. We walked into the shop, and it was hot. It must have been a hundred and ten degrees—just *stifling* hot. Pete still had on his white apron. He was so excited that he'd just come rushing over from butchering something for his restaurant, and he was covered with blood and spaghetti sauce. My business partner!

"So this guy introduced us to the inventor, who was about a hundred and ninety years old. You knew immediately that he was a health nut because his face looked halfway decent, but his body was shot! I didn't really know how old he was until his wife—who was just rusting away—came easing in, and she must have been two hundred years old, if a day.

"Well, this guy told us in this high creaking voice that he thought that we would be just the people to distribute this item of his in the United States. 'I'm primarily an inventor,' he said. 'I don't have time to distribute. If you like the invention, we can work out a price where you can take the whole thing over.'

"We said that was fine. We were in the vibrator business, and we were kind of cocky. 'You came to the right people,' I told him. 'We're in the health business ourselves. Sure, we'd be interested.'

"He said, 'It's upstairs in the attic. That's my workshop.' So we went up these real creaky wooden stairs. Man, miles up! At every step it got hotter—the sweat just pouring off, especially from Pete, who's short, and sort of squat; he was just sweating his ass off. So we walked in and the inventor said, 'Well, there it is.'

"It was a sort of revolving hospital examining table, like one of those Frankenstein movie tables the monster lies on. It was built up on a scaffold of little pipes, and it had leather Frankenstein straps that came down over the arms and legs.

" 'It looks sensational,' I said. 'What does it do?'

"The inventor said, 'Are you familiar with yoga?' From the way he pronounced it, I thought he was referring to Yogi Berra, the baseball player. But then he said, 'Well, the secret of yoga is the redistribution of the parts of your body. In other words, people stand on their heads so that the kidneys can rest at a different angle for a while. In this way, the blood that flows within the capillaries is replenished.'

"Pete Larco said, 'Of course. We know about that; we're in the massage business.'

"The inventor looked at him and said, 'What we do is put a guy on this slab and strap him in so that he can't fall off. Then we turn on the motor and gradually elevate him, head down, so that the blood begins to flow down from his toes and through his sinews to his head, and as he revolves he gets this splendid *flow*, back and forth.'

"I said, 'In other words, you slowly flip him over, like something on a spit.'

" 'That's the principle,' he said.

" 'Pete,' I said. 'Get up on the thing. Try it out. Let's see how it works.'

"Pete shook his head, but finally he agreed. He climbed up on the slab and we strapped him down. The inventor talked at him like a hospital nurse. 'How are we feeling?' he asked Pete. 'Are we feeling good and secure?' Then he stepped back and pushed the button. A motor began whining and the table slowly tilted up. Pete's eyes opened wide; the blood was beginning to flow out of his feet. Meanwhile, while he was tilting slowly in front of us, the inventor and I began to discuss details. 'How many can you build in a month?' I asked. He said, 'Well, that depends on production orders.'

"I waited until Pete was absolutely upside down, his feet at eye level, his head just off the floor, and then I said, 'Hold it a minute right there.' The old guy pressed the buzzer and the machine stopped—with Pete hanging there, his face just *glowing* red, his veins popping—and I said to the old guy, 'Well, my projection of sales is that they will be higher in winter, especially in Northern cities like Buffalo, because people don't get enough exercise in the cold to get that proper *flow'* . . . just gabbing on like that, this old geezer nodding and saying, 'Yes, yes,' and all the time Pete is hanging upside down. I said, 'Why don't we go down to your office to work out the details?' We started down the wooden stairs, and behind us Pete began to shout, 'Hey, you bastards, get me out of this goddamn thing.' He could barely speak, his head was so congested. He sounded like he had a handkerchief in his mouth. He might have died there. So we went back and the inventor pressed the button to get him back on an even keel again. Man, Pete was as red as a lobster. The veins in his neck were just banging away, and his feet were pale white, just *ghostly.* When we got him unstrapped he could hardly stand. 'I'm going to have a stroke,' he said. 'In fact, I think I *had* a stroke.' We practically had to carry him down the wooden stairs."

"Did you end up investing in the machine?" I asked.

"The old guy gave some fantastic figure for the proto-type," Karras said. "Twenty-five thousand. I told him that Larco and I would give it a lot of thought and talk it over with our accountant. Poor old Pete almost had another stroke right on the stairs there, when the old man said twenty-five thousand. He gave a little moan."

"Poor Pete," said Gordy. "He had enough to worry about with the Picomasters. His restaurant was jammed to the rafters with vibrators. His employees were always falling over them— the waiters, the cooks. 'The phone's ringing. Where is it? Where's the phone?' 'It's in that pile of vibrators. Just dig around in there. You'll find it.' Poor Pete, he did everything he could to clear himself of all that stock. He went everywhere with sam-ples. He'd be out in the back of the kitchen, shoveling out spa-ghetti, and he'd ask the waiter, 'Who's buying this order?' If it was someone he knew, he'd go right out into the dining room with a plate of spaghetti in one hand and a Picomaster in the other. He'd give a demonstration right on the spot."

"What was our national slogan?" Karras asked.

"TRY IT AND YOU'LL BUY IT."

"Jesus, I'm sick," Karras said. He was laughing so hard he could hardly speak. "We went everywhere with them. We hung them around our necks. We'd be playing golf with friends and they'd say, 'What's that?' We'd say, 'I'm glad you asked. Funny you should notice!' I used to walk into barbershops—we thought that was the big potential market for our vibrators—and I'd say, 'Hello, hello, I'm Al Karras. How ya doin'?' The barber would say, 'How you doin', Al? You want a haircut?' 'No.' 'What you got there in your hand?' 'Funny you should ask . . .' "

"I know what you said then," Gordy said. He was slumped hopelessly in his chair. You said, 'Here it is. The Picomaster. It's the *Cadillac of its field*.' "

"Absolutely right," Karras replied. "One time this barber asked me what would happen if the vibrator broke down. 'This machine is German, isn't it?' he asked. 'Do I have to send it to Munich, Germany?'

" 'No, no,' I said. I had so many Picomasters that I was panicky. 'If it breaks down,' I told this guy, 'we'll give it instant repair.' The barber said, 'What do you mean by "instant repair"?' So I said, 'I'll give you another one to replace it.'

"Everywhere I went, I had one in my hand. Oh Christ, I'm sick. We thought it was going to *work*. We thought we were going to be *billionaires*. People *fought* over the franchises. 'I can give you Idaho and North Dakota.' 'Gee, thanks.' 'Texas ain't gone yet.' 'What? Oh Christ, can I have Texas too?' Dave DeBusschere, who was playing basketball for the Detroit Pistons then, got the Pennsylvania franchise. *Man*, he wanted it. When things went sour, he didn't talk to me for a year. I knew he was mad because he wouldn't put me on his summer softball team."

"What's happened since?" I asked. Where are all the vibrators now?"

Karras said, "My father-in-law out in Clinton, Iowa, has five thousand down in the basement—down in his recreation room. He had to move the ping-pong table out. He can't have any parties in there; he doesn't have any room. He might be able to get three people in there, but no more."

"Damn," said Gordy. "I wish I'd known about your father-in-law's recreation room. Maybe I could have stored some of the 'Cry Out, Freedom' records down there."

The two of them were out of their chairs now, stalking

stiff-legged around the room, bawling with laughter. It seemed as good a point as any to bring the discussion on "business" to a close. I got them quieted down, and we went out somewhere and had some lunch. I paid the check. The fact was that both of them were much better at money matters than they ever let on.

9

"How often do Karras and Gordy come and see you?" a friend asked.

"Oh, every once in a while."

"Jesus, it must be great to sit there and listen in on those people talking about football. Jesus!" He was a tremendous fan. "You must be getting all this great stuff."

"The best thing is how funny they are," I said.

"Funny?"

He looked at me in surprise, as if the word were inappropriate. He seemed miffed.

Humor has always been a major and somewhat neglected constant in professional sports—perhaps not a particularly high quality of humor, but pervasive, though not much discussed or written about since the popular view of professional football is that it is what my friend imagines—largely a grim, dedicated business.

Yet the humor *was* everywhere—in the good stories one heard, in the quick ripostes and the one-liners, the constant joshing and put-downs, invariably bawdy and raucous—all of it a hedge against the boredom and regimen. True, the most elaborate level of the humor was often the practical joke, considered a lowly form in most societies.

Authorities consider the Americans the world's greatest experts at the practical joke, with the English a close second, the French a distant third, and no one else at all in the running. Latins are psychologically ill-equipped to perpetuate practical jokes, though they are splendid victims since an essential ingredient is the ability to *imagine* rather than witness the joke's denouement. The American sense of detachment is more constituted to this. For example, an American can crate up a large barber chair and send it to a family in Malaya, say, with no return address or sender's card—and sit back in his bath and bask in imagining the puzzlement of the family halfway around the world as the barber chair emerges slowly from its wrappings. The Latin, on the other hand, is too impatient to let his imagination satisfy him. He wants to be on hand to witness what is going on, and if he could, he would surely fly to Malaya to caper around in the flower beds outside the house, chinning himself so he can peer in over the window sill to watch the chair being unpacked and to check the reactions of the bewildered family.

Of course the foremost perpetrator of practical jokes on the Lions was Alex Karras. But the odd quality of his tomfoolery was that it was marked by a strong Latin flavor. He was intensely curious about the effect of the joke on his victims, and also, I think, he was self-centered enough to wish to indicate publically that he was the joke's author, which is not at all in the spirit of the true American prank.

For example, I remember Karras at the motel where Detroit stayed when they came to San Francisco to play the 49ers—lying prostrate on the bed yawning, and then reaching for the phone and asking for John North's room. North was the offensive end coach, a dedicated man with an abbreviated sense of suspicion, a fine dupe for someone of Karras' deviousness.

"John," Karras said. "The photographer from the *Chron-*

icle is up here. He wants a picture of you and all your receivers, a formal picture with blazers and ties. You better call them together. Where? Down by the swimming pool. He'll meet you there in ten minutes."

By and by, Karras swung his legs off the bed and pulled the window curtains of his room slightly ajar to peek out. "Hey, look at this."

Those of us in the room peered out on an Antonioni-like scene of seven or eight men, all with coats and ties, moving around the motel swimming pool, which was empty, in a San Francisco fog heavy enough to be classified as a drizzle.

At the window Karras' shoulders heaved as he giggled. "They've been down there for twenty minutes," he said.

We watched as one by one they drifted back to their rooms. The last to leave was a first-year man short on personal publicity, craving "ink," dragging his feet as he left the desolate fog-swept scene with its empty pool, looking back over his shoulder one last time for the photographer from the *Chronicle* as he swung the motel door shut behind him.

At this point in one of his jokes, Karras, never letting well enough alone, would begin to fidget. At the team dinner that night he would suddenly ask in a voice loud enough to be heard in most sections of the room, "Hey, what were you guys all standing around this afternoon in the rain for—in your blazers and ties and everything? That's pretty quirky. That's weird."

Those players who did not already know that Karras was responsible could tell by the cast of his voice, loud and merry and supercilious, that he was behind the joke, and they would look down at the remains of their steaks and potatoes, eyes narrowed, wondering at their gullibility in being tricked yet again.

It always seemed to me that Karras was putting his life on the line with such capers, because his dupes were invariably large people with quick tempers, and certainly possessing the physical wherewithal to dish out retributory punishment. Of course, Karras himself was large, and unbelievably powerful; perhaps this was a canceling factor.

The most dangerous of Karras' stunts, with the most

chance of severe physical retribution, was a ritual he occasionally put a few of the rookies through when he was still the proprietor of the old Lindell A.C., a somewhat seedy bar which he
was forced to divest himself of to get back into the good graces
of the Commissioner during the year of his banishment from
football. The bar was on the first floor of a run-down hotel with
about forty rooms, many of them occupied by skid-row bums
and people barely scraping along. Room 232 had a two-way mirror set in the wall, so that eight or ten people could pack into
room 233 and watch what was going on next door without its
occupants being aware.

The voyeuristic entertainment would be initiated by Karras sidling up to a Detroit Lion rookie visiting the bar for the
first time and saying, "See that girl over there?"

"Who?"

"That girl over there wearing the blue thing—hell, man,
the only girl in the place."

"Oh, her. Yeah, I see her."

"Well, she can hardly sit still, she has such eyes for you."

"Wha'?"

"That's right. In fact, she wants to meet you upstairs—
in room 232."

"No kidding."

So after four or five quick beers, the rookie would go up
to the room to see the girl—who was in on the gag, of course,
and knew that in the next room Karras and four or five others,
trying to keep their voices down, were sitting in hard-backed
chairs and looking through the trick mirror. Occasionally, she
would make faces at the mirror over the rookie's shoulder.

Karras said that often it was hard to keep from falling
off the chair from trying to contain one's laughter. The best to
watch were the country boys who came in shy and awkward,
and huge if they were tackles or guards, not knowing whether
to sit on the bed, which was the only piece of furniture in the
room, or to stand, and getting one shoe off finally and maybe
another, and often forgetting to get out of their shirts and ties.

When the rookie came back down to the bar, Karras
would be there waiting.

"How was it?"

"Great."

"Hey, tell me something. You always wear your socks?"

"Wha'?"

"And where'd you get that tattoo on your butt? The one with the little red heart that says 'Jody'? D'ja get that in Shanghai?"

The rookie's jaw would drop and he would hope desperately that the tattoo, which had been done in Duluth on the night of his high school graduation and was the bane of his life, was something Karras had noticed in the showers at training camp. But the divulgence about the socks was devastating, and he knew then that somehow he had been spied upon and the anger would begin to churn. It always seemed to me lucky that no one ever threw a punch at Karras at that moment, but no one ever did.

The old Lindell A.C. was finally condemned and the hotel, along with room 232, was torn down, which left the rookies with one less possibility of indignity to suffer through their first year.

Invariably, however, all of them were taken in by a far more wholesome practical joke, which was referred to as the Annual Turkey Caper. This involved making the rookie believe that it was a Thanksgiving tradition to receive free turkeys from a market proprietor named Milt Harris, a Detroit football fan of such intensity, they were told, that annually he gave the Lions these substantial tokens of his support and gratitude.

The trap was always set two weeks before Thanksgiving. Friday Macklem, the equipment manager, would write on the blackboard in the Tiger Stadium locker room: "Next Tuesday has been set as the day to pick up your free turkey at Milt Harris' store at Eastern Market. Specify weight, type of bird, if it is to be dressed, not cooked, or pre-cooked."

A pad was hung by a string from the board, and the veterans and coaches—all in cahoots, of course—would dutifully sign up, specifying such detailed orders as "Twenty-pound bird, with dressing, please include gizzard, and tail feathers for decoration."

The rookies would watch this activity with interest, and finally one of them would ask, "Hey, do we get in on this, too?"

"Hell yes. Why not?"

So the word would sweep through the contingent of rookies, and they would hurry to sign up. The talk around the locker room, and waiting for team meetings, and down along the sidelines during practice, began to feature the Thanksgiving meal. One rookie would ask another, "What kind of turkey did you ask for?"

"Well, I wasn't going to have anyone for dinner. I was going to have a turkey sandwich or something, down at the corner, and take in a flick that night. Hell, my folks are all down in St. Louis. But now, because of that turkey, I got them coming up for the game on Thanksgiving Day and afterwards I got some company coming in to meet them, and so I asked for a twenty-five-pounder with dressing. My mother's going to bring up this special cranberry sauce in a jar in her suitcase."

Then the other rookie would talk about the turkey *he* was getting, and who was coming to *his* party, and George Wilson, who was the coach then, got to hate the whole business because no one's mind was on football, though of course he played along with the veterans by signing up himself. The rookies thought of little else. Joe Robb, one of the veteran defensive linemen, once asked a rookie what sort of turkey he was asking for, and the rookie said he had put in his order for a thirty-pounder, because he had a lot of people coming to his place and he needed a big one. Robb said that he was having a big party too, but he was going to get two fifteen-pounders because they cooked faster and were easier to handle in the kitchen.

"Well, of course," the rookie said. "Why didn't I think of that. That's a great idea. I'm gonna do that too."

Karras told me that once a rookie had asked him the weight of the biggest available turkey at Milt Harris' store.

"The biggest?"

"Yeah."

Karras thought for a while and then told the rookie that he had heard that Harris had a special cornfed, double-breasted cackle-bird tom that dressed out at sixty-five pounds.

"Sixty-five *pounds*," the rookie said. "That's a big mother. Well, man, that's the one *I* want."

"How many people you got coming to dinner?" Karras asked.

"I ain't got nobody coming for dinner. I don't know nobody yet in this town," the rookie said.

"Well, what're you gonna do with that sixty-five-pound turkey?"

"I'm gonna set that mother right in the refrig'tor. All cooked, man. Then when I feels like it, I can swing open the do' and there that baby is . . ."

"Do you think you can fit a sixty-five-pound turkey in your refrigerator?" Karras asked.

"I ain't got nothin' else in there, except maybe two cans of beer."

This disarming admission suggesting the lonely state of a rookie, perhaps from a small southwestern college spending his first season in the big city, might have touched the sympathies of a lesser man than Karras.

"You may have to squeeze that big ol' tom to get him in," he said.

The rookie thought. "How long is a sixty-five-pound turkey?" he asked finally.

Karras brooded. "A sixty-five-pound turkey has got to be pushing four feet long."

"Four *feet*. Christ, man. What I can do is take out all the shelves and tilt that mother up on its end," the rookie said.

"That's a real good idea."

"Besides, I'm gonna eat a lot of the turkey, so she'll be thinning down right smart . . ."

On the day or so before the Tuesday pickup, Friday Macklem would post the rather complicated directions to the Eastern Market, which was on the far side of Detroit, and the veterans would groan and tell the rookies that there was no point in all forty members of the squad going out to Harris' place for the turkeys. Why wouldn't it be simpler if the rookies picked up all of them? Since traditionally they were sent on errands for the veterans, the rookies agreed, if somewhat sulkily, especially the one who expected to be wrestling with the sixty-five-pound turkey. He said that if he was going to have to worry about *other* players' turkeys he would have to hire himself a bus.

Karras said that it always took an enormous amount of will power to keep from driving out to the Eastern Market to hide behind the meat counter and bob up and peer over the top to watch what went on when a rookie, standing there with a long list in his hand, realized that he was involved in a hoax. Milt Harris was a no-nonsense party to it all, and when a player turned up in his store he would stare at him in feigned disbelief: "A free turkey? What are you talking about? You crazy or something? You got a *screw* loose? A sixty-five-*pound* turkey? You got to be thinking of an *ostrich!*"

Sometimes it took a lot of persuading before the rookie would accept the idea that he was being duped. "Listen," the rookie would say. "I don't care about *my* turkey. Forget that. But I'm supposed to bring back Coach Wilson's turkey. If I don't bring back his turkey, I'm going to be searching around for an assistant high school coaching job. Please. Now according to my list, he ordered a twenty-pounder, not pre-cooked, a chestnut dressing, and the giblets in a separate bag."

"Can't you get it through your head that you've been had?" Harris would shout. "There's no free turkeys here."

The rookies did not necessarily take the hoax with resignation. Bruce Maher, the peppery safetyman, was so fixed on picking up a turkey that he threatened to take Milt Harris' store apart if he didn't get one. Harris saw the look in his eye, and felt the rage boiling in him, and said, "Okay, okay, but for Chrissakes don't let on," and he went and got a turkey out of the freezer.

Another player, Roger LaLonde, a rookie nicknamed "Jug" because of his wide hips, was incensed enough to buy a live turkey, and on the Saturday after Thanksgiving he shut it up in Karras' locker, whom he considered the chief instigator, in among his spare T-shirts and a fine pair of knit golf trousers. Karras came in that day, thinking about the offensive guard he would be facing the next weekend, and when he looked in his locker, reaching in to get a sweatband, the big turkey sprang at him and scared him almost across the room. Karras said later that the turkey had all the moves required of a good offensive lineman: "speed, surprise, great lateral agility, and quick off the snap. Jerry Kramer of the Packers is a goddamn *wren* compared to that turkey of Jug's."

Karras bore no grudge against LaLonde. It was in the best spirit of the practical joke to suffer a reprisal gladly. Usually, though, he got away with whatever impertinences he wrought, largely because, unlike LaLonde, his victims had no idea how to retaliate. Since a consistent element in Alex's humor was to *startle* people, my own experience was that it was best to edge away at these times and let whatever he was doing take its course. Once I was sitting with him in a rather fancy restaurant and looked up to see that he was jabbing a fork loaded with lettuce into the center of his forehead. He was quite persistent, and eventually, from the force of the jabbing, a piece of lettuce fell off the fork, glanced off his nose and dropped onto the tablecloth. It was such a surprising sight that I was speechless. He noticed that I was staring at him. He put the fork down on his plate and asked, "Well, why does the mouth always have to get all the food? I mean, why can't it be passed around to other parts of the face?"

I could not think of much to say.

"It's unfair," he said. A piece of lettuce was still stuck to the middle of his forehead.

I managed to say, "Well, I would think that an ear or a nose might *work* better. At least there you have an aperture."

"The forehead has been neglected," Karras said, with a finality that put an end to the discussion, and we went on to something else. Throughout the evening the lettuce remained stuck to the middle of his brow, until just before we left the restaurant it dropped off as the waiter was bringing the change from the bill.

Karras stared at the leaf as if he had never seen it before. "Who's been throwing their salad at me?" he asked the waiter.

"I beg your pardon?"

"Someone in this café is throwing their salad. Look at

this. It just dropped off my forehead. Someone hit me smack-dab in the middle of the head with their salad. What sort of a joint are you running here?"

"I beg your pardon?"

Karras motioned the captain over.

"Yes, sir?"

"You've got someone in this restaurant who is throwing food."

"Sir?"

"Look at the middle of my forehead." The captain squinted at the faint spot still glistening slightly from salad oil, where the lettuce had stuck.

"Someone hit me right there with some salad," Karras said, pointing. "Maybe it's someone at that table over there." All of us wheeled and stared at an elderly couple sitting opposite each other along the side wall. They noticed us staring at them; their jaws stopped moving.

"They are eating the fish dish," the captain pointed out. "The sole meunière. They are not eating salad."

"Maybe it's the fish dish they threw," Karras said. "Or the lemon maybe. Whatever it was, it came from their direction. Did you throw your fish dish at me?" he called out. "Or the lemon?"

"Sir, sir," the captain was hissing. "You are disturbing the patrons. I must ask you to leave the premises. Please."

"Well, okay," Karras said huffily. "Do you think I have any interest in hanging around in a dump where the customers get peppered with food?"

"Christ, what a place," Karras said when we were out in the street. We strode a few yards, and then he said, "Hey, *you* didn't throw the salad at me, did you?"

"What?" I looked at him. "What are you talking about? You did that yourself."

"I did *what* myself?" He blinked convincingly behind his spectacles. "You mean I threw salad at my own head? What would I want to do a thing like that for?"

"Come on, Alex," I said. "You said that the mouth was getting all the attention and you felt the forehead had been neglected. You tried to get it to eat the salad, and you jabbed your fork into it."

"I jabbed my fork into my own *brow*?" Karras said. We walked along in silence. "You got to be kidding."

I took three or four steps and then said, "Well, I *am* kidding. I don't know what possessed me. In fact, I think it *was* the old geezer at that side table."

" 'Course it was," Karras said. "The guy had a hell of an arm . . ."

10

When I stepped out of the plane at the Flint airport, awkwardly because it was a small four-seater low-winged Cessna from which one clambered first onto the wing, then down to the ground, a representative from the airport staff told me that someone was waiting for me out front in a limousine. He said "someone" in a somewhat inconclusive manner, as if he were not at all sure of himself.

The only car in front of the terminal was a Cadillac of the "stretched" variety for use in funerals or weddings where it is provident to keep a family unit, however numerous, in one vehicle. At first I could see no one sitting in the cavernous rear section, but a chauffeur stepped smartly up and after relieving me of my golf clubs opened the door with a flourish, and I saw that perched in a far corner of the back seat, his feet sticking directly out in front of him, was a midget. He wore a gray fedora of the type cultivated by Chicago gangsters, and his face was largely obscured by an enormous cigar. I got in beside him, nodding politely, and the door shut behind me.

I said that it was very kind of him to meet me. He did not reply. Though his cigar was going satisfactorily, he produced a kitchen match, struck it on the heel of his shoe, and sucked in on the flame. Clouds of smoke began to thicken in the car, and the cigar tip glowed sullenly. I cleared my throat and discreetly lowered the window on my side. The car began to move. Where were we going, I asked. No reply. The midget stared straight ahead. Up in front the chauffeur tended to his driving. We began to move through the outskirts of Flint. I tried again. How were the preparations for the Karras golf tournament the next day coming along? More thick smoke. I gave up and looked out at the scenery.

The midget's appearance at the airport, and his silence, had obviously been cooked up by Karras and Buterakos to put me in the proper frame of mind for the second of Karras' weird golf tournaments held to benefit the National Cystic Fibrosis Campaign. For a month Buterakos had been calling me and telling me that the tournament was going to eclipse its predecessor both in scope and lunacy.

"Big Man!" Buterakos would shout over the phone. "The tournament's going to be the biggest thing in the country. We got a new slogan this year. 'The Benefit is one giant step forward for mankind and one giant step backwards for golf.' Guess who's coming?"

"Who?"

"Johnny Weissmuller!"

"Johnny who?"

"Weissmuller, goddamn it. The original Tarzan. He's coming with his chimp. He's got this chimpanzee he runs with. The two of them can't live apart. The chimp picks up his hat and hands it to him. He fetches the paper. I'm telling you, those two are going to set the tournament on its ear."

"What are they going to do?"

"Tarzan is going to yell," Buterakos said. "From time to time he's going to really *scream*—just as a competitor is at the top of his backswing. You know what else he's going to do? He's going to *swim*. The golf course has one water hole, and he's going to plunge in and emerge at the other end, dripping wet, and creep up on this poor guy playing out of the rough, and he'll say 'Ahem,' and this guy, this poor sucker who's coughed up fifty bucks to play in the tournament, is going to turn around and see *Tarzan*, soaking wet in his leopard skins, maybe holding the chimp by the hand, and man, it's going to blow the guy's *mind!*"

"I should think so," I said.

"That's right, Big Man. The tournament this year is going to be *big*. We got the biggest celebrities in the country coming. Joe O'Higgins, the sheriff who does those Dodge car commercials—*he's* coming. Not only that, but we got twelve midgets in from Chicago . . ."

I could not remember the other celebrities and events that Buterakos and Karras planned, but there were a raft of them. Once again I turned to the midget sitting next to me. "I hear there are eleven more of you," I said. The sentence seemed awkwardly put, and I was glad that he chose to answer it by once again striking a match to his cigar. We sat in silence. Up in front the chauffeur's shoulders were heaving—either from suppressed laughter or from the thick cigar smoke.

The limousine swept through downtown Flint and pulled up in front of the Durant Hotel. As the chauffeur hopped out and opened the back door, two men standing on the sidewalk leaned forward to see who was within. The midget stepped out briskly and spoke his first words. "Clear the way," he said. He was carrying a small cane about two feet long. He swept it back and forth. "We've got important business to conduct." His voice was astonishingly deep and husky. I stepped out behind him and we hurried into the hotel.

I followed him to the elevator, and the operator said, "Floor?"

"The Presidential Suite," the midget said. "Let's get this crate moving." He made another impatient move with his stick, and the operator swung the doors shut. He seemed annoyed. To make conversation I asked, "Has the Presidential Suite ever been used by the President?"

146

"Nah," the operator said. "But we had the president of San Salvador in here once. Stayed for three days."

We reached the top floor, and the midget led the way briskly down the corridor. The door to the Presidential Suite had a Presidential seal set in the wood. The midget swung it ajar. Inside, a big galvanized tub of ice and beer had been placed in the middle of the room, and around it, lolling back in armchairs, were a number of men, some of them wearing golfing hats, whom I presumed were tournament officials. As soon as the midget and I came in they started guffawing; apparently they were privy to my odd greeting at the airport. Having done his duty, the midget turned with a big grin on his face. "The name's Gus," he said, putting out his hand. I shook it solemnly.

The others all wanted to know what had happened. "Did Gus pick you up at the airport? What'ja make of that, huh? Did he blow the cigar smoke at you?"

"Yeah," I said.

"What'ja think?"

"I didn't know what to think. I guess it was a helluva idea."

They roared with laughter, then turned and asked the midget what *he* thought. "Tell us, Gus!"

"Well, I damn near got sick puffing on those cigars." He had a big grin on his face. "Puffed so hard I smoked my way through *three* of them."

They rocked back and forth in their chairs, snorting with laughter. "*Christ*, what a gas."

Buterakos came bustling in. "Hey, Big Man!" he shouted. "What'ja think of that, hey?"

"Well, I—"

"Did Gus meet you okay out there at the airport? Hey, Gus, did you meet him out at the airport? Did you give him the cold-shoulder treatment and all that stuff?"

Buterakos is one of those ebullient people who cannot wait for an answer to a question before hurrying on to another. "Hey, were you surprised?"

"Well, I—"

147

"What'ja think when you looked in the car and Gus was in there?"

"I didn't—"

"D'ja know where he was taking you?"

"No, but I—"

"What'ja think when he didn't say anything? Hey, Gus, you didn't say anything, did you? That was Alex's idea—for Gus just to sit there and puff smoke."

"Yes, I—"

"What'ja think when he puffed all that smoke at you? Huh?"

"I didn't know—"

"Blew your mind, didn't it? Hey, Gus, did you blow that smoke right in his face? Hey, what'ja think when he kept lighting his cigar when the cigar was already *lit*?"

"Well, I didn't really—"

"Did he tell those two guys in front of the hotel to clear out of the way? Did he swing his cane at them? That was all planned. What'ja think?"

"I didn't know—"

"D'ja bring your golf clubs? You're going to be playing in the biggest tournament that ever hit this state!"

By and by Buterakos calmed down and I was able to ask him if Karras was in the hotel. He told me that Alex was out at the golf course talking to the animal trainer. "We got a whole *zoo* coming tomorrow. That golf course is going to be *stiff* with animals. We got a goddamn llama coming. Not only that—" he gestured extravagantly at the ceiling—"the *sky* is going to be full—airplanes, balloons, parachutists . . ."

A tall man touched Buterakos on the shoulder. "Tarzan!" Buterakos shouted. He wheeled him toward me. "Big Man," he said solemnly, "this is Johnny Weissmuller."

We shook hands. "Howdy," he said. He was a silver-haired man with a florid, somewhat pocked face, and his voice was surprisingly high and squeaky. Though we were indoors, he was wearing a wide-brimmed safari hat with a leopard-skin band.

148

"How's the chimpanzee?" I asked, looking around, half expecting to see one lolling in an armchair wearing the usual circus ensemble of a little paper hat and a high-riding jump suit.

Weissmuller's face fell. "The tyke's sick," he said. "Ate something. When a chimp is sick, he sulks around. Can't do anything with them. Not much fun to have around. Give me a sick parrot anytime."

"That's too bad."

We fell silent. Buterakos was in the far corner of the room. To make conversation, I said, "I wonder how your chimp would get along with the midgets—I mean how he'd react. There are eleven or twelve of them in from Chicago. Has your chimp ever met a midget?"

"Most of these guys from Chicago are not midgets," Weissmuller said. "They're dwarfs. Actually they all like to be called 'little people.' " He leaned closer to speak confidentially. "Midgets are perfectly formed tiny people. They have high little voices, like they'd been breathing helium. Now dwarfs, they have near normal-sized heads and bodies, but they got these very small extremities, which are the arms and legs. The guy that come out to meet you at the airport was a dwarf. That's Gus. They tell me he's a family man—got a couple of kids."

"Oh," I said. "I didn't mean to be disrespectful of them, but I wondered what a chimp's reaction to them would be."

Weissmuller looked into the palms of his hands. "I'm no midget . . . er . . . *dwarf*. I'm no chimp, either." He laughed sharply. "But what I think is this: that a chimp can take them or leave them."

"I see," I said.

Buterakos drifted by to say that we all had to drive out with him to the golf course to see the arrangements for the tournament the next day. He wanted to show us the big tent they had put up for the golf dinner; also, there was going to be a practice balloon ascent.

"Balloons?" Weissmuller asked.

"That's right. Isn't that right, Gus?"

149

Gus, standing beside him, did not seem very happy. His cigar was unlit.

"We're sending Gus up tonight," Buterakos explained. "He's going to be the first midget balloonist. Right, Gus?"

Someone asked what sort of a balloon it was.

"It's a great big mother," Buterakos said. "With a basket. A hot-air machine pumps the son of a bitch with hot air and up she goes. We got the greatest balloon man in the world—Captain Phineas Phog, he calls himself—to come to town with his balloons. Tomorrow Karras is going to open the festivities by sweeping across the tops of the trees in the big balloon and throwing out the first golf ball. Isn't that a great idea? I'm telling you, this is going to be the biggest golf tournament this state has ever heard of. We got this *elephant* turning up. D'ja know that? The biggest elephant in Michigan."

A group of us agreed to go out to the golf course to watch Gus make his balloon ascent. He said he thought he ought to take along a sweater, so I went down with him to his room. The place was packed with some of the other "little people," and he introduced me to them. There were about six of them staying in the room, and cots had been set up. They were very excited, not about Gus making his evening balloon flight but because a few minutes before they had recognized Dick Butkus, the great Chicago middle linebacker, walking down the hotel corridor to his room with his golf bag on his shoulder. They had all followed him, turning a corner, and then one of them had shouted, "Hey, Butkus, where's your ball and chain?" He had wheeled around, the clubs clinking in his bag, and had stared at them briefly, the group of them poised like prairie dogs, one or two of them just peering around the corner, and then one of them from the back called out, "Hey Butkus, where's your cage?" Their temerity had scared them, and as soon as the question was asked they ran pop-pop-pop-pop, swaying back and forth on their dwarf legs in their haste, giggling, until they reached the sanctuary of Gus's room. They had closed the door and bolted it, reaching up to do so. They told Gus three times what they had done: "You should've heard Jake. Jake sings out, 'Hey Butkus, where's your *cage*?' Gus, it was grand. Oh, Gus."

"I wish I'd seen it," said Gus. He walked over to his suit-case and pulled out a sweater. The others wanted to tell him again. "Hey, Gus. Gus!"

"I got to go." He looked at them. "I'm going up in a balloon," he said mournfully.

On the way out to the golf course, Buterakos talked non-stop. Gus was sitting beside him in the front seat. I was sitting in the back with Weissmuller. I could just see the top of Gus's head. "Gus," Buterakos was saying, "you're going to be the first of the little people to fly in a big balloon. It's going to make headlines! History! You're going to make history, Gus. You know something? You got to have a *uniform*, Gus. I should have had an air marshal's uniform made for you. I should have thought of that, but it's too late. You got to go up in your civvies. But you can salute, Gus, and act like an air marshal. Hell, Gus, you can *bomb* somebody. Why didn't I think of that before? Gus can drift over some dude working in his garden, humming to him-self and planting some goddamn little shrub, and Gus can *bomb* him . . . just drifting over this guy's garden, quiet as smoke, and Gus can call something down, very quiet, and the guy will look up and see this tiny face looking over the edge of the basket of this big mothering balloon, and he's holding this bomb, maybe a paper bag full of water, and it comes down *blam!* And hits this guy right in the kisser. Blow his *mind,* right?"

It was evening when we reached the golf course. An occasional warm puff of air turned the leaves backside to, and they showed silver. Swallows in their swift sweeps for insects were flying close to the ground. The air had that tremulous quality that comes before a storm.

"Hey, Gus. You oughtn't to go up," I said as we got out of the car. "There must be thunderheads around."

"Oh, I don't think anybody's serious," he said.

I was not so sure. Buterakos was striding ahead of us across the golf course toward a group of people on a level fair-way beyond the eighteenth green. I could see Karras among them, his head tilted back, drinking a beer. The fabric of a bal-loon was spread out on the grass. "Captain Phog!" Buterakos was yelling. "What's going on? You're behind schedule. Haven't you got the balloon pumped up yet?"

A thin, fragile-looking man wearing a yachtsman's cap with braid at the brim detached himself from the group and hurried over. He looked harried. "We're just getting things ready," he said.

"Well, I should hope so," Buterakos said. "Gus here is pining to get aloft. He's got itchy feet. He wants to fly—isn't that right, Gus? How much longer do you think it's going to be?"

"Maybe fifteen, twenty minutes," Captain Phog said.

When the balloon had enough hot air inside to lift the canopy, we walked through the opening at the base and prowled inside, stepping carefully on the nylon fabric. Captain Phog did not seem worried about the conditions outside. He bustled here and there inside the balloon, its interior lit by electric lamps, bellying out the canopy with the palms of his hands so that it would rise properly. Above the roar of the motor producing the hot air, the distant thunder murmured. "It won't be a free flight," Captain Phog was explaining. "We'll send him up but keep him anchored, and then we'll bring him down."

I went outside. A few feet from the expanding canopy was the balloon's basket in which Gus would ride, the hot-air device attached to the overhead framework. On the ground next to the basket were six coffee containers. "Just got them. They're filled with water," Gus told me. "Those are my bombs."

"I suppose Buterakos prepared them."

"Sure," he said. He looked unhappy.

The half-inflated balloon suddenly rose in a slow heave, stirred by a puff of the warm fitful air, and then subsided to the ground. But it was awake now, and the hot air roaring from the blowers moved it anew, sending shivers across its plastic skin. It heaved again. "Won't be long now!" Captain Phog shouted. The scene took on a bizarre atmosphere of emergency, as if the balloon were on hand to evacuate personnel from a siege—the flashlight flickering on the gasbag as it expanded, the shrill cries of Captain Phog to his crew, and across the fields the ominous flickering of lightning, like artillery flashes.

The thunder rumbled. The entire stretch of horizon to the west was dark with line squalls. Buterakos' shouting lent an additional sense of urgency: "Phog, go to it! You're going to be the first balloon man to get one of the little people up into the air. You're going to be famous, Phog! You're going to get that son of a bitch full of hot air and *up*, Phog!"

"Look at that!" someone shouted.

A quarter of a mile away a solid bank of rain emerged from a background of black clouds and began moving swiftly toward us across the golf course. Shrubs alongside a distant fairway bent double, their branches lashing.

"My God," Captain Phog shouted. "Line squalls! Get her down!" He rushed for a rope. "Pull the safety panel!" he shouted. "Get the air out of her!"

His people rushed around, but it was too late. Drumming hard across the turf, the rain squall reached us and took a hand—the wind picking up the balloon and shaking it violently, lifting it off the ground with a series of loud canvas-like flaps, and the canopy opened a rip which soared up the surface like a flame. The guy ropes ripped and slashed. We did what we could to help the frantic captain, but the wind had shredded the canopy, so that we were like a crew at sea trying to retrieve a vast spinnaker split and trailing to leeward like a streamer.

"I can't believe it," I heard Captain Phog berating himself. "What the hell was I doing?" He seemed utterly puzzled.

In the jumbled roar of the storm I could hear Buterakos crying in the wind like some mad Ahab: "Phog! What's going on? Can't you get that balloon up? Gus is waiting. We can't let him down. Let's proceed with the launch, goddamn it!"

I went over. He was grinning enormously, almost beside himself at his own powers of persuasion. "My God," he said. "Did you see me *motivate* that man! Captain Phog? Did I not pump him up? He was being motivated so hard, he didn't know what he was doing."

"You lost him a balloon," I said.

"He can sew it together again," Buterakos said blithely. "Besides, he's got another one."

153

I felt relieved for Gus. I strayed over. He was standing in the shelter of the circus tent looking out at Captain Phog, whose black slicker glistened and flapped in rain-strewn gusts of wind. He was still trying to collect what gear was left of his number one balloon. "Man, you're lucky, Gus," I said.

He did not reply for a second or so, and when I looked down I saw that he had a wistful look on his strong farmer's face. "I love a good time better than anyone," he said in his solemn voice. "I'd have gone up in the balloon, I think. That would have been something to remember, eh? You know something? I was sort of sorry when it blew away."

"Damn, Gus, you could have disappeared forever. You could have been blown clear to Iowa. That was a damn powerful line squall."

"Sure," he said. "Still, it's too bad. Buterakos really tried."

"That's for sure," I said. "Buterakos has a tendency to overdo things, doesn't he?"

The two of us got a lift back to Flint, and on the way Gus told me how Buterakos had come to a convention of little people in Chicago and given one of his inspirational talks. He had thrown out a lot of props, and yelled at them, and told them they were the "biggest" men around, and they stood up and cheered for him for ten minutes. "He really made us feel good. I'd have gone up if he told me to," Gus said. The rain had stopped. The headlights glistened on the wet macadam. He stirred in his seat. "Of course, I don't really understand what this golf tournament is all about."

I told him that my own theory was that both Karras and Buterakos played such atrocious golf themselves that, perhaps subconsciously, they were taking their revenge on the game and against the solemnity of those who swore by it. Someone had described the tournament as the "Black Mass" of golf, I said.

"I can see why," he said.

I asked him what had been planned for him the next day. He told me that Buterakos had somehow managed to persuade the local National Guard commander to loan the tournament a small military unit. "He's put me in command," he said. "He's got me a uniform and a pearl-handled revolver. I'm riding in the lead vehicle, which I think is a General Patton tank."

"Is this for some sort of parade?" I asked.

"God, no," he said. "We're supposed to dart out of the forest onto the golf course with this unit and surprise people. Buterakos told me, 'Try to emerge'—that was the word he used: 'emerge'—'from the forest at the top of the guy's backswing. That's the best time.' "

When I saw Gus later that evening, I asked him how the little people had reacted to the news that he had not made his balloon ascent. "They weren't interested one way or the other," he said. "They were into something else. They were all carrying on and planning to knock on Dick Butkus' door at midnight, and when he answered it they were going to gang-tackle him, just for the hell of it—all eleven of them."

The thought of this plan stayed with me through a night's fitful rest, and the next morning when I saw Butkus out in front of the hotel, a golf bag over his shoulder, I was tempted to ask him if the midgets had attacked him the night before. But it was such an odd question to put to someone so intimidating. One had to assume that the midgets had thought better of it.

The tournament started at ten o'clock. Captain Phineas Phog's reserve balloon floated serenely in the summer sky. Already a large crowd had collected. Many had come because they had heard of the hijinks the preceding year, expecting better this time; others because of the celebrities, again most of them from the Detroit professional teams—the Pistons, the Redwings and the Lions. Many of the children had autograph books. I saw Johnny Weissmuller, outfitted for his golf game in his safari clothes and hunter's hat, and we waved at each other.

About fifteen minutes after the tournament started, Gus put in his appearance. We could hear the motors of his military unit, and the crackling of branches and small trees going down as he approached. His lead vehicle, it turned out, was not a Patton tank but a huge amphibian, heading a procession which included two jeeps and a number of one-and-a-half-ton trucks, one of them a fuel carrier. Gus rode in the prow of the amphibian. He had indeed been provided with a uniform, a weird General Patton outfit; he was top-heavy in a helmet, tank-driver goggles, and a chestful of medals. He brandished a riding crop. Throughout the day, his unit turned up at the most unexpected times and places, bursting through the underbrush that flanked the fairways with Gus yelling in his startling low voice that boomed above the roar of the motors, "Clear the hell out of the way! The Eleventh Armored is coming through!" From time to time he hit the side of the amphibian with his riding crop. Some of the golfers felt that it was the single most surprising sight of the day—to hear the approaching rumble of motors, the crackling of bushes, and then to see the nose of the amphibian poking through, the tiny goggled figure perched atop the huge machine, waving his riding crop.

I was pleased to note that many of the traditions established in the tournament's first year were continued: each golfer teed off for the first hole in a wail of amplified sound from a loudspeaker system—animal roars, machine-gun fire, steamboat whistles and the like; the single-minded man in the sombrero was back, who moved across the fairways to the greens to sing "The Mexican Hat Dance" and inspire the golfers' putting. Other music-makers had been hired, or more likely persuaded, perhaps even *motivated* to join the festivities—including a jazz band on a cart that was pulled around by a tractor. But the musicians I would truly remember were the soloists who wandered around the golf course: a lovely girl in a hippie gown, who stood by a sand trap singing ballads in a gentle voice that carried barely six feet; an old man in a bowler hat far too small for his head, who played a vague *plinkety-plank* banjo out on the far reaches of the course. One came across them and their music suddenly, around a tree, like figures in a Fellini landscape.

Karras was beside himself with delight. Later that morning he took me on a tour of the course. He was dressed in white coveralls, with his name in big red letters on the back. He took big puffs on his cigar. "We've really doctored the course, much more than last time," he said. He showed me a green which had been pocked with six cups and flags. The flags, red cloth, snapped in the wind from their thin bamboo poles. "A golfer's delight, this hole," he said.

"Yes," I said. "Does the player have his choice here?"

"He does," Karras said. "Any cup. It's an easy hole because of all those options. In fact, it's the low-handicap hole of the tournament. No one gets a stroke here—not even the highest scoring of the midgets." He puffed enormously on his cigar.

There was another green he wanted to show me, and we set out across the fairways.

"Look at that!" he exclaimed, pointing at what I thought was a large boulder. "That's a three-hundred-pound turtle."

We stood and stared at it. It moved its beaked head, inspecting us with ancient eyes, then, uninterested, resumed its nibbling on the fairway grass.

"You can hear it eating," Karras said. "Swear to God. If you kneel down there and put your ear up close, you can hear that grass getting *chomped.* He's moved about ten yards since he was set down there an hour ago. We expect him to have a hundred-yard day. He's one of our what we call 'movable hazards.' Of course, he's one of our slower movers."

"What are some of the faster movers?"

"Well, you remember last time I was hoping to get some llamas," Karras said. "Well damn, we *did* get one. Not only that; he's a nervous llama. He hasn't stopped running since he got here, and he goes through foursomes like he imagines he's a stampede. He's the fastest mover we got.

"We had hopes for our zebra. Actually, he's really a Shetland pony painted with white stripes. It didn't come out right; he just looks like a painted Shetland pony. He's not much of a mover. Neither is the Indian elephant, which is named Wanda. Big eater, though. Then we got a goat, a cow and a couple of donkeys out on the course. But they are not your fast movers; they're not worth a damn as fast movers. Neither are the chickens, which are all hanging around the eighteenth green. But the llama has been making up for all of them. Have you seen him run? He's got this strange rocking-horse gait, with this tiny head on a long thin neck which sticks straight up like a wooly sort of periscope, and I swear to God he *materializes*— he's just everywhere. I heard that this one guy was so startled seeing him that he toppled backwards and broke his golf club in half. The llama's doing fine. Of course, he's got a long day in front of him."

"Who provided all this stuff?" I asked.

"An animal keeper. He's around here somewhere. He's got his hands full today. Over on the eleventh fairway he's got a pen with a couple of baby wolves in it, and a leopard and a little tiger cub. The pen was supposed to be a hazard in front of the green there, but the children packed in so tight wanting to pet the babies that he had to move the whole works off to one side. The keeper will get you just about any animal you're looking for. I wanted a crocodile, a big mother, for the water hole, but he finally balked at that. Wouldn't do it. So we got a corpse in there."

"A corpse?"

"It's a storefront mannequin dressed up in old clothes and wearing a wide-brimmed gangster's hat. It floats on its stomach in there amongst the cattails. Gives you a big turn when you spot it. It looks like it had been dumped in there a month ago by the Luchinni brothers and has just floated to the surface."

As we reached the sixteenth green, Karras lowered his voice. "Now we've done a job on this green, a *real* job. There's no flagstick here, because if the caddy took it out of the cup, it would be about fourteen feet long. The cup goes down *eight* feet. Damn right. They dug it out last night and put it back together again, and you can't hardly tell. So what happens is that the player rolls in a long putt, maybe a thirty- or forty-footer, and he strides up with this big grin, reaches into the cup to get his ball back, and in he tumbles, his arm right up to the shoulder in the ground. Helluva sight."

A foursome was toiling up to the green. "Look at them," Karras whispered. We watched them make their approach shots. One of the golfers had to make his from an enclosure immediately in front of the green, with a low fence around it, which included, besides his ball, six ducks. "Robert Trent Jones couldn't have placed a hazard better," Karras whispered. "People have been knocking their shots in there all day long." At the golfer's backswing, the ducks tilted back on their feet, spread their wings and chattered noisily as the shot glanced weakly off the club face. The golfer swore and climbed over the fence.

"You know, Alex," I said. "Some of these golfers don't look especially happy."

It was true. This foursome looked particularly grim. "Hey, Alex," one of them called over. "Does that llama bite?"

"No, but it sure kicks," Karras said.

The foursome reached the green. The first putt rolled toward the cup, stopping within an inch or so of the lip. Karras tensed. "Damn," he whispered. "The guy may notice." The golfer stepped up to tap his putt in, and then stopped short, peering down the hole.

"Hey!" he called. He motioned the others over. "Jesus Christ! How far down does that son of a bitch go?" one of them asked. They stood in a tight group, looking down. "What's in there?" another asked. The others looked at him. "Damned if I'm putting my hand in to find out," the first man said. "He's probably got a mess of snakes down there." The four looked over, aggrieved. "Goddamn it, Karras," one of them called. "Whatcha trying to do—steal our golf balls?"

"I'm telling you, Alex," I whispered. "Those guys are huffy. They are not amused."

"Yeah," said Karras, turning away. "Who are they, anyway? Who invited them to my tournament?"

One astonishing aspect of the day was that despite the wandering spectators unfettered by marshals, the noise, the doctored greens and the movable hazards—especially the excessive bouncing about of the llama—somehow the golf scores were often respectable, and low in many cases. Lem Barney, the Lion cornerback, shot a seventy-three, and his legendary predecessor at that position, Night Train Lane, shot a hole-in-one on the

159

eighth hole. It was witnessed by a small knot of people who, seeing the ball land, take a big bite and backspin into the hole, began leaping up and down.

Later, I asked Night Train, "What were your emotions when the ball ran in?"

The English language has always had a gentle love affair with Night Train. "Well, my commotions were that I had gone to the wrong club. I used a wedge."

"Wrong *club!*" I said incredulously. "My God, Train, you got a hole in *one.*"

"Yesterday I lost my nine iron," Train went on unperturbed. "Might have put it in someone else's bag. I should have gone to the nine iron." He shook his head sadly.

In the afternoon there was a considerable amount of aerial activity; besides Captain Phog's hot-air balloon, it included a flyover by two National Guard jets from nearby Selfridge Field, two stunt planes maneuvering loudly and threateningly over the golf course, a drop by two parachutists and, perhaps most memorable, the catatonic arrival of a crop-dusting plane which roared down a few feet over the heads of the crowds on the fairways and let loose fog clouds of vapor.

"There was a little disappointment in that department," Karras told me later. "The real hope was to completely sock in the golf course with that crop duster—such a heavy cloud of fog that the golfers wouldn't be able to see each other. The pilot said he couldn't produce like that. Then the idea was to drop clouds of colored dye so that right before your eyes everyone would turn, you know, *red.*"

Throughout the afternoon helicopters dropped in and out of the tournament. Joe O'Higgins, the sheriff in the Dodge automobile television commercials, stepped out of one of them— the celebrity of the day, judging from the delighted shouts of the children and the thickets of paper thrust toward him to sign. But from time to time over the loudspeaker system it was announced that an even bigger celebrity than O'Higgins would be arriving. Tantalizingly, he was referred to as "The Big Man." "Get your autograph books ready!" we were informed by the amplifiers. "The Big Man is coming."

Finally, the helicopter floated in at about two P.M. An enormous circle of people waited for The Big Man to get out, craning their necks and calling, "Who is he, who is he?"

The man who stepped out of the helicopter was indeed large, and he was wearing a yellow windbreaker with the words THE BIG MAN stenciled on the back. He alighted with a big grin and a wave. Everybody was shoving to see. "Who is he? Who is he?"

I did not recognize him. I went over and stood beside Karras, who was doubled up. "Look," he said, "the disappointment is just *intense*. 'Who is he? Who is he?'" His hand flew up to cover a giggle. "All these people shoving and pushing to see The Big Man, and then he gets off the plane and he's nothing. He's nothing at all. He's just fat. Oh, it worked just beautiful."

"Well, who is he?"

Karras looked at me, startled. "Oh," he said. "Why, that's Gene Mitchell. He's just a friend—an insurance salesman from Birmingham. He's a fat friend, that's all."

"A fat friend?" I repeated.

Karras said, "We were thinking of getting the rumor started that he was a big celebrity who had just gone through a big face-lifting operation and didn't *look* the same—you know, the new and bigger Mickey Rooney, or something like that. Johnny Weissmuller was going to go up and say, 'Mickey Rooney, as I live and breath,' and shake his hand vigorously. But the trouble is that Mitchell doesn't look the part."

I agreed. People were drifting away. The "Big Man" excitement was over; there were other things going on. A cannon went off behind the first tee and someone yelled, probably a golfer bending down to put his ball carefully on the tee.

I wandered over to the eighteenth green to watch the foursomes finish. The chickens searching for picnic scraps moved among the spectators. I stood watching the late starters straggle in, coming slowly up the fairway. The revelry was beginning in the big tent. I could not stay for the entire awards dinner. What I saw of it was raucous with shouting and carrying-on, big hands reaching for yellow pitchers of beer set in rows on the wooden tables. Night Train Lane got the big prize for his hole in one on the eighth hole—a 1951 Oldsmobile, donated by a used-car dealer. Three other used cars were donated or auctioned off. Karras and Buterakos had planned to award an Edsel, which would turn out to be a six-hundred-pound woman of the same name, but like John Weissmuller's pet chimpanzee she had fallen ill at the last moment.

A high school kid drove me out to the airport. I told him about the cigar-smoking midget who had met me the afternoon before. He shook his head. "You're being returned to normalcy," he said.

11

In the spring of 1967 a movie producer named Stuart Millar called me and asked if I would join him for dinner with Marty Ritt, a brilliant director who had just completed *Hud*—a highly praised film set in contemporary times in the Texas Panhandle. Ritt, said Millar, was now interested in making a film about football, and the two of them wondered if I had any general opinions on such a project and, specifically, if I knew of any "properties" which they could use.

We met in a midtown hotel. I did not keep notes on the dinner, though I remember Ritt as a large and solemn man who saw football as the background for a deep and personal film study of a very "American" sort of tragedy. It would happen to an aging star (*Death of a Quarterback?*), played out against the violence and grimness of the sport, suggesting something of the correlation between the national character and ferocity; the whole thing would be very real and stark, with the sort of dramatic pertinence that had been done about boxing in *Champion* with Kirk Douglas. What did I think?

I remember being disappointed. I had hoped that perhaps they had called me because they were interested in the film rights to my own light-hearted study of football, *Paper Lion*. Apparently not. I remember saying to Ritt that I didn't know anything about the sort of thing he had in mind—that in my limited experience the atmosphere around a professional football team was buoyant rather than somber, and that I could not think of either Earl Morrall or Milt Plum, the two Detroit quarterbacks, as Willy Lomans. The really tragic people in football were the ball park ticket-takers who were cooped up in their booths half listening to the great roars coming over the rim of the stadium and were never able to see a game.

The three of us sat looking at each other, turning our drinks in our hands.

Well, perhaps the tragic figures in football were the *owners,* I went on to try. Perhaps a film should be done about *them.* Here were these weird men who had pots of money and power complexes, which was certainly an American phenomenon, and look what they did with it: they bought football teams, though only one owner each year, out of all the franchises, would win a championship. The odds made it all so futile. Someone had once said something excellent about owners —what was it? Oh, it was awfully good. Yes: "What dark past would compel a man to arrange his life so that he could sit up in the back of the press box with a good-luck hat on his head and watch his team on their eleven yard line break the huddle with third down and thirty-five yards to go?"

"Or take Harry Wismer, the fellow who owned the New York Titans before they became the Jets," I went on. "On the Titans was a scat-back—Tiller? Was that his name? Jim Tiller—and Wismer's wife was always crazy to see him run. He wasn't much good, but Wismer knuckled under, and he'd make the coaches send in plays for this guy. The trouble was that Tiller ran laterally and occasionally backwards, but rarely forwards. Still, he ran long distances, from one side of the field to the other, which was exciting, and Mrs. Wismer would sit next to her husband and cry, 'Oh, they're going to get him, they're going to get him,' and they would, and it was terrific for her. But what had driven her husband to accept this sort of thing? And what about her; what was their relationship? Highly tragic stuff."

We turned the glasses around in our hands some more.

"I guess it's not very filmic," I said finally.

I never saw Ritt again, but Millar stayed in touch, titillated by the notion of doing *Paper Lion,* and finally one day he called and said that he had signed to produce it in conjunction with United Artists.

Naturally, I was excited. In the beginning, I had the vague notion that perhaps I could perform in the film myself. I thought about it from time to time, daydreaming, and let Millar know that I was available—for a "draft," I think I described it. But Millar had other ideas. He felt that a documentary drawn straight from the book would not work, that the text was too static for filming. Some extra ingredients had to be added; specifically, to use a word that was bandied about constantly, the material had to be "Hollywoodized." To this end he hoped to find a big-name star to play my role in the film—dashing that forlorn hope that I might be able to play myself as well as anyone—which would help at the box office.

To attract an established actor Millar adapted the film script to give "fuller dimensions" to my character, and I found myself transmogrified from a somewhat shy and introverted reporter to a brash, rather kooky fan (one rarely had the sense that the character *was* a reporter, since he never carried a notebook or asked a question or even *listened*) whose motivation at one point was that he really believed he could make the Detroit Lion team—such a bizarre fancy that had I ever expressed the thought at training camp I would have been requested to catch the next train out. It was hoped that Jack Lemmon, the comedian, would be intrigued enough by this dipsy-doodle character to accept the role, but it turned out that he had other commitments and could not accept.

Millar looked around further and finally picked a young Broadway star named Alan Alda—a polished performer with a thin and wiry frame which looked vaguely athletic, perhaps a quarter-miler's, and whose facial features were thought by many people to bear the dubious distinction of resembling mine. I met Alda a few times. He was personable, and the football players liked him enough so that they felt easy joshing him ("Is that the fastest you can run?"), but his football experience was even more limited than mine. He had played two weeks in high school before his mother made him quit on the grounds that contact was bad for the braces on his teeth. He could never quite get over what he was doing—a feeling with which I could sympathize. He told me, "To think that three weeks ago in a touch football game in Central Park I was going after an eight-year-old quarterback. I got chopped in the larynx by his father. That was bad enough, but now I'm supposed to stiff-arm Karras."

Most of the filming of *Paper Lion* was done at a private school near Boca Raton, Florida. The winter months had gripped the Cranbook School in Michigan, the locale for the text of the book, so that Millar had to forgo the unique beauty of that opulent campus—the swans, the pine forests, the brick walks, and the halls and dormitories, with their fronts of ivy, and the quiet of the place, the sprinklers ticking back and forth on the lawns—all of which struck such contrasts with the physical intensity of a professional football team in training, and which would have been fine to suggest in the filming. With a schedule to keep, he was forced to look elsewhere, in the clement weather of the south, for a simulated training camp.

The Florida school he had found was set in flat, sun-parched barrens, palms set about haphazardly amid barracks-like school buildings, so that one had the sense that the classes were held outdoors, the instructor leaning up against the bole of a palm tree with his students around him. Next to the gymnasium was an outdoor swimming pool which was continually in use —whistles going, the constant thump of limbs against water, and, whenever one looked, a young face turning, streaming water, to suck in a tortured breath of air through a mouth grotesquely ajar, then facing down in the water again to pursue those endless laps—driven by new hope of one day winning a race and a tiny medal with a ribbon attached.

I went down to Boca Raton a few times to see what was going on. I had no official capacity with the film, though Millar was kind enough to show me the script every once in a while, and we fought about what was in it, especially a fabricated scene in which I knocked myself out running into a goal post.

The first time I arrived, I could see a big crowd of Lions in football gear standing in the middle of the practice field. It turned out to have nothing to do with the film. The players were surrounding two linemen crouched opposite each other in their stances, as if on the line of scrimmage. Alex Karras was one of them; the other was Roger Shoals, an offensive lineman known as "The Turtle"—chiefly, I think, because his neck was so thick that it continued the dimensions of his head, a very large one, down into his body, so that he seemed to be peering out from the carapace of his shoulder blades. Apparently the two of them had bet fifty dollars that playing head to head The Turtle, who was an offensive tackle, could keep Karras from reaching a point seven yards behind him—the average distance a quarterback drops back to pass—within three seconds. The Turtle was sure enough of his abilities against the pass rush to put up twenty dollars of his own; the rest of the fifty was gathered from fellow offensive linemen who were skeptical but loyal enough to their own kind to back him.

Karras had not bet on himself; he said that was against his principles, which, as everyone knew, were rock-ribbed and airtight, but his side of the bet had been quickly covered by teammates from the defense.

Someone on the side barked out the signals, and at the simulated hike, The Turtle, with a hard concussive series of grunts, jigged back with quick ferocious steps and set himself up, hands cocked, for Karras' rush.

It was difficult to follow Karras' moves. Invariably, as one remembered from watching him in games, it seemed the opposing lineman's *clumsiness* that let Karras through, because The Turtle was left on one knee, off balance, grimacing in despair; of course what had put him there was something Karras had done to him in a quick blur of motion, a feint and heave. I could hear the crack of a hand on a helmet, and then Karras seemed to scuttle past in a maneuver that a master of Tai Chi, the most advanced and subtle of the Oriental martial arts, would have applauded. He reached the designated spot in well under the three seconds, almost as if he had scampered there unimpeded, and the players began to josh and rail at Shoals. Someone said he played his position like a guard on the taxi squad of the then enfeebled Philadelphia Eagles.

Karras saw me standing at the edge of the crowd and trotted up to say hello. His big peaceful face stared out of his helmet. "To think," he said, "that it's only taken two and a half seconds to destroy the confidence of a man built up over six and a half years."

Karras had come to Florida for the filming with suitable props: a director's chair shipped down with his name and four stars stenciled on the back; a red beret that he either hung off the back of his chair or wore at a jaunty angle—usually when he had his football uniform on, which gave him an oddly paramilitary look, as if he were a weirdly armored reconnaissance scout for the Green Berets. From time to time, during the shooting on the set, he took to shouting out the orders associated with moviemaking: "Slate it! Roll sound! Quiet on the set!" And especially, "All right, everybody, it's a wrap!"—the standard Hollywood phrase for calling it a day, which Karras would usually announce just five minutes or so after the day's shooting had *started*. He practiced an equivalently exquisite sense of timing with "Quiet on the set!"—bellowing it out when it *was* quiet, with everyone in their positions, and tense, and the camera just about to roll. "QUIET ON THE SET!" and everyone would jump and say, "Oh for Chrissakes, Alex."

The man most agonized by this sort of behavior was Alex March, the director. He was a lean high-strung ex-TV producer who had shifted to directing because he suffered such pangs handing over his shows to someone else to give them expression. He felt he could do as well, and for seven years he had been directing on his own, largely television dramas. He told me that in those seven years of directing, his voice had dropped practically an octave. *Paper Lion* was his first motion picture, and he expected that by the time he had done with it his voice would drop out of audible register, as if off the bass end of a piano.

"What's the trouble?" I asked. He had invited me over to his motel on the edge of the school grounds. He sat with his hands folded over his stomach, staring up at the corner of the ceiling.

"I love athletes," he began. "I'm a great fan. Once I went up in an elevator in the RCA building with Willie Mays. I was supposed to get off at the eleventh floor, but I recognized him and went all the way to the forty-fourth, where he was getting off, hardly even daring to look at him I was so excited. I feel the same way about great football players. But this film has been a nightmare.

"Football players are such opposites," he said mournfully. "They're big adults to look at, but really they're not: they're children. That was the first revelation. So I decided I'd *treat* them like children. But that didn't work. I tried to coax them. No. I yelled at them. No. In fact, I don't know *how* you handle them. Football players are supposed to be supremely disciplined people, since what they do is predicated on the notion of supreme discipline. But they're *not*. If I try to get them together for a scene, it takes hours. They mill around like cattle; they don't listen; they all talk at the same time. And Christ," he said. "The vulgarity. The incredible vulgarity. It's as thick as steam, and after a while you damn near get suffocated by it."

"What seems to be the main problem?"

"Well, for one thing I can't get them to *exert* themselves," he said. "We get the cameras trained on what is supposed to be a red-hot scrimmage, and it looks as though they're doing a mime, a gentle sort of ballet. Sometimes the defense pops; *they* do all right. It's instinctive for them, I guess; when they look across and see someone carrying the ball, they want to get him. Still, I can't get anyone to *sweat*. And no one will take out his false teeth. They all look scrubbed and clean. Hell, I don't think anyone even has to take a *shower* at the end of the day. After the morning's shooting, almost all of them lunch in the cafeteria in their football uniforms. Helluva thing to see a guy in shoulder pads tucking into a little cup of fruit salad. And of course the lack of exertion on their part shows up in the rushes. On the screen this training camp looks like everyone's getting ready for a pinochle tournament."

March told me that the first scene he had tried with the Lions was symptomatic. On paper it had seemed simple enough; it called for Joe Schmidt to motion Karras out of a group of players running in from practice to tell him in a sentence or so that a writer from *Sports Illustrated* was turning up in training camp to join the team.

"Fifteen takes. To begin with, I couldn't keep the players —and they all looked scrubbed, not a grass stain on their uniforms—from looking into the camera as they ran by. Finally, after I got *that* straightened out, I discovered that as soon as they were out of camera range, they'd turn and hustle up behind me and the camera to watch Schmidt and Karras—ribbing them, obscene hand motions and so forth.

"I don't understand them. Their private *personae*. Christ! They go out all night and come dragging in at dawn. It's hard to imagine what they find in this strange octogenarians' town of Boca Raton. I think they go just out of habit, and lean up against buildings.

"And on the set. *Christ!*" Reflectively, he said, "You know, moviemaking is a dull business, really. I mean, it's boring waiting around for your scene, and then the retakes. So most of the people I know in show business find rather normal ways to pass the time—they play chess or cards or read a paperback or play liar's poker. But you know what these football players are doing?"

"I can't imagine," I said truthfully.

"A lot of them have got these magnifying glasses." His voice rose. "There's a whole rash of them around, and the players are always lying around in great heaps out there in the sun and trying to burn each other's body hair off with these magnifying glasses."

I expressed appropriate surprise, and then I asked if he thought any of his charges had potential ability as actors.

He was dubious. "Alex Karras could be a Nat Pendleton —a funny heavy. As for the rest of them . . ." He shrugged. "If they learn the lines, they sound like schoolboys. As for improvising—well, only the best actors can do that. But you know, sometimes I think they could do much better than they let on, that somehow I'm involved in a tremendous put-on. There's a terrible intelligence that shines out of their eyes, like the look you sometimes get from cats. For example, Karras had this line in which he had to mention Park Avenue. But he kept substituting other places for it: 'Hyde Park,' he'd say. So we'd start again. 'Dobbs Ferry.' 'Grosse Pointe.' I mean, what was he *doing*?" His voice was rising. " 'Memory Lane.' What did he have in mind? Did he have some sort of psychological block about Park Avenue? Take after take. Or a scene he had with John Gordy. Twenty-nine takes. They just giggled at each other."

March looked at his watch and sighed deeply. "Joe Schmidt's the only one who can handle them." He went on to describe one of the low points in his own attempts to keep order and decorum: the occasion of the big jello fight between many of the players lunching in the school cafeteria. To no one's surprise, Karras was the instigator, apparently with a spoof of a television commercial current then, in which tea is shown being poured over ice cubes into a tall glass. "Harry, this iced tea is so good on a hot summer day," Karras was saying in the exact words of the commercial, "that I can't get enough of it . . ." But he kept continuing to pour the tea until it overflowed the glass, spread swiftly out across the cafeteria table, and over the edge onto Roger Shoals's legs. "Just can't get enough of this super-tasting tea," Karras kept intoning. Shoals reached for his plate and, cupping his portion of jello in his palm, he lobbed it onto Karras' lap. Karras retaliated with *his* jello, and the contagion spread from table to table—largely, I was told afterwards, because of the hugely pleasurable feel of jello as a projectile. "There is a technique," I was told. "You can't close your fingers around it or it'll slip out between your fingers. Your true jello shot is a lob. The jello quivers through the air and lands just great. Beautiful!"

Because of the jello fight, in which a lot else was thrown too—milk from jugs, pats of butter, rolls, a dish of mashed potatoes, celery stalks—Joe Schmidt called the team together that afternoon, told them that he was disappointed in them and ordered them to behave like gentlemen henceforth. At the end of the talk, just as if he were appealing to their football instincts, he told them to dedicate themselves to the film, "to give one hundred percent to these motion-picture guys."

Poor March; he was a harried man. The team was at the Boca Raton location for almost a month, and on the last day of shooting a few of the players picked him up and threw him in the pool to celebrate the end of their stay there, much in the same spirit that the crew of an eight-oar shell picks up a coxswain and throws him into the river after winning a race. But March, who did not cotton to the idea at all, struggled desperately in the grasp of the players, cursing at them, and as he was tumbled into the water he fractured a couple of ribs on the side of the pool. "I'm broke!" he shouted, his mouth half full of water.

"He was real mad," one of the players told me. "He couldn't take it as a joke."

What the player remembered best about throwing March in was that the regular activity in the pool never stopped; the kids kept doing their laps, though they must have seen him—this man thrashing around, fully dressed, with his shoes on. They just kept going up and down, the swimmer in March's lane swerving slightly to avoid him. "Great dedication," the player said. "Man, that's *it*."

The morning after I had spoken to March, I saw him direct a few scenes, and I understood his torment perfectly. In the first one I watched, Pat Studstill, the team's flanker and punter, had one line to deliver—"I got a haircut," just a throw-away line for background effect, in essence—but he had stewed over it and practiced it, and when the time came he said, "Stand back, everyone; I'm kind of nervous." Then he delivered the line with such heavy, portentous emphasis that he seemed to be announcing that rather than a haircut he had a serious, very communicable disease. March threw up his hands. There had to be a number of takes to tone down Studstill's delivery.

Another instance of an ill-delivered line occurred in a scene in which Jerry Zawadzkas, a tight end, was cut down by Bruce Maher with a block, and John North, who coached the receivers, was supposed to yell out a reprimand and tell Zawadzkas to get off his tail. As a player, North had a reputation for being especially rough, with a lot of gold in his mouth as a result of reprisals, and he has always had an appropriately foul mouth to go with his deportment. But he found the camera completely intimidating, and at March's cry of "Action," he leaned forward and gazed out at where Zawadzkas had been dumped somewhat gently by Maher. "Gerald," he cried mournfully. "You're supposed to take the linebacker to the outside." Each word was carefully evoked from memory with immense formality.

"Son of a *bitch*," he said later, with more characteristic fervor. "I've set this mothering industry back one hundred years." He was beside himself. " '*Gerald!*' Can you believe it? What the hell got into me?" He snorted scornfully. "Christ, I don't even call that guy 'Jerry,' much less 'Gerald!' I don't even call him 'Za . . . Za . . .'—whatever the hell his name is. I might call him 'you dumb Polack' or maybe 'you son of a bitch,' but '*Gerald!*' Christ!" He was shaking with dismay.

Among the Lions, however, one player had had considerable "practical experience," as he called it, in "motion-picturing." Night Train Lane, the greatest of the Detroit cornerbacks, was now retired and working in the Lion front office. I was delighted to see him again. He came running up in a bulky sweat suit. All bone and tendon in his playing days, he had now abandoned the training regimen that kept him slim and his weight had ballooned to over two hundred pounds, though it was not disproportionate distribution of weight: he had simply turned into a big man. After the opposition began to beat him too often for him to continue as an active player, he stayed on with the Lions, working at one thing and another. He affected a pipe —a heavy, odd-looking meerschaum, a Sherlock Holmes type that weighed down one side of his face and gave him a somewhat strained expression. The Lions had him doing some scouting for them and gave him a little office at their headquarters where he kept his charts and scouting reports. Dick LeBeau, who collected Night Train anecdotes, told me that the place was full of craftsman's tools and slide rules, and that walking in there was like being in the chart room of an ocean liner. "The charts he kept on the players he scouted were so complicated that he had to be kept around just to *decipher* them," LeBeau said. "Either that or bring in a Ph.D. I once asked him what it all meant and he said it was nothing but a 'grading code,' but you could tell by the way the smoke poured out of his pipe when he showed you around his office and the way he'd reach down and touch one of those slide rules that he was pretty proud of how it all looked."

Also, at that time, LeBeau told me, Night Train was involved in "motion-picturing." During pre-season training he was in charge of making video tapes of practice scrimmages to help the coaches pick up flaws. He worked on the top of a thirty-foot scaffolding set on the sidelines of the practice field.

"How were the films?" I asked.

"Well, they started out kind of blurry," LeBeau said. "Like he'd done them in a snowstorm. He had trouble with the sun at first, and he said he didn't know how to 'down-focus the meter,' which he said was very important. They got the thing working pretty good finally, and the players began calling him 'Cecil B. de Train.' "

Apparently, the one peculiar disadvantage of having Night Train as a cameraman was that if rain was in the area, or there had been forecasts of thunderstorms, an uncertain jiggle and swaying would turn up in the video pictures—or, more likely, the taping would be suspended entirely. Though utterly fearless, Night Train was unnerved by lightning. The players knew this and twitted him about it, and they referred to the scaffolding as "Train's lightning rod."

If the weather forecast had been uncertain that morning, Train would get up in his scaffold and revolve slowly, like a lookout in the crow's-nest, scanning for storms, peering out from beneath the brim of his golfing hat. If a cloud began to loom on the horizon, the smoke would begin to puff more nervously out of his meerschaum pipe, and soon, after pacing around up in the little platform, he would call for assistance in getting the apparatus down. "No common sense t'all to let this stuff get all rusted up with rain and thunder," he'd call out. He had a young kid to assist him, who was usually sleeping under the big shade trees that lined the practice field, and the players would grin and call up to Train that the cloud was hurrying up on him fast. So Train would struggle with the equipment himself, busying himself in the bright sunlight. According to LeBeau, he'd kept himself in great shape scurrying up and down the scaffold to keep clear of the lightning.

The fact that he had been involved in the "motion-picturing" business gave Night Train a certain air of authority at Boca Raton. He took me over to look at the big Technicolor cameras on their rubber-wheeled sleds. "Look at these babies," he said.

"What would you point the camera at if you were in charge here?" I asked.

He squinted slightly. "The *best* thing to show in a film about football is what the people *don'* see, so in the the-ater they is surprised, and they say, 'Oh my, so *that's* what it's all about.'"

"What are some of those things?" I asked.

"The behind-the-scenes is what I'm touchin' on," said Train. "How to keep a team high on the steam. Now a very serious thing is the tapin' . . ."

"You mean taping ankles?"

"Correct," said Train. "A very essential business. Tapin' shot. That's what I'd do. Jes' get the camera in the trainin' room and crank away. A nice close shot of the fellow's *foot* and the trainer smoothin' the tape. You get a little scene like that an' you tell somethin' 'bout the danger—it *indicates* it—and it's interestin' 'cause the tape goin' around the ankle is so clean and smooth. And what about the fellow *doin'* the taping—what about him? Why just what this fellow *says* is very important— puttin' the people he's workin' on at *ease,* if that's what he thinks is right, or maybe gettin' them riled up if he thinks they is shuffling too easy-like, maybe, or moseyin'. Why, we had this trainer on the Cardinals, Joe Dollar, who is a chiropodist in Florida now, and while he was doin' your tapin', why, this man would fin' somethin' to say, somethin' 'bout your ancestors, maybe, that'd snap you out of droppin' the ball durin' the game. He had a jillion lines. One time he says, 'Don' go down there with your head in the *crowds*'—he was talking about showboatin'. He was always sayin' little things like that to get you jes' right."

"That's very nice," I said.

"Another thing the movieman can focus on is the little things like the habits that a lot of ballplayers have, like chawin' tobacco. Just mosey the camera down into things like *that*."

I pointed out that I had not seen much tobacco-chewing among football players.

"That's true," Night Train said blithely. "You don' see so much of it around no more. But I remember this time when Joe Strydahar bent over with this chaw stickin' out of his back pocket, and Ben Sheets sneaked it out of there and took a bite out of it for a joke. Well, Ben Sheets was deadly sick and they had to pump it out of him. That's the type of thing I mean," he said triumphantly.

"Let me give you another. You have Erich Barnes down there on the field, the cornerback of the Cleveland Browns, and when he gets pass interference called on him he goes into a big confrontation with the referee. You see him down there hoppin' and jawin' to beat the band. That's when you get your camera crankin' on him, and you see Barnes leaning right up to an *inch* of that referee, and his mouth goin' at him. He's a mad rooster, but what is funny is that he can't *touch* that referee. If he does, it's a two-hundred-dollar fine, and Barnes, he *knows* that. So he may be awful mad, but he's not *that* mad. He got to keep his hands under control, and his feet too, because if he stomps on that referee's toe, even by mistake, he's goin' to be hurt plenty in the pocketbook. That's a fine thing to catch on the film—all this fire and fury, his fingers all jibbery wantin' to collect a referee, and yet that poor man is all flummoxed; he can't do *nothin'*. And the other fine thing on film is that the referee knows that *too*, so you see him standin' around as solemn as a church and 'bout as safe too, just achin' for that cornerback to stub him with a toe so he can balloon up as big as a thunderstorm and say, 'You *touched* me, man! Get on off this field and that'll be two hundred singles. You'll be hearing from the Commissioner . . .' "

The other Lion who was having the time of his life in "movie-picturing" was, of course, Alex Karras. In fact, he began behaving like a star, but with all the pique of an ingenue. "Look at Friday Macklem," he said to me indignantly, pointing at the Lion equipment manager. "Not a damn thing out of him all season long. Players have to get down on their knees and beg for a shoelace. Now look at him—throwing jocks around, and sweat shirts, and yelling commands and looking worried when the camera's on, like he's got sixteen tons of responsibility. He's in every goddamn shot." I resisted pointing out that Karras' outburst was delivered as he sat in his own director's chair, with its four stars, wearing his actor's beret.

In fact, almost as soon as the filming began, Karras could see that potentially he was a good actor, as March had suggested, and that it could provide a funnel for his constant, near obsessive need to perform. We talked about it one afternoon after the day's shooting. Was it something he might consider after finishing football? He was skeptical, though intrigued.

The sun was overpowering, and we moved to the shade of a palm tree. He began talking about films. His favorite film was *Zorba the Greek*, which he had seen three times because, as he said succinctly, it was about ugly Greeks. The good-looking matinee idols disturbed him, and he felt that men like Tab Hunter and Rock Hudson—he referred to them as "those funny guys"—should be supplanted in romantic leads by potato-faced actors who looked like Wallace Beery. "Of course there are some scenes," he said, "that might embarrass audiences: say, a big, Beery-looking guy with whiskers making love to a Norwegian girl. We might have to hide him a bit. We might have to enclose the two of them in a sheet."

"What sort of roles do you see yourself playing?" I asked.

"Robin Hood," said Karras. "I've always wanted to wear a pointed green hat with a long feather in it. I also see myself as a Pepe Le Moko type who speaks a terribly thick foreign language. In the film I come into this room full of big high furniture where a beautiful Norwegian girl is struggling in the arms of a duke who looks like Rock Hudson. Church bells are ringing, and you can hear a big crowd shouting outside. Some sort of a revolution is going on. I lean up against the back of an armchair. I say something very suave. Nobody knows what it means. *I* don't know what it means. The duke looks over; he's puzzled. But whatever I'm saying in this thick accent, the girl says, 'Yes, yes,' and she pulls away from the duke and comes towards me. Her eyes are shining. She says, 'But first we will have a cocktail in the lounge of the Villa Caramba.' She has a sheet in a little handbag."

"Naturally," I said.

"But the role I really want to play," Karras went on easily, "is in a Western. First of all, it would have nothing to do with your usual Western. Not at all. I'd have a different sort of name. I wouldn't want to be called 'Slim' or 'Tex' or 'Wyoming Bill,' or 'Monte.' Nossir."

"Well, what would your name be?"

" 'Ace Zerblonski,' that's what I'd like to be called."

"Ace Zerblonski? Why that?"

"There's been a big ethnic void in Westerns," Karras said grandly. "Ace Zerblonski would help fill it. And another thing: I wouldn't want to be one of your tall, gaunt Western stars, always looking into the sun and squinting. Nossir. To begin with, I wouldn't wear a cowboy hat. I'd be the first bareheaded cowboy star in the history of the cinema."

"What would you do about the sun?" I asked. "The desert sun gets awfully hot."

"Well," Karras said, "I'd have this little parasol—maybe a little Japanese parasol. It would be in a carrying case on my saddle if it was cloudy or I was traveling at night. Then when the sun came up, I'd take it out, snap it open—click!—and the people in the cow town would see the silhouette of this guy with a parasol on the horizon and they'd shout, 'Oh, for Chrissakes, it's Ace Zerblonski,' and they'd run into the meeting house and ring the bell.

"Besides, a parasol is a good prop," he went on. "All the best Western characters had their props. Bat Masterson had his cane; Dan'l Boone had his coonskin cap; Ace Zerblonski has his parasol. When the townsfolk see that parasol coming out of the tree line, everybody begins carrying on because they know that Ace is under that parasol and someone around there is going to lose their stuffings!"

"Is Ace a brave man?" I asked.

"Christ no," Karras said. "My style as a gunslinger is very different. I shoot people in the back."

"Oh, come on, Alex!"

"That's right," he said. "Just ease up to them from the rear and let 'em have it."

"Is that reliable?" I asked. "Don't you make mistakes that way?"

"All the time," Karras said quickly. "Sometimes I walk up to these people after I've shot them in the back and they're lying on their stomachs in the middle of the street, and I turn them over with my toe and I say, 'Oh Lordy, that's not Buck Jones *at all*. It's the *preacher*, isn't it? Amen! Damn shame!' I *brood* about mistakes like that. But in the long run, if you shoot enough people in the back, you're bound to get the one you're after. It's just a question of time. Of course it has a big effect on the cow towns in the area where I hang out. I've shot so many people in the back that the folks in those parts are always wheeling around to see if Ace Zerblonski is *behind* them. If a guy steps off his front porch and goes down to the saloon for a drink, he *revolves* down the street. That's one of the things you remember out there—these little cow towns where everyone's spinning around and walking quickly in circles. Then you know that Zerblonski's been through."

"What sort of a gun do you use?"

"It's very loud and powerful. Terrific kick at both ends. I have a great callus right here on my shoulder. But you know something? It doesn't bother the horse at all when it goes off. He's used to it. Doesn't even jump. Just ho-hum stuff for him. Of course, maybe he's deaf."

"What do you call him, this horse?"

"His name is Great Big Elephant. It's a very good name for my image," Karras explained. "It makes people think that I'm about a mile tall and dangerous, sort of like a rock slide. It has a nice effect. I mean, when the word gets around I'm coming into town they think I really *am* on a great big elephant. So they cry out, 'Martha, get the buckboard! Pack up the hens and chickens. We're pulling out. Ace Zerblonski is coming through the pass on his great big elephant!'"

"Had you thought of doing a television series about Ace Zerblonski?" I asked.

"No." Karras said. "I think of Ace Zerblonski as being in a mammoth super-Western one-shot that'll play in the drive-ins. The kids will look up from lying on top of each other in the back seats and see me on the huge screen in the night riding into town on Elephant and holding my little parasol, and they'll stir themselves and say, 'Jesus Christ! Put on your shoes, Kitty, here comes the Ace. Let's watch Ace Zerblonski.'"

The sun, orange and huge, was sinking toward the flat Florida horizon, and an evening wind began to rattle the palm fronds.

"Tough life, this. Show business is hell." He yawned. "It's hard to believe a guy can get through to the next day. I suppose I could get into it—I mean *truly* get into acting or something like it. When you play football, you always think of what's next. But it's never predictable. I always tell myself that when football's over I'm going to leave Detroit, pack up my family, move to Clinton, Iowa, and help my father-in-law run his bowling alley. Of course I could do something else," he said pensively. "But my father-in-law's bowling alley—that's solid. The days would be predictable. I could put my legs up on the desk and listen to the bowling balls rolling down the alleys. There would be things to do. That would be all right, wouldn't it?"

"I would think so, Alex."

We looked across the playing fields toward the school buildings. The whistles were still blowing by the outdoor swimming pool.

"They really work, those kids," I said. "Hour after hour."

Karras stirred. "When we're done filming," he said, "we're going to throw Alex March in that pool."

"That's absolutely predictable, is it?" I asked.

"Absolutely," he said.

12

That fall, Karras, swept by a sense of civic responsibility that somewhat startled those who knew him, became a head coach in the Bloomfield Hills Pony League, which was composed of a number of teams named after NFL franchises—the 49ers, the Rams, the Raiders, the Vikings, and so forth—and restricted to youngsters nine to ten years old. Originally, he had been offered the job of coaching even younger kids in the Bee League, where seven- and eight-year-olds played, but he felt there was probably "too much crying down there for me to take on the job."

Karras' team was the Bloomfield Hills Jets. His second son, Alex Jr., played on it, as did one of John Gordy's two sons and Joe Schmidt's son, Billy. It was an oddly frustrating experience for Karras. The Pony League teams played each other on Friday afternoons or on weekends, which meant that Karras, involved in his own turbulent football wars, was often away when his charges had their games. He did the best he could. As soon as his own game was over, he would hurry down the ramp to the locker room, lob his helmet into his cubicle, and reach for the phone to call home.

"Hey, Alex, that you? How'd the Jets do? . . . You *lost!* To the Chargers? What happened? . . . Six fumbles!" and he would sit and listen to his son's explanations, his face torn with despair despite the fact that around him his own teammates might be shouting and carrying on about their own victory, and that some fifteen minutes before he himself had been scuttling around in a real-life adult backfield, reaching for the quarterback with self-satisfying success.

During the autumn, I came out to Detroit to watch the Lions play a few of their home Sunday games, and on one occasion I arrived a few days early in the hope of watching Karras' Bloomfield Hills Jets in action. Alex gave me directions, and in the late afternoon I drove out to the high school grounds where the Jets were going through their last drills before playing the Bloomfield Hills Vikings the next day.

I stood on the sidelines and watched. Wearing his golf hat, Karras reared above his team like a derrick. Almost immediately I could see that there were a number of distinctive characteristics about a Karras-coached team. After a run-through of each offensive play, the Jets center was required to form the huddle by stationing himself at the proper eight- or nine-yard distance behind the line of scrimmage, raising his arm aloft so it could be seen, and shouting at the top of his lungs "Hud-*dle!*" —apparently an attempt to get the players grouped quickly around their quarterback. It was a cry one could hear across a couple of fields, as echoing and forlorn as a loon's, and it indicated to anyone in the vicinity who followed Pony League activity that Karras was at work with his team.

I took a few notes. Almost all the players looked like choirboys, an appearance that was not even belied by the accouterments of football warfare; they stared out from beneath the rims of their helmets with enormous gentle eyes, and their high voices, clear as whistles, were as unferocious as bird calls in the evening. All of them were required to wear plastic mouth guards, which were attached to their helmets, and when they set them in place they seemed en masse to have regressed to the use of pacifiers.

Some of them, of course, did not like what they were doing. After every play involving contact, an inevitable grasping at imaginary wounds would occur, usually the elbow or wrist; or a sudden limp would devastate a player, and he would come hobbling up to Karras and say, "Sir . . ."

"Puffer, what the hell's wrong? You're wetting in there like a little girl. No one even hit you. Go on back."

"Yessir."

Not only was Karras tough on his charges, but predictably he was not above keeping his team on edge with his own brand of needling. At one point his quarterback, a youngster named Reardon, complained after an unsuccessful pass that he could not see his intended receiver. "Mr. Karras, I can't see Brookmeier. He's too small."

Karras blew his whistle to stop practice. "Brookmeier," he called out. A helmet atop a small boy turned. "Brookmeier, your quarterback can't see you. *Grow!*"

On another occasion, Karras called out, "I want the pass-return team over here. Quick!"

The youngsters milled around uncertainly.

"I want the eleven people who are on the pass-return team over *here*. You all know who you are."

A group began to form around him.

"Well, it's about time," Karras said. "Our special teams must have pride. Okay, let's hear it for the pass-return team."

"Yay!" they cheered.

"What is the best of the special teams?"

"The pass-return team!"

"Are you proud to be on the pass-return team?"

"Yessir!"

"Well, you dummies," said Karras. "There *is* no such thing as a pass-return team." The youngsters looked at him, betrayed, eyes solemn and large in the shadows of their helmets. Karras shook his head.

"All right," he called. "Everyone gather round." The entire squad moved in around the forlorn "pass-return" team, Karras in the middle, towering above them.

"Okay, that's enough practice for today," he said. "But first I have some questions. Who are you playing tomorrow?"

"The Vikings!"

"Once again."

"The Vikings!" they all shouted in unison.

"Who are a bunch of turkeys?"

"The Vikings!"

"Who are we going to slaughter?"

"The Vikings!"

"Dismiss," said Karras.

He watched them troop off toward the sidelines. A few mothers were standing in the gathering darkness. Back in the high school parking lot other mothers waited in their cars, the headlights on, and the youngsters moved reluctantly, as if what each had been playing at—aping an adult pastime of ferocity and hitting at each other—should not properly conclude by going to one's mother, perhaps (the ultimate indignity) to be clasped briefly and asked if he was "all right" before being driven home, holding his helmet in his lap, in the family Chevrolet.

Karras, his son, Alex, and I walked to his car. "I'm wrung out from psyching my team up," he said. "There's nothing left for *me*. I'm playing Green Bay on Sunday. What kind of a game am I going to have against them! Jesus!"

"What sort of personnel do you have on the Bloomfield Jets?" I asked as we headed for home. "Certainly you've got a lot of football heritage," I pointed out, thinking of his son, and Gordy's, and Joe Schmidt's.

"They're okay, those kids," Karras said. "But the squad is very weak in reserves. Wait until you see them in action tomorrow. The rule is, they all have to play. Did you see the one called Puffer? Puffer is about one foot tall and he's all voice. He's very bright. If Puffer could play the game he talks, no one else would walk out on the field; they'd all go home and hide in their basements. He wears number one, and he's the single worst football player I've ever seen. I don't think he's made contact with *anyone* this year."

"What position does he play?"

"I think he plays somewhere in the line," Karras said. "It's hard to tell because he sidles away from the guy carrying the ball. He doesn't want to get involved. He wears glasses. He's *very* bright. He's going to be Secretary of Commerce one day . . . When I was playing football at his age, the kids had names like Slivovitz and McTawney and Bragodnic, really tough Polack and Irish and Eyetie names, and nicknames like Turk and Hammer and Jughead, and some of them had already lost their front teeth. Puffer," he said in despair.

From the back seat Alex Jr. said that a lot of the kids didn't really like to play. A couple of weeks before, the guy opposite him in the line of the Bloomfield Hill Raiders had said, "I'm really going to get you. I'm really going to push your face in the dirt." Alex blocked him properly on the first play and the kid had broken into tears and gone back to his bench.

"I'll tell you one thing," his father said. "Those Raiders didn't *all* break down and cry. They beat us about one sixty-eight to nothing."

I asked, "How have the Jets been doing?"

"What's our record?" Karras asked, turning back to look at his son. "We beat somebody, didn't we?"

"Oh, Dad," Alex Jr. said from the back seat. "We beat lots of people."

"I have all sorts of problems as a coach," Karras went on. "My best player, a kid named Robertson, came up to me before the last game and said, 'Mr. Karras, I can't play.'

" 'What?' I said.

" 'I've got a French horn lesson at four-thirty on the day of the game.'

"Well, I near fainted away. A French *horn* lesson. We finally solved it. We moved the French horn lesson up a half-hour and the teacher allowed Robertson to come dressed in his football outfit, shoulder pads and all. He sat in her parlor on a straight-backed chair with the music stand in front, and when the hour was up he took out the French horn mouthpiece, clapped in the football mouthpiece and came running out to play. He had a *horrible* game. It's not the way to get ready for The Big Game."

I stayed for dinner at the Karras house, standing out in the kitchen having a drink with his wife, Joanie, while she occasionally turned a spoon in the stew. Drawings by the two youngest Karras children were pinned to a cork board—square-shaped houses with big windows, and chimneys with lines of smoke coming out. I asked her how much she herself could get involved in football—whether she let it permeate her life as much as it did the males in her household.

"Oh, no," she said. "The wives and mothers have to stay on an even keel. They can't get wrapped up in games the way the males do—it would drive a household crazy."

Her husband was in the living room playing with the younger children. Was he easy to live with during the season?

"There are always the sullen silences if things aren't going right," Joanie said. "It's unpleasant to live with, but it's common enough. During the season, the first few days of the week are calm, but then the pressure begins to build. One night Al climbed out of his side of the bed, dragging the comforter with him. He draped it over his shoulder and looked at me sleepily and said that he was off to play the Green Bay Packers. That's because of the pressure. It's great that a football team spends the night before a game in a hotel, even if it's a home game. Why, they might jump up in bed and kick us wives to pieces."

"What about after a loss?"

Joanie turned back to the stew. "Oh, after a loss there's usually a half-hour of blowing off steam when he gets home, but he feels fine after that. Once I remember I took the family to pick him up at the Detroit airport after a big loss, and we went to have supper at a Howard Johnson's with Nick Pietro-sante, Jim Gibbons and his wife, and some others, and every-one was grousing and staring into their shrimp cocktails and really *beside* themselves, until finally Alex Jr., who was just three then, piped up and said, 'Well, back to the old drawing board.' No one could believe it."

After dinner, I left for my hotel. With The Big Game in the Pony League coming up, the Karras household went to bed early. When I returned the next afternoon, driving through a slight rain, I found the house full of tension. Alex Jr. stood in the hall, fully dressed in his football paraphernalia and wearing his helmet. His father was pacing through the rooms. Even Joanie seemed affected. She shook her head and told me that her days had been full enough of gossip and chatter about the NFL as it was, and now, like opening a closet door and finding someone standing there, the Pony and the Bee Leagues had suddenly made their presence known.

"The kids have their ups and downs about it," she said. "One time young Alex came to me and said, 'Mom, I have a bad shoulder. Do I have to go to practice?'

" 'Yes, Alex,' I said. 'Put on your uniform. Think of your father. He played five games with two torn cartilages . . .'

"You know what young Alex said to me? He said, 'Yes, but he had Novocaine.' "

Joanie stayed home with the smaller children. Peter Karras had gone off earlier to play in *his* league. Alex Jr. sat in the back seat of the car. "Are you going to give us a big pep talk, Dad?"

"Why, what's wrong? Didn't you like the one I gave you last week?" Karras turned laboriously from the wheel, maneuvering his big shoulders around so he could glance briefly at his son.

Alex Jr. did not answer. He was looking out the window at the passing scenery. "Mr. Stump usually gives the pep talk," Karras told me.

"Who's Mr. Stump?"

"He's the defensive coach. His first name's Dick, but I call him Mr. Stump. I give it a 'Mistah Stump!' He cried out the name in the car like a sea captain calling for his boatswain's mate. "Mistah *Stump!* Sometimes I think Mr. Stump is putting everybody on with his pep talks." He shook his head. "Wait till you hear him. Couple of years back *I* gave a pep talk before my old school. At Iowa. They had the worst team that year. I went back for a homecoming, and they asked me into the locker room before the game to talk to the team. So I thought, Shall I give them a real Win-It-for-the-Gipper sob talk, or a big long Vince Lombardi scream and knock over a few lockers and act like a gorilla? I gave them neither; I looked at my feet a lot and mumbled a few things. What I remember is that there was a black guy right in front of me—Levi Williams, hell of a good tight end—and while I talked he had on this big grin, like I was telling him the funniest thing in the world, some great honky joke that really grabbed his ass. I couldn't figure him. So the team went out on the field and they got beat something awful. A real horror. But this fellow Williams came up after the game and he *still* had this same tremendous grin on his face—and hell, he'd really been *laced* out there; Iowa was beat about forty to nothing. I said, 'Hey, man, you all right?' He told me that he liked what I'd said in my pep talk. I said, 'Hell, man, you got beat forty–nothing.' He said, 'Hell, man, you *not* give that talk and maybe we get beat *eighty*–nothing.' He was one grand man, let me tell you."

When we reached the playing field it was overcast and threatening rain. Karras had left his rain gear at home; he was wearing the golf hat that read JEWISH OPEN and brightly polished cowboy boots. Alex Jr. stood beside him and looked across the field at the Vikings. "They're all big," he said.

Karras collected the team on the high school gym steps for his pep talk. "We better hold on here a bit," he said. "No one seems to be here," he explained to me. "Just reserves. Where are my stars? I'm missing my quarterback and my best running back. No sense in panicking; they're only half my starting back-field. The quarterback is probably washing dishes . . . Mistah Stump? Do you have a few words for us?"

His assistant coach stood up. He was a big man who wore a trench coat, and he had a Coke in one hand. "Men," he said. "We're going to win this one . . . and we're going to win it big. I don't want crumbs. I'm not interested in crumbs. *You're* not interested in crumbs. I want the whole slab of bacon." He took a swig of his Coca-Cola. "I want you to hit them out there. We want blood, sweat and tears—otherwise you can go home. This game isn't milk and cookies. Nossirree, it's blood and *guts*." He sat down.

"Thank you, Mistah Stump," said Karras. He rose for his own pep talk. "Boys, I'm tired of losing. Are you?"

"Yes!"

"Now the Vikings have lost three games this season. After we're through with them this afternoon, how many games will they have lost?"

Everyone shouted, "Four!"

"I want this one. Do you?"

"Yes!"

"Now, tomorrow's Halloween. I don't want anybody thinking about Halloween. I want you to think about winning and hitting the other guy and bringing home the bacon. Right?"

"Right!" they all yelled.

A latecomer came hurrying up wearing his helmet, his mouthpiece inserted, and a big number one on his jersey.

"It's Puffer," said Karras. "Boy, are we glad to see you."

Puffer removed his mouthpiece. "Did I miss anything?" He had a clear, bright voice.

"You missed Mistah Stump's pep talk. And mine," said Karras.

The boys began milling around. There were only a few minutes to go and they began aping their elders' pre-game rituals—boxing each other on the shoulder pads and running in place. Puffer stood off to the side. I watched him, a small vigorous figure with a pale intelligent face and a spotless uniform. He was chattering away to himself. "Puffer is here," I heard him whisper. "They'll tremble in their boots when they hear that Puffer is here." He looked across the field at the Vikings. "They're not so big," he said. "Puffer is going to stomp them and ring their bells." He walked over to his coach. "Mr. Karras," he said, tugging at his sleeve and looking up. "Their shirts are going to run *red with blood* when Puffer gets ahold of them."

"Yes, yes, Puffer," his coach replied.

"Mr. Karras, their brains are cooking with the awfullest fear."

"Puffer, sit down and calm yourself."

"Mr. Karras, when I tackle them, I'm going to put their light bulbs out."

"Sure, Puffer. Now just don't burn yourself up thinking about it. Save yourself."

Puffer sat down on the gym steps, his hands in his lap. Across the field the referees' whistles began to shrill. The team was quiet suddenly as they trotted across to their bench. Their captain, the middle linebacker, a youngster named Simon, chugged out under his oversized helmet to the center of the field for the coin toss. Karras had instructed him what to do. "He's a good player," he said to me as we stood in front of the bench. "He's three feet tall and he weighs thirty-three pounds, but he sticks like a burr."

Apparently the team lost the toss, for the referee signaled by extending his leg that the Jets were to kick off, and then, turning and catching an imaginary ball, indicated that the Vikings were to receive. But when Simon came trotting back to the bench, he allowed that he had actually *won* the toss.

"Wha'? Wha'? Well, then, why the hell are we kicking *off*?" cried Karras. He looked betrayed under his golfing cap.

"It's psy . . . psy . . ." Simon stuttered.

"Are you trying to tell me there was a *psychological* reason?" Karras exclaimed. "Jesus Sweet Christ!"

To avoid hearing more, Simon turned and scampered out to his team, drawn up in a line and waiting for him to kick off. At the referee's whistle he ran forward and, perhaps frantic in his anguish at having made a tactical error, sent a wobbly kick down to the ten yard line, where it bounced and eluded some potential receivers who looked forlorn and not especially anxious to fool with it until finally the least nervous of them picked up the football and ran it up to the twenty-three. Simon was one of the tacklers.

"Nothing wrong with that," Karras said, looking pleased. "Shows what a heady team leader can do."

The Vikings moved for a few first downs before kicking eighteen yards, and then the Jets' offense took over.

Karras sent in the offensive plays by shuttling quarterbacks. It would have given him the greatest sense of power if they ever turned out to be what he expected, he said sadly. He would instruct his quarterback to call "The power left on 'go,'" pat him on the back as he ran out for the next play, and stand peering forward through his big spectacles in the hope of seeing his orders translated into a recognizable physical facsimile. Instead, the play itself would convolute and heave, with perhaps a fumble for good measure, and when the quarterback arrived back on the sidelines Karras would ask, "Now, damn it, what in God's name was *that*?"

"Oh, sir," the quarterback would answer, "they're kicking us and *everything!*"

The second time the Jets got possession of the ball, they did better. They made a first down, but then stalled with fourth and six to go. Since the team was on its own thirty-five, the situation seemed to call for a kick, but Karras sent in an end-around play. "I don't believe in punting," he told me. "These people can kick the ball just about fifteen yards. Only the very suave coaches call for a punt. The Viking coach punts. The Viking coach is very suave."

His tactic worked; the end-around went for twenty yards and the Jets had a drive going, supported with high-pitched yells from the bench. Before every play the Jet center raised his loonlike yell of "Hud-*dle*," and finally after one distant grouping down at the far end of the field, we saw the Jet players run a short plunge and then leaping up and down, barely discernible in the gloom. We had scored. All of the Jets began slapping each other's palms as they trotted back toward the bench, a massive imitation of the familiar ritual practiced by their elders involved in a score. The try for the extra point failed, but there was still general jubilation.

"Damme, Mistah Stump!" cried Karras. "Have we got ourselves some champions?"

Mr. Stump's face glistened happily in the rain.

After receiving the kickoff, however, the Vikings began marching steadily for the Jets' goal line. Seeing his defensive charges wilt before the Viking onrush, Mr. Stump was beside himself; he took off not only his trench coat but his suit coat, so that in the considerable chill and rain he was wearing no more than a sleeveless white shirt, patched against his body, and a black string tie, looped loosely to his neck from nervous tugging. "Come on! Jets! You gotta have guts to play this game," he cried. He leaned over the border of the sidelines, jackknifed, as if he were poised on the edge of a swimming pool. "Oh no! Make him go inside of you." He turned away and strode frantically in front of the bench.

"Mistah Stump!" cried Karras. "What is transpiring?"

Stump shouted at Karras. "What can you do? You ask them to move just a little bit to the outside, maybe a step or so, and they shift twelve *yards*." He turned back to the game. "Plug up those holes. No more *flinching*, damn it!"

His cries were to no avail. The Vikings scored on an end run. Their extra point try failed as well, and the score was tied six to six.

The time it took the teams to make the two scores used up almost the entire first half, which in the Pony League consisted of two ten-minute quarters. With all the emotion and concern invested in the game, it seemed we had just barely settled down before the referee came over to Karras on the sidelines and said, "We've got one minute to go to the half."

"What are you on, Greek time?" Karras said querulously. His team had possession of the ball and were moving in Viking territory. The two men glared at each other. In the background the cry of "Hud-*dle!*" arose. "You heard what I said," the referee remarked. "One minute." He was wearing all the proper accouterments of his profession—the striped shirt and the whistle suspended from a bleached cowhide lanyard. A bead of rain wobbled on the brim of his cap. "You want me to say it again?"

There it was: they had just a few seconds in which to establish the adult prerogatives—in the case of the referee, who probably taught math in the third grade, his authority in a profession in which the man he was trying to face down was probably the most famous tackle in the country.

Karras stared at him and found nothing to say. The referee turned almost immediately and trotted swiftly toward the Jets, now breaking the huddle and moving up to the line of scrimmage. "What's with that guy?" Karras muttered. "What's wrong with Greek time? Hey?"

In the second half the teams began to slip in the mud. I was hoping to make some notes about the playing of the Detroit Lions' progeny—Bill Schmidt, the Gordy boy and young Karras —to detect whether they reflected their famous parents on the field, whether one could tell from the boys' mannerisms—the hunching of shoulder pads under a jersey, the position of the hands on defense, the profile of their stances—that a Gordy was out there, or a Karras, or a Schmidt. It turned out to be impossible to tell, not only because of the mud and gloom but because at nine or ten the boys' frames were as thin as ropes and bore no resemblance to the quick heft their fathers carried around. As Karras said of them, "They get into positions like snakes."

The teams churned back and forth, neither scoring. Behind the Jet bench a few girls stood watching the game, shifting their weight from one long, thin leg to another. "Is that your brother?" I heard one of them ask in disgust. "He fell down. He's gross."

"It's raining. Why not?" said the other defensively. "But he *is* gross," she added reflectively. She bent and began speaking earnestly into the face of an Irish setter, cupping its head in her hands. "I'm going to petrify you tomorrow," she said. "I'm going to leap out at you with a Halloween mask. Are you prepared to be petrified?" The dog moved its tail uncertainly. His haunches lowered and he began to tug against her grip. She let go. "Stupid," she said to him. "Big stupe." She stood up. "What's going on? Who's ahead?"

"Who knows?" said the other girl. "Maybe it's a tie. Your brother fell down again."

I moved out of earshot as the team toiled on in the semidarkness. Behind us a group materialized and stood at the bottom step of the stands in back of the bench. With a start I recognized Joe Schmidt, the Lion coach, standing under a large black umbrella, his face impassive. He was there to watch his son. The rain began to pelt down harder and his wife moved in closer to share his umbrella. I wondered whether Karras was aware that Schmidt was watching. Rumors had it that recently the two were not on the best of terms.

With only a few minutes to go in the game, Karras called out, "Has anybody not played yet?"

A number of hands went up along the bench.

"Jesus Christ, Mistah Stump, we've got about ten of them," Karras said grimly. "Mistah Stump, begin sending in the reserves!"

His assistant substituted at every opportunity. The last one sent in was Puffer. A small tidy figure with the big number one on his back, he ran out with quick, busy steps that carried him along quite slowly. Karras watched him go. "Okay, Puffer!" he called. "Turn out their light bulbs."

"See if you can figure out where Puffer plays," he said. "It's somewhere of his own choosing."

I watched. The Vikings were on the offense at midfield, and when their fullback moved forward with the ball I could see Puffer receding from the play, falling back from the line into his own backfield. I was reminded of a shore bird, one of the plump plover family, retreating up the beach from a line of surf.

Still, Puffer's presence on the field did not result in any change in the score. In the gloom, the game finally ended in a six–six tie. On the sidelines Karras asked, "Is that the end? Okay, everybody. Go over and shake hands with them."

The players began walking slowly back toward the gym, winding down, I supposed, their emotions about the game. I moved along with them, my notebook open and smudging slowly in the faint rain. I could not resist leaning down and asking the superficial questions that reporters put to players in post-game interviews. "What about the Vikings?" I asked Morton, the Jet center. "What sort of a team?"

He looked up, startled. "Well, they defense good," he

said, aping the locker room banalities of his elders—his voice husky from the effort he had put into crying out "Hud-*dle!*" "They're a real good ball club. They come off the ball real good."

The boy walking along next to him said, "We proved one thing, though: the Vikings put on their legs . . . er ah . . . at a time."

"You're saying that they put on their pants one leg at a time?"

"That's right," he said. "They can be beat. We just didn't get enough points up on the board."

"What was the problem?"

The boy shuffled along. "We couldn't get enough points up on the board," he said again, keeping to that familiar platitude, so incongruous because it was delivered in a high-pitched fluting voice. "They defense good." Then he began to have trouble. "Er ah . . . Brookmeier . . . and then there was that time . . . well, *you* know, when . . . and what about when . . . and he *kicked* me, that big guy . . . and the rain . . ."

"But most important . . . ?"

"We just couldn't get those points up on the board"— this clear and positive.

I fell into step alongside Puffer. "Puffer, what is your opinion of the Jet coaching staff?"

"I think Mr. Karras is the new Chubby Checkers," he said, in reference to the somewhat stout pop star of the day. I jotted this comparison down in my book. I continued, "Puffer, did you put out any light bulbs?"

He did not answer. He walked with his head down. My heart sank.

"No," he said softly. "I ran away."

I had no idea what to say. "It's all right, Puffer," I said finally. "One day you're going to be Secretary of Commerce."

He stopped and looked at me out of the depths of his helmet. "Isn't that funny," he said cheerfully. "That's exactly what Mr. Karras tells me."

13

In the long run of the history of the NFL, John Gordy may be remembered less for his considerable skills as an offensive guard (selected three times for the All-NFL team) than for his contribution as a prime mover in the formation of the present-day version of the NFL Players Association. There had been a Players Association before Gordy got himself seriously involved, but it was thought of as being little more than a social club. Representatives elected from each club would meet once a year to draw up a list of grievances, largely to do with minimum salaries and cases regarding complaints about injuries. These would be presented, usually by letter, to the owners, who would sulkily acknowledge receipt and promise to get back in touch with the Association. That was about it.

What led to the strengthening of the Association's hand was the attempt in 1963 by the Teamsters Union to organize the football players. Their chief organizer was Bernie Parrish, the former Cleveland Brown defensive back, described by Gordy as being as aggressive and determined off the field as he was on it. In addition, said Gordy, he was very, very bright. "What he wanted to do originally—backed by Harold Gibbons of St. Louis and the Teamsters there—was to organize *all* of sport," Gordy told me. "The whole works—baseball, hockey, roller derbies, what-have-you, into a sort of conglomerate. He came to see me about this in Detroit. At that time I was the vice-president of the Players Association. I was skeptical and told Parrish that I thought that football had its own problems and should concentrate on setting its own house in order."

Parrish went back to St. Louis without Gordy's support. At this point, the Teamsters apparently thought better of their conglomerate plan and Parrish was sent out to concentrate solely on organizing football. He traveled to the NFL cities and began getting affirmations from the members of a number of teams. Gordy received a progress report in Detroit which dismayed him. Unable to understand the value of a match-up between the Teamsters and the players, he decided that if the drift of the NFL players continued toward absorption by the Teamsters, he would resign his vice-presidency. He announced his intent at a meeting in Hollywood, Florida, where the NFL players' annual golf tournament—just the sort of a social occasion the organization had become known for—was scheduled. Gordy stated his reasons for resigning so effectively and with such concern that the entire roomful of players rose up, and by the time they were done Gordy had become their new president —with a mandate to struggle to keep the players out of the Teamsters.

At first it did not seem an easy fight, because the Teamsters listed a lot of pie-in-the-sky demands that they claimed would be pressed on the owners. In vying for the players' support the Gordy group was much more contained, not wanting to make promises they knew they could not deliver on. Eventually, a poll of the players of the league showed a ninety percent vindication of Gordy and the Players Association, and a vote *against* professional unionization. The latter, Gordy had always felt, was a concept that football players regarded as antithetical to the sacred notion of being rewarded solely on how well one played the game.

But the owners were fair targets, and in January 1968 the Association flexed its new-found muscles and hired an obscure Chicago labor lawyer named Dan Shulman, an energetic and cheerful public relations man from Houston, Texas, named Tom Vance, and Mal Kennedy as a business manager. These were the civilian advisers; Gordy's negotiating committee drawn from the players consisted of himself, quarterback King Hill from the Eagles, fullback Ernie Green from the Browns, tackle Bob Vogel from the Colts, and Dave Robinson, the Green Bay linebacker. As the chief negotiator, Gordy worked at such a pitch that he remembers seeing his family only about twenty times between January and the day in July when the issues were finally resolved.

Twenty-one conditions were presented to the owners. Some of them involved small beefs such as an increased out-of-town meal allowance, and permission for players to purchase two good tickets before the public sale began. The three main demands were a $5,000,000 contribution to the pension fund, a $15,000 minimum wage for a season's work, and $500 per game for pre-season exhibitions.

"The pension payment was the biggest bone," Gordy told me. "What we were trying to do was to make football's pension plan equitable with baseball's." At that time baseball owners contributed $4.1 million each year, whereas the NFL owners put in about a quarter of that figure. They had found out that Frank Howard of the Washington Senators, who played in the majors for ten years, would be getting a pension of $1,287 a month when he was sixty-five, while Gordy, after the same number of playing years, would receive only $656. "Those figures are memorable, let me tell you. Even at the age of fifty Howard will be getting paid five hundred dollars, and I won't be getting anything. I remember at one of the players' meetings the salary and pension potential of a guy named No-Neck Williams who played with the Chicago White Sox was a chief topic, and when they heard what he was getting, there was a vote to beat him up and take his share!

"Of course the owners' position was that they couldn't afford our demands. But we'd done a careful study, using the Green Bay books, which are open to scrutiny since they're a public corporation, and it was fair to assume that the costs of other operations in the NFL were similar. We knew that profit estimates in 1972 totaled forty-four million dollars. Our position was that if the owners were making a ton, we wanted a *quarter*-ton.

"So we sat down with them. My background in negotiating was simply zilch, and none of the other players—King Hill, Ernie Green, Bob Vogel—knew very much either. What we *did* have was an instinctive ability, and of course a firm belief in our cause, which was to do something for the players. The most important thing to remember was not to say too much. There was an awful lot of psychological maneuvering. I always tried to have some great superstar sitting behind me, so that when the owners began lambasting me they'd look up and see Bart Starr sitting in the shadows, glowering at them.

"The owners' negotiator was Ted Kheel, the great labor dispute arbitrator, and he is simply the best there is. Damn, he was so bright, and he could tie you up in knots. He knew every trick there was. So the best thing to do was to retreat, play dumb, not say much and always fall back on football, which is what I *did* know, and leave him hanging. It must have been exasperating for him—to offer these seemingly plausible and articulate observations, beautifully put together, and requiring *some* sort of response, and have them go winging past this guy sitting opposite with his mouth hanging slightly open, a real dumb-ass; his brilliance must have seemed so *wasted*. But I had to be so careful. There was hardly a sentence I could say that Kheel couldn't turn around somehow."

I once had the opportunity to ask Kheel about the negotiations and Gordy's part in them. He was very complimentary about Gordy's abilities. It was not surprising, he said. "Time and time again I've seen guys come out of the rank and file, completely untrained, with such intuitive ability as negotiators that they can hold their own, and even sometimes outwit the professional lawyers opposite them. Gordy was one of those people, and he also had the qualities of a natural leader. I once told him, 'John, you have the makings of a great union leader—you're absolutely unscrupulous.' "

"What did you mean by that?"

"Oh, I didn't mean it unkindly," Kheel said. "All I meant was that Gordy was able to say something he didn't really believe, in order to enhance his bargaining position."

I said that Gordy had talked about silence being a weapon.

"It *is* a weapon," Kheel said. "It requires great discipline, because the temptation to resist answering what the other fellow is saying is enormous. But if you can stick to it, it's effective because the other side doesn't know whether you're speechless or have something to hide."

I reported this later to Gordy; he laughed and said that "speechless" was the correct word for the state he was in most of the time.

"What about the owners?" I asked him.

"Kheel did almost all the talking for them. In fact, Coach Lombardi, who was representing Washington then, paid Kheel the highest compliment by referring to him as 'Coach.' But the owners—I'm excepting Lombardi—weren't any good. Many of them had always talked to their players as if they were talking to dogs—*nice* dogs—and had no idea how to deal with them as equal negotiators. It was like coming down to breakfast to find your Labrador sitting tending the toaster and he asks you to pass the jam. Of course, Lombardi was not like that. He was the toughest to sit across the table from, because I thought he was the greatest individual in professional football. I'd been coached by him once in a Pro Bowl game and had seen that amazing ability to take athletes and give them momentum, to channel and maintain their abilities. Now here I was opposite him and still feeling this awe, and knowing I couldn't act scared. That was another reason I was so quiet—I mean, suppose I opened up my mouth to say something to Lombardi and out came this little canary noise?

"Well, the negotiations went on and on, and I began to learn the language. But it was awfully taxing on everybody, and boring. I remember that at one of the player-rep meetings Tom Vance, who was doing public relations for us, suddenly noticed Dick Butkus from the Bears motioning him over. Butkus shoved a pad of paper at him and whispered, 'Draw me a squirrel.' He'd heard somewhere that Vance once went to art school or something.

"Vance said, 'What?'

" 'A squirrel. Right here on this pad. I mean it. Right here.'

"So Vance took his pencil and laboriously, because he was out of practice, drew a squirrel. All this while, somebody from the Players Association was droning on with his lecture. Vance said he was nervous as hell because Butkus kept leaning over the pad to see how the drawing was coming out.

" 'Well, there's your squirrel.'

" 'Draw me a rooster,' Butkus said.

"Poor Vance said, 'Oh, come on,' but Butkus insisted, getting quite noisy about it, and Vance drew a rooster, and then a pig and a large cow, and he was working on a horse when the session finally adjourned and Butkus let him go.

"But most of the time, of course, it wasn't anything like this at all; it was very serious stuff, and nip and tuck too. The licensing fees we'd arranged for players endorsing products came in just in time to pay off our office and telephone bills. The final stumbling block was the pension plan. In July, just before the training camps were to open, the owners made an offer. They'd accepted the other twenty points, though all of them with compromises, but not our demands on the pension deal. When they finally made an offer, I turned it down. I felt the players would want me to. It was quite a step, because it meant that as head of the organization I could face ten to fifteen years in jail for calling a work stoppage and defying interstate regulations. But we polled the players and discovered that they were behind us. The owners retaliated by closing the training camps. They remained closed for ten days, until finally we met again in the Waldorf Astoria and the owners agreed. It was over! We'd got the three big things we wanted. The minimum wage was hiked to twelve thousand dollars a year for a two-year player and thirteen thousand for a three-year player. We finally got good money for playing in exhibition games. And the great thing was that we got a three-million-dollar pension plan, which just about doubled a player's pension benefits. There'll be increases in the future, but it was a start. What a relief!

"The best part was when Coach Lombardi took me aside and patted me on the back and said that I'd done a helluva job. That meant everything—it's one of the great times in my life, though I've never figured out whether it was because it was all over and I could start thinking again about simple things like knocking a man down with a cross-block, or whether it was because of the pat on the back from that man. Anything he ever said, he *meant*.

"It *was* an honorable agreement, and it was good for football. It cost the training season ten days, which wasn't much of a price, was it? I mean, that's not too much for getting good security for players when they get older, do you think?"

14

Despite his efforts on the pension plan, and his concern for players once their playing days were over, Gordy had ambivalent feelings about old-timers, at least regarding reunions and becoming part of the ritual of nostalgia. Alex Karras felt the same way.

"I've never even thought about being an old-timer," Gordy told me a year after he had left football. "When you quit, it's hard enough to learn how to be a fan, much less an old-timer. Besides, who wants to go to reunions?"

"What's the problem?" I asked. "Wouldn't you enjoy seeing your teammates again?"

"I'd be scared of the failures," Gordy said. "Life ain't easy, and once out of a football uniform they might all look so *vulnerable*."

Karras had a more particular reason. It was his fantasy

that an old-timers' reunion would be crowded with wizened and shrunken men who would stare at each other and read each others' name tags, squinting forward to see, and then one of them would sing out, "You're the guy I knocked the crap out of in nineteen thirty-six, and I can do it again." So the two of them would go off in a corner and throw pathetic cuffs at each other with arms like sticks until finally the waiters would sigh and step in and lift them up and put them down in their chairs for The Big Meal, which was applesauce and zweiback. The old-timers would eat in silence. Then someone would say, "Ah, Tittle, you were never any good." The great quarterback would look up from across the table, pick up a piece of zweiback and take careful aim. The throw, across four feet of tablecloth, would miss. The old-timers would look up, but their attention span was short, and quickly the scrape of knives and forks would rise again in the quiet dining room.

I was under no such compunctions, myself. So when an invitation arrived to attend a Lion alumni reunion I packed a bag and went to Detroit. The occasion was held in a large, dimly lit clubroom in a hotel in a Detroit suburb. Everyone wore plastic-encased name cards. Some of my contemporaries were on hand: Terry Barr, Night Train Lane, Tommy Watkins, and Darris McCord (who told me regretfully that his hayrides were a thing of the past). Wives were there, and some lively dancing was done to a three-piece orchestra that played in a corner of the room.

The more venerable old-timers sat at tables around the dance floor, gossiping and looking out at the younger people like parents chaperoning a high school dance.

I wandered around. I overheard Night Train telling a Polish joke. "Why don' Poles ever commit suicide? Because," he said, "outhouses ain't above two stories high." He slapped his knee. "It's all right for me to tell jokes like that," he confided to me. "I'm an ethnic."

I sat down at a table next to Jim Steen, the president of the Lion alumni association. He introduced me around. ". . . Dutch Clark? You heard of this great one?"

"Certainly," I said.

"Look at ol' Dutch," Steen said with tremendous affection. "He was the greatest runner that football ever had."

I stared across the table at a kindly-looking man, his jaw working just slightly on gum, tieless, with a yellow shirt buttoned up to the neck and ill-fitting glasses that with a recurrent gesture he would push back up to the top of his nose.

"He was the slowest runner you ever saw, but every step meant something," Steen said. "Isn't that right, Dutch? There was a standing joke: if you missed a block for Dutch, you didn't have to worry because by and by he'd be back, still on his feet, and you'd have another crack at helping him. Isn't that right, Dutch? He was the passer for us—wore wool gloves, which made Potsy Clark, the coach, good and angry. He'd say, 'Get those gloves off, Dutch, how the hell can you pass with those gloves on?' And Dutch would say, 'Potsy, my hands are cold.' Isn't that right, Dutch?"

Clark finally stirred. He had been listening to these rapid-fire comments with no show of interest or reproach, as if it were an established part of his social existence to be forced to sit within earshot of people telling stories about him. Clearing his throat, he said softly, "My fingers were all broken and white and stiff, so I wore gloves. I couldn't pass worth a damn."

"He's the number one Lion," a wife at the table said loudly.

"Naw," said Clark. "I had a bad left eye. On defense I played safety, and they used to shoot down on my blind side."

"The worst guy on pass defense was Father Lumpkin," someone said.

Dutch Clark said, "Quite right. He couldn't cover *anybody* on pass defense. A pass would get completed in his area and he'd stand there holding his head in his hands in horror. He got confused; he was too independent-minded, I think. But on offense he was great." He pushed his glasses back up to the top of his nose.

"Why was he called 'Father'?" I asked.

No one seemed to know for sure. Someone said, "Well, he was certainly no priest. Off the field he was sort of meek and

206

quiet, a slim-built guy; maybe that was why. He was also called 'The Ramblin' Wreck' because he came from Georgia Tech, and he *looked* like one, too. He had a cauliflower ear, and towards the end of a game he'd rip off his helmet and play without it. He couldn't find one that fit. Maybe it hurt that ear of his."

Clark said, "He was a great blocking back. He was a wrassler and he loved to knock people down. We never had huddles in those days. I called the plays at the line of scrimmage, and Father Lumpkin would turn around and look at me with this pleading look, as if to say, 'Please call the one where I can run and really give the other guy a lick.' Oh my, he loved the offense."

"What did he play on defense?"

"Linebacker. He was fine on running plays because it gave him a chance to knock people down. When he wasn't knocking people down on a football field, he was off somewhere *wrassling* them down. He'd disappear, and Potsy Clark would yell like hell, and Father Lumpkin would turn up in Charleston, wrassling someone. He did what he felt like. He was finally dropped from the Lions because he wouldn't give up professional wrestling."

"What I remember about him," Jim Steen said, "was that during the season he never wore socks. He taped up his ankles on the first day, and then wore that tape until the last game. When the tape got dirty, he just slapped on some more."

"He was quite a character," Steen's wife said. "He came and stayed with us once. He slept on top of the covers in the guest room. I know, because I went in there to wake him up for breakfast and he was lying fully clothed and with his hands folded over his stomach, like he was lying on a slab. But it took him forty-five minutes to come down for breakfast. What do you suppose he was doing up there?"

None of us could arrive at an answer.

"He never got hurt playing without that helmet?" I asked.

"Probably," said Clark. "But people *had* to play hurt in those days—at least when I began—because there were so few players that you *couldn't* substitute. On the Portsmouth Spartans we had a fourteen-game schedule and fourteen players. Why, I remember one time we were playing the Philadelphia Yellow-Jackets, or the Staten Island Stapes, one of those teams, when this kid called Harry Ebding, who played end for us, got hit so hard in the eye that it just absolutely swole up with blood so he couldn't see. So at half time somebody run down to the drugstore to get some leeches—"

"Leeches?"

"That's right, leeches to put on that kid's swole-up eye so the blood would get sucked out and he could see good and proper."

"Lord Almighty," I said.

Everyone at the table looked puzzled that I should be startled by this information.

"Well, we *had* to get him out there," Clark said, pushing at his glasses.

A thin slight man named Aid Kushner, who had been the trainer for the Lions in the late thirties, said that the best thing for swelling had always been ice, he didn't want any leeches around, nossir, and he could remember when Lloyd Cardwell had gotten his face busted up by the Bears and they had used the snow off the field to pack the bruises and he'd finally gone back out and played a whale of a game.

"I don't think today's players can play through pain the way they used to," he said. "People don't walk enough; too many escalators. They get hurt easy. There are a lot more injuries now because the players don't go the full sixty minutes and aren't physically prepared."

Leon Hart, the great Lion end, leaned forward and said that *chance* had a lot to do with injuries, that he had once been injured running up out of the dugout in Baltimore for the pre-game introductions.

A wife said, "Yes, I heard that."

"It's true," he said. "Coach Buddy Parker wanted me to play in that Colt game real bad. I had pulled hamstrings, but he decided to chance putting me in the starting line-up. We were supposed to run out between a line of girls with pompoms. When I heard my name over the loudspeaker, I took that first step up onto the field from the dugout, and the muscle popped. I couldn't even get to the center of the field; the next guy being introduced ran past me. I hobbled to the sidelines and told Parker. He said I must be the first guy ever to be injured in the introductions."

After the chuckling and nodding had stopped around the table, I said that I was curious about what it was like to play both ways for those sixty minutes, and wondered if players who had done so had a preference.

Jim Steen said that since hitting was the name of the game, linemen usually preferred defense, because they could freewheel and really sock people.

Leon Hart disagreed. He said that he always thought of the offense as being constructive, something that had been carefully put together to perform a function; there was great pleasure when it worked as it was supposed to, and it was terrible when it was destroyed. "I just don't approve of ripping things apart," he said. "That's the trouble with defense—it's destructive. It made me uncomfortable playing it."

This struck me as a sensitive observation, and admiringly I wrote it down on a napkin so I could remember it. But later, wandering around the room, I heard Hart telling someone, "There's only one way to tackle quarterbacks, which is to come in high on them so you have the chance either of, *one*, destroying their passing sight, or *two*, you might break an arm."

Towards the end of the party, Hart saw me standing at the edge of the crowd watching the dancing. He came through the press, a huge-shouldered man who wore thin steel-rimmed spectacles. "Hey, I've got something to tell you about."

We sat down at one of the tables. "God, the football stories are great," I said. "Dutch Clark told me that they're all the same, but that every year they get better."

Hart laughed. He said he had been listening to an awful lot of them because he was an official of the NFL's Alumni Association, which represented old-timers like Dutch Clark.

"That's what I wanted to talk to you about," he said. He told me that the Alumni Association was involved in a bitter scrap with the Players Association and the owners.

The gist of the fight was that nearly six hundred NFL veterans—many of them in the Hall of Fame—were barred by a technicality from participating in the benefits, especially pension benefits, enjoyed by the members of the Players Association, which, ironically, many of them had helped found. The bylaws of the Players Association stipulated that the only players eligible for the pension and benefit plans agreed to by the NFL owners in 1959 were those who had played for the five years from 1955 to 1959 inclusive—which denied benefits to any players who retired before 1959.

"Why that particular date?" I asked.

Hart leaned across the table to make his voice heard above the dance music. He said that he had always assumed the date was arbitrarily set, probably by an actuary, and chosen because of the funds available at that time and the economic conditions that prevailed. But of course these had changed enormously since then. Television income and the rising popularity of the sport had substantially increased the resources for pensions, but the 1959 date had remained the same. The NFL Alumni Association had been formed in 1968 to do something about it, but they had been largely rebuffed. The only help the Players Association had offered was to organize an exhibition *basketball* game to raise money so that the old-timers could start their own pension plan.

As a result, the old-timers had decided to bring legal action against the NFL owners and the Players Association. Some months ago they'd had an emotional meeting at which Rocco Cavelli, a 350-pound former middle guard who had played for the Philadelphia Eagles and then the Boston Yankees, and was nicknamed "The Walking Billboard," had jumped to his feet and cried, "Let 'em have it! Sue! Throw the bomb!" and the cheering had started, and someone else had cried, "Let's go for six," and another, "Clothesline 'em!"—a series of football exhortations erupting from men so excited that they had regressed to the phrases of the profession of their youth.

The Alumni Association was going to have a meeting in Las Vegas a couple of weeks later, Hart told me, at the same time when the defendants in the suit, the Players Association, would be meeting just across the street. Hart thought I might be interested in coming out. Many of the great names of football would be there—Marion Motley, Alex Wojciekowicz, Bruiser Kinard, Dante Lavelli, Eddie LeBaron, a whole bunch of them—and the confrontation with the younger stars would be dramatic.

"Will I get the chance to hear some stories out there?" I asked.

"Will you hear stories? Holy *God!*"

When I returned to New York I called John Gordy to tell him that I was going out to Las Vegas for the meetings, and to see what he had to say about the cutoff date and the dilemma of the old-timers. He groaned and said that while it seemed paradoxical that the great stars of the past were not benefiting, the fact of the matter was that to have the pension plan include them was not actuarially sound. The report from Ed Garvey, the executive secretary of the Players Association, was that the players would have to bargain for an additional $10,-000,000 to fund such a program. The money would have to be paid out immediately, since many of the beneficiaries had already reached retirement age, whereas the 1959 cutoff date allowed the money in the pension fund to work for twenty years or so and pile up interest before it began to be tapped. Besides, it didn't seem to him that present-day players should be responsible for their elders; why not the owners, the twenty-six millionaires, who had made such a lot of money off them in the old days? But hell, he was out of it now; maybe the situation had changed. He had passed on the leadership to John Mackey of the Colts and the others I'd be seeing out in Las Vegas.

The NFL alumni were meeting in Caesars Palace. When I arrived, I noticed that the team representatives of the Players Association were across the Strip in the Flamingo, and that much was being made of their stay. A floodlit sign announced their presence, and each player had his name on an individual sign set into the grass in the traffic island in front of the hotel.

About forty-five of the NFL alumni had turned up at Caesars Palace, many with their wives. When I met them, I discovered that the topic of the moment was not the organization's legal action, but its pride in the singing voice of Rocco Cavelli, "The Walking Billboard," who had been persuaded to perform during the Frank Sinatra, Jr., supper show at one of the hotels on the Strip the night before. Someone had tipped off the management that he had a fine voice. At first, there was consternation that the stairs leading up to the stage would not bear his weight, which was 350 pounds, so he had sung from his table, in a sweet soaring voice, picking up in quality and volume after a somewhat nervous and quavering start. "D'ja hear Rocco last night?" I was asked by an old-timer on the way through the hotel to the alumni breakfast. "Well, man, you sure missed something great!"

The breakfast was held in a purple-carpeted meeting room with high ceilings, a buffet table set at one end and large round tables set for eight or ten places, on each a centerpiece of an individual long-stemmed rose in a thin glass.

Leon Hart took me over to a table and introduced me around: to Alex Wojciekowicz, the center famous for his absurdly wide stance over the ball, who had been one of the Seven Blocks of Granite from Fordham whom everybody, to my relief, referred to as "Wogy"; Ray Monaco, who was an ex-Redskin; Bill Dudley, who played his famous years with the Steelers; Marion Motley, the great Cleveland running back; and two or three players' wives. Other people came and went, sitting down with their coffee cups and listening to the stories, perhaps contributing some, before moving to another table where the same sort of conversation was going on. Motley was the only black in the room, and I realized how few old-timers *would* be blacks because of the discriminatory practices of their times.

The conversation started up again after the introductions. They were talking about the hardest hitters they had faced. Motley said that Chuck Bednarik of the Eagles was a bitch, and so was Wojciekowicz (who looked across at him and grinned), but the worst was Tom Kennedy of the New York Giants. "He followed me everywhere. When Otto Graham called a trap play in the huddle, I always said, 'Oh no,' because I knew that I'd find Kennedy waiting for me in the gap. What a war we had! In his house, which is in Maryland somewhere, I'm told Kennedy has a photograph hanging on the wall showing the two of us in a play in which I knocked out all of his front teeth. He's got this brass plate underneath which reads 'Marion Motley Knocking Out My Teeth,' with the date. He was a rough one."

Someone across the table said, "You had a rough one over there in Cleveland in that guy Chubby Griggs, that three-hundred-pound tackle. Why, he'd have your brains out if you *looked* at him."

"You know something?" said Motley. "You know who kicked the extra point in Philadelphia for the Cleveland Browns in the championship game?"

"Wasn't it Lou Groza?"

"Groza had hurt himself. He picked up a fumble and headed for the goal line. There were some people in front of him." Motley got out of his chair to demonstrate. "He wanted to move *this* way, and then he wanted to move *that* way . . . but what happened was he didn't go any way at all. He crumpled like a napkin was thrown down." He threw a napkin on the table. "He pulled some muscles, so he couldn't kick. The guy who came in for him was Chubby Griggs, that's who."

"Is that so? That guy who weighed three hundred pounds could *kick*?"

"That's so."

Ray Monaco said, "Big mistake for a lineman to pick up the ball like that. I remember a guy called Eddie Ulinsky, an offensive guard on the Browns, who picked up a fumble in a game against Washington, and he got hit by every Redskin there was—just *bam bam bam bam*—and after it was all over he pulled himself up and he said to this running back, 'Man, I know you get *paid* for running the ball, but Jesus *Christ!*'"

The laughter rose around the table. Motley slapped his knee and revolved the cigar between his teeth.

"What did Ulinsky weigh?"

"Oh, he'd go two hundred and thirteen pounds. Six-footer. Maybe a touch shorter. He was bald-headed the first time I ever saw him, which was when he was barely twenty-one. Big hairless bastard. Excuse me, ladies."

Wojciekowicz stirred and said that he could remember the one time he had tackled Motley. As he told the story, he spoke about it as if Motley were not sitting across the table, referring to him by name rather than addressing him personally: "What happened was that they gave the ball to Motley and he came right up through the middle, just *pounding*. I was playing linebacker off to the flank, and I knew I was going to have to tackle the bastard from the side. That's not good for me; I like to kill a man from the front. That's the way to handle power— to whipsaw these power-runners like Norm Standlee and Motley and get 'em under the neck, and backwards they go. Of course, if you hit 'em in the shoulder or the knee, then *you* get killed." He wiped his mouth with a napkin. "Well, as I was coming at Motley from the flank, I kept thinking, How'm I going to *do* this, where am I going to hit him? So I got to where I could throw myself in front of him." He looked up. "How much did you say you weighed?" He seemed to be noticing Motley for the first time.

"Two forty."

"Well, I'll tell you something. After I made the hit on Motley, I didn't want to get up. I lay there and I thought, Well, I've heard a lot about Motley and now I know why."

Motley nodded as if to thank him for the compliment, and said, "At two forty I was the oldest and biggest guy on the team. I started when I was twenty-six."

"Bigger even than the defensive tackles?"

"Well, Lou Rymkus was the biggest of the tackles and he weighed two thirty-two. I was the biggest guy until Ernie Bland came along and then Chubby Griggs."

"Ernie Bland," someone said with a sigh of recognition. "He was what?"

"Oh, he ran about two forty-six, around in there."

"I'm told he was living around Baltimore and died recently of bladder trouble. I never seen a guy so afraid of a woman. A woman would come around training camp and the

214

big man would hide behind a tree and peek out like a buffalo was waiting for him."

I sat enthralled. There seemed to be a number of distinctive characteristics to the ritual: each storyteller always got undivided attention from around the table; no matter how preposterous or exaggerated the tale might seem, there was never any dissent or wonderment, but rather an occasional remark of "That's right" and a nodding of heads in accord; the players described in the stories were usually identified by their weight, invariably to the last digit—such as "Well, Mayberry, who was two sixteen, maybe two seventeen on a cold day . . ." and everyone would nod because they had a clear physical picture of the player involved. The stories usually divulged that the old-timers had all played on both offense and defense, which was the custom before the platooning system, and many of them had played both ways for the full sixty minutes of a game. They were very proud of that fact. Ray Monaco told me during a pause in the storytelling that at a football players' golf tournament in Fort Lauderdale, Florida, a foursome of three old-timers and one young player, Chuck Mercein, a Yale graduate who played with the Packers and then the Giants, had got to talking about playing "both ways," and Mercein piped up and admitted that he didn't know what "both ways" meant. Gary Fincemelti, an enormous old-timer who had played defensive tackle and offensive guard for the Eagles, was so upset by this ignorance that he hit two drives into a pond, missed his third attempt completely, and left the golf course to go somewhere and sulk.

Mayhem was almost invariably an ingredient of the stories. "It took thirteen years before I lost any teeth," Wojciekowicz was saying. "It happened in an exhibition game against the Chicago Bears in the Milk Fund game in nineteen fifty. I was with the Eagles then. Chuck Bednarik, who played middle guard, came down with the flu, and Greasy Neale took me aside and said, 'Wogy, old man, it's going to be like the good old days; you've got to play sixty minutes, both offensive and defense, but remember that it's only an exhibition game and you can pace yourself.' Well, I did a damn fool thing. I told Ken Kavanaugh about it, who was playing offensive end opposite me, thinking maybe they'd go easy on me, and he went back to the Bear huddle and they ran every play at me, until finally their fullback Osmanski came ripping through and his elbow caught me in the mouth and out came two teeth. I still had to go the sixty minutes, but everyone had their adrenaline going by then and we beat the tar out of them. I had the best game I ever played. I tried to kill Kavanaugh and everyone else too." He slammed his fist into his palm. "I *love* to play tough against the Bears."

"That guy Ed Sprinkle of the Bears was a tough one," Motley said. "I fixed him one day. Coach Paul Brown warned us about him. 'He'll hit you anywhere and anytime.' Well, early in the game Sprinkle hit Tony Adamle a terrible blow on the Adam's apple and then ran off the field laughing."

Everybody nodded.

"That's right. He was holding his sides he thought it was so funny. Well, when we got back on offense, I told Otto Graham in the huddle to call a pass play which would put me into Sprinkle's area. It was just fine. I got to him and *tried* to get him in his Adam's apple but something went wrong and I got him far south of there, if you catch my meaning. Excuse me, ladies."

After the chuckling had died away, someone said that the guy who really got Sprinkle was Charley Trippi of the Cardinals, who got so angry that he pulled Sprinkle's helmet off with one hand, just like lifting the lid off a pot, punched him with the other, and then walked off the field.

From the other side of the table Leon Hart cleared his throat and said, "Well, you all remember who gave Charley Trippi *his*—John Henry Johnson, that's who. What a headhunter he was. He hit Trippi with a roundhouse right, his arm extended, and the plastic surgeons had to redo the whole of Trippi's face—jaw, nose . . ."

Beside me I heard a wife suck in her breath.

"You know, there's a fine line between being *nasty* and being *dirty*," Hart was saying. "I don't know whether Sprinkle was nasty or dirty, but John Henry was just plain dirty. There was a time in San Francisco when I caught a pass, and some defensive guy got me by the ankle and I was dragging against him. Out of the corner of my eye I caught sight of John Henry coming for me, getting set to clobber me with that roundhouse right, so I shifted the ball to under my left arm and as he came in I gave him a short pop with my right fist and down he went before he could get that punch of his uncorked. Really cold-cocked him. The referee said, 'Okay, Hart, that'll cost you fifteen yards.' I cried out, 'But didn't you see what he was going to do to me?'

" 'Sure,' said the ref. 'And I probably would have done the same thing you did. But you did the hitting, so it will cost you fifteen.' " Hart laughed. "I'm probably the only guy who ever carried the ball on a play and got penalized fifteen yards for unnecessary roughness."

"The hell you are, man," Motley said. He was beside himself with delight. "The same thing happened to *me*. In a game against the Redskins. Can you believe it. The gun had gone off at the half and I'd run the ball out of bounds and I was turning around to give the ball to the referee." He jumped out of his chair to demonstrate. "The play was *dead*, but Eugene Pepper was coming at me, hell-bent, and he was getting ready to hit, first with his elbow, then with his fist. Like this. Well, I countered before he could do anything, and I hit the nose guard of his helmet and broke all my knuckles."

On the other side of the table Bill Dudley rocked back and forth in his chair. "That's right. You got thrown out of the game!"

Motley turned his cigar in his mouth. "Ox Emerson came in for me, and he had a big heyday."

"What did Eugene Pepper weigh in at?" someone asked.

"Oh, two thirty—right in there."

"That was like Pepper," Dudley, who had played with the Redskins for a short stint, said. "I mean, to try to smack Motley when the play was dead. His timing was always way off. He was the guy on the team who was supposed to pretend to be hurt so that they could get the clock stopped. But his act wasn't any good—it looked like he was having a convulsion—and his timing was terrible. He'd fake his injury just after the gun had gone off and the game was over."

"That's right."

"Or he'd be thrashing around on the ground and the ref would come rushing up and ask, 'Are you hurt?' and Pepper would forget and say, 'No, of course not.'"

Wojciekowicz leaned forward, the ballroom chair creaking under him, and said, "You know, sometimes you *got* to crack someone. When Hunk Anderson came to the Lions from the Bears in thirty-nine, and co-coached us with Gus Henderson—this was before I went to the Eagles—he said there was only one way to handle the Bears. He ordered us to slug them for the first three plays of the game—every lineman in front of us. We did it. You could hear the punches, *bam bam bam* all the way down the line. We got penalized three times fifteen—forty-five yards—back to our thirty-five yard line, but that's as far as the Bears ever got that day. They were supposed to be the big bad bears and we were supposed to be the meek pussycat lions, with our paws up, and they were *surprised*. Bulldog Turner, Joe Strydyhar, Musso, all those big people—they couldn't believe it. They kept ducking. We beat them ten–nothing, right there in Chicago!" He made a convulsive motion in his chair which jarred shivers across the water in the glasses, and the ice clinked. "Golly, I *love* to play against the Bears."

An announcement was made that the room down the corridor was ready for the meeting, and that it was time to get down to business. The players around the table rose and stretched.

It was a closed meeting, but that afternoon I was invited to the final session. Jim Castiglia, a former back who had played with the Redskins, Eagles, and Colts, spoke from the rostrum. First he mentioned and commended Rocco Cavelli's singing performance at the supper show, and Cavelli, an enormous tublike man, rose to raise an arm in acknowledgment to shouts of approbation. Next, the Wogy Award was given: a bottle of bourbon to Buck Evans, the oldest veteran in the room. The award seemed to serve no other purpose than to indicate the warmth and good will for the white-haired, slightly stoop-shouldered gentleman. He was a Harvard man, class of '23, who had played with the Bears. He had an old Bears game program with him which he had shown me before the meeting. In it was a column of news notes from around the football league, and we had both admired the fact that the Dayton Triangles had a Chinaman playing for them who was called "Sneeze" Achui. Evans rose and addressed the group from the rostrum, speaking in a soft stutter; he said that he was going to be seventy-three in April, which was as good a time as any to start thinking about a pension. He grinned and said that he hoped that everyone would oblige and arrange one for him. He sat down to a storm of applause.

Jim Castiglia then reviewed their meetings and the progress of their struggle with the Players Association. He was confident, he told them. Four years ago the Alumni Association had twenty-one members; now they had eight hundred. Their cause was justified. There was so much money in the NFL pension fund that the opposition was thinking of lowering the retirement age to forty-five, at which point a veteran who had played ten years—subsequent to the cutoff date of 1959—would receive in the neighborhood of $50,000 annually! And yet the old-timers, who had formed professional football and played for $20 a game, were left out in the cold. It was a mockery. If Vince Lombardi hadn't died, things might have been different; he had pounded his fist and told the owners that they *had* to include the older fellows. Well, now the Alumni Association had taken things into their own hands. They would prevail with their law action. "The vehicle is there," Castiglia said. "It's on the expressway."

When the meeting broke up, a few of the old-timers asked me to join them for dinner, but I said I was going to see some friends from the Players Association.

"You going over to the other place!"

"Just to visit," I said.

"We've met them. All they think we want is a handout. They don't care. All they want to do is finish up their meetings so they can go out and play some golf and get some desert sun so they'll look better for the girls they'll find in the evening."

"Aw, the kids can't concentrate right anymore," another old-timer said. "How can they? Got all these goddamn billion-dollar contracts, and they wear hats indoors and buckles on their shoes and clothes fitting for a whore. Why, I saw Dan Pastorini, that kid who plays quarterback for the Oilers, over in the lobby of the Flamingo Hotel, and he was wearing these two- or three-inch stilts on his shoes. Now why? He's a big tall boy in his bare feet. What in tarnation is he wearing that kind of shoe for—less'n he wants folks to take him for a basketball player."

"Hey, do you know who he reminds you of?"

"Who you talking about?"

"Pastorini . . ."

"He reminds *me* of someone?"

"That's right. He reminds you of Bob Waterfield in his good years quarterbacking the Rams, that's who. He'll be a great quarterback if he survives."

"Now don't you be telling me who reminds me of who! A kid who walks around on built-up shoes reminds me of *no one!*"

I went across the Strip to the Flamingo. Evidence of the presence of the Players Association was everywhere. Placards on wooden easels directed the press to different conference rooms. Some of the players were in the casino. Bill Curry of the Colts was wearing a buckskin jacket. Pastorini of the Oilers did indeed have stilts on his shoes, which raised him up to six-four or -five. He was wearing a gold chain around his neck.

I sat around for a while with a group of them. The matter of the Alumni Association grievance was not even on the Players Association agenda. "What's wrong with you guys?" I asked. "What they're asking, as I understand it, might cost everyone playing maybe ten dollars or so more a month."

None of them seemed to know much about the alumni demands. "They should get it from the owners," someone said.

"These people are all your old heroes," I said. I said Karras told me that he kept a picture of Bronco Nagurski on his dresser.

"Is he over there—Nagurski?"

"No, but Marion Motley is."

Bill Curry remembered that Motley had been one of the

coaches in the East-West game some years before, and he had taken Ken Willard aside, a very bright undergraduate who had been an All-Scholastic fullback, and said, "Young fella, you got your foots lined up all wrong."

"That was Ken Willard's introduction to professional football," Curry said, not unkindly.

Ed Podolak, the great running star of the Kansas City Chiefs, asked, "Hey, did they tell you how they played both ways and how they folded up their helmets and stuffed them in their back pockets?"

They looked out at the action around the tables.

When we left for dinner, everyone walked very slowly through the gaming room, like cowboy stars, and the young girls looked up from the keno tables . . .

15

One day Karras and Gordy turned up in the apartment and began talking about the differences between the teams of the National Football League. They were in town for a game; the Lions were going to play the New York Giants the next day up at the Yankee Stadium. John Gordy's contention was that the personality of each team was so marked that a player could tell by remembering the feel of a game just who the opponents had been. The Giants were invariably neat and surgical; so were the Baltimore Colts. The great Giant teams of the past decade had the additional characteristic of playing somewhat undistinguished games, and then making long, improbable, but precisely executed run or pass plays in the waning moments which produced a win for them. On the other hand, some teams tended to possess simple brutal philosophies: the Rams and the 49ers, for instance; also Minnesota and Atlanta, probably because of the hard-hat attitude of Norm Van Brocklin, the coach who had put together both clubs. With his teams, both offense and defense tended to run straight over people. The Chicago Bears were that sort of team too, their defense notoriously rough, and invariably big and quick-tempered, conceived in the George Halas mold and perpetuated by the "Monsters of the Midway" sobriquet which conditioned them to think of themselves as brutes both on and off the field.

"The Bears hang out in Chicago bars you wouldn't advise your worst enemy to go to," Karras said.

"That's right," Gordy agreed. "They spend their time seeping up ill will. They're the most vocal and loud-mouthed of the teams out on the field—just a stream of vilification. There's method to all that yelling, too: shouting like that across the line can break the rhythm of the quarterback's signals, and it's effective, especially against teams which use staggered rhythm calls. It makes opposing linemen jump offside."

"The Monsters of the Midway . . . helluva name," Karras mused. He shook his head.

"On the field they're even rude among themselves," Gordy went on. "Really cussing each other out. It was a terrific thrill to beat that kind of team, to shut them up—like beating up the bully down the street."

"What about Green Bay?"

"Green Bay is the team I always love to play," Gordy said. "Except that they win. You never get the sort of physical beating you take playing the Bears or the Rams or the Falcons, because Green Bay's mark is finesse and perfect execution, and you never seem to get bruised by it. On pass rush they get around you and you never touch them. They get by you somehow, and you look around and the Green Bay front four are sitting on the quarterback with these big grins. Or on a running play, you're out in front running interference, looking for someone to block, and Ray Nitschke filters through behind you from his linebacker's spot and gets the runner down, leaving you thundering along thinking the play is still alive and just aching to knock someone down. It's very embarrassing. You come back to the huddle, really puffing hard, and someone gives you a scornful look and says, 'Hey, give the ball to Gordy, he's really tearing up the ground with his cleats. He's running forty yards on every play!' " He laughed. "No, Green Bay was good. It was always terribly frustrating to play Green Bay because I always felt we should come out on top. We always seemed to lose to them in some jerk way."

"That's right," Karras said. "Green Bay is like Notre Dame was when I was playing in the Big Ten. When we played Notre Dame, we annihilated them, and at the end of the game we'd come off the field feeling good until we looked at the scoreboard and saw we'd lost. It worked the other way, too. When we played Purdue, they just beat the crap out of us. We'd walk off the field feeling maybe we'd been beaten one hundred to nothing —but we'd won. That's how Green Bay is. You beat them physically, but they always seem to beat you on the scoreboard.

"I'll tell you another thing about playing at Green Bay," Karras went on. "The showers are cold. They get you up there into that freezing frontier town, beat the crap out of you and then make you take a cold shower. Three years in a row they haven't had any hot water. Of course I've been in some weird visitors' showers in the NFL—some of them have shower heads that must have been set for midget woman wrestlers, the water hitting you about navel height. Everybody on the team has to crouch like baboons on the tiles to get any water."

"Baltimore is a team like Green Bay," Gordy said. "You always have the feeling that you are being treated kindly until you get on the team bus to go out to the airport and realize that you've been whomped."

Gordy went on to say that some teams had schizoid personalities. Kansas City had a deft brush-block offensive which seemed to leave the opposition still on its feet after a play, standing around and wondering what had happened; yet its defense was massive and corrupting.

"What's the key to stopping a clockwork offense like that, and Green Bay's?" I asked.

"There was only one thing to do with those great Lombardi offenses," Karras said, "and that was to gang-tackle and try to mess up that mechanism by going for the ball in swarms."

I asked about the Philadelphia Eagles, who had been in

the doldrums for a number of seasons. Both Karras and Gordy agreed that the one distinguishing feature about playing the Eagles was that fistfights were almost sure to erupt.

But doesn't a team character change as its personnel changes? I wanted to know. Were the Eagle players doomed to fistfights year after year?

Both of them demurred, pointing out that obviously while a team had its ups and downs, its character remained surprisingly constant. For example, Green Bay had always been the scourge of the Central Division under Vince Lombardi; they never played a bad game. But Lombardi was gone, and the Packers had begun to lose. But they still had that grand aloofness that Coach Lombardi had instilled in them, though from time to time it would crack, and across the line the Lions would hear the bickering and the name-calling that suggested that the team's composure was deteriorating. "It's such a sweet thing to hear a Packer linebacker bad-mouth one of his people," Karras said. "Especially at Green Bay. We'd never heard anything like it before. They beat you with this terrific superior aloofness, like they'd all been born in some great palace somewhere and it wasn't worth considering that they might lose. They were elite."

"But the point is," Gordy said, "the Packers'll never lose that elite character, unless there's a huge shift of ownership or they get moved to Orlando, Florida, or they trade everyone who's ever had a sniff of it; they'll have their bad seasons, like now, but the team character will remain, and it's very valuable. A lot of it has to do with that crazy town up there that they all work out of. And the support they get from their fans."

"What *about* the fans?" I asked. "What was it like playing in Chicago, for example? Do they behave like the team?"

"The Chicago crowd is unbelievable," Gordy said. "For one thing, Wrigley Field seats are built right up to the edge of the field, so they're all on top of you. They really let you have it. I don't know what sort of language they learned at their mothers' knees, but this isn't it."

"They're very good on your background," Karras said. "They told me about things Greeks did that I didn't even know."

"There was this one time," Gordy went on, "when Erich

Barnes, who was playing corner for them then, intercepted a pass out by the pitcher's mound, and when I rushed over to tackle him he ducked his head and I went sailing over him and got him solid in the head with my knee. It must have looked like I'd kneed him on purpose, because the Chicago bench emptied and we all had this big shoving match out there on the field, the kind of thing that usually happens in Philadelphia. A photographer snapped a picture of me with my fist under George Halas' chin, just a freak picture that made it look like I was going to punch that nice ol' man. Well, he's a *tough* old man, but sure as hell I never wanted to hit him. That's how it looked, though, and it got published in the papers. The Chicago fans have the memories of elephants, and the next time we played them, you wouldn't believe the abuse . . ."

"Five years after my suspension for gambling," Karras said, "they still remembered. I'd run out on the field, and I'd hear these cries drifting down: 'Hey, you Greek fat-ass. Wanta place a bet for me? Who you betting on today?' "

"Is there no recourse?"

"Oh, I'd yell back at them sometimes. 'I'm betting on your mother,' I'd shout. I don't know quite what I meant by that, but it seemed to disturb them. I'd see them rocking back and forth up there, their fists up."

Gordy got up out of his chair. "Hey, you remember that time when the Chicago crowd came running out on the field, and everybody started to slug everybody? It was catching, like some sort of quick-moving disease. Jim Martin was standing over on the sidelines. He was our place-kicker, and he'd been in the Marines, and he was a Notre Dame man, and he was a little crazy, too. While he was watching what was going on, a cop came up alongside, Martin saw him, turned, and hit him with a short, stiff right hand. Absolutely great punch. The cop went '*boing*' and down he went. I don't know why Martin did it —maybe because he'd always had a hankering to hit a policeman and it seemed as good a time as any. Playing in Chicago always drives you a little nuts anyway."

"Fans have always scared me," Karras said. "I don't know anything about sitting in the stands. I've only been up there a couple of times in thirteen years. I sat up there once at a baseball game with four men and I was scared to death. Beer drinkers."

Gordy said intensely, "It's the frustration. They take out their frustrations through what we do on the field. They can't go around hitting people. They're scared to, or they don't want to—it's barbaric—so they pay football players to do it. But the trouble is that the game doesn't really rid them of their frustrations. I'm not even sure that a *win* satisfies them, but a loss makes them grotesque. They wait for you at the end of a game. They hang over the fence, their faces twisted with hate, and shake their fists—these *little* people."

He was visibly upset. He began pacing around the room. "You can feel the mob rule ticking in these people. I don't ever want to look at them—bent double over the fences screaming down at us. That's what scares me more than anything: a mob scene. In Mexico once, when I was there with my family, they were having an election and a riot started. It was just at the time of those "Yankee Go Home" scenes. They came pouring down the street. I was in the car with my family. Man, I wanted *home*. I was scared to death. I started up the car, but they closed in around us. I could see that they had no control over themselves. Man, I was through, I was just *finished*. A man started pounding on the window. I had no choice; I rolled it down. He leaned in, a big, swarthy guy. I shrank back, and he said, 'Hey, Joe, you wanta buy some watches at the market?' "

Both Karras and I laughed, but Gordy's face remained grim. "No, no," he said. "This is very serious. The snowballs come down with rocks in them. I've seen these guys who are sedate businessmen, and they've got a Caddy out in the parking lot and a big house in Grosse Pointe to drive home to, and a wine cellar, and all they have to worry about are their golf handicaps —and I've seen these guys hanging over the runways with the hair hanging down in their eyes, and their faces blood-red, screaming insults, like you were a bug and they wanted to exterminate you . . .

"It's like they have no concept at all of what a football player goes through out there. I remember I got hit in the throat one time, going down after a punt. It was against the Giants, the team we're playing tomorrow. I went down on both knees and put my head on the ground, and it was as if somebody had cut me open and taken everything inside of me and pulled it out of my open throat. I was hit right in the Adam's apple and I had nothing left. I wanted to go straight to the locker room and take off my football equipment and never, ever, *ever* hit anybody or be hit again as long as I lived. Well, no sooner had I got myself supported to the sidelines when the ball changed hands and I had to go back out there again. I remember thinking, If only all those people knew what it was taking me to get myself back out there . . . Or the time I hit Eddie Meador of the Rams; as I blocked him I pinched every nerve I've got in my body. Goddamnedest thing! I was knocked out, lying flat on my back on the ground, and my arm was frozen, *pointing straight up,* the nerve locking it there, like I was pointing up at God or something. What do you suppose the people in the stands thought? They probably thought I was pointing at a pigeon. 'Look at that lazy dumb-ass lineman lying on his back and pointing at pigeons.' When I came to, I still couldn't get the arm down. It was locked, absolutely numb, and when I walked off the field it stuck straight out in front of me like a Hitler salute."

Karras and I were laughing again.

Gordy was beside himself. He strode about the room. "No, no, no, no, it's terrible. When something like that happens to you, and the pain, and all the grief of losing, you come off the field and you want to get to your family, and you hurry through the tunnel to get away from the crowd, and you hear them screaming at you, and you think about where you can go to eat in a place where nobody knows you, and all the time you're wondering how you can be *hated* so much for going out there and trying your best."

He collapsed in a chair; it squeaked sharply under his weight. He put his legs out in front of him. "Aw, to hell with it. The crowds shouldn't mean that much anyway. They have nothing to do with the great satisfactions of football either. Jesus! Sometimes it's fun to see that mob take it on the chin. Do you

remember the game—I think you wrote about it in *Paper Lion*,"
he said, looking at me. "The one in Baltimore where in the last
minute of the game Lennie Moore of the Colts made this fantastic touchdown pass against Night Train Lane?"

"Yes," I said. "And Earl Morrall came on for the Lions
and—"

Karras stirred in his chair. "Christ! I'll never forget it.
Lennie Moore went six yards in the air *parallel* to the ground,
I swear. He caught the ball just on his fingertips, the most fantastic catch I ever saw in my life. I ran down the field. I couldn't
believe it. Neither could Night Train. His whole spirit left him;
he turned *white*. And then this whole ant army of Baltimore
fans came down on the field, and they knocked Train over and
they were yelling and screaming. The announcer came on the
public-address system. It was almost impossible to hear him,
and he was saying, 'Okay now, you've got to get off the field.
This is Baltimore's greatest hour. Please don't ruin . . .'

"Well, man, I was hot. I got to the sidelines and these
three Baltimore fans started giving me the needle. One of them
called me a 'fat-ass something-or-other' and I took my helmet
and hit him '*whap*' in the head with it. He went down, and one
of the other two guys pulled a knife. I stared at it bug-eyed and
began swinging my helmet back and forth to keep him away
from me. Jimmy Butsicaris was there, a friend of mine from
Detroit. He came rushing up and pretended he had a gun. He
put his hand in his overcoat pocket and shoved it out with the
index finger forward and said, 'I've got a gun, you mothers.'
They turned and ran. Christ, all he actually had on him was a
bench pass!"

"Remember Gil Mains?" Gordy said. "He just waded
into the crowd. He almost killed one of them."

"What was going on out on the field?" I asked.

"There were still twenty seconds left," Karras said.
"When they finally got the crowd moved, Baltimore kicked off
and we had time left for one play. There was only the slimmest
chance of winning it—being what? Five points down?"

Gordy nodded.

"Out of the corner of my eye I could see Coach Wilson,"

Karras continued. "He was behind a row of fans on the sidelines, jumping up and down like a kid trying to see over a fence. The poor guy couldn't even see what his own team was doing. As for me, I didn't care about the game. I was still running around holding my helmet by the strap trying to bop the guy who'd pulled the knife on me. The whole place was going crazy—the damnedest sound."

"That's right," Gordy said. "The acoustics in that stadium are weird, and it funnels the sound right down to the field. 'The Baltimore Boom.' Sometimes it's so loud that the quarterback has to scream in the huddle."

"And then suddenly all that noise stopped," Karras went on. "It was like all those mothers had been throttled. There wasn't a sound. I pulled up. I thought maybe I'd gone deaf. Just like that—*blam!*—the whole place went silent."

Gordy could hardly contain himself. "Christ!" he said. "I was out there." He spoke in awe, as if he still could not believe it. His voice squeaked. "There were six seconds left after we'd run the kickoff back," he said. "Earl Morrall gave us the pass play in the huddle. We went up to the line, and I had Art Donovan to contain, and Willie McClair, playing offensive tackle for us, had Gino Marchetti. Man, that's a tough game for both of us. At the snap, Donovan and Marchetti did a loop—what they call a 'twist' at Baltimore—and they ran *into* each other. Well, that neutralized them just for a second, and then they came on—too late. Morrall hit Jim Gibbons over the center and he got to the sidelines and ran into the end zone and scored as the gun went off. Willie and I looked all over for penalty flags going down. No flags!

"Christ, we'd won it. But then came the scary part. There was that quick awful silence. The crowd moved onto the field again, and it was like they were coming for us. We jumped up a few times in the air when Gibbons scored, but then we stopped. No cheering by us, nos*sir*. You had to weave your way through them to get back to the locker rooms. They wouldn't move. If you got near them on the field they'd elbow you, and you'd look into these crazy, mad, *quiet* faces, and it was the scariest thing in the world. You have to step down into the baseball dugouts at Memorial Stadium to get to the tunnels that lead back to the locker rooms. The crowd was so thick and surly around the dugout steps that I asked a cop to help me through. The guy *shoved* me into the dugout, real hard, and I smacked up against the dugout wall. A policeman! I didn't say anything. The whole town was furious. They had to drive us to Washington to catch a plane back to Detroit; they were afraid to take us to the Baltimore airport. Oh, yes, we stuck it to the crowd that time."

We sat there, turning the scene over in our minds, and then Gordy said, "Of course, the same score that stuck it to the Baltimore fans made the people in Detroit go crazy with delight in front of the TV sets—spilling their beer and leaping up and down and scaring the hell out of the family cat. Well, I don't care if they're Baltimore fans or Detroit fans—they *all* scare the hell out of me."

16

The next day, for that bleak mid-December meeting between the Lions and the Giants, the producers of *Paper Lion* wired up Gordy and Karras with microphones, and from time to time the tape machines were turned on to eavesdrop on them. The hope was to get authentic background sounds for the film. The tapes were later transcribed by a pair of embarrassed secretaries— the language is constantly blue and violent—though they turned out to be useless for the film. A year later, the producers were kind enough to send the material around for me to listen to.

I found them fascinating, perhaps because I am an eavesdropper at heart. I despair not knowing what is being said just beyond my hearing—what it is that has produced a roar of laughter in the far corner of a cocktail party. At spectator sports I find myself feeling the same way—in baseball wondering what is being said at the conference on the pitcher's mound, or in football what the coach is whispering to the quarterback on the sidelines. Football is particularly frustrating since so much of the game is verbal: voice signals, both offense and defense huddling to talk things over, spotters and assistants outfitted with microphones and headsets, hurried conferences at critical moments, and especially the exchanges that must erupt between men in close quarters under violent stress—all of which, to the despair of the football fan, goes on out of earshot.

The fidelity of the Karras-Gordy tapes is extraordinary, recording not only the immediate sounds of the two players' voices, but also the quarterback's commands, the defensive signals, the constant warnings from the officials ("Linemen, keep your hands in!"), smatterings of conversation on the bench, and the concussive sounds of the plays themselves—the grunts, the crash of padding, the sharp, near-expiring gasps of players smacked hard to the ground, along with an occasional word of comment between the combatants.

In the background, the roar of the crowd, varying in its intensity, provides a strong clue to what is happening on the field, further illuminated by the public-address system over which the stadium announcer's voice, shredded slightly by the wind, intones: "Tarkenton's pass . . . complete to Crespino . . . brought down . . . by LeBeau . . . first and ten . . . on the forty-three." It is easy, listening to the tapes, to conjure up a visual picture of the proceedings.

Also in the background, providing a wrench of authenticity, are the occasional jangled and tinny strains of a banjo-dominated musical group known as "Your Father's Moustache." The Christmas season was almost at hand, so on the tapes one hears the startling contrast of "Jingle Bells" and other such carols plinking over the brutal yawp and heave of the proceedings on the field. By some mysterious and perverse edict, Your Father's Moustache—a small collection of portly musicians housed in a little shelter down at the bleacher end of the field—has been playing at the stadium for years. I suspect that if a change were made, if their plinkety-plinks were supplanted by more traditional band music, a great outcry from the traditionalists would go up and they would come to the support of Your Father's Moustache with all the zeal of a dowager dog-owner defending the character of her ancient mongrel.

That is an odd corner of Yankee Stadium: above, the bleachers with its raucous citizenry (invariably fights break out); the Moustache group playing in front of the bleacher wall; and in front of *them,* down on the field, long lines of patients in wheelchairs who are trundled in by attendants at the beginning of the game to watch from behind this corner of the end zone, the worst vantage point in the stadium. Invariably, just at the beginning of the fourth quarter, whatever the situation in the game, the patients are wheeled out. They seem to go without complaining, with rarely a head turned to watch as they are rolled away, or a cane raised in protest. Perhaps they consider it a relief to get away from the sounds of bleacher strife and the ragtime assault of Your Father's Moustache.

When I told Karras I had the tapes, he said that he doubted they'd be of much use, pointing out that he rarely talked to the linemen opposite him. He remembers his private wars with Jerry Kramer, for instance, the offensive guard of the Green Bay Packers, as being absolutely silent struggles. He recalls only one instance when they had words—a weird occasion when the left side of Karras' nose guard, or "cage" as the players refer to it, came loose and somehow, as the two of them bulled at each other, *hooked* into Kramer's cage, so that their two helmets were stuck fast, the players jammed up against each other, their faces within inches, staring at each other, with neither able to pull himself loose.

"It was crazy," Karras said. "We must have looked like a terrible, snake-like animal, two-footed at each end, some kind of big inchworm writhing about."

"And you had words during this?"

"Damn right. Kramer kept shouting, 'What the hell are you doing?' I guess he thought I'd hooked up to him on purpose. He looked a little scared. I mean, we were really stuck."

Finally, Karras was able to disengage himself by skinning out of his helmet and backing away, leaving it hanging off Kramer's nose guard like a huge morsel dangling from his jaws. "Yeah, he talked that time. He still thinks it was a sly maneuver I cooked up to intimidate him."

"So other than a rare case like that the offensive guards keep their mouths shut?" I asked.

"My brother Teddy," Karras said, "played offensive guard like Jerry Kramer, and he once told me that he never said anything to the guys opposite because generally they were twice as big, being defensive tackles, and twice as strong. He said, 'Why should I say anything? They'd kill me.' Once when he was with the Chicago Bears, he was playing against Big Daddy Lipscomb, the huge linesman who was with Pittsburgh then. Big Daddy was one person it was *good* to talk to, because maybe you could tone him down a bit if you said, 'Hi, Big Daddy, how are you today?' and a lot of friendly crap like that. So Teddy was trying it. 'How's the family, Big Daddy?' he'd ask, and in the meantime Big Daddy was just kicking the crap out of him, and Teddy'd say, 'Oh that was good, Big Daddy. I've never seen such moves. *Gee*, you're good.'

"Finally, on this one play, Big Daddy went offside and he just killed Teddy who was still down in his stance. He hit him alongside the head so hard—WHOP!—that Teddy thought he had forgotten to put on his helmet. He went back to his huddle and asked, 'Where's my helmet?' His teammates looked at him and said, 'It's on your head, man.' So on the next play Teddy's temper got lost, and when Big Daddy came at him, he hit him alongside the head with a right hand as hard as he could. It didn't even budge him, but Big Daddy must have felt it because he said, 'I'm going to get your ass.' Teddy said, 'Any-time you want to fight me, Big Daddy, I'm ready. Any*time!* I'm tired of your bullshit. If I ever catch you off this field, I'll kick your ass.' After he'd said it, he felt like slapping himself in the face. It was like he was listening to somebody else talk. Big Daddy looked at him, leaning in to be sure he'd heard right, and then he said, 'Well, I'll see about *that*, boy.' Teddy heard himself replying—and he couldn't believe what he was saying— 'Don't call me "boy," you son of a bitch! I'm *Karras!*'

"Well, in the hotel after the game Teddy was coming down to the lobby from his room. He was alone in the elevator, and at the tenth floor the elevator stopped, the doors opened, and standing there was Big Daddy. When Teddy saw him, he turned and faced the corner of the elevator like a dunce in the schoolroom. The elevator gave this big creak when Big Daddy stepped in. He's huge! Big Daddy said, 'How you doin', boy?' Teddy said, 'Fine, Big Daddy. How's the family?' He could hear Big Daddy breathing—high up back of his head! The elevator started down. Teddy couldn't believe how slowly it was moving, especially with all that weight of Big Daddy in it. Well, Big Daddy made him sweat for nine floors. Then, just as they got to the lobby, he said in this deep voice, 'I know that's you, Karras.' Teddy just about went to his knees, he was so frightened, but then Big Daddy started to laugh, and so did Teddy, a real high-pitched laugh of relief, and it was all right."

John Gordy was not sure about the value of the tapes either, and questioned what could be gained by wiring up players. He remembered that a scientist who was doing a serious paper on what he called "impact structure"—a study of the kinetic violence of football, how hard players hit each other—had come to Los Angeles for a Pro Bowl game. He reasoned that the middle linebacker probably dished out and took more punishment than anyone else, so Joe Schmidt, then an All-Pro at the position, was persuaded to play the game rigged up with a number of measuring devices. According to Gordy, the trouble was that Schmidt had a terrible game, or perhaps opportunities to make primary tackles were rare that day. At any rate, he did not make one solid tackle, and when the tapes were transcribed on graph paper, much like a seismograph chart, hardly a wiggle showed up to suggest the concussive nature of football. "The scientist read his charts," Gordy said, "and as far as he could tell from them *ballet* was just as full of contact as football."

Of the two tapes the movie producers sent me, the Karras transcript is the more extensive. Gordy keeps his mind largely on the business at hand, while Karras characteristically lets his faculties freewheel somewhat more extensively, though

236

much of the verbiage is directed at himself. "Stay tough" is a constant self-goad. Still, there are certain outside catalytic forces which command loud verbal observations—European place-kickers, for example. Karras is roused to a sort of wild, half-serious frenzy by the steady encroachment in football of European players whom he refers to as "tiny, foreign soccer-kickers" who are summoned from the bench (the coach calls out, "Hey, Boris . . .") and prance onto the field in their spotless uniforms shouting, "I am going to keek a touchdown, I am going to keek a touchdown." On the tapes the first words Karras speaks to any member of the Giant team are addressed to Pete Gogalak, the Hungarian-born place-kicker, who appears for a field-goal attempt early in the game. The monologue is not without bite. Of course the quarterbacks (in this case Fran Tarkenton of the Giants and, later in this game, Earl Morrall) are traditionally targets for Karras' comments, and there is always abuse for opposing linemen unfortunate enough to have been raised in the south. Karras has always felt that southerners, being overly sensitive to criticism, can be intimidated by verbal attack.

The Lions won this game rather handily, scoring two touchdowns and a field goal in the first half and thereafter never being seriously threatened. They received the opening kickoff, Mel Farr carried nine yards on the first play, and the team went on from there to score. Karras spent this first offensive drive on the sidelines, of course, and since he does not see well, much of the early section of the tape consists of his asking, "What's going on?" "What was that?" "Did he pick up any yards?" "Who's that?" "What down is it?" "Was that Amos Marsh who ran the ball?" At one point, he stumbles into a fellow player on the sidelines who accidentally steps on his foot. There is a sharp cry and Karras' voice says, "Oh Christ, my foot's gone, and I haven't even been on the field yet."

"You all right?" a voice asks.

"Yeah, yeah."

In the background, another voice says, "Alex, they ought to give you a white cane so you can tap your way up and down the sidelines."

Then the Lions kick off, and the tape picks up the creak of Karras' gear as he trots out onto the field.

KARRAS:

(*Steady roar of crowd in background. Voice of middle line-backer, Mike Lucci, calling defensive signals: "Four four three; blitz; blue!" Crack of hand slaps as defensive team breaks huddle*) Come on, come on. Start it good. Fix 'em. (*Concussion of play; heavy breathing*) Jesus! Again! My foot's smashed again! Oh my! Christ! First play and my foot's smashed. Christ! I'm a hundred and twenty-three years old. Keep moving. Keep moving. (*Lucci's voice calling next play: "Four three; blue."*) Play tough. Let's go, fellows. (*To himself*) Killer, here we go. (*Concussion of play; grunts*) Beautiful! Jesus Christ! Beautiful! Good position. Yumyum. Who ran that ball? Young rook? (*Lucci's voice: "Four three; blue."*) Once more. Yeah. (*Enticingly*) Come on inside here, baby. (*Crash of gear; heavy breathing*) Okay, okay! Nice. Nice. That was beautiful. He tried to come out and he had to go back in. (*Voice in background: "Yeah, yeah, I know." Announcer's voice: "Gogalak for field-goal attempt."*) Now who are you? I said who are you, you little pisser. You from Rumania? Latvia? No? Well, then, are you from Finland? You lending *class* to the league? From England? That's why you're in here? Lending *class*? (*Concussion of play; heavy breathing; stadium announcer's voice: "Gogalak's attempt failed. Detroit's ball on the Giant twenty."*) Go on back to the bench, you little pisser. Hey! Unscrew your foot and stick it down your throat, that's what I said, you little Slovakian pisser. Jesus!

(*Creaking of gear as trots to bench. In background, tinny band plays "Jingle Bells"*) Nice going. We're gonna get some points. (*Cheering the offense*) Run, Melvin [Mel Farr, Detroit running back], run, baby, run, you mother, beautiful. Man, look at that offense move! Mel Farr's the sweetheart. He'll go a thousand yards this year. Man, it's raining touchdowns. I can't believe it. Who scored that touchdown? (*Voices: "Kickoff team get ready."*)

(*Back on defense, Lucci's voice: "Four three; red."*) Okay, killer, stay tough. Here we go. (*Concussion of play: heavy breathing*) Oh, you mother! You stomped my foot. You took care of my toes! Christ! (*To Lucci, hurt on play*) Hang in, Looch. Get up, Looch. Hey, Looch! (*To John McCambridge, defensive end playing alongside*) Hey listen, Johnny, Looch is staying in, but he's hurting. I'm gonna play a little tight there, right? (*Lucci's voice in huddle: "Four four; blue."*) Right. (*To himself*) Okay, killer, here we go. (*Referee's voice: "Watch your feet; watch your feet!"*) Yeah, yeah, yeah. (*Another play; heavy panting*) I shoulda had him. Jesus! Oh Christ! I had the mother. I shoulda had him. Jesus!

(*On next play Karras tackles Giant quarterback*) D'ja like that, Fran? Hey, Fran, d'ja *like* that? Hey, Fran? Hey, Fran? Hey, Fran, watcha think? (*Announcer's voice in distance: ". . . tackled by Karras."*) Oh yes. Oh my.

(*On bench*) Sweet. Sweet. It's like a bunch of bees out there. Really swarming. No fun being a halfback today. Gang-tackling. Real bunch of bees. They'll try to run some fast screens. Is there any water? Water? C'mon. C'mon. Lace their ass out there! Lay it on them! (*Band plays "Rudolph, the Red-Nosed Reindeer" in background*) Run, baby, run. I'm going to tell you something right now; it's *nice*. It's nice sitting here in New York on a wood bench in the sun with your team doing fine. (*Unidentified voice: "Man, I got a good bunch of Tarkenton that time. How's your man coming?"*) He comes strong. They were right during the week with those scouting reports. Dess [Daryl Dess, Giant offensive guard] uses that forearm. He's good. He's rough to get by. They got anybody to come in for him? Some kid from Tennessee? (*Crowd noise rises*) Christ! What was that! Horrible!

(*Back out on defense. Lucci's voice: "Four four three; blitz; red." Referee's voice: "Watch your feet!"*) Stay tough. Yumyum. (*Crash of play*) Double twist! Great! Great! (*Calling to linebacker*) Good position, baby. Beautiful. (*Unidentified voice: "Okay, let's keep 'em back in the toolhouse."*) Hey Jer [Jerry Rush, tackle playing alongside]. Jer, there's a little trap on me. (*On next play, Karras reaches Tarkenton again*) Hiya, Fran. Howdeedoodee Fran. Hey Fran, you like it out here, hey Fran? Hey Fran baby? Nice. Nice. (*Lucci's voice: "Four two; blitz; blue."*) Double twist! (*Lucci yelling: "Open right! Open!*

Open!") Hold him up! Get that guy. (*Loud applause and shouting; distant cowboy yell*) What happened? What the hell happened? What's going on? Christ! Hold him up for Chrissakes. (*Snorts violently*) Come on, boys. One more play. (*Play called in huddle*) I screwed up on that one, Jer. Should have had the son of a bitch. Give me room and keep outside this time. I'm going to play him a little tight. Come on, Jer. (*Concussion of play; thudding; heavy panting*) Nice, nice. Yes. Yes.

(*On way to bench; announcer's voice: ". . . brought down by Karras."*) All ri-ight. Right at me. Way to go, Paul [Paul Naumoff, outside linebacker]. Yumyum. Real sweet out there. Isn't it the quarter yet? Run, baby! Beautiful! Get some points. Christ! (*Tries to clear throat*) I got this upper respiratory problem. I got a headache I wouldn't wish on Khrushchev. Killing me, just killing me. What down is it? Third? Third and what? (*Announcer's voice, with slight Continental inflection: ". . . carried by Farr."*) D'ja hear that? (*In heavy British accent*) . . . bawl kerried by Melvin Fah of England. That's what I like. A lot of class in football! Carrying British stadium announcers. Quite! Splendid! What the hell is wrong with Amos [Amos Marsh, Detroit fullback]? Tired? I wish I could get tired anytime I felt like it, walk off like that and sit down. Put him back in. Get the *force* out there. *Got*damn. No more scrambling, gang. Let's lay it on them. Block that man! Knock his dick off. (*Ragtime band in background: "You've Got the Sweetest Little Baby Face"*) Keep it up. Oh my. That's lousy. That's horrible! (*Announcer's voice: ". . . tackled by Lockhart."*) One foot. One little foot. That's all they had to make. (*To himself*) A foot. You know how big a foot is. (*Announcer's voice: "Fourth and one."*) Twelve inches. Couldn't make *twelve* little inches, so I've got to go back to the pressure cooker. (*Crack of gear as runs back onto field*) The pressure cooker. Christ.

(*Announcer's voice: "That's the end of the quarter."*) Hey, you hear that announcer from England? Quatah! Quatah! What class! (*To new Giant guard*) Hello! Who are you? I'm a hundred and twenty years old. Y'all from Tennessee? You one of them cotton-pickin' hillbillies? Well, fry my ass, I do de-clare. What's a li'l ol' Southern boy like you doin' out here in this mess?

Y'all lookin' to get your dick knocked off? (*Line judge calls: "Offensive linemen, keep those hands in. I'm going to call it on you. That's a warning." Concussion of play; Karras gets to Tarkenton*) Hiho, Fran. What are you doing on the floor? (*Announcer's voice: ". . . brought down by Karras."*) Hey Fran? That's some li'l ol' Southern boy you got yourself for pass protection—mah *good*ness! (*Lucci calls play: "Four three; blitz; blue."*) Hello, hello. You still in here? Goodness. What you breathin' so hard fo', li'l boy? (*Concussion of play; heavy panting*) What's that for? Ref! What you throwing down that flag for? Wait a minute! (*Yelling*) He was on the ground already! Holding face mask? Oh that's horrible, ref, that's a horrible call. He was on the ground. The play was over! (*Players arguing*) Shut up! I'll talk. Shut up for a minute. I'm the captain. I'll talk. Don't tell me *not* to talk. (*Voices calm him down; one says, "I'm with you, Alex."*) Okay then. (*Calmer*) Okay. Okay. (*Lucci calls defensive huddle: "Four three; blitz; blue."*) Okay, Jer. Let's get them. (*Crash of contact*) You *held* me! You held me, you motherfucker! You hold me again and I'll punch your goddamn hillybilly head off. Get off me, you piss-ass hillbilly. (*Heavy breathing*) Motherfucker! (*Next play; crash of gear*) Nice. Nice. Come to me. That's it . . . go to your knees!

(*Announcer's voice: "Fourth down." Lucci's voice: "Double twist. Special set." On way to line Karras and Rush hold whispered conversation about which will be primary attacker in looping maneuver by two tackles*) Me first? (*"Sure, you."*) You? (*"No, you."*) No, *you* go ahead. (*"Quit kidding, Al. You go."*) Okay, man.

(*Signals called; crash of play*) Man, you hillbillies can't block worth . . . hey . . . hey! He's *clipping,* hey ref! (*Whistle*) Damn right. Give 'em five yards. Five more. That's right. Five *more.* Hey, hillbilly, you're doing your team real good in there. A fifteen-yarder. Yumyum. (*Lucci's voice: "Safety blitz."*) Jerry, your man is pop-blocking, isn't he? (*Muffled reply: unidentified voice: "It's what? It's what?"*) Safety blitz. Safety blitz. (*Crash of play; whistles; referee's voice: "Get your hands off him, number seventy-one. You're hitting him late. That's a warning, number seventy-one."*) Christ! (*To himself*) Must have heard that a billion times. "Get your hands off him." "Don't spear him." "You're hitting him late." "That's a warning." Goddamn quarterbacks. What are we supposed to do: stand around and *gawk* at them sons of bitches? (*Lucci's voice: "Double twist. Special set. Reverse." Crash of play; grunts*) Hey, Mike! Did you call the twist? Yeah? Well, I didn't twist. No. I didn't hear. That's my fault.

(*Back on bench*) No, coach. I didn't hear. But I'm glad I *didn't* twist. I got him. He came right to me. (*Announcer's voice: "Farr carried the ball; tackled by Lockhart." Players begin yelling along the bench*) Flag's down. Damn right. Cheap shot. Give them fifteen yards. If I did that, they'd give me twenty-five yards. Hell, they'd throw me out of the park. Hey, *water*. Let's have some water up here! (*Drinks; spits*) Hey, Looch. We've got the game. Ease up on the blitzes. Let the linebackers help out with the backs. (*Lucci's voice: "Okay. I'll talk to Jim [Jim David, defensive coach]. Announcer's voice: "Two-minute warning."*) That's good. The soup is getting cold. (*Band begins playing "Four-Leaf Clover." To show discontent with Giant head coach Allie Sherman, crowd begins to sing "Goodbye, Allie" to tune of "Good Night, Ladies." Singing drowns out band, though plinkety-plunk of banjos still discernible*) Man, they can boo here too, can't they? Listen to them. The great American fickle fans. Hey, Carl? The Giant team is second in its division, isn't it? Six wins, six losses, and they're second in their division! Damn tough division, this Eastern Division, whooo-eee!

(*Back on defense. Lucci in huddle: "Double twist; outside double."*) Yeah, yeah. Okay. Play it tough in the middle. (*Concussion of play; grunts*) That's a wham, baby. (*Breathing hard*) That's a wham on me. They really came down on me. But it's okay. That's the way to hold up. Hustle all the time. (*Lucci in huddle: "Double twist; special set."*) Okay. The soup's getting cold. Time for the big reach. (*Referee's voice: "You guys are playing a tremendous game. Don't spoil it. Keep your hands in." Unidentified voice: "Aw, man, git out of here." Lucci's voice: "Over right! Over right!" Concussion of play; Karras reaches quarterback*) Howdy, Fran. Why, it's *not* Fran. Who've I got here. Earl? That you? Earl Morrall. Well. God*damn*. How sweet it is.

> (*Gun goes off, ending game. Karras trots to bench. Unidentified Lion says, "Hey, Alex. You still wired up?"*) Huh? (*"You still got a microphone on?"*) Yeah. (*"Well, can I tell you something?"*) Yeah. Go ahead. (*"Yeah? Where do I speak? I mean, I want them to hear this."*) Right here. You speak right into my chest. (*"Okay, Alex. I wanted to say what a shame it is, being wired up and all, that today, of all days, you had to have the worst goddamn afternoon of your career. I mean, man, you stunk!"*)

The laughter goes up, and on the tape the listener can hear the creak of Karras' shoulder pads as he takes a retaliatory cuff at his persecutor. The voices of the autograph-hunters take over: "Hey Alex, would you sign this 'To Tracy'? And maybe put 'A swell guy' after it. Right here on this napkin."

The Gordy tape is substantially the same—the exhortations, the panting, the violent shifts of mood, though Gordy coughs more and spends most of his time on the bench trying to clear his throat and nostrils. He says far less on the field than Karras, presumably because his work, leading the interference, leaves him spent at the end of each play, so that he gasps out his sentences as if trying to speak while being garroted. His accent becomes far more Southern than it is in usual conversation, and his grammar sometimes collapses. At one point, suddenly aware that the microphone has picked up an ungrammatical entreaty to the defensive unit ("Hey, big D., don't give them nothing"), he lowers his voice abruptly and says, "I wonder if I could correct that. Please substitute: 'Please, don't give them *anything!*'" At another point, he shouts out, "Get them motherfuckers," and immediately says, "Get *those* motherfuckers . . . sorry, and maybe you'd better leave out the last part, too."

GORDY:
(*On sidelines, to Karl Sweetan, Lion quarterback*) Hey Karl! They're stunting off that four four. Anything in the four or five

243

hole is no good. Is there any water? Water! (*Hawks and vomits*) Christ! (*To himself*) How come I got to throw up during the game? Happens every damn time. Pass the word down. Everybody hustle. Hey, are they going to try a field goal? (*Frantically, to Jim David, Lion coach*) Hey, Jimmy! It's going to be a fake. Honest to God. This guy I was out with the other night said that they had practiced the fake field goal all week. Honest to God! (*Stadium announcer's voice: "Gogalak's attempt fails . . . Detroit's ball on the twenty."*)

(*Creak of gear as Gordy runs onto field for offensive series*) Okay. Four good downs here. Let's go. (*Sweetan's voice calls play in huddle: "Opposite right thirty-four on two." Sharp handclaps as huddle breaks. Line judge's voice: "Keep your hands in. Last warning." Sweetan's voice at line of scrimmage: "Four. Set. One nine A. Hut! Hut!" Crash of play; tremendous grunts from Gordy*) Oh Jesus, no! (*Loud yell from crowd; referee's whistle; big pileup. Referee's voice: "Okay, everybody relax, except you with the ball. Relax. Relax. Detroit ball." Gordy spits*) Christ! Where was the MBU on that. Jesus! What the hell. I got to take the guy in the gap. (*To Ed Flanigan, Detroit center*) Come on, Ed! Get him inside, hey? Okay. Let's get a good play. Let's get some blocks. (*Following next play, to Chuck Walton, Detroit offensive tackle*) Hey Chuck, what was that? A four four. Want me to take the guy in the gap? Call me a signal, because he can keep you from getting out. Or I'll call "George." (*His voice hops and breaks*) Then you can step out. If you call the signal, say "left" or "right" in case I forget which direction I'm supposed to go. (*In huddle*) Okay, babies, let's go. (*Concussion of play; sharp, staccato grunts from Gordy as he runs; crash of his block*) Christ! Get off my hand. You stepped on my hand. Oh, Jesus, you broke my hand! (*Heavy swearing*) My fingers are all gone. My hand's broke. (*Unidentified voice: "Shake it off, Bear."*) Did you see what that guy did? He went and stomped on my hand. (*His voice calms*) What did he want to do that for? (*Ragtime band in background: "Hello, Dolly." Sweetan calls end sweep in huddle; his voice sounds healthy and chipper above Gordy's puffing. Tremendous grunts from Gordy as play commences and he pulls to run interference*) Huh

huh huh huh huh huh huh huh huh . . . (*Crack of gear as throws block*) Crap! Nowhere! Jesus! I should've had the guy. (*To Amos March, Detroit running back, on way to huddle*) Hey, Amos. I thought I had him. I blew it . . . I blew it . . . if I had a little more in me I would have had him, but I didn't . . . my fault. (*Blows nose; Sweetan calls running play in huddle; concussion of play*) No. No. Please no . . . Please! (*Detroit fumbles; great roar from crowd as Giants recover*)

There is one greatly poignant moment on the Gordy tapes. Following a running play, in which Mel Farr's signal to carry the ball is called, a sudden, sharp scream erupts over the crash of padding and the heavy grunts of the players. Gordy's voice cries out, "Mel, what's wrong. Mel! What's *wrong!*"—a voice so tragic with concern that, listening to the tapes, one conjures up a quick image of a crippled running back lying askew on the field with Gordy standing over him in despair. In the background, Farr's voice is barely understandable, but it is reassuring; he is all right. Gordy's reaction is startling: his voice shifts abruptly from anguish to rage. "Bastard! Don't you be yelling like that. You mothering bastard. Don't you *ever* yell like that. Don't you ever scare me like that, you bastard!" The temper of his voice then shifts once again, as in his relief he suddenly sounds close to tears: "Mel, baby. Please don't scare me. What the shit am I going to do without you out here, baby?"

Farr's reply is audible. Startled by Gordy's outburst and the sweep of its emotion, he says in a high, almost querulous tone, "Damn, John, I don't know. I don't know."

Both Karras and Gordy came around to my apartment to hear the tapes played on the machine. It was the following year. The effect on them was quite different. At the time Karras was still in football, so the sounds—that shredded roar of the crowd, the tinny background music, the whistles, the thuds, the signal-calling—were as uninteresting to him as a phonograph record of barnyard noises might be to a farmer. Most of the time he stood at the window and watched the big tankers easing up the East River toward Hell Gate. "Any bodies float by?" he asked.

"I suppose so," I said. I was changing the tapes on the machine. "I've never seen any. Traditionally, most of them are outfitted in cement boots so they go to the bottom quick and stand there."

"Well, look close the next time you see a bunch of floaters going by and you'll see they're all old washed-up football players. They can't afford cement boots. And they'll all be linemen," Karras said. He stared moodily down at the currents and sighed. "Quarterbacks and tight ends die comfortably, in big beds, and the Irish setter is whimpering on the other side of the door, and someone is mowing the great lawn outside the big mansion. But the linemen give it up in these little rooms in the poor sections. They wake up on a cot in a room the size of a closet, and they look at their pushed-in kissers in the little mirror, and they pull their old football jerseys with the number on the back out of the bottom drawer of the beat-up dresser, and they put them on and go up to the bridge there—what's the name of it?"

"That's the Triboro."

"The Triboro. And they drop off the Triboro and float down here." He leaned forward. "There goes one. That's Ed Glurk, number seventy, good journeyman tackle for the Eagles in the fifties. Always was a nice guy. Look how he rides nice and high in the water. Just behind him, that's Al Woekowski— good Polack kid who played guard for the old Yankees. He's got his jersey on inside out. Look at him turn in the water. He always had classy moves. Now who's that coming along now?" His voice rose in mock excitement. "Why, is that John Gordy, that old has-been from the Detroit Lions, number seventy-*five*? Why, I do declare I believe it *is* . . ."

"Can it," said Gordy. Hunched over the next tape, he turned the volume up on the machine and the roar of the crowd in Yankee Stadium shivered in the room.

For Gordy, out of football for a year, the sound track re-created scenes for which he had such nostalgia that the muscles began working in his throat and I thought he was going to cry. Afterwards, he took the tapes and edited a composite for his own use. I thought of him occasionally, sitting in his small

New York apartment (he had left his family in Detroit and was involved in the bitterness of a divorce action) playing his tapes, the volume up on his machine, lost in the re-creation of that cold December afternoon in Yankee Stadium.

What did it give him, I asked.

Oh, it took him back. "But the main thing," he said, "is that I am in awe of myself. I think, 'Jesus, what it took to go through that.' I'll tell you something: it makes me feel proud."

"Do you play the tapes a lot?"

"From time to time," he said. "Sometimes I play them for other people. Sometimes alone, when I'm down. It has a big effect on the girls." He laughed and shook his head. "It fills them with awe, too; they look at me different after they hear them. This man went through *that?*"

17

Just about the furthest thing from my imagination was that I would ever again hear firsthand the sort of sounds that we had listened to on the tape recorder in my apartment. When I left the Lions, I thought I was done with it forever. Friday Macklem, the equipment manager, had given me a few mementos of my experience there: a couple of gray sweat shirts inscribed DETROIT LIONS in blue on the front; a helmet with the Lions decal on each side, which I hung above a door in my apartment. Occasionally I wore one of the sweat shirts around the apartment. Once, on a cold fall day, I put one on, with a couple of sweaters over it, and went out to Central Park for some exercise.

The best type of communal exercise in the Park if you don't want to jog around by yourself is to play in the pickup touch-football games, which are quick, often violent, and very competitive. Many of the players wear cleated football shoes, and often the faded jerseys of their college football days. The procedure to enter such games is to stand along the sidelines, especially if the teams playing are not evenly matched, either in numbers or ability, and when you can get someone's attention, to call out, "Hey, you want anybody?"

The Central Park touch football games are imbued with ritualistic procedures. Such a request is never acknowledged as far as one can tell. The heads turn and look, like cattle at a sudden noise, and then the huddle forms and the game continues. But the request has been absorbed. After a while, unless you have an obvious physical problem, such as being on crutches, the heads will come up and turn toward you once again, and a voice will sing out, "Hey, you!"

Almost invariably the new player trotting in, lifting his feet high to try to give the impression he was once a college hurdler, is placed at center. It is the position of least authority on the field. The key figure is, of course, the quarterback. Since all the plays are improvised on the spot, it is he who instructs the others, and if he is a good quarterback, with a sense of public relations, he involves all of them in the possibility of glamorous participation in the play: "Harry, you go long; I'll be looking for you. Tim, cut across diagonally on a fly." To a stranger wearing a number on his jersey: "Ninety-eight, you go ten yards down and circle like this." He kneels down and scrabbles a design in the dirt. "Pete, hold the rush up and then slide off *here* for a safety valve, just in case I got to unload the ball. On two."

This last is directed at the center, the only instruction he will get, unless possibly: "Try to hold up that big guy, for Chrissakes. He's coming in like an express train."

For the new player at center, the position affords the others on his team to chance to judge the way he moves, his ability to catch the ball, if he should get the opportunity, and whether he seems to know what he's up to. There is always the chance he'll be promoted.

In my case, our team's quarterback had to go home ("I've got to take the goddamn kids to the goddamn zoo") and a man wearing a heavy knit sweater said to me, "Hey, do you want to run a few plays?"

249

"Sure," I said easily. "Just a couple."

In the huddle I said, "Look here, let's do this. Harry, you go way long. I'll look for you. Tim, a diagonal cut. Ninety-eight, ten yards or so, and then buttonhook. Pete, a little blocking and then slide off to the side in case I got to get rid of it. On two," I told the new center. A squat figure in heavy dark glasses, he was wearing a Beethoven sweat shirt and had been standing on the sidelines for ten minutes.

The play worked. Tim's diagonal cut carried him out beyond a defensive back who was probably thinking of something else, perhaps that he ought to be getting home for lunch, and as our man ran between the two piles of coats and gear marking the goal posts, someone said, "Man, hell of a pass."

It *had* felt good, a clean spiral and a good trajectory, and I had come up on my toes to savor the last steps of the receiver's run. I felt warm, so I trotted to the sidelines to remove a sweater. As I started to skin it off, I thought, Well, why not, so I took off both of them, revealing the gray shirt with DETROIT LIONS on the front. It was sleeveless and I felt the cold prick the skin of my arms. Still, I should have known better than to think the shirt would make an impression on my teammates; they could not help noticing it, but there were no reactions, no gasps, no double takes, no one saying, "Well, for Chrissakes, why didn't you let on?" One of the players said, "What's the play, man?"

"Harry," I said in the huddle. "Why don't you go long. I'll be looking for you. Tim, take that diagonal cut of yours . . ."

The huddle broke.

Somebody on the opposing team wearing a tattered gray fedora stepped in front of Tim, arched his neck and, reaching high, pulled in my pass. He ran a few steps and fell down. Our defense held, and I was allowed to continue. This time, on the first play, the man in the Beethoven sweat shirt let his man brush by him. As he came on, I retreated, back-pedaling to keep away from arms that reached for me like a film monster's, until I was leaning so sharply backwards that when I released the ball, it rose almost straight up in the air. It came down in the hands of the man in the fedora, who caught it in full stride and ran for a touchdown.

A change was made, initiated by the *éminence grise* on our team, the slightly built man wearing the heavy Shetland sweater which exuded a slight but noticeable odor in the huddle. I noticed that everyone deferred to him. Perhaps he owned the ball. He said, "Hey, Tim, why don't you take over for a few plays." The Beethoven man was shifted out to flanker to take Tim's place, and I, wearing my DETROIT LION shirt, went back to center. It was very cold. I stayed until I felt I could say with a certain amount of grace that I was required elsewhere. "I've got to go to the goddamn zoo," I said, and trotted off the field to the warmth of my two discarded sweaters.

I had always assumed that this kind of Central Park football would remain the highest level of the sport at which I could ever expect to find myself. But then a television production company, Wolper Productions, got the DuPont Corporation interested in backing a series of TV hour specials utilizing my services as an amateur trying a number of different professions —struggling as an aerialist in the circus, for instance, or as a race-car driver, or as a comic on the Las Vegas stage.

Football was high on the list of professions the television people wanted me to try. Pete Rozelle, the commissioner of football, had been approached and had agreed to allow me to quarterback four extra plays in a pre-season exhibition game which would be photographed in the TV special. DuPont and the production company were very excited. Doing the research for *Paper Lion* I had been allowed to play in an intra-squad scrimmage (losing twenty or so yards); this time I would have a chance to play against an honest-to-goodness enemy.

I was not as enthused about the prospect as the production company and DuPont, but they said, Oh come on, this will really be the true test—something you've always wanted to do.

Well, I wasn't so sure, I told them.

I had assumed that I could rejoin the Lions because my old friend Joe Schmidt was now the coach. But when I had lunch with him in New York, he shook his head and was skeptical. I could come out to the training camp and hang around just as I had done before, he said, but he didn't want the place cluttered up with the electronic equipment and crews of a television company; it would be too much of a disturbance. He had always felt that the Detroit Lions' absorption with the movie *Paper Lion*—the opening nights, parades, personal appearances, all the hoopla—had been a factor, if a slight one, in blunting the team's competitive edge in the 1968 season, and he was not going to let anything like that happen again. I could play *against* them, if I liked; that would be just fine.

So we had to look elsewhere. Eventually I was accepted by the Baltimore Colts organization, partly because I knew Carroll Rosenbloom, the owner. I had tried the Colts years before, but Rosenbloom had asked me to write about another team, or wait a year, since Don Shula, in his first season with Baltimore, would not want to be afflicted with an extra quarterback of my dubious quality. Now, however, the Colts had won the Super Bowl the year before, a seasoned team that Rosenbloom told me could surely accept my presence without falling apart.

I thanked him for interceding in my behalf, adding that the big question was not whether the Colts would fall apart, but if *I* would.

In the meantime, it was worked out by the television people and the Commissioner's Office that in the pre-season game I would indeed play against my old team—four extra plays at half time in the Colt-Lion exhibition game scheduled for August 22 in Ann Arbor in the great saucer-shaped stadium there that seats over 100,000 people. To prepare for it, I was to train with the Colts for a month. Don McCafferty, the head coach, called up and said that he was going to work me hard and that he expected me to gain some yardage against the Lions. "It's been my observation," he said, "that ballplayers have their best games against their former teammates."

Once my connection was established with the Colts, letters began to arrive in early July from the Colt front office—directives addressed *Dear Baltimore Colt* . . . very heady mail—and I ran hard in the sands along the beaches of Long Island to train; I began to have dreams which woke me up early in the dawn, though I could never recall them exactly except that they

252

involved quick movement and the sounds of concussion and that I had done some shouting. My throat always seemed sore . . .

Are you going to record your adventure down there? my friends asked. After all, the cameras will be recording it for the television show.

I'll keep a diary, I told them. A kind of journal. The television crew was limited in what it could do. There would be an awful lot that the camera could not catch . . . I told them that I would force myself to start writing as soon as I got there.

The Baltimore Journal

Arrival

July 14   I arrived at the Colt training camp on the campus of
Western Maryland University in Westminster, Maryland, carrying a flight bag with a tennis racket packed in it, the handle
stuck out the end. I wore a floppy tennis hat. My hope was to
get a game with Jim O'Brien, the Colt place-kicker who had won
the Super Bowl with a field goal the year before. We had played
against each other in a doubles tournament in Ft. Lauderdale,
Florida. Sporting a red bandanna to keep his hippie-length hair
out of his eyes, he had caromed around the court playing a
joyous, slapdash game, full of confidence (occasionally pushing his professional partner, Bob Lutz, out of the way to make a
shot), and though he had picked up tennis only a couple of years
before, he assisted his partner formidably enough for their team
to prevail. The defeat still rankled.

My dormitory room is on the ground floor. The walls and ceiling are painted baby-blue, and the floor is brown linoleum. A naked light bulb hangs from a wire in the center of the room, and two wooden desks with the drawer knobs missing stand against the walls. The windows look out on a row of pine trees, with the parking lot beyond, and as I write there is the high whine of a model aircraft being flown in a tight wired circle in some distant field. The room has two low cots, with mattresses that sag only a foot off the floor, but I have not been assigned a roommate, which is a relief. Training camps always abound with stories of incompatability. John Gordy once told me that he and Karras had been forced to room together because they both still had their tonsils and slept on their backs and snored steadily in such roaring gusts that neither, conditioned by the considerable sound he made himself, seemed to be bothered by the other. Joe Schmidt had hung up a sign on their door reading MENAGERIE, which stood as much for the sounds that emitted from the room as for the fact that The Mad Duck and The Bear lived within.

The oddest strain I've heard of between roommates at Detroit was that between Bill Swain, one of the linebackers, and Roger LaLonde, a big offensive guard. Swain noticed that LaLonde wore calf-length Supp-Hose socks to bed. It bothered him so much that he mentioned it to LaLonde, who told him that he had worn socks to bed all his life and couldn't break the habit; in fact, he couldn't *sleep* without a pair of socks on. For some reason this idiosyncrasy disturbed Swain's sensibilities to such a degree that he fessed up to LaLonde, if very politely, that he didn't think they could go on together.

I stowed my gear away and went off to find O'Brien to see if he'd like to get in a set of tennis before the first team meeting. I found him. A Snoopy doll was propped up on his roommate's bed. When I asked him about the tennis game he became very nervous. Had anyone seen me carrying a racket into the camp—by any chance was a coach looking out the window?

"I don't think so," I said.

"You haven't talked to any of the coaches? McCafferty?"

"No," I said. "Not about tennis." He seemed so concerned that I found myself lowering my voice so as not to be overheard.

"Christ Almighty," he whispered back. "The idea here is that they work you so hard that by the end of the day you're supposed to drop. The coaches calculate it that way. If they saw you after practice leaping around the tennis court, smashing and lobbing and carrying on, you'd be doing fifty laps the next day. I wouldn't play tennis fifteen miles from here."

"Oh," I said.

"Tennis is not a good word around here."

"I see."

When I got back to my room I stowed the racket in the back of the closet. I put away the floppy tennis hat too, just to be on the safe side.

John Gordy

Gordy also arrived today. The television people had wanted a technical assistant and I asked if we could take him on. His knee had been brutally racked up during the Lion's training season the previous year, and after the operation and half a year of thinking about his future, he had decided to retire. Part of it, I think, was to get out of Detroit; he was separated from his wife and involved in divorce proceedings. He took a small apartment in New York and we saw each other occasionally. No longer having to keep his weight up to buttress the force of his charge across the line of scrimmage, he had lost thirty pounds and was taking to wearing fancy weaved slacks and letting his hair grow long in a sort of Hamlet style. We had lunches in places like the Italian Pavilion. I saw him around town with tall girls with names like Marsha and Wendy. He had founded an audio-visual communications company at which he worked hard and sensibly—conditioned by what he continued to refer to as "The Lionburger School of Hard Knocks." Then he fell in love with a girl from New Jersey, whose family also had a place on the shore of Long Island Sound with a tennis court and a schooner moored at the local yacht club. At a lunch when I planned to ask him to become a technical adviser, he kept talking about the Block Island race.

"The spinnaker . . ." he said. "I'm telling you, I'd rather face Leo Nomellini than a spinnaker."

"John, guess what I'm doing," I interrupted.

"What?"

"I'm playing again."

"You're *what*?"

"I'm a last-string quarterback again—this time for the Baltimore Colts." I told him about the television project.

"Christ Almighty," he said. "Why not the Lions?"

I told him that Joe Schmidt had said he did not want his training camp messed up with television crews.

"That figures," Gordy said.

"John, the project needs your help. They want you to become a technical assistant."

Gordy looked dubious. "Well, what would I do?"

"Advise," I said. "You can show the television people where to point their cameras. You've always wanted to promote the activities of linemen—how skillful they are, and just what goes on in the line—and here's your chance."

"I'm really out of it. I'm going on yachts quite a lot," Gordy said.

"John, you've got to see me through this. It's not only the television people—hell, *I'm* the one who needs a technical adviser."

"I'm playing a lot of tennis," he said.

"Yes, I know that."

"Where are the Colts training?"

"In a place called Westminster, Maryland," I said. "I'm going to be sent into a pre-season game against the Detroit Lions at Ann Arbor, Michigan."

"God Almighty," he said. "*Against* the Lions. Well, that's something. Well, damn," he said. He turned a water glass on the table. "Well, we sure as hell have got to get you ready for

257

that." He snorted, and then grinned enormously. "Of course I'll come down. It'll be good to be involved. Damn right I will . . ."

We had dinner the night of our arrival in Westminster. At the far end of the dining room a group of Methodists joined hands at their table and sang a soft prayer. The college is host for a number of such groups, who come there for conventions and seminars; another such party using the college facilities consisted of more than a hundred deaf-mutes who had been around for a month's stay. We watched a table of these semaphoring to each other. Gordy said, "Good-looking bunch of Colt rookies, especially those guys singing and holding hands. You've got me involved with quite a team."

First Meeting

July 16 The first day has been predictable: going through the medical tests, getting weighed and being outfitted in the football accouterments laid out in separate piles on the gymnasium floor. I spent a lot of time at the helmet pile, hoping to find one which was snug and could be drawn on and off without my ears suffering excruciating pain. But there must be something wrong with the conformity of my head; I had the same trouble at Detroit. The only solution will be to wear the helmet at the beginning of practice and not take it off until the end, which means that it's going to get hot in there, and the sweat will drip into the eyes, and I will hear everything as if it were coming through cotton.

There are two, sometimes three team meetings a day; invariably one is in the morning at 9:00 A.M. They are held in a subterranean classroom in the cellar under one of the dormitories. Upstairs in their rooms the students occasionally have their phonographs going, the beat of the music drifting outside and down through the cellar window wells. Bubba Smith, the great defensive end, sits over there, his head nodding to the faint distant pump of rock. The college R.O.T.C. unit meets in this room; a map of Vietnam hangs to the left of the blackboard, and in the back corners of the room are banks of steel drawers with military maps inside, an appropriate place to plot football campaigns. The chairs have kidney-shaped writing arms, and when the players sit down and shift around, the legs shriek against the concrete floor. Flies drone about in the summer heat. Just in front of the coaches' lectern is a big floor fan which stirs the air; the quarterbacks sit up in front of the class. I do not sit with them; they are right under the eyes of the coaches and questions are constantly put to them, so I have taken up a *querencia* in the back of the room, seated alongside Dave Lee, the punter.

At exactly the stroke of the meeting's scheduled start, Don McCafferty walks through the classroom door to the lectern, looks back over his shoulder at the clock above the blackboard to check, and then begins by calling the roll. He is a tall man (a former New York Giant end) with a military bearing, close-cropped silvery hair and a deep, commanding voice one would associate with military academies, yet he is universally known as "The Easy Rider" for a principle of coaching that is supposed to be more benevolent than authoritarian.

He seems awfully tough to me; he started the first meeting by fining a number of his ballplayers. Occasionally, the final decision on individual fines is left to a vote by the entire team—perhaps this is why he's called The Easy Rider—thumbs up, thumbs down. At the first meeting Bubba Smith and a rookie defensive back named Leonard Dunlap from North Texas State were to be fined $100 each for missing the previous morning's 9:30 A.M. weigh-in unless they could plead their case convincingly. Dunlap got a thumbs-up show because he said that while he'd gone over to the gym at the wrong time and found no one there, he'd gone ahead and weighed himself anyway. A roar of approval, the thumbs went up and Dunlap had won himself a reprieve. Bubba's turn. He couldn't even get started on his plea; he rose enormously to his feet, coughed, and in a chorus of shouts and laughter was voted thumbs-down before he could get a word out. He was probably very guilty. He waved a big hand at his teammates and sat down with a grin.

McCafferty then called the classroom to order and asked that each player stand up in turn to announce who he was, his position, and where he had played college football. The procedure gave everyone a chance to look at their fellows, and for the newcomers to put a face to the Colt names that were so familiar: Mike Curtis, the All-Pro middle linebacker, slighter in stature than I expected, with a handsome sharp face that seemed perpetually creased by a straight tight-lipped smile; Bubba Smith, a big gap between his front teeth when he smiled, sitting by the window well with a long string of keys dangling from a belt and wearing a Big Apple hat; Bill Curry, the blond center who played under Vince Lombardi and whom everyone thinks of as the team's spokesman; Ted Hendricks—"The Mad Stork" they call him, for the conformity of a tall (6'7") skeletal frame combined with a ferocious freewheeling style of attack from his linebacker position. His head is small, with the skin tight and almost transparent over the high cheekbones.

The veterans horsed around with the procedure. Unitas got up pretending a rookie's shyness and stuttered endlessly over his name ("U . . . U . . . U . . .") and his college, which was Louisville ("Lou . . . Lou . . . Lou . . ."). Dan Sullivan, an offensive guard who was a Boston College graduate, announced in a rich Boston patois that he was Sullivan of Harvard. (Dave Lee whispered to me that Billy Ray Smith, a defensive tackle from Arkansas now retired from the Colts, who wore a cowboy hat indoors and out, had always used this as *his* line at the first team meeting: "Ah'm Rabbit, y'all, and Ah'm from Harvard.")

The rookies were much less innovative; they stood up and barely whispered their names. The only stir came when Don Nottingham, the Colt's final draft pick and thus the last man picked in the entire league, announced his name and school (Kent State) in a high, piercing, near-girlish voice. Eyebrows went up, and several of the Colts turned around to look at him. (Actually, it is surprising how unexpectedly high athletes' voices so often are: the near-squeak of Willie Mays, Deacon Jones, Roger Brown and Tom Matte . . . especially the larger people— weight-lifters, big wrestlers, football linemen—though one would assume that such large frames would contain a large enough voice box to produce low thunder. I have been told that the reason for this is that athletes in their exertions invariably breathe from the chest rather than from the diaphragm, the latter being the area that actors cultivate for their sonority. Of course there are too many exceptions to make it the general rule: Bubba Smith, for instance, has a voice that reverberates out of his 295-pound 6'7" frame as if his enormous dimensions were as hollow as those of a bass organ pipe.)

When the team introductions were done, McCafferty introduced Ed Block, the trainer. It was evident he is the team character; he has been with the Colts for seventeen years; he is short of stature with a melancholy clown's face, and he speaks in a strange, declamatory manner, drawing each word out as if to test it thoroughly. A man of orderly habits, he categorizes what he has to say into numerical or alphabetical divisions.

"Thank you for the ovation, gentlemen," he replied to the affectionate chorus of catcalls that greeted him. "I should like to start by giving you a few maxims adapted from Murphy's famous laws. *One:* left to themselves, things will always go from bad to worse. *Two:* in any field of athletic training, anything that can go wrong *will* go wrong. *Three:* it is my experience that Mother Nature is a bitch. *Three and a half:* it is best not to play with the crutches in my training room, or you may indeed end up on them. *Four:* if everything seems to be going well, you have obviously overlooked something.

"Now gentlemen, some friendly advice. *A:* If you are hurt, report it. We can't cure you if we don't know what ails you. *B:* No roughhousing in the training room. It has been my observation that things get broken—valuable machinery, such as whirlpool baths, and usually the bones of your teammates. *C:* Ice is the great restorer for those of you who insist on bruising yourselves. *D:* Don't use too much soap in the groin area when you take showers. If the natural antiseptic oils in that area are washed off, pimples will appear."

At the end of Block's dissertation, McCafferty asked if there were any questions or problems. Hendricks raised his

261

hand and said that because of his height he was having such trouble sleeping that he was either going to have to ask Ed Block for sleeping pills or get a longer bed.

McCafferty suggested that the Stork put another mattress on his bed which would raise it so that he could let his feet dangle over the end.

Sullivan raised his hand hurriedly and complained that this was an exceptionally bad solution. "The Stork's feet snore," he said.

That was enough for McCafferty. He blew his whistle and sent us all out for practice.

On the Field

We come up the steps from the cellar, cleats crashing on the cement, across a service road, past the tennis courts, down an embankment on which the spectators are already sitting out on their picnic blankets, and onto the practice field. I can see our television crews on the far sidelines. The practice starts with a lap of the field, the creak of gear, many of the players conversing as they run; I run nonvocally, puffing. The sun is up and already I can feel the heat building up inside my helmet.

After calisthenics the squad breaks into its various components, each under its respective coach: quarterbacks; flankers and receivers; running backs; the offensive line; the front four; the defensive secondary; and down at the far end by the goal posts the kickers and punters—all working at their specific duties. Slowly, as the morning progresses, the components come together as the quarterbacks join the flankers and receivers, and the defensive units combine, until finally for the last three quarters of an hour the entire squad is together, often with a scrimmage between the Big O (for offensive) versus the Big D. The players of each unit stand on the sidelines and exhort their fellows who are out on the field: "How to go, Big O." I didn't know what "Big O" meant the first time I heard it; I assumed everyone was referring to "Big" O'Brien, the place-kicker who takes a regular rotation at the flanker position, until I saw him standing next to me. Surprised, I whispered to him, "What's the Big O?" He looked at me. "Big O for Offense," he said. "Christ, that's what *you* are. You're a member of the Big O."

During practice I stick with the quarterbacks, slipping into the early drills every once in a while when McCafferty nods at me, trying a handoff, or a pass play when the receivers join us and their patterns are within my limited range. I take a turn only occasionally because it is important not to disturb the flow of the practice session. But McCafferty is working me much harder than they ever did at Detroit. In a few days' time, when the full-out scrimmages begin, he's going to put me in one so that I can get "blooded," as he puts it.

Sometimes I go off to the sidelines with Bill Curry and practice receiving the center's snap from him. Today I asked him if he could tell by the feel of the quarterback's hands just who was standing behind him in that coupled relationship of the T-formation—quarterback and his center—and he said, "Oh, sure. Earl Morrall, for example, puts his hands much further under than most and presses up against me so that I know just where he is. Unitas, on the other hand, has a light touch, and I have to reach back for him with the snap. One of the easiest quarterbacks to center the ball to is Joe Namath. I played with him once in a Bowl game just after we got out of college. He has his hands so far under that all I have to do is hoist the ball up to him. Now *your* touch is very tentative."

"Well, I've not had much practice at it," I said, "and it's not a situation where one wants to go wrong."

From time to time I go down to the end of the field with John Gordy and we work on the patterns of a bootleg pass play we hope to try against the Lions, in which the quarterback fakes a handoff, hides the ball on his hip and scoots in the opposite direction from the flow of the play, hoping desperately to fool the defensive end into falling for the fake, because if he *doesn't*—well, the quarterback is naked, like a man loitering through a pasture who looks up and finds the bull there.

The nomenclature of the bootleg play is enormous. In the huddle I am suppose to call out, "Flank right split fake thirty-nine flow bootleg right off end comeback eighteen," and then give the numbers on which the ball is to be snapped; it's quite like reciting a difficult line of Gerald Manley Hopkins poetry, and I often stumble over it in my practice run-throughs with Gordy and have to start afresh.

In fact, Gordy has not been very hopeful about the success of the bootleg. I have one gimpy foot from a long-ago ski accident; the tendons tighten sharply, and on occasion I break into the stumble of someone who has stubbed a toe. Gordy tells me that the run is so pathetic-looking that I'm going to be swarmed under just on general principle: "They'll want to put you out of your misery," as he puts it grimly.

Inspiration

July 17   The television crews have been on hand in Westminster for a few days to get the lay of the land. William Kronick, the director, and I have done some television specials before—one a documentary on a circus in which he had suffered through my attempts to become a trapeze aerialist—and we get along fine. He came to see me in my blue room.

"I've got a terrific title for the football show."

"Oh?"

"Get this: 'The Great Quarterback Sneak.' It just came to me."

"Yes," I said admiringly. "That's really very nice."

"Of course," said Kronick, "it means that you'll have to incorporate that particular play into your repertoire. You can use it in place of that bootleg play you've been having problems with. I see you running it as the last of your four plays against the Lions. An absolutely terrific climax."

"Oh. Well, have you come up with any other nifty ideas I should know about?"

"Not yet," he said. "But we will."

The Quarterback

July 18 Tonight, lying in the blue room, I've been thinking about John Unitas—his presence on the field, how not only the rookies glance across at him, stunned that they are in the same company, but just about everyone on the practice field, looking over at some point in the day to see what he is up to, so that one catches oneself, jaw slightly agape, staring at The Main Man, which is what they called the superstar when I was at Detroit and which is the same here. Sometimes they call him "That goddamned Ukrainian," or sometimes "The Man," but usually it is "The Main Man." He is practicing the drop-back from the center to test his weak ankle. Hundreds of times a day he does it, those seven savage quick bustling steps on pipestem legs back into the protective pocket, his shoulders hunched forward under the high pads, the white helmet with the horseshoe turning first this way and then that, and the pale small face within—an utterly familiar process to Baltimore people, as ingrained in them as the taste of crab cakes from the Chesapeake. Of course, some of the attention paid to him these days is clinical rather than rapturous: the arm is not what it used to be; the long ball is not in his repertoire any longer, they say, because it has a "rainbow" quality—a high arc—which is undesirable. Perhaps this is because he cannot stride off that weak ankle into his proper throwing motion. It is easy enough to see. By comparison, Karl Douglas, who is being given a chance at quarterback and will be the first black in the league at that position if he makes it, has a young, strong arm that the writers around town keep referring to as a "rifle"—a cliché, but an appropriate description nonetheless. Standing behind him when McCafferty calls a long pass pattern I can hear the laces whistle when Douglas lets the pass go, and the football bores quickly off into the distance like a projectile launched by some device other than a human arm. He has such natural ability that, seeing the passes fly out and connect at the end of a low trajectory, like a string pulled taut between quarterback and receiver, the veterans whistle and call out, "Hey, Karl, how to throw that thing, baby!" And yet there is only one quarterback on the field, and I have the feeling that it will continue to be so, however tortuous Unitas' return to complete recovery may be.

Jim Brown, the great Cleveland fullback, once told me a story about superstars such as John Unitas. Both he and Unitas were invariably picked to play in the Pro Bowl. In 1964 the East squad was coached by Allie Sherman. He met his players for the first time on a Los Angeles practice field, and he clapped his hands and called out, "All right, let's have a first team line up over here." Sherman had no list to refer to; he was suggesting that out of all those stars the right players would amble forward. *Which is just what happened.* A team materialized with hardly a word spoken, or even a sidelong glance. The players *knew* where they belonged; they could evaluate themselves in some private, yet universal grading system.

I thought this extraordinary. "But suppose . . . I mean, suppose a great player was humble?" I asked.

"The others would wait for him," Brown replied. "The position would stay open until he walked in and filled it."

"Damn, that's something," I said. I thought of such a humble player, perhaps working a piece of grass in his teeth, lolling up against a tackling dummy, maybe testing his fellow players with his reluctance before he picked up his helmet by the strap with a faint shrug to come forward and take his place. "That's something," I said again. "I'd have imagined that a shoving match would start when Sherman said that—a couple of centers, say, heaving and pushing right in front of everybody . . ."

Brown laughed. "Ballplayers know," he said. "Can you imagine another quarterback, no matter who the guy was, shoving *Unitas* aside to get into a line-up? No, man, no way."

The Specialists

July 19 At *Sports Illustrated* the half-serious conjecture by the editors has always been that the brightest athletes were long-distance runners because they had so much free time in which to exercise their minds. The equivalent on a football squad would be the specialists, the kickers in particular—especially if kicking were the only ability they had. Being a resourceful athlete, Jim O'Brien is a reserve flanker, and the classroom work is important to him. But Dave Lee, the team's punter who sits in the back of the classroom next to me, can't do anything but kick, and his only duty in class is to reach behind him and click the wall light switch when the coaches want to show films. His chair is situated so that he can turn off the light without turning around to look, just reaching up behind him, *ho hum*, and *click* . . . very smooth, and he never misses.

We chat back there, waiting for the meeting to start. I've suggested that he should be writing a novel, or studying a foreign language, utilizing his time, but Lee says that he doesn't mind listening to the coaches and taking an occasional note because football fascinates him, even if he can't perform any of the positions being discussed. Besides, football is his profession and livelihood, and it makes him cringe to think of the coaches' discovering that his playbook has a *Popular Mechanics* hidden in it, or a beginner's Spanish language text.

Lee did admit to me somewhat ruefully that if it weren't for his kicking ability he'd obviously be doing something else— selling insurance, probably, or teaching school. "The players sometimes call me and Jim O'Brien 'Easy Money,' " he said.

"They're probably envious."

"Each person out there is proud of the job he has," he said solemnly. He told me that he had found out he could kick when he was about six years old; he'd worked to perfect it, but he felt it was really a natural gift.

I asked him what had always puzzled me: why was it that kickers in the NFL weren't trained to kick the ball out of bounds, the tactic known as kicking for the "coffin corner."

Lee said that at high school he'd been trained to drop his kicks into hula hoops set along the sidelines far downfield, but in the pro leagues it was different. The notion was that if done properly a downfield kick not only had increased distance but could force a fumble. It had all been figured out. If the punter could hang the ball up in the air for 4.1 seconds, giving the defense an opportunity to get downfield, the chances were heavy against a runback. So when Lee was practicing on the field, often a coach would stand alongside with a stopwatch which he would click when Lee's foot came through the ball with a *thonk*, and click again when far downfield the punt was gathered in. "It's funny. I can tell a good kick less by the sound the punt makes coming off my foot than by the fact that you don't feel it as much if it's a good one. A bad kick will make your foot sting. Of course, the noise a crowd makes will tell me what the ball is doing in the air; you can hear the disappointment or joy."

On the field Lee has a number of personal habits that identify him quickly. He carries a football everywhere, from the moment he leaves the locker room to the end of practice, turning it in his palm so that it is totally familiar to his touch and no doubt because its texture is a sort of security blanket. He tells me that he never sits down on a bench at practice or during a game—a habit he has developed to keep his leg from stiffening up.

During practice I sometimes stand beside Lee and watch him arch long kicks into the summer sky. If anyone asked me what position I would accept if I had the ability, it would be Lee's. Kicking is something I've always felt I could do—if I *worked* at it. It was always the final refuge of those who realized when they were growing up that they did not have enough ability ever to become crack athletes, and so they would dream of sneaking onto a squad by developing some specialized skill—an extraordinary baseball pitch, such as Frank Merriwell's "double shoot," which curved in both directions on its way to the plate, or an unstoppable tennis serve, or punting or kicking field goals in football. It was important to fantasize about such things. When I was a youngster away at school in New Hampshire, I soon realized that I had no stomach for the collision aspects of football, and that I was not much of an athlete anyway, but I thought perhaps I could develop the arcane art of *drop-kicking* field goals to such a degree that I would be an indispensable asset to any college team. It was only a question of practicing. A classmate named Buzz Merritt and I would go down to the playing fields and drop-kick field goals in the evening after supper until the moon came up over the line of trees down by the river and a good kick would disappear over the crossbar into the darkness and *thump* on the other side. On the way back to our rooms, we walked past dormitories with lighted rows of windows behind which our classmates were studying Euclid, Horace and Boyle's Law, but we did not feel the slightest bit competitive because we knew that one day on some college field the head coach would say, "Well, what can *you* do?" and Buzz or I would ask for a football and shyly ask him which of the many goal posts across the reaches of the practice field he wanted to have the ball kicked over. He would laugh sardonically and say, "Oh, *that* one," pointing at a structure sixty or seventy yards away, and would start to go *haw haw haw haw,* but the laugh would die away as the drop-kick soared easily toward the distant crossbar, turning over very slowly in that sure sign of the long boot. I don't know about Buzz's daydream, but in mine the coach usually fainted and had to be brought back to consciousness by his assistants. There were professional scouts standing in the shadows under the trees. All this was predictable —we dreamed too much about it for it not to be—and so it was all that seemed important on those late fall evenings as we walked back along the paths, the snap of winter beyond the dark line of trees behind us . . .

Earl Morrall

July 20 I had lunch with Earl Morrall today. He was with the Lions when I was there—and he seems just the same, not a jot different in character or looks. Down on the field, hearing his strong, strident and familiar voice calling signals, it takes an active jolt to appreciate that I'm not back once more with Detroit.

There is one small change. Sometimes Morrall looks at me slightly quizzically, as if wondering why on earth I didn't have enough of it the first time, and what am I doing back at it again. But he's always helpful. He advises me, and pushes me to do better, and in the wind sprints, the so-called gassers which the quarterbacks always run together, he springs out ahead and laps me eventually, and I'll hear his voice coming up behind me. "C'mon, George baby, c'mon, c'mon."

At lunch I asked him if he felt that a quarterback's skill improved with age.

When he choked over his salad, I hastened to add that I wasn't referring to myself.

He recovered and said that it was difficult to say. The mental skills—the keying, reading of defenses and so forth—improved, but the defenses changed from year to year, so that one was never really on top of the situation. What did improve, and only by a fraction of a second, was the ability to shift from the main receiver and throw the pass almost instantaneously to an alternate. John Unitas had always been the best at that: finding the main man covered, *boom,* he'd go to the alternate, and he seemed to get better at it as the years went on.

"What do you think I'm going to see out there?" I asked.

"Well, one thing you don't want to have happen is to let the motion and action of the line in front of you mesmerize you as you drop back with the ball," he said. "That often happens with rookie quarterbacks. They see all this ruckus and commotion, and they lose their concentration. Either they pull up short to throw too quickly, or they keep dropping back, way back, when they should stop at exactly those seven yards to get in that protective pocket."

"I'm the guy whose feet will keep moving backwards," I said.

"Well, that's broken concentration, or maybe panic. Established quarterbacks do that seven-yard drop-back automatically, and *boom,* they throw." He chewed thoughtfully. "I wouldn't hang on to the ball too long," he said. "Not a terribly good idea . . ."

"No."

"You don't seem to be eating much," he added.

270

"Well, sometimes it's an effort," I said. "Around here sometimes food doesn't exactly lie easily on the stomach."

"Hell, the game's four weeks away," Morrall said.

"Don't you ever get queasy?" I asked. "With all that responsibility?"

"It's very important for the quarterback to relax and not show that his stomach is flip-flopping," Morrall said. "On the day of the game you don't want to go into the locker room john and throw up. It's all right for linemen and running backs to do that kind of thing, but some of the team's confidence might be a bit shaken if they heard you getting sick in there."

"I'm sure you're right," I said. "It's like the field marshal saying to his staff, 'Men, we will attack at dawn,' and then vomiting over his maps."

"Right on, George baby. Right on," Morrall said.

The Office

What I envy on the practice field as I stand around watching, scared that McCafferty will send me in, is Earl Morrall's tremendous confidence in voice and demeanor, his voice so loud and distinctive that a team across a couple of fields could respond to his signals.

It has not always been so for him. The Colt offensive system is extremely complicated, and when Morrall, who has played with four other teams (San Francisco, Pittsburgh, Detroit and New York), arrived at Baltimore he found himself overwhelmed by the sheer number of plays and formations he had at his disposal, and flummoxed because all of them were identified by a relatively haphazard nomenclature which made them difficult to learn. Among the pass plays, for example, is a Q series, so-called because Raymond Berry, the great Colt receiver who invented them and refined the pass routes, picked an identifying initial which had no meaning other than it had popped into his mind at the time. Some plays have the play assignation first

("Ride 38"), others the running assignments first ("34 Wham"); in addition, the numbering system along the line of scrimmage is the opposite of what it is in the system of the other NFL teams. Almost all clubs designate the holes to which the ball carrier runs by even numbers on the left of the center and odd numbers to the right, following a system devised by the Chicago Bears in 1930, so that a play called in the huddle with the numbers 3-4, say, indicates that the number three back, running from a halfback position, is to slant into the number four hole between the left end and tackle. But the Baltimore system is exactly the reverse, and one can imagine the initial despair of Morrall after ten years of playing the standard variations. Indeed, in his early games he often spun the wrong way and offered his handoff to the open air, while behind his back the runner thundered by, his fingers groping, eyes popping in surprise at the unexpected vacuum in front of him.

So complex is the system at Baltimore that John Unitas once kiddingly assured a mournful quarterback candidate that he was going to try to get the Players Association to insist that football terminology be standardized—an unlikely gesture since he often joked that he would be quarterbacking the Colts long into his fifties because he was the only one who could master the playbook; the more complicated and abstruse it was, the better for him.

Tom Matte told me that one of the reasons he got to play so much was that he had such a total knowledge of the Baltimore offense that Don Shula sent him in to help Morrall call his plays. If Morrall got stuck and began hemming and hawing in the huddle, Matte would say, "What do you want?" and Morrall would say, "Well, I want to hit an O pattern to the out end." Matte would say, "All right . . . Out left flank right sixty out end O," and Morrall would repeat it to his men in the huddle.

Of course, by now Morrall has been with the Colts for four years, so he isn't surprised by much anymore. This is the vast difference between what I see when I walk up toward the waiting ball, and what is in Morrall's field of vision when he calls his play and breaks the huddle. What he sees is absolutely commonplace to him: the row of jerseys moving toward the line of scrimmage, then his people getting set, while beyond them the enemy shifts and jockeys about, the defensive calls directing them. Nothing anybody does, at least in the quiescent period before he unleashes a play, surprises him. The analogy that always comes to my mind is that it is his "office"—and that everything is as predictable to him as what a businessman sees when he opens his office door to start a day of work: a hatrack off to the left at which he sails his hat, hardly looking, and it catches, and spins on the peg; in the center of his big mahogany desk are the yellow legal pads; his mail is opened and waiting; his secretary, Miss Smithers or whatever her name is, steps forward and offers the same stiff smile and greeting she has for ten years. The day's work will probably not surprise him either.

Of course, Morrall's office can become a prickly place if things go badly against him, but such afternoons are an occupational condition of his profession. If a reporter commiserates with him about a bruising game, he is apt to reply, "Well, it's all in a day's work."

There's no such equanimity for me. It's an utterly foreign world I step into every time McCafferty calls for my services—very much as if that same businessman walks through his door one morning to find himself in the engine room of a submarine, the pipes slick with moisture, with his secretary transformed into a worried subaltern who is saying, "Sir, six Jap destroyers are closing at three thousand meters."

What is required, of course, is enough experience so that the strangeness of what I'm doing will dissolve into a vague confidence. Obviously, I'll never get enough opportunity. So after the huddle breaks with a crack of hands I always keep my eye on Curry, the center, never sure that I won't step behind the haunches of another lineman by mistake. My brain is nagged by any number of such uncertainties: whether I can perform the physical requirements of the play called in the huddle—to spin in such-and-such a direction, the football in this-or-that hand, to be delivered to one-or-the-other halfback, who will be ripping past from either left or right to disappear into such-and-such a hole—all of which must be executed with dispatch and finesse. The sheer weight of this burden is such that the picture of what I am supposed to do is poised just at the edge of my consciousness, part of it out over the void waiting to drop off, which would leave the landscape of my mind utterly blank.

It is always a relief when the practice is over, when McCafferty calls us around him and gives his précis of the day, and then says, "All right, everybody up the hill." For me, suddenly the pressure is off, the possibility of my mind going embarrassingly blank is postponed. It is like shutting the office door, with papers heaping the desk within, and with a sigh of pleasure heading off for the weekend.

Helmet

This afternoon after practice I walked up the hill to the gymnasium with George Hall, a big blond-haired lineman with a pale face that the sun reddens and blisters, especially the end of his nose. Both of us have problems with our helmets. He helped me off with mine today, heaving at it, and then he got his palms under the earflaps and pushed up, practically lifting me off the ground with his effort, the people around staring as the two of us staggered around. Finally it came away, past my ears which burned as I rubbed them. Hall hasn't ever found a helmet which fits properly; every time he hits someone two small holes are dug into his forehead, and soon they open up and bleed in two lines like rust stains that run down each side of his face onto his jersey. We decided that we're not going to look like much after a while, since I'm losing my ears and his forehead is slowly being chipped away.

Sullivan

July 22   Dan Sullivan was the offensive guard who would be facing Karras on that Sunday afternoon nearly a month off. I couldn't resist asking whether he thought he could contain him. It was a personal matter, I said.

Sullivan grinned and said that it was a personal matter with him too. "You know, Alex is quite different from the brute-force guys," he went on. "As you know, he's lighter than many of us offensive guys, but he has extremely long arms, tremendous strength in the upper part of his body, and a low center of gravity. I've never known a guy who's quicker. He gives you a little shuffle with his belly which gets you committed just ever so slightly, and he's flipped you. Honest to goodness, I don't know the best way to block Alex. Perhaps the right way is to stay away from him and challenge him to run over you. If you get too close to him, he's going to flip you right over; that's the end of you, and he's almost surely going to get to sit on top of the quarterback. Which is neither pleasant for the quarterback nor for the offensive guard."

We looked at each other.

"Well, I wish you terrific luck when the time comes," I said.

"I know you do," Sullivan said.

The Press

July 26 The four or five reporters assigned to training camp stand on the sidelines, looking out at us. I feel awkward about them, because theirs is more properly my fraternity and I should be standing among them writing notes in a little loose-leaf notebook that folds back on itself. I've heard that one or two of them are resentful; here they've been coming out to practice for years, restricted in their movements, hardly allowed to put a toe across the sidelines onto the field, and now this guy has come down from New York to loll around out there in forbidden sanctuaries, actually wearing a Colt uniform and privy to what they have always been denied. It was downright unfair. Hell, it was only the first or second time the guy had ever *been* to Baltimore, and he probably thinks of the place as a nickel town, a Washington suburb, and what makes him so special? And it is not only on the playing field that this interloper enjoys extended privileges, but throughout the camp—the team meetings, the evening outings down to Oz and Jenny's, the poker games, the conversation along the length of the benches in the locker room, and even in the dining room where the press had to sit at its table over by the windows and wonder what Ted Hendricks and Tom Matte and this New York guy are roaring with laughter about as they pick at their cups of fruit salad.

In fact, however, what is going on out of earshot of the reporters is almost invariably of no consequence whatsoever. Out on the practice field the groups of helmeted Colts standing around a coach listening to him are almost weak-kneed with boredom; sometimes, for lack of anything else to do, Tom Matte will take a long stem of grass and, reaching around behind a player's neck, inserts it in the helmet earhole on the far side, very deftly, so the player thinks a bug has crawled in there—or worse, a bee—and he jumps and shouts, and maybe slaps his helmet hard; the best reaction, of course, is if he rips off the helmet and looks inside to see what's there. I have been a constant victim. I wear my helmet throughout practice, because it is too painful to my ears to take it off, and I am in dread of being sent to do something by Coach McCafferty and being unable to put it on.

Tom Matte did this trick with the grass so often that if he was in the vicinity, he was immediately suspect. After twitching his head, the victim would turn and say sharply, "Goddamn it, Tom, cut that out!"

"Cut what out?"

"Cut out putting that damn thing in my damn ear."

"What damn thing in what damn ear?"

The reporters along the sidelines cannot tell what has caused the curious flurry of movement among the players and are too far away to hear the scintillating exchange of words. Is a fight about to start? Why are they all staring at Matte? What was being discussed out there? Perhaps a new-fangled play that Coach McCafferty had suddenly decided to install (which would be big news); or perhaps the personal peccadilloes of one of the players were being talked about (just the sort of thing they could use to juice up next morning's column). If they could only hear! They tap their pencils against their pads and gaze enviously at the clumsy-looking quarterback standing out there with the others, who just at that moment has cracked himself on the side of his helmet, spinning crazily to look behind him. "What's with that goof?" one of them says. "He just hit himself in the helmet. Geez, you'd think they'd at least give a *normal* the chance he's getting. Kee-rist!"

Collision

July 27 Today I watched Bubba in the scrimmage. Enormous, steatopygic rear high, he waited for the center's snap. Down in his three-point stance, he often rested his free hand on his left knee, which is a bad habit, like a fighter cocking a fist back on his chest rather than keeping it forward and poised, and Coach Sandusky kept yelling at him to keep the hand free and ready. "Git that hand off there, Bub, god*damn* it!" Bubba bridles under that sort of needling, and perhaps he's a better ballplayer for it —smoldering and taking his anger out on the fellow opposite. I did not notice who this was—a rookie probably, because he was having an awful time containing Bubba. Toward the end of the scrimmage Bubba got to Tom Matte as the halfback was trying to sweep the end, and put him down in a quick convulsion of movement, rather like that last second of quick flurry and stillness when a big cat pulls an antelope down on the African plain. As Matte fell, there was a sharp popping crack and he screamed—a quick abrupt *yell* that froze everyone in his tracks. On the field it was suddenly quiet, as if a door had been slammed on a noisy party, and then we heard Matte's high giggle and he said "Holy Christ!" and we saw him get up and test his knee and we knew that he was all right. What had happened was that the scar tissue and adhesions from his knee operation the winter before had popped under the stress of Bubba's tackle, but it was harmless, like the cracking of the spine of a stiff book being opened.

Such incidents, especially in a scrimmage, and the terror they invoke, make it impossible to forget the considerable risks the coaches put their charges to every time the order is for pads and contact and the players come down the hill to slam at each other. Perhaps injury is inevitable, but it is always such a mockery when it happens in practice during the training season.

Last night, lying in the blue room and thinking about the violence of the scrimmage that afternoon, Colt versus Colt, I remembered a story Dick LeBeau, the Detroit Lion corner-back, had told me when the two of us were standing on the sidelines watching a scrimmage in which Karras had sent Mel Farr, the Lions' star running back, hobbling to the sidelines with an injury. "Crazy times, isn't it?" LeBeau had said. "The coaches sending in these superstars from the same team to belt at each other. You know why? I'll tell you the real reason. You remember the story about the fellow walking along a country lane and he sees his neighbor plowing up a field with a pair of beautiful breed bulls—not the kind of work that bulls like that are used to, and the plow is yawing all over the lot and these bulls are ripping up the field something fierce? The fellow asks, 'Man, what are you doing that for?' 'Well,' the neighbor says, 'I just wanted to show these fellows that *life is not all play.*' That's the principle behind putting in these great players from the same team and having them beat the hell out of each other; it's just to show them that life is not all play . . ."

The Garbage Man

"The Garbage Man" is the nickname Alex Karras invented for Tom Matte, because of his infuriating aptitude in picking up an extra yard here, or a couple of yards there, just enough in most cases to grind out a first down. Matte never broke loose on a flashy long run . . . it was just this dumpy sort of thing. I had a particular empathy for him. Though the comparison might seem invidious, for him too the most challenging time of his career had come when he was plucked out of his humdrum existence—the halfback position where he did his garbage work—and lofted into the glamor of quarterbacking when both John Unitas and Gary Cuozzo, the backup quarterback, were injured, and Ed Brown became ineligible. It was a position quite foreign to him. He had none of the characteristics of the true quarterback; his voice was high and squeaky, his build was squarish, and a round baby face peeked out of his helmet. But the Colts simply had no one else. To his credit he had a football mind of the highest quality and a fine understanding of the voluminous Colt playbook. It was a proper move, for he quarterbacked the team through two extraordinary games at the end of the 1965 season that caught the imagination and fancy of the country—winning 20–17 over the Rams to tie the Packers for first place in the Western Conference, but losing the last, a sudden-death thriller, to Green Bay in the play-offs.

I asked Matte about this experience, feeling this kinship, and he understood why I was so interested and tolerated my questions. Besides, he likes talking about it, since it had been a good time for him. He told me that he'd hardly had time to worry about taking over. When Unitas hurt his knee, which elevated Cuozzo, Matte knew that he was next in line, but this possibility seemed so remote that it was all a joke; on the practice field he told Cuozzo that if he tried to come off the field hurt, he was going to beat him back on with a stick. Cuozzo laughed because he too never seriously believed that a team could lose two quarterbacks in a week.

But it happened. In the next game, against the Green Bay Packers, Cuozzo separated his shoulder and Matte took over the club.

"Christ, what did you do?" I asked. "What was the first play you called?" We were sitting on the embankment looking down on the practice field.

"There was a time-out on the field," Matte recalled. "As I ran out to take over, I decided that right off I'd try a pass and really surprise the Packers who reckoned, quite correctly, that I'm not a very . . . um . . . efficient passer, you might say. So when I got out there I looked over at Jimmy Orr and asked, 'Jimmy, watcha have over there?' He said, 'Well, I'm on the wide side of the field and I doubt you can throw the ball out that far. So the answer is that I don't have anything for you.' Then I looked at Raymond Berry, the other receiver. 'Raymond, do you have anything?' "

"What does that mean exactly?" I interrupted. " 'Do you have anything?' "

Matte explained that sometimes a receiver will come back to the huddle and say to the quarterback, "Listen, I've got a side line at ten yards. The guy's playing off me; right now it's open."

"Those were the words of wisdom I was hoping to hear from at least *one* of those great receivers. But not at all. Berry said *he* didn't have anything, either. Then he said, 'Why don't you call the Ride Thirty-eight.' So I asked him why he was suggesting *that* play. 'Hell,' I said, 'that play runs on the other side of the field from you. You don't have to do anything. You don't even have to *block*.' He said, 'I don't feel like blocking right now.' "

Listening to Matte, I made a clucking sound of sympathy. "What a nightmare," I said. "Do you suppose they'll say that sort of thing to me at Ann Arbor? 'Sorry, George, we just don't feel like blocking for you.' Jesus."

Matte laughed, and then said that actually what Berry had said wasn't indicative: in fact, the offensive line had performed so well on pass plays that he had never once been dropped by the opposition during those two games.

I was relieved. He looked at me clinically. "You know, you've got some advantages," he said. "You're tall, which is good in a quarterback. I'm relatively short, and I always remember that when I quarterbacked against the Rams, with that huge Fearsome Foursome front four they have—all of them six-eight and six-nine—after I'd hunched down behind our center I couldn't *see* over them into the defensive secondary. Even when they lowered into their stances their eyes were at my level, looking at me out over their helmet bars, and they were growling and snorting like the cattle they are. Frankly, it scared the hell out of me."

I asked him if having to be the leader had changed his

character during those games. "Did you become authoritarian?"

Matte shook his head. "I think the opposite happens. Whoever the quarterback is, the club takes on something of his character. In my case, I'm a jovial type—'the fat little quarterback,' they called me—and when I took over, there was more levity, more of a relaxed feeling around our club than any of us could remember."

The disturbing thought crossed my mind that if indeed one did inflict one's character on the team, then during my quarterbacking stint the Colts would become a skittish and frightened group, shying away from contact and generally behaving like sheep in a thunderstorm.

Matte rocked back and forth, laughing. "I'll tell you something," he said. "I don't think you'll be around out there long enough to infect anyone."

The Playbook

July 28 They still play jokes, of course. Today I left my playbook on top of a filing cabinet in the back of the classroom rather than carrying it back to my room, and when I came in for the evening class it was gone. I looked behind the cabinet where perhaps it might have fallen and then sat down feeling low, envying everyone else opening and shutting the big blue books with the Colt insignia on the front, and putting play sheets in and snapping the big clasp-rings shut.

McCafferty came in and after making a few announcements he looked at me in the back of the room and inquired, "Where's your playbook?"

I mumbled that it had disappeared. A few of the players in the front of the class turned in their seats to look at me. McCafferty held up my book. It had been "found," he said, by one of the coaches, and that would be a fifty-dollar fine.

I could have protested or made a flip remark, but the playbook is traditionally such a serious symbol in the football fraternity that it was best to let the matter drop. The book was passed back to me. It felt good to have it again—the security blanket which meant that you truly belonged. When a player is cut from the squad, the first request is that he hand in his playbook, a gesture as awful and ceremonial as the ripping off of an officer's epaulets when he is being cashiered on the parade ground.

Actually, my own book is not worth much. The average book has two or three hundred different plays, but the Baltimore coaches had only entrusted me with six sheets describing and diagraming the plays I would be attempting. I suppose they never could quite dismiss my past with the Detroit team. It always struck me as such an odd notion that the coaches could imagine me furtively calling Joe Schmidt from a phone booth.

"Hey, Joe, I've got it."

"You've got what? Who's this?"

"Is this Joe Schmidt of the Lions?"

"Yeah. Who are you?"

"Well, maybe I'd better not say, because this line could be tapped, but where I am is in a phone booth on the Harrisburg Pike and I've got a *Baltimore Colt playbook* in here with me. Have you got a pencil?"

"Hello, hello, who is it, anyway . . . the connection's bad," etc. etc.

"Joe, let me start with a play called the Eighty-four Air Hook. It's in the game plan for Sunday. Under the diagram are these instructions: 'Zip, basic to flanker; ind. to Cut End. FB check pattern.' Got it? Do you want me to describe the diagram?"

"Who is this? Why are you talking that way?"

"I'm whispering. Joe, I've got it here in *front of me . . .*"

Dave Lee, sitting next to me, sometimes slides across a play sheet from his book so I'll have something new to look at while the coaches drone on. The diagrams with their X's and O's are simple enough, and so are the arrows indicating the running assignments, but the notes accompanying each diagram are more difficult. For example, here are the following instructions directed to the fullback on a play called the "84

Fan Dig": "Check Weakside plugger and go. If LB'r is in a walkaway position, go right now." And here is what the half-back on the weakside end is instructed to do on a play called the "Flank Right Split Motion 40." "You are responsible for the WSLB'r; if lined up inside call 'GAP!' and block down. If not, M cut and hook up."

Esoteric stuff. The only phrase which sticks to my mind like a burr is "check weakside plugger and go." As I sit swaying back against the classroom wall during these sessions, I have an occasional fantasy that a rookie will come rushing up during practice and shout, "Man, my mind's scrambled; what do I do on the Fan Dig," and I clear my throat easily and say, "No sweat, man. Just check the weakside plugger."

In truth, it is difficult to gauge how helpful information of this sort would be to the opposition. Far more valuable, obviously, would be the play list, which is a carefully selected group of plays designed to take advantage of the particular weaknesses of the other team. Karl Sweetan, who was a Detroit backup quarterback for a while, and was then traded around the leagues, finally ending up with the Los Angeles Rams, tried to sell his Ram playbook to the New Orleans Saints for $2,000. He was caught at it, but the prosecution finally dropped the case because it was too difficult to determine the value of a play-book. Paul Brown, the Cincinnati Bengals coach, said that the books were worthless, and that any of his players who were leaving the club for a coaching job were welcome to them.

Sweetan! It would have raised a laugh if I had replied to McCafferty that I suspected Sweetan had snuck into camp and filched my book. He was quite a character. I remember meeting him when I once went back to visit the Detroit players at training camp. He was reputed to have a lively private life reminiscent of Bobby Layne's. One lunch, as I was coming through the serving line in the dining hall, Sweetan tapped me on the shoulder and asked me if I would do him a favor. "Sure," I said.

"Could you carry a tray of food down to the boiler room of Page Hall?"

"A tray of food?"

"If they see me carrying the food out of here, they'll be

suspicious. But *you* can get away with it; they'll think you're carrying it back to your room."

"What's down in the boiler room?"

"Well, I've got a girl there. I got some bread and cheese down to her last night."

He loaded up a tray and gave me directions. I took it out, walking self-consciously across the quadrangle lawn, through an entryway, and down into a long gallery-like cellar lit by a series of dim light bulbs. "Hello?" I called tentatively.

The girl emerged from behind a cluster of thick asbestos-coated pipes. "I heard you coming. I thought you were the superintendent. You gave me a terrific fright," she said. "Christ, I'm hungry."

"At your service," I said.

She was very pretty. A red ribbon tied her hair back in a thick cluster behind her neck. She took the tray and turned for a packing case by the boiler. She wore blue jeans that were dusty in the seat.

"Did Karl give you any messages?" she asked.

"No."

"What a man to be stuck on," she said. "He's a big raft of laughs, but he's not what you'd call dependable. He could forget, you know, and just leave me to waste away down here. It's not very interesting. It's damp. Things drip," she said. "But I stick around. He's very persuasive."

Whatever his powers, Sweetan would have had a hard time unloading a playbook as skimpy as my Colt book. The only interesting thing about it is that someone had used it last year, but it's hard to tell who because the hints left in the book, on the paper of the clip-in folders, are thin. I think about him occasionally. He was probably a flanker or a tight end because on one page under the heading "Cuts" he lists the nomenclature of such pass-receivers' patterns as "O.H. comeback, C.I. Max, Q and T.O," and draws diagrams to show each of these. There are other notes of a more personal nature: telephone numbers; a drawing of a house, simple as a child's, with two windows on either side of the door, and smoke coming out of the chimney.

There is also a small shopping list: 1. *Teddy Bear*   2. *Ball*. Presumably a family man. Out of football now? Or perhaps in some distant training camp, having been traded, he is sitting in a classroom, the hum of summer outside the window, making new lists of that club's pass patterns, and maybe a toy or two to be reminded of.

I could not resist it. In my playbook I wrote in a tremulous hand: "I am very very scared. I do not like it here. I am involved in a sad case of mistaken identity. I am a violin teacher."

That will give someone pause one day.

The Oklahoma

July 30 Trouble today. Coach McCafferty announced at the morning meeting that the first practice session would conclude with the Oklahoma Drill—at which news a sustained groan went up from the team, many of them rocking back in their chairs with dismay. When everyone had quieted down, McCafferty went on to say that the drill would be filmed from atop a portable scaffolding so that each player could be graded on his performance. "I don't want any holding back—you're to go full out." Everybody looked grim.

Sitting with my back against the rear wall, I must have looked simply puzzled, as if someone had suggested a mysterious parlor game. ("All right, everybody; we're going to play Democracy.") I leaned over to Dave Lee. "What on earth is the Oklahoma Drill?"

"Don't worry about it," he said. "The specialists aren't involved. It's too damned dangerous. Don't do any volunteering. Always remember: 'Think specialist.' "

The Oklahoma Drill turned out to be an invention of Bud Wilkinson's, adapted from a play called the Oklahoma Dive —a drill exercise in which a pair of tackling dummies are set up about six feet apart and between them, facing each other, two linemen square away just as they would on the line of scrimmage.

Behind the offensive player, five or six yards back, a running back is poised, and at a coach's signal *"Hut!"* he receives a handoff and runs full-tilt forward, hopefully over or past the defensive man who is wrestling with the player opposite. The back's running room is restricted by the two tackling dummies, and the trick is to read which way the offensive lineman is playing the defensive man opposite and to make one's cut accordingly. It is a brutal exercise for all three participants, especially for the defensive player, who must fend off the blocks of his opposite number and also try to make the tackle on the running back.

There are a number of NFL players who look back on the Oklahoma Drill ruefully—the most famous of them being Tucker Frederickson, the New York Giant fullback, who damaged his knee badly during the drill (which the Giants called "The Nutcracker") and was never the same player thereafter. Randy Minniear, Frederickson's teammate, had his leg broken. But the drill delights the crowd, of course, sitting on the slopes surrounding the practice field, lolling back on beach blankets, the girls wearing straw hats with embroidered designs, and such messages as "Hi" stitched into them, and the men in Bermuda shorts and fishermen's hats with long visors, leaning forward and chewing gum rapidly when contact is made out on the field.

I remained as removed from the Oklahoma as the fans on their beach blankets, standing at the perimeter of the players and peering over the shoulder pads of a teammate. The barbaric nature of football is never more graphically evident than when the action between two or three of the linemen is isolated—the grunts, the self-goading cries that erupt from within the helmets —with everyone standing around as if watching bull mastiffs in a pit. I would have none of it. But then one of the coaches looked over and asked, "Hey George, do you want to try it?" and I saw the helmets turning, and the grins, and the players I had been standing with step back so that I was all alone, everyone looking at me, and I said as follows:

"Hell, yes."

Once declared—by some stranger in residence within me to whom I had not been introduced—there was no means by which I could gracefully withdraw. It would have been too embarrassing to announce that I had changed my mind. So I stepped into position. I never found out who the offensive guard in front of me was; in his three-point stance he settled into the anonymity of a wide stern, and the reach of his back under a numberless jersey with the tail half out and the smooth surface of his helmet were all I could see of him as he dug in for his charge. Opposite him, though, looking at me through the bars of his helmet, was Billy Newsome, the first reserve of the Colt front four, who weighed 250 pounds and was just on the verge of being first string himself.

At McCafferty's signal, I launched myself toward the tackling dummies and the two men between them heaving at each other, Newsome throwing his man around and staring at me as I came at him. I was moving somewhat tentatively, by subsequent accounts, like a man tiptoing up to look over a high fence. Newsome reached around his blocker and collected me. I felt his strength as I was picked up and shaken, and I recall sensing, in that instant, a power so kinetic that I did not associate it with human potential but rather with something mechanical and quick, like a huge spring. I was flung down, discarded, and the ball slipped loose and skittered across the ground. A faint sound of laughter drifted through the earholes of my helmet as I heard McCafferty call out, "Next, next," as if to get on with the drill so that the unprofessional mess that had just occurred could be scooped up and removed.

Humiliation settled in, and also a rising indignation at my performance. Shaming! I scrambled to my feet. Possessed once more, I heard my inner voice carping that I would have to vindicate myself. I got back into line to do it again. I could scarcely believe what I was hearing myself say ("Well, we're just going to have to try that until you get it right") or that my legs were moving me into the line of fullbacks and halfbacks shuffling forward to the instant of their commitment—for all the world, some sensible part of me imagined, like captors being herded toward the pirate's plank.

When I got to the head of the line, I saw that this time the defensive player was Ray May, the first-string linebacker, substantially lighter than Billy Newsome, for sure, but hardly a slouch at the destructive impulse required by his position. Again I did not see who the offensive player was.

McCafferty was surprised to see me back, poised to go as if in the starting blocks, and his eyebrows arched. At the "*Hut!*" I tucked the ball under my arm and launched myself forward once again, lifting my knees higher this time, and I ran those eight yards at a determined gallop, urging myself forward with a thin and barely audible nasal whinny. Ray May held his position against the offensive man's push, and side-stepping him just as I passed the tackling dummy he hit me from the side; the breath was knocked out of me with a rush, the ball bounded away, and I was driven down at a trajectory much the same as if May had thrown a spear into the ground immediately in front of him. The first point of impact was my right thumb which, with my weight bearing down on it, was driven back into the hand. The pain was instant. I sat up and looked at my hand. The rear joint of the thumb was pushing up the skin on the back of my hand in a high mound, like an extra finger trying to break out. Eyes staring in horror, I slapped at it, as if swatting at a grotesque insect, and drove the thumb back into place.

I got up; I ran over to Ed Block, the trainer, and held my hand out to him as if I were carrying a package. "The thumb came out!" I called wildly. Heads turned on the embankment, spectators craning to see.

Block is quite deaf, especially in one ear, and he said, "No, it's no fun."

"Thumb! Thumb!"

He took my proffered hand and began to knead and test the thumb. "Dislocated, most likely, maybe broken." He took a roll of gauze tape from his hip pocket and began to bind the thumb fast. "I'll drive you up to the hospital and we'll get it x-rayed."

I sat next to him in the car, uncomfortable under the glances of the Westminster pedestrians looking in to see an adult decked out in football togs, his shoulder pads enormous in the front seat.

"What did you do that for, anyway?" Block asked.

"Oh Christ, I don't know," I said. "Lee and O'Brien have been telling me, 'Think specialist.'" I looked at my thumb. "It's on my throwing hand, and the game in Ann Arbor is only three weeks off. Jesus!"

"I've never seen a quarterback do the Oklahoma," Block said.

"Something gets into me," I said. "In fact, it's worse than that. Some*body* gets into me. He roams around in there. He sits down at desks and rearranges the papers and dictates these lunatic orders into the dictaphone. *He* was the one who shouted out 'Hell, yes!' when McCafferty asked if I'd like to do the Oklahoma Drill. It wasn't me. This guy inside me just opened up a window and yelled out with a bullhorn. He's going to be the death of me. He wanders around. He goes to directors' meetings, where everything's all solemn and orderly, and he bursts in and yells things and intimidates the directors and sends them home. He sits in the chair reserved for the Chairman of the Board. He picks up the phone and gives orders to blow up one of the plants—'I want that thing wiped off the face of the earth by next *Tues*day!' That's the sort of person he is. I can almost hear him treading around inside me. Very destructive."

"It's not a doctor you should be seeing," said Block after a long silence. "It's a goddamn exorcist."

Playing Hurt

Tonight Ray May looked into my room and said that he was sorry about the thumb. "Ho, ho," he said sympathetically as he looked at the gauze-enveloped appendage. "Hey, man, I sure didn't mean to jack you up."

I thought it was an odd and rather nice way of putting it—a garage phrase, as if I were up on a hoist for repairs—and told him so.

Later Gordy came by and inspected the thumb. "Shucks," he said derisively. "You're lucky, being a quarterback. Injuries aren't the same for linemen. If a halfback is hurt—oh my! A halfback—they'll rush to take him out of the game. Hell, a halfback can look over at the bench and *act* mournful, and they'll pull him. Receivers, halfbacks, quarterbacks—they're all pampered in practice, especially in contact work, whereas a lineman would be chastised if he ever asked to be pulled. A lineman just doesn't leave a game unless he's been knocked out cold—and even then, they'll stand around and wait for him to wake up. Part of it is the tradition that linemen are tough and can shake anything off; also, of course, a hurt lineman can perform more efficiently at his position than an injured halfback can. I mean, I can pass-protect and block straight forward, and even run interference with a groin pull far better than what a halfback could do if he had an equivalent injury. Linemen just don't get hurt."

I asked Gordy what the worst injury was that he'd played with.

"Let's see." He cocked his head back and looked at the ceiling. "I've played with a dislocated toe. That doesn't sound like much, but for eight games I had to have shots of Novocaine in both sides of the toe and in the bottom of my foot to keep it dead. I've played with a broken hand several times, and many times with broken fingers. I've never bothered with casts for the fingers. The calcium fills in and they'll set eventually. I've played with cracked ribs, and with torn rib cartilage—which hurts much more than a cracked rib, by the way. A pulled groin is awful. Alex had one so bad that even when he coughed he could feel it. He played with it, and I've played with them, too. I've played with chipped elbows. Of course, you always play with pinched nerves or twisted ankles or bad shoulders. I guess the worst for me would be the problem I had with my ear. In one game against Washington, Fred Williams, who was the Redskin tackle I was playing opposite, kept hammering me on the head with his right hand, a head slap, which is a common enough tactic—but in this case it caused the cartilage to tear loose on the inside of my ear and a big blood clot began to form and puff up. That's the way a cauliflower ear starts. Well, I didn't want to walk around with a cauliflower ear, so I had it operated on at the Ford hospital. The doctors put a drainage tube in on a Monday, and when next Sunday came around they wrapped my entire head in bandages smeared with vaseline so that my helmet, which had a special pad inside, could slip on. That was the procedure for about four or five games."

"Anything to get you in there," I said.

"I remember that at the time there was a friend of mine in the hospital who was pretty sick. I went to see him, walking into the hospital covered with so many bandages that I looked like the Spirit of Seventy-six. The nurses jumped when they saw me, like I'd escaped from one of the wards. My friend was lying in bed looking bad. I sat down beside him, and for some reason we started talking about injuries. I went through all the bad hurts I'd had and the operations, and by the time I was finished I was feeling right sorry for myself, and the other fellow, my friend in bed, he was beginning to perk up and feel less sour about things. He began to feel sorry for *me;* he felt we ought to change places, and I should slide into his bed . . .

"Yeah, they'll do anything to get you out there on that field. Once I had this strep throat on a Monday, and I didn't get out of bed or hardly eat until Saturday afternoon. On the morning of the game they filled me with B-complex to give me strength, and Dexedrine to pep me up and keep me alive. We were playing the Colts that day and we beat them, one of the best games we ever had. I played left tackle on the offensive line. During the game it was like being in the twilight zone. Afterwards they took me to the hospital and fed me intravenously because I was so dehydrated; halfway through the bottle I started feeling good—a combination of glucose and Dexedrine and the B-complex and everything. I decided that if I had played in that great game, certainly I could handle the celebration that was going on at Larco's restaurant. So I crept out of the hospital, and when I got to Larco's I walked down the steps and called out, 'Hey, all you guys, I'm here,' and pitched forward like a sack of potatoes and hit the floor out cold. They had to carry me back to the hospital."

"God Almighty."

"I've just been talking about the serious stuff," Gordy

went on, "because of course there are all the superficial injuries. For example, you won't find an offensive lineman who hasn't got a permanent scab on the bridge of his nose from putting his face into the opposite guy's number and getting the helmet bar jammed back onto his nose. Then, I've got scars on all my knuckles and joints—hell, I *have* no knuckles; they've all been hammered flat in the hand-fighting. Sometimes the injuries are weird. Once I got my little finger caught in a guy's shoulder pad, and when he kept running, my finger got laid back alongside my hand."

I cringed in sympathy.

"That's nothing. Superficial. That's what you have," Gordy said, "a superficial injury."

Violence

I have found myself much less at ease with the violence of football than ever before—perhaps because I myself am more fragile and gimpy, and the thumb throbs, but also, I think, because the second time around seems to require that I look at it more clinically and personally. The general temper of the times —the war in Indochina and the vast unrest, tipping over into brutality and rage—is itself so violent that it is impossible to accept the metaphor of football, and its popularity, without wondering whether it reflects some of the country's excesses.

It was very likely tedious for the players to be asked so many questions about violence; it was an obvious part of their business, after all, and they had come to terms with it. It was a fact of their lives, and they must have thought my nagging persistence in asking what they thought about it much like a busboy in a seafood restaurant who is worried about the future of the trout swimming in the glass tank.

Tonight I was sitting out on the dormitory stoop with Bill Lasky, one of the linebackers. He looked at my thumb and said, Well, it was too bad, but it was the occupational hazard of those who craved violence.

"You went to the well once too often," he said.

"Bill," I said, "since you're always trying to knock some-one's head off, suppose it actually *did* come off and was rolling around on the ground. What would your emotions be?"

"Jesus, man. Well, some people might feel bad, but personally, if it was a clean shot and legal, I couldn't feel *that* bad about it. Deep down inside, I know it's part of the game, and so does the other guy."

"Is there ever a temptation to take an illegal shot at someone just to get him out of the game?"

"Sometimes, but of course it's much better to hit a guy legally, as hard as you can, and if you happen to injure him you feel okay because you've been able to do it cleanly. But if you're twenty or thirty yards away from the play and take a cheap shot at a guy, a clothesline, and down he goes, knocked out or injured—well, that's one of those incidents which you creep away from; you feel rotten inside. Of course, sometimes you get so worked up that you can't help yourself; you just take that shot. It's just as Mike Curtis says: the football field is the only place where it's socially acceptable for him to go around hitting people."

"What's the reaction of a player's teammates if they see him take a cheap shot at someone?"

"His teammates will always stick up for him, but they all know that one day he'll get his. If a guy on your own team gets a cheap shot, the coaches will run the film back and forth in the classroom, no one saying anything, but everybody's filing it away in their mind who the other player is, and his number. So a player who delivers a cheap shot walks off the field a little sheepishly, a little guilty—and very worried."

The screen door swung open behind us, and Bill Curry came out and sat down. I said that we had been chatting about violence, and that Lasky had been talking about illegal shots.

"Football's *supposed to* be performed under the stric-tures of rules." Curry said. "I remember a play against Alan Page of Minnesota. He was hanging on to one of our backs, and I belted him loose, and the guy with the ball went on for a long gain. I thought it was an excellent block; Page had to be helped from the field—ribs probably—but he was back after a few plays and I wouldn't have thought a thing of it if I hadn't seen in the Tuesday films that I had just about murdered him: it looked like a playground mugging. Our runner had already broken away, and I hit Page while he was lying on the ground. Very illegal. So I sat down and wrote Alan a letter and apologized."

"A letter?" I said in surprise.

"Did you ever get a reply?" Lasky asked.

Curry shrugged. "It probably surprised him, getting that letter."

"Bill, do you actually consider yourself a violent man?" I asked.

"I'd like to think of myself as a gentle person," Curry replied, "but I *am* violent. You couldn't be a lineman in pro football and not be violent. Everyone has this same facet somewhere in their personality. It's often exposed—the player in a controlled situation venting his hostility on the field, and the fan up in the stands, with his yelling, doing just the same thing . . . and for both of them the effect is cathartic."

"Would you search it out if you didn't play football—I mean, would you look for fights in bars?" I asked.

"I used to get into fights in grammar school, but I got beat up enough to stop that. No, I don't think I'd get into fights in bars, because that's a question of maturity and knowing that no good can come of it."

"What about the off-season? Do you find yourself getting edgy and wanting to hit people?"

Curry laughed. "My wife is dreading my giving up football, because—and I hope she's kidding—she doesn't know exactly what I'm going to be like when I can't hit anymore."

"Does someone take naturally to this concept of violence?"

"There are two kinds of people," Curry said. "Some kids love to hit right from the start; it's just natural to them. I wasn't like that at all; in fact, I hated the game. I went out there because at my school you were a sissy if you didn't play; I didn't see any point in getting in anyone's way, until the coaches embarrassed me to the point that I began to do it. I learned that if I hit the other fellow harder than he hit me, I came off better, and then I began to enjoy it."

Bill Lasky stirred and said that he had really loved the contact right from the beginning. But he had made a bad mistake: he had started out as a running back, which meant that he was being hit rather than hitting. He had taken his lickings through high school and college, but now as a pro he had shifted to linebacker, where he was dishing out punishment as fast as he could to make up for lost time.

Had there ever been a great football player who didn't enjoy violence, I asked.

Curry grinned. A lot of the great running backs disliked contact and avoided it skillfully, which was why they were great, he said. Of course there were other great running stars who loved contact; it was all a matter of style.

He paused. Something had been disturbing him. "Look," he said, "when I was talking about violence before, and the need for it, and what it's done for me, I was talking about *football* violence. I'm very much opposed to the sort of violence that's going on in Vietnam now, or in the college streets, or the ghettos, but in the context of the football field I think violence can be healthy."

He looked at my bandaged thumb. "Well, *reasonably* healthy," he added.

Critique

August 1   At the meeting this afternoon we were showed films of our performances in the Oklahoma drills, the whole series spliced together. The entire team stayed in the classroom to watch them, and to expedite matters the critiques on the three players involved in each drill were delivered simultaneously—a strange babble of sound through which the defensive tackle, say, would distinguish his coach crying at him, "Sam, you're letting that guy *dictate* you," while the guard would hear *his* coach complimenting him on his charge, and the running back would be lambasted for not taking proper advantage of his offensive man's moves: "*Cut* off that block, damn it, Tom, you're loafing." Then the next group would appear on the screen and the voices would rise once again in unison. Toward the end of the film three figures appeared on the screen, but this time there was no comment and I realized with a start that it was the episode in which I had lost the use of my thumb. Sure enough; my efforts as a running back *did* look like a man tiptoeing up to peer over a hedge.

"Any comment?" said McCafferty.

There was none.

Evening Talk

August 3 (A transcript of an actual classroom dissertation— with Red Miller, the offensive line coach, in front of the screen on which is shown the diagram of a play. This is the type of thing we listen to, evening after evening, the chairs squeaking under the weight of the players, and outside the distant shouts of students out on the quadrangle lawn throwing frisbees)

MILLER: Men, does everyone have the Fifty-two–Fifty-three Draw in their notebook? This is a new play we're going to take on tonight. Pay attention, because this is a timed-up play;

there's a little talent and technique involved here, so let's get it now. So far in our playbook we have the Fifty-four and the Fifty-five Halfback-Fullback Lead. This play is our draw off the flank formation. Now as it is drawn up here, we'll be in our flank formation. We like to run this play against the four-three defense with the middle guard deep. When the middle guard is deep, we want a good quick set off the ball. You've got to be a good actor and a good faker. Quick set off the ball, and then we go into our regular trap action off the set. Center: take that good set and seal back on the backside tackle. Guard: set, and you're trapping the first man on the strong side. Now here is the key block, right *here*. Tackle: you can't be too late or too early on the block. You have to set and go . . . that is the strong side tackle. Don't pop out; set, and here you're coming down to clear off the middle linebacker. Now the two blocks here are combination blocks. If he sets too quick and pops back, the middle guard will read it and will be up in the middle before the tackle can clean it up. So you have to time it . . . set, and block. Tackle: set, and come down in here on that middle linebacker. We'll area-block the backside, and we'll pop it up in there in the middle. It's a fullback draw. It would be a good play for Bulaich, and it might even be one of the plays Plimpton will call with our team when he's in there on a scrimmage. ("Gulp!") Now if they go into an odd defense, our center, if he can't get the block back, will call "straight" against the over-strong and the under. If you can get the block back, if it's off set, then center, you get the block back and keep the trap on. If you can't, just call it there. The worst you can get on any front is a one-on-one situation. You got that now?

Now, while that play has averaged for us four yards a carry, we want to make it better. Every play has got to be better this year. We want five yards a carry from this play. It's a timed-up play, and it's going to take a lot of practice out there on the field. Now are there any questions? You got it? If it's an over, what do you call now?

CHORUS: Straight.

MILLER: Straight! And then the snap, big man on big man. The uncovered guard on the middle linebacker. You might have to come around on the wheel block, but we'll get that part out on the field.

QUERY: When the MLB drops off, do you want us to come over to the strong side or stay?

MILLER: We'll have to drop. Come back and wheel up the middle on the MLB. Okay?

QUERY: You want a set and then attack that defense, or do you want us to go after them right away?

MILLER: This has got to be a set. We want a quick set off the ball, so we'll get this defensive tackle reading pass. Make that hit, come up, and then we'll trap him, and then you (*to the right guard*) get an inside-out look on that end. Of course, a stunt, a twist or something like that, can hurt us on the play, but we hope we can attack that four-three defense with this drop. Now, another thing: center, if the MLB crawls up in here and they got tackles out with the MLB up strong, then we're going to have a straight call because we'll never be able to come down that line and get him with that tackle. Just call straight, and we'll divide the hole. If you take a set step and go after the MLB, we've got a real nice play in there. Okay? All right now, and when we go out let's have some good time and let's run that football tomorrow. Okay?

Girls

After an evening class of this kind, the Colt players sit on the entry stoops of the dormitory in the twilight and watch the Western Maryland summer school students throwing frisbees and footballs up and down the quadrangle lawns. The young males play with enormous intensity, attempting catches that require leaps or long sprawls, obviously aware that they are being watched by the great Colt athletes, who look out at them as bored as lions peering sleepily across the veldt. In front of the dormitory across the way, the girl students collect in small groups, giggling sharply, leaning their lovely heads in on each other to gossip, their long polished hair falling forward in bells. Occasionally, one of them comes halfway across the lawn, the frisbees and footballs sailing around her head, and stares unabashedly at the players, who lean forward just perceptibly and rumble in their throats. There is a very strict non-fraternization rule; an imaginary line runs down the middle of the quadrangle lawn, and neither the students nor the football players are supposed to cross it to socialize on the other side.

But last evening a girl kept on coming, right up to the front of the stoop where I was sitting with some of the Colts, trying to imitate their arch superiority. The girl said, "Hey." We all looked at her, astonished. She was looking directly into my eyes. "I've got something for you," she said, holding out a box tied with kitchen string. I stumbled to my feet. I said, "Oh, well," and I stepped down and walked her quickly away from the group; feeling their eyes, and knowing that they were working up remarks to make, I hurried her along, one hand under her elbow, so that her shoes slipped on the gravel walk. "Hey," she said. "I just have some cookies for you."

I slowed down; we were out of earshot.

"You're terrifically full of impestuosity," she said. "Wow!" She laughed. She was very young, and wore pale Levis and a light-colored man's shirt tucked in by a wide belt with a big circular buckle. I was the only one of the Colts she could imagine cooking a batch of cookies for, she said.

"Oh?"

She laughed again. The twin rubber bands of her braces showed at either side of her mouth. "Have you ever walked down on the golf course?" she asked. We meandered along. I held the box of cookies by the string.

The golf course bordered one side of the campus. "This is the twelfth hole," she said. "This is where they 'do it.' You've never heard of the twelfth hole?" She seemed genuinely puzzled. "I mean, wow! You must have been born yesterday. This is where everybody comes down with their blankets, and they 'do it.' I have a friend who has a room on the corner of her dorm, and she can actually *see* the twelfth green from her window. She says she sees the wildest things. It's really quite gross. She invited me to come watch."

"Did you see anything?" I was intrigued.

"I drew a blank," she said wildly. "It had to happen to me, natch! I looked through her field glasses—they're about twelve-power—and all I saw was Mr. Rabinowitz. It was getting dark, but he was sitting there on the grass, thinking and occasionally writing something in a notebook. Perhaps he was writing poetry. He teaches the piano. No one else came; Mr. Rabinowitz probably scared them off. It was terribly frustrating."

We continued across the fairways. I asked her what she was studying.

"Social relations," she said. "But I'm going to shift. I want to study Chinese. The real reason I want to study Chinese is to see the expression on Daddy's face when I tell him. He's always asking me what I'm going to major in. You know, this very bored voice at the breakfast table when I come home on vacation: 'Christina, I don't suppose you've come to any decision about your major . . .' and this time I'll say, 'Well, Daddy, I've decided to major in Chink.' It will drive him right up the wall; he's a terrific anti-Communist. He'll think I've been corrupted by some sinister Chinese commissar. He might just drop dead when he hears, right there at the breakfast table."

We had reached a circular bandstand set among a grove of trees. We sat on a bench. The air was thick and sultry, and almost as soon as we were seated, mosquitoes, heavy and lazy, began to float around us, the thin whine of their excitement quite audible.

"God Almighty, these mosquitoes . . ." I said.

Christina said, "Just about everybody who comes out on the golf course—y'know, to 'do it,' or just to walk around—well, they absolutely souse themselves with bug spray. Do you know the bug spray that comes in a greenish can? That's the kind that smells sort of lemony. It's sort of groovy. The other kind comes in an orange can that has a bug lying on his back with his feet up in the air, who is dead, and that spray tastes sort of *blah*. Did you know T. S. Eliot?" she asked abruptly.

"No."

". . . *measuring out lives in teaspoons,*" she said. "Hey, that reminds me. I've got this absolutely fierce exam tomorrow." The two of us rose. The mosquitoes were almost as thick as mist.

We started up toward the college. Just before we got to the twelfth green she stopped. "Sssh. Do you see anyone?"

"No."

"Hey, would you do me a big favor?" A faint odor of soap drifted off her, or perhaps it was the "blah" bug spray.

"Sure."

"You won't be embarrassed?"

"I don't think so."

"Well, I want to meet Jim O'Brien."

"Who?"

"You know, the Colt place-kicker. He's neat. I'm sort of desperate to meet him. You could arrange it, couldn't you?"

"Couldn't you do it yourself?" I asked. "Every evening he sits on the dormitory steps. You could just walk up to him."

"I'm shy." She giggled sharply. "Hey, will you do that?"

"Okay," I said. "I'll tell him about—I'll tell him that you make these terrific cookies."

When I got back to the blue room that evening I opened up the box of cookies and had one or two. They were all right. It was hard to eat them without thinking of the girl unsnapping the rubber bands of her braces and collapsing backwards on her bed to think about Jim O'Brien.

Karras would have been amused by what had happened; so would Gordy. Being linemen, and hefty, and non-Lotharios, they were not as susceptible to the windfalls that came along for the more glamorous players.

Karras had once told me about a gentle-looking girl he met somewhere on a road trip during exhibition season. She looked at him in the hotel lobby and came up and touched him on the bicep with a long finger ("She looked like some kind of ballerina," he had said, "all hands and feet."). She never spoke a word, and Karras figured it was a mistake; she had thought he was someone else. He was woozy from exhaustion, and so he took the elevator up to his floor. She took the next car up, and when he looked over his shoulder she was coming down the corridor, eyes averted. For an instant he thought that it was a coincidence—that she happened to live on the same floor. His heart thumped. He decided to make a gesture to indicate that he was aware of her presence. A wink, perhaps; a suave tilt of the head; a gracious motion of the hand. He turned. The wink was unsuccessful—more of a grimace, he felt, with one whole side of his face constricting so that his lip curled up in what he realized was a leer. The suave tilt of the head was no better —an awkward exaggerated hitch, as if a wayward neck muscle had pulled his head down to his shoulder. The gracious hand gesture was a sharp military salute. Appalled, Karras turned for his room. Inside, he peeked out; she was still coming, walking very slowly, seeming to inspect the numbers on each door. Now what? Should he leave the door ajar, so that when she came by she could glance in and see him standing by the bed, full of nonchalance? No, too obvious. Perhaps plumping up the pillows, looking back over his shoulder with a wide grin. On the other hand, perhaps it was a mistake to leave the door open at all; her sensibilities might be hurt. She should have the option of knocking if she really wanted to come in. He rushed for the door and almost closed it on her fingers.

"Oh," he said. He backed away and she came into the room. Neither of them looked at the other, except in quick furtive glances. She touched the bedspread. She was as thin as a rail. She sat down on the bed, reached down and slid off a shoe.

Karras said, "Carfadrink?" A friend had left a pint of Scotch somewhere—in the bathroom, he thought. She looked at him, puzzled, then flipped off the other shoe and walked in stockinged feet first to the corridor door, which she closed, and then to the light switch, which she clicked off. A shaft of light shone into the room from the bathroom. "I'll take it," he said vaguely. He stepped into the bathroom, closing the door behind him, turned off the light and immediately lost his bearings in the pitch-blackness. As he turned he knocked what sounded like a soap dish into the bathtub. It clattered enormously. "You all right out there?" he called. His hand fluttered across the wall unsuccessfully for the switch. He paused to listen; did he imagine the rustle of her dress coming off? He felt an enormous urge to pee. He did so in the darkness, through a washcloth, squatting awkwardly above the bowl to disguise any sound which might embarrass her. He hummed loudly. "Everything okay?" he called desperately through the door. To wash up, he managed to find the basin, the faucets, and also, just by chance, his friend's bottle of Scotch from which he took a tremendous draught. He worried about his breath. Groping in the darkness, he found his toilet kit; he squeezed some toothpaste on his finger and rubbed vigorously inside his mouth. The Scotch was having an almost immediate effect. He knocked a hairbrush to the floor. He felt dizzy. The darkness was as enveloping as black wool. His head buzzed. His hands searched for the bathroom doorknob. Slowly he turned it. In the soft glow of light from the bedroom window he could see the girl standing by the bed, her hands crossed over her chest. "Breex?" he asked, and stepping toward her, tripped over the doorsill and toppled forward, face down, with a considerable crash; his stomach worked convulsively a few times, and his mind, out of embarrassment more than anything else, suddenly turned off, and he passed out.

"They woke me up the next morning, pounding on the door," Karras recalled crisply. "I looked around and found that she had taken with her a wallet, a watch, a tiepin, and my friend's bottle of Scotch."

John Gordy's best story about linemen's girls involved a party in a Shaker Heights motel where a group of Lions were staying. They were playing in an off-season golf tournament in Cleveland the next day. A number of local girls turned up at the party, some of them wide-eyed at the thought of being around football stars, but others more calculating. Not long after the party started, the prettier girls disappeared with the halfbacks and flankers, leaving a few big-breasted, jolly girls, often giggling sharply, who had a residue of linemen lolling heavily in chairs to pick through. The biggest of the girls chose Gordy; she sat on him, which nearly collapsed his chair, and asked him what his favorite astrological sign was. At two A.M., with the room empty and nothing of the refreshments left except some collapsed potato-chip bags, she persuaded him to go swimming in the motel pool. Gordy announced that was a fine idea except that he had not thought to bring his bathing suit. The girl gave a snuffling laugh, and subsequently, when Gordy stood at the pool's edge, tastefully down to his undershorts, she hooked a finger into the waistband just as he launched himself into a dive; the shorts came away with a rip, and Gordy shot from them clean as a squeezed watermelon seed.

"It wasn't much of a dive," he recalled later. "I sort of curled up and hit the water with a big splash. But that was nothing to the splash *she* made—jaybird-naked, just acres of her hitting the water with a big smack."

The night was warm, with a full moon out, and the two of them gamboled around, snorting with laughter, the girl moving slowly after Gordy, her body an odd ivory texture in the dim underwater lights. The water, from their commotion, sloshed over the gutters out across the lawn. Gordy came up after a dive, grasped the pool's edge, and found himself looking up at the hotel porter, who was staring down at him in awe from behind his spectacles.

"Man, I'm telling you," the porter said, his voice low and hoarse with anxiety. "You must re*move* yourself from there. You must get *out!*"

Gordy said, "But we aren't doing any harm. Everybody's asleep."

"Man, we got an underwater bar down below. It has portholes that look in on the pool underwater, and there's a small crowd down there, and it's getting bigger, and I'm telling you, you must remove yourself from this heah pool, *please!*"

Gordy came up out of the pool with one quick thrashing motion, as if he had been told he had been in there with a school of barracuda. He and the porter between them managed to hoist the girl out. At first she did not understand what was going on, and she pulled playfully at the two of them from the water, nearly dragging them both in. The porter yelped, dug his heels in and hauled.

"What the hell's the matter?" she asked when they finally got her out.

It was explained to her. "So that's where everyone is," she said. "Down in the underwater bar." She did not seem at all abashed. "Let's go down there and have a nightcap. You too," she said to the porter. "You look nervous. You Aquarius? Let's go. We'll have a Pimms Cup. I'm into Pimms Cup."

Gordy, who excused himself and went to bed, said he could never remember a jollier girl. "When I think of Cleveland," he once told me, "I think of Gene Hickerson, who was an offensive guard, and Bill Glass, a helluva defensive end, and the way Jim Brown ran, and then I think of how that whole pool exploded when that fat girl hit the surface."

Parties

August 5   The Colts have certainly turned out to be a gregarious group, and the tedium of training camp has been broken up by a number of social occasions. After the first cut, the team had its traditional rookie show in an abandoned V.F.W. hall on the outskirts of Westminster, a converted Quonset hut with a wood floor and an old piano at one end with half its hammers missing. After a barbecue feast on tables set up under the big oak trees outside, the team trooped in to see the show, carrying big pitchers of beer. There were a number of musical acts. Don Nottingham, the Colts' last draft choice, sang "The Yellow Rose of Texas" in his high piercing voice with considerable élan, because he had been playing very well in practice and had been singled out by the coaches. Indeed, throughout his song the veterans threw beer at him, which was a good sign; he was being baptized into the family.

I had written a skit in which a number of the veteran Colts were depicted paying a visit to a local house of ill repute, which was represented by a sheet hung across the middle of the stage area. The rookies wore wigs and Colt game jerseys to indicate which veterans they were. After a few lines of banter on stage, they stepped behind the sheet through which an occasional sound of intimacy would rise, punctuated by Ed Block's voice offering medical advice, usually his familiar cry of "Ice!" Sitting out in front of the sheet, I was the madam. I wore a woman's hat and carried a fan I had found in the college props department, and from time to time I blew a small child's trumpet to try to keep order. As the rookies appeared onstage I would offer up a line or so to describe the veterans they represented. I had been prompted by the veterans themselves as to the sort of thing to say—some peccadilloes, some little divulgence about their fellow players, and when one of these was delivered it would set the audience to simply *bellowing*, rocking back and forth, throwing beer on themselves in ecstasy. It gave me an extraordinary sense of power to announce, for example, that coming down the street was Dan Sullivan—played by a rookie wearing number 71—just in from "the cornfield," and have this statement greeted by a roomful of grown men almost weeping with laughter. I never discovered what the connection was between Sullivan and a cornfield, but obviously it was common knowledge among the veterans. The rookies were just as surprised by this as I was. The Sullivan rookie, who had predictably been upset by the paucity of the line I had given him ("Is this all I'm supposed to say—something about a 'cow in a cornfield'?") basked in the storm of laughter greeting his line, his lips finally parting in a self-congratulatory grin.

A great deal of beer began to be thrown during the skits, much of it by Coach McCafferty—first at the actors, and then quite a lively exchange started in the audience. At the windows the neighborhood kids, attracted by the noise, were leaping up and down to peer in, their heads bobbing up, then disappearing, then up again, eyes wide with surprise as they glimpsed their heroes at play—the great yellow arcs of beer in flight, the rookies mournfully reciting their lines, one of them holding his violin aloft to keep it out of the strife, the audience lost now as the chairs tipped backwards and the beer-throwing began in earnest.

Last night there was a much less strenuous team party, a crab feast and horseshoe-pitching contest at the home of a

Baltimore fan who works in the tax division at the State Treasury Building in Maryland. His name is Romeo Valianti, a super-fan, very nervous, and so thin that the Colts pick him up, pass him around and josh at him: "Hey, isn't this Romeo?" "Right." "Didn't he give us a party?" "Right." "What do we need him for now?" "Nothing. Throw him away."

Valianti has three passions in his life. One is a myna bird he keeps in his house. Second is John F. Kennedy, about whom he has collected clippings which fill a scrapbook the size of an elephant portfolio. It weighs twenty-eight pounds, he said as he staggered out under it to show it to me. He turned the stiff pages lovingly. Some were pinned with campaign buttons. We looked at a picture of Caroline Kennedy standing with one small foot in her mother's shoe. Romeo told me that he had got the President to sign the book, rushing up to him in a big crowd outside the 5th Regiment Armory bent almost double under it.

Valianti's third passion is the Colt team. This was the nineteenth straight year he had held the crab feast and horseshoe contest for the players. In the backyard stood long tables and tubs full of crabs, and at the far end was the horseshoe pitch. Fred Miller, in charge of the contest, kept a flashlight in his back pocket to search for errant shoes when darkness had fallen. The contest would be a long one.

I was eliminated early. I returned to one of the long tables, where the players' jaws were munching steadily; the carcasses of the soft-shelled crabs were beginning to pile up amid the dishes of sauce and melted butter. Ted Hendricks reached into a tub and showed me how to get the crabs ready for eating and how best to get to the meat. The crabs were delicious. Bob Vogel, sitting next to me, had a different method. He took issue with Hendricks. The two argued. They prepared crab after crab to demonstrate the benefits of their methods, and I ate a number, trailing off after a while. I coughed carefully and had some white wine from a jug. I told them I'd had enough.

I fell into conversation with Vogel. A huge pale man with gentle eyes and nothing in his demeanor that suggests what he does for a living, he has been playing offensive tackle with the Colts for nine years. It turned out that we shared a common interest in bird-watching. He said that he had become interested in birds while looking for ground hogs and had seen a Baltimore oriole sitting on a branch; he was stunned by its beauty and annoyed that he knew nothing about what he was looking at. He was an apt student, and very intense about it. On one occasion, while visiting a friend's house, he had glanced out the picture window and spotted an evening grosbeak. He leaned out of his chair, his eyes staring, and let out a small cry. His hostess, who was sitting with her back to the window, involuntarily let out a louder cry; from Vogel's intensity she assumed that something awful was out on the lawn behind her— perhaps something that had escaped from the zoo.

Fred Miller called Vogel to the horseshoe pitch, and I sat and had some more wine. Across the table a few of the veterans were roaring with laughter as they reminisced about a post-game celebration at John Unitas' Golden Arm in 1968. They were talking about Alex Hawkins, who was a big betting man and who had wagered someone $1,500 that a girl could ride naked on a horse from the Golden Arm down to Sweeney's, a bar a few miles away, without being arrested. The girl who was willing to do this, a quite pretty girl, bore the nickname "Hard Times," because she complained constantly of her difficult lot in life. ("Yes, I do too have leukemia. I have all the symptoms," etc. etc.) The wagering swept the length of the long bar in the Golden Arm and the pros and cons of the girl's chances were discussed endlessly. Finally Hawkins called an end to the betting, and everyone trooped out to the parking lot and the warm evening air; Hard Times reached for her wide leather belt to unbuckle it. But where was the horse? Heads craned. Apparently in the intensity of the wagering no one had been detailed to get a horse; it had simply been forgotten in the excitement. Hawkins was besides himself. A half-hearted attempt was made to get Hard Times to walk to Sweeney's on foot, but she demurred; she felt an ache coming on.

I walked up to the house. Bubba Smith was in the living room, his face against the myna bird's cage. "Bubba, Bubba," he was saying to it. The bird, "Stoney," was named after the ex-Colt linebacker Steve Stonebreaker because it so often bit people, "putting the hit on them"; it said "hello," and whistled a lot, but it apparently would not say "Bubba." "Bubba, Bubba, Bubba," the big end intoned carefully. He picked up the cage and shook it gently, the myna bird within teetering back and forth and whistling sharply. "I've been an hour working on him today," Bubba said, his eyes behind the black spectacles never wavering from the bird. "Bubba, Bubba."

Romeo came in. "How's it going, Bubba?"

"Bubba, Bubba."

Romeo shook his head. "Bubba sometimes just drops by unexpectedly to see Stoney," he told me. "He's very determined, you know. We're in the kitchen and I hear this deep voice saying, 'Bubba, Bubba,' out in the living room, and we rush out, thinking maybe Stoney's learned it, but no, it's always Bubba himself, kneeling on the floor, working on the bird."

We watched Bubba's attempts for a few minutes. "Hey, Bub. I think you're too close to the cage," Romeo said. "You're making him nervous."

"I'm trying to *will* him to say it. It takes my concentration and personal attention."

There was a sudden convulsive movement, a quick flap of wings in the cage, and Bubba jumped. "Christ," he said, "I got bit." He looked aggrievedly at his finger. The myna bird, hopping from perch to perch, whistled again. "That bird's had his mind messed with," Bubba said, rising to his feet. "Romeo, the next thing I'm going to do to that bird is eat him."

Oz and Jenny's

When the parties aren't going on, the most popular place in Westminster for the players is Oz and Jenny's pizza joint, a shanty-town structure ten minutes from the campus and housing a large low-ceilinged room with a square bar in the middle.

Booths are set around the perimeter of the room; often the deaf-mutes take over two or three of them, which quiets the place down, though after a few beers the semaphoring of the hands and fingers becomes more agitated.

Bed check for the Colts being at eleven o'clock, the players only have an hour or so after class to socialize and play at the long shuffleboard table. Everybody drinks his beer quickly. No dawdling. The conversation is almost invariably about football.

Tonight Tom Mitchell, the big tight end who is called "The Crocodile," came over and dumped a pitcher of beer on my head. Seeing our group—Hendricks, Bulaich, Curry, Nowatzke—at a table eating pizza, Dave Lee, sitting next to Mitchell at the bar, had apparently dared him to do it. The Crocodile had stepped up and poured the beer over me, easy as nothing. I rose, soaking wet, and The Crocodile pushed me back down into my seat, grinning at me enormously.

"I hadda do that," he said. "The Stork was gonna throw his pizza at you," he went on mysteriously. He turned and went back to the bar.

"Christ!" I said. "What was that?"

"The Crocodile is inscrutable," said Curry.

"God Almighty!" I said, getting angry.

"Cool it, man," Hendricks said.

"What was that about your pizza?" I asked.

He shrugged. "I've eaten most of it."

"He's as mad as a coot," I said, glaring over toward the bar. Mitchell was looking back. His smile had disappeared. "But I don't see any reason why I should tell him that to his face," I said.

"No," said Hendricks.

"In fact, the thought makes me ill."

It's a lot calmer when the coaches turn up at Oz and Jenny's.

They usually appear at 11:30, driving over on occasion

after the bed check to relax, drink a few beers and take their turn at the shuffleboard table.

Tonight I stayed on after the players had left. I knew that the coaches would give me a lot of jawing when they saw me waiting there ("Hey, rook, that'll be a one-hundred-dollar fine"), but it was worth the joshing to sit with them and hear their gossip.

Tonight, while McCafferty and John Idzig, the offensive backfield coach, played a shuffleboard match against a local team, John Sandusky and Hank Bullough, who coached the defense, talked about the striking differences in the characters of players, even those who play the same position. For example, Mike Curtis and Ted Hendricks are linebackers, but they were described as having quite different attitudes about winning.

Sandusky said, "Even if the team wins, Curtis will get peed off because we didn't win big; we just *won*. Well, Ted's a much more happy-go-lucky guy. That doesn't mean, though, that he may not be the best outside linebacker there ever was."

"You know, that strange 'stork' size of his is a great asset," Bullough said, "because he's got these great long arms, with enormous strength in the hands and wrists and shoulders. He's like a great hillbilly, one of those guys from the mountains with long skinny arms, with the veins popping out of them, and you're always told as a kid, 'don't fight those people' because they're so damn strong. Well, that's what the Stork is like . . . He may be six-six or -seven in height, but he's got such great strength and leverage in those arms that you can't cut him down because you can't get at his feet."

I asked, "If you could construct the perfect ballplayer, what would you start with—the sort of physical ability that The Stork comes by naturally, or the competitive spirit of someone like Curtis?"

Bullough said, "You know, I don't think there's any such qualification as 'physical ability'; there are so many great guys playing without much physical ability at all. Take Billy Ray Smith, who played so well in the line for us—well, he couldn't run a hundred yards. He was the slowest guy we had. If you picked a team by what you read off a stopwatch, Billy Ray would have been on the next bus out. Actually, it's very seldom that a big-muscled, body-beautiful guy turns out to be a great lineman. He's more likely to be flabby-muscled, smooth, loose-footed."

"Look at Dan Sullivan," Sandusky said. "He's sure not a great physical specimen. Look at the weight on him. But when you watch him work, you see that he's got these very quick feet and great intelligence. He gets things done with his feet and his mind, but he looks so unlike a super-athlete that people mistake him for an assistant personnel manager, maybe, gone to seed and living high on the hog. I'll tell you another— Art Donovan, one of the best football players we ever had here, a Hall of Fame guy. His nickname was "Fatso." He *was* fat. He couldn't run the forty-yard dash if you gave him from ten in the morning till two in the afternoon. He was always being kidded about it. But what a fine player—quick, strong, and great balance. No one could knock him off his feet. You very seldom saw him on the ground."

"Of course he had that tremendous competitive drive," said Bullough.

"Also, he could play hurt," Sandusky said. "That's another attribute—to have a great pain tolerance. Donovan could play with a broken bone. I remember one day we asked him about an injury he had; did it hurt? And he said, 'Yeah, in between plays.'"

"Unitas has that quality," Bullough said. "He's been hurt for years, and right now he's playing off that Achilles tendon injury. You know it hurts him, but when you ask him how he feels, it's 'fine!' like he's never had an injury."

"So in a football player, physical attributes aren't that important?" I asked.

"Right."

I drove back to the campus that night wondering how much of their denigration of physical talents was said in deference to my own precarious state—gimpy-footed, the thumb still encased in gauze. It was nice of them to have answered the question as they had . . .

Nightfall

At night the television crew packs its equipment into station wagons and moves down to the motel for the night. They cart the stuff into their ground-floor rooms for safekeeping. Then they're done, their day's work caught in the emulsion on miles of film. They sit out behind their rooms with a portable grill on which they cook steaks, and after supper they throw a football back and forth.

During this time, if I don't have classes or the group isn't down at Oz and Jenny's drinking, I sit in my blue room, working a pencil, often holding it in both hands because of my bad thumb, putting down awkward notes that one day will have to be wrenched into something. I'm tired, and bored with the task, and yet I feel no envy of my television pals down in town, their work in round tins, sealed and done. What luck they have to have! It's easy enough to set up the interviews, to point the cameras at the scrimmages, and to move in for such close-ups as the muscles in Mike Curtis' smooth jaw working swiftly on gum, and his smile. And perhaps the contrasts can be caught: a Mickey Mouse balloon floating motionless above a child, tied to his wrist with a long white string, the transparent rubber face above large and lunatic, the one below small and solemn, the two of them looking down from the embankment at the grown men struggling over the brown ball. But how much is missed! Selectivity is dictated by where the camera is and whether it is loaded and working properly, and whether the scene captured mirrors what the director and cameraman have seen in their mind's eye. Of course this is what the writer faces too, but at least his eye is a more manipulative camera, with no need to be focused, and it can be put in operation by a quick turn of the neck. The material collected is boundless—anything that falls within the range of eye or ear—and sitting in my room I can shift it all around in my mind and select what I want, and probably lie a bit, too.

Now what is it I'm trying to remember? My thumb throbs and I'm awfully tired. It was some object, part of a short but interesting list of jetsam that Bill Curry has spotted in the grass during his years of looking down at the ground before centering the ball. A Spiro Agnew watch, was that it? I can't remember. It might be an absorbing list, if one really did a lot of research and asked a number of linemen what they had discovered in the grass over the years. It's unlikely that any area of ground is surveyed as consistently as a football field, with a dozen or so men staring down in the huddle, and as they take their stances. I must remember to ask Karras and Gordy if they've ever found anything, though of course Alex can hardly see his own shoes in the grass.

I'm going to put the pencil down. It can all wait. I will barely have enough strength to pull the cord on the light hanging from the blue ceiling.

Dream

August 8   I had a really sharp dream last night—which is rare because usually mine are fuzzy and I don't remember them well enough to describe what went on. I was out on the field at Ann Arbor in front of an enormous crowd, a great bowl of people stretching away on all sides, and in the huddle I had just called the first of my four plays against the Lions. As the huddle broke and I began to walk up behind the center, Karras suddenly came offside, bolting across even before I had got to the line of scrimmage, and crushed me to the ground four or five yards behind Curry.

"Hey, you can't do that," I shouted in a muffled voice. "That's not fair."

Nothing, however, was done about it. I scrambled to my feet and looked at the referee, who scratched his head and said he had never seen anything quite like it before—the act had taken place such a long time before the teams were set that it seemed quite beyond the scope of regulations. "I'm sorry," he said.

The next time Karras tackled me *in the huddle*. I had

regrouped the Colts and had just repeated the Ride 38 play when he got me from behind—he had circled the huddle—and drove me forward into the ring of Colts, who stared down at us lying amidst their legs. "Hey, goddamn it, that's not fair," I shouted once more. I got up and pushed my way through the Colts and approached the referee. "It's anarchy," I said. "He can't—"

He was scratching his head again. "It's unusual for a lineman to commit himself so quickly—*very* unusual. It's like he went and tackled you in the training room when you were having your ankles taped. I don't think the action lies within our jurisdiction."

Just then, while the referee was intoning this solemn judgment, I heard a quick scuffle of feet behind me, and yet again I was tackled and driven to the ground at the referee's feet with a sharp shoulder block that got me in the small of the back.

"Well, I don't know about Mr. Karras' timing," I heard the referee saying. "But I'd call that a good *clean* tackle. Yessir, Mr. Karras."

Very odd.

Dave Lee's Big Idea

"Hey, why did you get The Crocodile to throw the beer on me the other night?"

We were sitting in the back of the classroom. Dave Lee said, "Well, you've made me feel guilty about sitting back here and not using my mind properly. So I decided the other day to use it."

"And that's what you came up with?"

"That's right," he said. "I worked on it all day. Boy, it didn't take The Crocodile a long time to make up *his* mind, did it."

"Almost instantaneous," I said.

"He'd throw beer at anyone—except maybe the coach. He loves throwing beer."

I began throwing the ball again today. "Shot-putting it" might be more descriptive of what I was doing, since the thumb was still stiffly bandaged and throbbed after each toss. John Mackey, the tight end, fifteen yards down the field, would gather in my lobs. Each time he would turn the ball and tuck it under his arm before shoveling it across to Unitas who was standing next to him. Quarterbacks did not like to catch the ball for fear of jamming a finger. Then Unitas would whistle the ball to Sam Havrilak alongside me, who would sometimes rifle it to Mackey (since he was a reserve quarterback himself) or lob it to me so that I could rear back and with a little *eeep* of pain arch the ball downfield.

I did this for a while and then joined Unitas and Mackey. "You do that every time?" I asked Mackey, watching him tuck the ball under his arm after a reception.

"Got to groove it," he said, "so it's completely instinctive —so that when you catch the ball it ends up in the proper, safe position no matter what else is on your mind."

The ball thudded into Mackey's palms. It seemed to arrive almost before it left Havrilak's hand, the nose just a touch down, as steady in its flight as a dirigible, yet swift as a dart—a quality which I envied, since my passes, however often I experimented with the grip, wobbled like a schoolboy's punt. Once I had asked Leon Hart, the ex-Lion tight end, if he could distinguish from the *feel* of a ball coming into his hands who had thrown it; one always heard of quarterbacks who threw "light" or "heavy" balls. "Oh, yes," he said. "Bobby Layne threw a very light ball, almost like it had helium in it and had to be pulled down. But Tobin Rote threw a ball that came at you with steam, and catching it was like blocking a heavy punch. I think it was because Rote was a javelin thrower in college; he had a huge wrist and a snap to his throw that gave it that heavy quality."

The thought crossed my mind to ask Mackey if there was a distinctive feel to my tosses, but I resisted it. There were some Colts you could ask things like that, half in jest, and some you could not. Mackey was a very serious competitor. He had taken off his Super Bowl ring when he arrived in training camp. "I figure there are twenty-six teams starting off even," he told me. "If I want a place to put another Super Bowl ring, I got to have the ring finger empty, right?"

Mackey once explained to me how easy it was for him to get psyched up for a game: he just let himself get hungry. He ate a Saturday night meal, but skipped everything on Sunday and just sat around getting angrier as he got hungrier. He was an awfully good man to have on your side.

Telephone Call

August 10 I gave Freddy the news. Behind her voice I could hear our four-month-old daughter murmuring. I told Freddy that the thumb was coming along fine and McCafferty was probably going to test it in a line scrimmage in the next day or so.

"A big moment for the Colts."

"Absolutely."

"Where are you calling from?"

"Same place. A public booth here in the dormitory. How's Medora?"

"She's right here. She said a few things today that sounded like words. Perhaps she'll repeat them for you."

For a while I listened to the child's soft breathing.

"Nothing?"

"Not really," I said. "Would you like to listen to my thumb? It throbs. Can you hear it? I've got it up against the mouthpiece."

"The connection must be bad. What's your room like?"

"It's blue—baby blue. One light bulb hangs from the ceiling. The beds are steel cots."

"Can we come down and visit?"

"No, they have bed checks. You and Medora would add up to a two-hundred-dollar fine at least."

She laughed. "I'm glad Medora's not old enough so that I have to try to explain to her what on earth you're doing down there."

"I have a hard enough time explaining it to myself," I said.

"Do you need anything down there? I feel I should pack up a CARE package for you. A transistor, or something?"

"There's enough music around here as it is. But you know something crazy? It's not always to sooth the savage beast. The players use it to pump themselves up for a game. Bubba Smith uses Motown soul, and after a while he's ready to kill someone. Mike Curtis told me today that—"

"Who's Mike Curtis?"

"He's the middle linebacker. He's the guy right behind the line—"

"I remember. What sort of music gets *him* ready?"

"*Any* kind of music will do for Curtis. That's the odd thing. Sometimes before a scrimmage he listens to a hard-rock station; at other times it's classical. What he does is turn the radio dial up in his room until something comes on that begins to pump him up."

"Did he do your thumb?"

"No, that was Ray May. But Curtis knows I have another thumb left. I have the feeling he's got his eye on it."

"You should be careful not to sing in the locker room."

"What?"

"Don't sing. It might get someone pumped up."

"Don't worry."

"Don't they listen to music for pleasure?"

"Oh sure. When Bubba's not on the practice field he's usually sitting in his big pink Continental with the white Texas plates, and he drives out to the country somewhere grooving to the cassette player turned up loud. His favorite is 'Save the Babies.' He keeps to the beat, and the whole car rocks back and forth. We went to listen to some music in town the other night. He keeps his money in his shoe because he's got no pockets in his pants. We had a great time. He's quite a sight to see out on a dance floor. He got bit by a bird a couple of days ago."

"He what?"

I explained it to her. After we talked some more she put Medora on the phone again to try to say goodbye, and I listened to the quick breathing.

"Nothing?"

"Not really. But it's a good sound."

"Well . . . good night, all you music lovers," she said.

Training Room Scene

August 12 I came into the training room to get my ankles taped. It is the social center of the club, and performances go on while the players lounge around waiting their turns on the tables. Yesterday Roy Hilton, the defensive end, gave a monologue about a Baptist preacher and a whale that went on for so long that some of the players resting over in the dormitory heard about it and came over to listen to the end of it.

Ed Block usually presides over the room, talking nonstop as he stands at the end of the training tables taping ankles. Since he is deafish, it is difficult to interrupt him. Today he was saying, "Everyone is spoiled these days about pain. Not so many years ago an old piece of shoe leather used to be sufficient to bite on. Now everybody's got to have a silver bullet."

Jim Duncan hopped up on the table. He has a bruised ankle. The trainer kneaded it. "Tell me where the gold is hidden." His fingers probed and Duncan yelped. "Ah, so that's where the treasure is. It's no wonder, Mr. Duncan. Your ankles are too slender. My canary bird's got thicker ankles than you do, and he's barely able to stand on his perch. He topples off from time to time. Now, the first and only question is whether you can *run* on this ankle. The test goes as follows. *A:* Can you chase a girl who is fully dressed with this ankle? *B:* Can you chase a girl who is topless with this ankle? *C:* Can you chase a girl who is completely nude with this ankle?"

Duncan laughed. Leaning forward on the table, he said, "Well, Ed, I'd bait a trap."

"You'd do what?"

"I'd bait a trap."

"Oh, you'd bait a *trap*. With what?" Block asked.

"Worms," Duncan said. Block was an avid fisherman, and Duncan knew this would produce a reaction.

"Worms?" Block said sorrowfully. "That shows you the new generation. In the old days anyone doing such a thing would use a Gray Hackle or at least an Uncle Ben's Popping Plug."

It was my turn on the table. Block looked at my thumb. "Using ice on it?" Ice is the Block cure-all.

"Absolutely."

He began the taping. "Now, George, we're going to want the tape on your ankle a little *tighter* than normal, because you're going to have a full scrimmage this afternoon and the grass is slippery. In fact, I think I'll give you an X-support right here. The ankle strapping that we use here is called the Gibney method, supposedly invented by Dr. Gibney in the Civil War. Actually, he said he didn't invent it. He was very firm about that, though all the books say he did. Most of your ankle-strapping was invented by the Egyptians. They invented tape, balaam of Peru, and of course they used it on their mummies. You look at any mummy's foot and you'll see an X-support just like the one I'm putting on here. How does that feel? Good and tight? All right, go on out there and don't fall down."

Scrimmage

Sure enough, McCafferty did send me in to try the last three plays of the scrimmage. He wanted to see what I could do with two handoff running plays, the 34 Wham and the Flow 38, and he didn't see why I shouldn't finish up with the quarterback sneak, just to get some idea of what it was going to be like in Ann Arbor against the Lions.

I practiced the sequences in my mind most of the afternoon. Gordy kept hammering at me. "On the sneak, keep low so you don't get snapped upright when you get tackled."

During the long wait I kept glancing at McCafferty, wondering if perhaps the whole notion had not slipped from his mind and he'd finish the practice and send us all up the hill without putting me in. But with ten minutes to go, he shrilled his whistle and motioned me over, and together we walked into the offensive huddle.

"Okay," McCafferty said. "Let's start off with the Thirty-four Wham. Call the play." He stood next to me to listen.

I leaned forward amidst the waiting Colts and announced, "Frank light stiff."

"Come on, do it right," McCafferty interrupted.

I tried again: "Flank right split; thirty-four wham; on two; break!" and the unit wheeled away from me and started toward the line of scrimmage. The defense began yelling as soon as they saw me coming. "It's The Gimp," I heard someone yell. "Here comes The Big Thumb."

Stan Hansen was the center. Bill Curry told me later that his snap was slow. An enormous hole opened up which could have been exploited had the timing of the play developed as it should have, but when I got the ball in my hand I revolved to hand it off with such heavy turnstile solemnity that Tom Matte, who was playing the running back that afternoon, had to practically come to a halt to gather it in, rather as if we were exchanging a satchel of valuables. The hole had long closed by then, and Matte churned helplessly at the line of scrimmage until he was dragged down.

The second play was the Flow 38, a sweep into the eight hole by the number three back which required that the off-guard pull to lead the blocking. It was a play that had been in my repertoire at Detroit and had always caused me trouble because the speed and patterns developed so quickly that I never could seem to get out of the way of my own blockers, who would bowl me over before the defense ever had a chance to get to me. In fact, the defensive people used to complain about this, and plead that the offensive team let me stand up long enough for them to get at me at least once in a while.

The same thing happened this afternoon. After getting the ball from the center, I began the spin toward the running back but found myself still in the path of the guard coming down the line to lead the interference. He bounced against me heavily and the ball popped loose, jarred so hard that it sailed out of bounds. The defensive players stood around and hooted with pleasure. Humiliation began to settle in. I trudged back to the huddle. John Unitas was standing with McCafferty, and he came over. "You're letting the ball hang out there where things can happen to it," he said. "Pull it in and get it under control." He demonstrated. "You have to haul a girl toward you before you kiss her, for Chrissakes," he said.

Back in the huddle, I called the quarterback sneak. Bill Curry had come in and substituted himself for Hansen, thinking that I would have an easier time with the snap. I announced the play and walked up behind him to the line. The defense was sure it was going to be the sneak. "The Gimp's gonna try the sneak. Watch it, everybody." I glanced to the right and left, but not over Curry's back into the area where Mike Curtis was waiting, perhaps subconsciously fearing that I would see that straight-lipped grin behind the face bar and be unable to call the signals.

My sneak made perhaps a yard. I scrambled forward, legs driving, eyes shut tight, hearing the crash and heave of gear, and almost instantaneously the whiplash of hands being laid on. It is such a surprising feeling to suffer the sudden, violent clutching of unknown people, and one's first reaction is of indignation, as if one's person had been violated. Hammered down, I found myself at the bottom of a pile that grew, players from both sides hopping on like children roughhousing, and the giggling began, and the weight of them on me so fearsome that I offered up a muffled shout, "Hey!" and I heard McCafferty's whistle blowing and his cheerful call of "Up the hill, everybody."

I walked up toward the gym with Curry. "Thanks for coming in like that," I said. "It meant a lot."

"It's better to have a center you're used to," he said.

"It's not going to be like that in Detroit, is it?"

"What do you mean?"

"I mean there won't be any horseplay and laughing and carrying on, will there?"

"No way," Curry said. "No way at all. That's another ball park . . ."

The Reporter

August 13 Sometimes after practice an onlooker who turned out to be a writer would come forward out of the crowd carrying a big legal pad, or perhaps a tape recorder. Almost invariably he wore a tie in the summer heat, and his shirt would be discolored by stains of sweat. In the old days the news profession all wore hats; now it's ties.

"Christ, it's hot," one of these guys said. "Mind if I ask you a few questions?" We sat under a tree on the slope leading up to the gym. I held my helmet by the strap. I felt awkward. A group of onlookers collected to listen in. The reporter, who was from the county seat local newspaper, clicked a button on his tape recorder and asked: "What's the difference between this team, the Colts, and the team you used to play for, the Detroit Lions?"

It was a good question and one which I had thought about. "I think back on the Lions as a group of very distinctive individuals," I said, "such a variety of characters that I often wondered if—well, if a weird casting director hadn't been at work. Look who they were: Karras, Gordy, LeBeau, Night Train Lane, Joe Schmidt—each of them affected by the legacy of Bobby Layne, who was such an individualist himself. The Colts, on the other hand, seem a more cohesive group; if one had to find a single word to describe them, it would be something like 'solidarity' or 'love' or perhaps 'family.' The Lions were a crew of vigilantes, a bunch of guys out of the Old West who'd taken over a cowtown and laid the whole thing to waste. With the Colts there's a sense of common effort which is much more apparent, and there's more confidence . . . maybe a quality which comes along with being champions."

In the middle of this, I was aware that the reporter was not listening; he was wondering whether his tape machine was working properly. He peered to see if the spools were going

323

around, then looked up, his eyes glazed. "Yes, yes," he said. Now he was beginning to worry about his next question. I rambled on nonetheless. When I finally finished, he cleared his throat and asked a question which had nothing to do with what I had been discussing: "What is the *real* John Unitas like?"

How rarely sports reporters had *conversations* with their subjects. The procedure was as formless and clinical as a questionnaire put to a traveler coming through immigration: "Where do you live? Are you carrying any fruit?"

The temptation was to spice up the answers in the hope of getting a visible reaction from the reporter—if you could only get him to respond, "My God, I never knew that!" I never had the temerity to try to hoodwink one with a goofy answer, despite my doubts that he would catch on.

"The *real* John Unitas?" I would say. "Well, John Unitas has this incredible habit. He likes to sink his head into goldfish tanks. Don't ask me why. But if you're with him at a party in a house where there are goldfish, before you can reach for a canapé you'll see John at the far end of the room, leaning over, with his head in the goldfish bowl. That's why he wears his hair cropped short; it's so the strands won't get in his eyes and disturb his vision. I don't know why he does it. Maybe he drinks a bit of the water. I think he likes those little alabaster castles set in the sand. He looks in the windows . . ."

You could keep up this sort of nonsense indefinitely, carrying on with whatever flights of fancy came to mind, and as long as you pretended seriousness and maintained a certain portentous tone, the reporter would nod happily, and behind the glaze in his eyes it would be apparent that to the exclusion of all else he was hard at work phrasing his next question: "What about Bubba Smith? Have you had a chance to get to know the *real* Bubba?"

The interview with the county seat reporter lasted about fifteen minutes. Some of the questions were excellent, though disjointed. I sat in the heat and did my best. Finally he came to the end. "That'll do it just great," he said. He clicked off his machine. All of it trapped in there, I thought mournfully. "Well, thank you very much," he said.

324

I walked up toward the gym past the tennis courts. In the corridor was Ted Hendricks, already dressed. "Hi, Stork," I said.

"What did you tell the guy?" he asked.

"The reporter? I told him that Unitas drank the water out of goldfish tanks."

The Stork raised an eyebrow. "So what's new?" he said.

Bubba

"It's hard for me to hang out with ballplayers because when many of them reach a certain economic bracket they become something they aren't. Most blacks don't want to go back where they came from. I can't think like that. I sit on the hood of my car, and it'll take me home to Beaumont, Texas, and if you're on a happy horse like that, it gives you a chance to think and not get your mind too messed. Home is the Golden Triangle of West Texas and Beaumont, which they began calling the football capital of the world because it's produced so many great football players—Mel Farr, Jerry Levias, Miller Farr, Warren Wells, and then all us Smith brothers that came out of there. That's where I began to think about football. The best thing about football is that it's all I know. From the beginning guys would hang around the house and talk football, and Daddy, who was the coach of Charlton Pollard High School since nineteen fifty-seven, talked and *thought* about football all the time, and at five A.M. he'd come to the bedroom doors and get his sons up and say, 'What do you think of this play?' and then he'd tell us. We'd say 'Yeah, Daddy. Can we go back to bed now, Daddy?' That's all people thought about down there. We'd get three hundred out to watch a high school practice. Why, even when we went down to the parks at six in the morning to exercise and run a few plays, always in the swings over by the playground there'd be a few kids sitting there who'd gotten up out of bed at that time and come down to watch. They were crazy about it. The night before each game we'd take our football shoes home to shine them up, and those kids would turn up the next day and walk along beside us and say, 'Hey, man, can I carry your shoes to the game?' The shoelaces were snow-white and the black leather was shining. So they carried the shoes for you, walking along beside, and it was maybe the biggest thing that had happened to those kids for a month. The guys from Beaumont were their heroes—not Lenny Moore or Gale Sayers. On the street when they make a few moves it's always, 'Hey, watch me, man—I'm Miller Farr, I'm Bubba Smith.' Now they'll be saying it about my brother, Tody, who's out there at the Dallas Cowboy camp. He's a great player, but the Dallas coaches are messing with his mind. He got there late, so they put him on the *ninth* team and he's got guys in front of him who can't hold his shoes. I'm on the phone all the time to tell him he can play and to help him from going crazy. He's always been very uptight. He's got knuckles like cement, and when he was growing up he went around hitting walls with karate chops—that's right—and he split the wood-work in the house while he was in high school. My mother said, 'Hey, Bubs, look at this,' and she showed me where it was done and we called him 'El Toro the Ferocious.'

"But it was my older brother, Willie Ray Jr., who was the best of all the Smiths—a running back who was with Kansas for a while—and every time I watch Gale Sayers running I see a lot of Willie Ray. He had a knee. He had five operations. When he was cut from the Colts my rookie year, I almost quit. I knew they had nobody who could run like him. Then he went to the Packers as a free agent, but his knee puffed and they cut him. I idolized him. In elementary school I said, 'I want me a horn,' but when they gave me a saxophone Willie Ray said, 'Hey, li'l bandboy,' and I never picked up the sax again. I knew when Willie Ray ran the ball, that was the only thing that meant anything. I wanted to block for him. I was at the All-Star game when he was cut from the Colts, and Daddy was with me. I said, 'Daddy, let's go, we're going home to Beaumont.' Daddy talked to me in his li'l ol' soft voice. He was always the absolute king, the Coach. He was gentle and wise, but he was very rough on us kids too. He whipped us when we did wrong on the football field. Originally, the whipping was done with a bicycle tire outer tube, but by the time I was in my junior year at Charlton Pollard he made himself a paddle about twenty inches long with a handle that fit his hand real good, and everybody called it 'The Board of Education.' We saw a lot of The Board of Education. Once we skipped school and went over to Bear's house with some girls. Daddy found out, and he arrived in no time at all with his board. He and The Board of Education, they came through the door *together*. But it was on the football field that we was most familiar with The Board of Education. *Everybody* was familiar with it. He'd use it. You'd get five licks if you messed up the same play twice. A lot of people came out to watch us practice, standing along the sidelines, and if everybody was getting a beating from The Board of Education, I'd get a beating too—just on principle, so that people wouldn't think Daddy was beating up on everybody else and excusing his own son. One time I went to Mother and told her that I was going to quit football, that I was gettin' beat something awful just to satisfy the people watching; she probably spoke to him about it, but it didn't change nothing. Sometimes she was the coach, too. When I was a kid she sent me down to the bench with these notes to give the coach that she'd written up in the stands—'Try the Quickie 5.' One time, later on when I was playing, I came off the field at half time for a hot dog to eat, and up in the stands I heard her whistle. She had a note for me to take to the coach, and on the way to the bench I opened it. It said, 'Hit Bubba alongside the head.' The next game I heard her whistling at half time just like before, but this time I just kep' walking; man, I didn't even turn my head, and she could whistle like a calliope.

"Those were the days. We played the game on hot dogs and potato chips and soda water and mother cooked beans and two-cent corn muffins, and the kids walking home came by the house to eat. When we got older, after the ball game we'd meet at Lilly's and Elma's on Irving Street, and we'd sit on the curb and talk about what we did in the game. We lied a lot: *That big man, why we jus' run him home.'* The cheerleaders sat on the curb with these bitty dresses on, so their panties showed, and the hats with the plumes, y'know, next to them on the sidewalk. Right then I began to think about playing football all my life.

"Then I began to get real big. When I started the tenth grade I weighed two hundred pounds and I was six feet tall. Then the pants started creeping up my leg, and by the spring of that year I was six-seven and weighed two forty-four. I had a roommate at Michigan State who'd never seen a black person, except maybe on TV, and when I jumped out of the top bunk to say hello, I 'most scared him half to death.

"When I left Michigan State I hoped maybe I'd play in the west. I'm crazy about California. That's where my brother Willie Ray is living now, in Los Angeles. I go out there all the time and stay with him. I'd like to play for the Rams. One time I turned up at the Rams' training camp, just visiting, and there was this guy checking everybody in and he said, 'Can I help you?' I said, 'Well, Coach Prothro told me to come and try out.' 'What's your name?' 'Ralph Jones.' So he looked at his list and said that he had no Ralph Jones. 'Are you under contract? I can't give you a room unless you're under contract.' I said, 'All I know is that Coach Prothro told me to report.' He said, 'I better call Prothro.' So he telephoned and I heard him say that there was this real big cat standing around in the office who said he had a tryout, and sure enough Prothro turned up, and he took a gander and just about fainted. 'What are you doing out here, Bubba?' 'I dunno,' I said. 'Maybe wishful thinking.' Maybe *he* was wishful thinking, too. I'd like to play there. But when the season starts it don't make no difference where you play—you get crazy again. Dr. Jekyll, he's being eased out and Mr. Hyde is coming in. You walk around all cool, but Mr. Hyde is getting ready to take charge and make your head twitch and your body all fiery. John Mackey's that way—real fiery. He'll call up: 'Hey Bub?' 'Yeah?' 'This is eighty-eight.' 'Yeah?' 'I'm fired up. Let's go work out. Let's run.' 'Hey, eighty-eight, it's one in the morning.' 'No excuse.' And he goes out and runs through the night with his equipment on. But his knee never came around that year. He sat on the bench, which killed him, and his wife Sylvia, too, because she was the only one he could talk to about it. But me, man, I can talk to my brothers, and my mother, and my daddy. Then *this* year Mackey's knee came around strong and he called up: 'Hey Bub?' 'Yeah?' 'This is eighty-eight.' 'Yeah?' 'I'm fired up. The weight's right. I'm not pregnant no more. I lost my baby. Come on over so's I can run you.' 'Hey, man, it's one in the morning.' 'So, man, come on over.' He's real serious. You know, that type of attitude spreads like fire on a team—'What do you mean, *lose*?'—and you *got* to have it; it makes you champions because everybody starts playing over their heads. Mike Curtis is like that. He spreads the fire. He's a very good person. He doesn't believe in unions. I mess with him. I sit there and look across the locker room and watch him. He won't let nobody tape his hands. I feel close to him. He makes a lot of facial expressions; his teeth shine and I know he's ready. I've got to get *myself* in high gear, and having people like that around helps. The first time I ever played against Forrest Gregg of Green Bay I asked Bill Curry what he was like to go against, and Curry said that he was the nicest human being that God had ever put together. On the first play Forrest Gregg set back and did something to me and I fell down. He helped me up. 'Bubba,' he said, 'you got to use your hands more. If you don't . . .' and he talked at me, just about with his arm around my shoulder, and I thought, This *is* the best man ever put together by God. He is a disciple! So for a while I put my hands on Forrest Gregg and he said, 'Oh my, Bubba that's much better,' and he kept helping me up all the way into the fourth quarter and, you know, I'd never even come *close* to the quarterback at all. So it finally came down to a play where it was fourth and seven to go for them to get a tie, close in on us, and I forgot what Forrest Gregg had been telling me about using my hands, and I ran over him—*splat!*—and the nicest man that God had ever put together became unglued in the mud—right?—and I sat myself on the quarterback.

"Oh, it's a fine thing. You get up on Sunday and you know how important it is, and you go down and eat the pregame meal and a lot of guys are sitting around trying to bullshit and laugh the tension away, and you go back to the room and sit there and listen to that music, that soul music, that Motown that jumps, and it helps perk me up, and before long I'm ready to kill someone. Don Shula never knew that about the music. One time we were playing Dallas in Texas and they had this great band out on the field that was playing this jump music and the brothers were all standing around soaking it in, stomping and moving their heads and stuff, and Shula yells at us to start warming up and to pay attention. He never knew we *were* warming up. He messed with my mind. The next training camp I came in with love beads and a big beard and gone all *hippie*, and I wanted Shula to say one word. But that time he fooled me.

"When I can no longer do what I do best, which is to come fast off the snap of the ball, I got to go. As soon as my legs leave, I got to go. I'd like to play football forever, but there's this li'l ol' bitty man hanging around, and every year he grabs at you and sometimes he gets aholt of your ankle and keeps you from getting off as quickly. And then one year he jumps on your back. Sometimes you can brush him off, but every year he gets heavier and grips harder. We call him 'Rigor.' 'Mr. Rigor Mortis.' I don't feel him now, but I've seen him riding the backs of others. He's right around here somewhere. Look yonder—he might be just behind the door. Maybe he's behind that curtain over there. If he started to bother me on Sundays, I'd lose my mind."

The Other Camp

August 16 The television crew went up to Michigan to film the Detroit team at practice, to see what was on Karras' mind, and to establish a portrait of the opposition. John Gordy went with them, and had the following exchange with Joe Schmidt, the Lion coach:

GORDY: What do you think about George playing against your team?

SCHMIDT: If he wants to play against us, that's up to him. We'll give him a good day's work in Ann Arbor. We'll get after him.

GORDY: You won't let up on him?

SCHMIDT: There's no way you can do that without a chance of injury. If he thinks they're going to go easy on him, he just might be surprised.

330

GORDY: What four plays do you think George is going to run?

SCHMIDT: I wouldn't have the slightest idea. Does he? I hope he tries to throw the ball and that Unitas and Morrall have taught him a quick release.

GORDY: Have you got any advice for him?

SCHMIDT: The only advice I can give is that I hope he's in good shape, and that he's able to run.

Gordy also interviewed Karras:

GORDY: Do you think you'll be able to control your violence when George is on the field?

KARRAS: Well, I don't think there's any such thing as "controlled violence"—at least as regards the play of a defensive lineman. *I* don't know what it is myself. If offensive linemen are thanking God every night as they go to bed that the violence is controlled, then I don't know what they're doing it for, because I've sure never seen anybody controlling himself on *our* side of the line. There's certainly a lot of banging going on out there which looks to me like an all-out effort to knock the other guy's head off. Now it's true that offensive players have to control their violence because they can't use their hands. By the rules they're restricted to the use of their shoulders. I don't know how they do it. Imagine the frustration! I'm sure that at night they go home and get into their closets and scream—maybe for an hour and a half. I wouldn't be able to control my violence like that.

GORDY: So when George appears on the field . . .

KARRAS: I'm going to knock his head off. It's just a question of whether I'm going to maim him a little first . . .

The foregoing were the *official* remarks Karras prepared for the television show—he and Gordy walking along the pink brick paths of the Cranbrook School and chatting easily, the camera crew crouched in front of them and backing up as the two players strolled toward them. Subsequently, Karras, Gordy, and Bill Kronick, the director, found themselves unable to resist filming an additional segment. It started off innocently enough:

GORDY: I know how you feel about quarterbacks, but George

331

Plimpton is your friend. You named your youngest son after him.

KARRAS: That's true. But it may have been a mistake. Look at the funny clothes George wears—those thin ties. I'll bet he was pampered when he was a kid; I'll bet his mum and dad took him to ice-cream parlors and dressed him in knickers.

GORDY: Does that mean you're going to be easy on him?

KARRAS: No, I'm going after George. I want him to know that I'm a real tough football player and that if he gets in a football game in the NFL he's going to find out that we don't just screw around.

GORDY: Alex, do you think George can physically stand that sort of pain?

KARRAS: Yes, I think he can stand the pain. In fact, I think that when they got home from those ice-cream parlors, his mum and dad used to beat him up with a knobbly whip—and so now he *digs* pain. That's the reason he tries to get in all these physical professions. He says he wants to write about them, but that's not true; he wants to be beaten up. That's why he came back to football. He probably wants one of the players to beat him up in the shower, or something like that. The kid is definitely a freak. I hate to say this, but I've seen him checking peckers out in the showers. He's a pecker-checker.

GORDY: Good heavens! You mean . . .

KARRAS: Any quarterback who enjoys going up there to the line of scrimmage and putting his hands on a fat center's crotch has those tendencies, and whenever I've seen George doing it, his eyes are lit up.

GORDY: That might explain one thing that happened when we first got him down there in Baltimore. It had been a long time since he'd been in a group of football players, and he put his jock on over his head.

KARRAS: He likes to smell jocks. He's a jock-smeller and always has been.

This piece was spliced into the regular film for a special occasion or two, and in the instances when it was shown it created quite a furor. One of the people who unexpectedly saw it was an official from DuPont, the sponsors of the TV show, who had come out from the Wilmington, Delaware, home office to Hollywood "to see how we are getting along." He was ushered into the screening room at Wolper Productions and supplied with a drink. The doctored version was deliberately fed into the projector, and when the Karras-Gordy scene flickered on the screen he began shifting around, squeaking his seat in agitation; finally when the part about jock-sniffing appeared, the plastic glass cracked in his hand and ice fell to the floor. "Hey, wait a minute," he said. "I don't know how Wilmington is going to go for this stuff." He was very upset, and I was told that it took quite a while to convince him that the segment was a spoof.

Scene at Elaine's

August 17   I came back to New York for a week, breaking the regimen of training camp. Gordy was in town too, seeing to his fledgling audio-visual business, and we had dinner at a restaurant called Elaine's, which is uptown on Second Avenue. The place was packed, and we stood at the bar in a heavy press of people. Gordy had been to a cocktail party beforehand, and was now weaving a bit and being amazingly belligerent. "Now goddamn it, George," he said. "The game at Ann Arbor is only a week off. You've got to start getting psyched up for it. You're going to get a touchdown against the Lions, or else I'm going to beat the crap out of you."

"John, you must be kidding." I grinned at him.

He was absolutely serious. "What are you talking about, *kidding*," he said scornfully.

I looked down into my drink. "Well," I said. "I'm not sure that threatening to beat me up is the right psychological approach."

"The Colt team is going to bust their ass for you," he said. "You've got to perform for them. Now on that Thirty-four Wham play, you got to do it faster, you got to spin real quick." He spun amid the crowd at the bar to demonstrate; people were jostled; there were cries of alarm. "The thing you have to remember is to keep low and crouched, so the ball is hidden as you turn. Look, like this." He bent over as if he were going to leap out at someone. ("What's *wrong* with that man?" I heard a girl ask.) "You got that?" Gordy said. I nodded. "Well, try it." I crouched, but I did it subtly, and turned slowly. "You look like you're hiding behind a bush," Gordy said loudly. "Your body's got to be full of tension—cocked like a trigger. Try it again."

This time I put more into it, holding my hand over the top of my Scotch and water to keep the ice from slopping out, and Elaine, the proprietor of the restaurant, came over and said, "I don't know what you two are doing, but can you calm it down a little?"

She gave us a table. The people at the bar stared. Gordy took out a felt pen and began drawing Lion defenses on the cloth. "Now if they defense you with a four-three, which they probably will, here's the sort of thing you should look for. This guy here"—he tapped the tablecloth with the tip of his pen—"may cheat a bit this way. Which means that—"

Nick, a waiter, appeared at his shoulder. "Gentlemen, the specialty tonight is veal parmigiana with a nice Marsala sauce . . ."

"Just bring us some chops," Gordy said. He turned back to the drawing. "Now if you see him cheat, you can take advantage of it by—"

"It doesn't do me any good to see that," I said.

"It's everything. Goddamn it, George, if you can read what they're doing . . ."

"John, Mac hasn't taught me any automatics. I can't change the play at the line of scrimmage. I don't know enough to do it properly. If I call the Thirty-four Wham, that's it, even if Bulaich or whoever gets the ball from me on the handoff sees the four hole plugged with seven Lions. You know that, John."

Gordy made some furious marks with his pen on the cloth. "I gotta speak to Mac about that; it's not right. If you don't know a few automatics—well, I don't know about your *moving* the ball. We got to get you scoring, not running Bulaich into seven Lions. Jesus!"

I tried to calm him down. "Look, John. I'm going to do the best I can. Sometimes I think more about survival than scoring touchdowns, I admit, but I'll do my best."

He looked at me and his voice dropped. "I want you to beat those people so bad," he said.

Gordy's attitude was much more than that of simply wanting a friend to do well. I was never able to figure it out, and I'm not sure even he could fathom that odd, turbulent love-hate relationship with his old team. Perhaps one reason was that all the activity, the familiar rituals, the camaraderie that he had once been such a part of now belonged exclusively to others—all of it denied him, like being abruptly kicked out of a country club. It rankled. What made it so ironic was that *I* had become his surrogate for taking it out on them, his instrument of revenge, the only one he had. So he urged me on.

It was an unlikely position for me, but I did my best to humor him. As the chops arrived at the table, I said with conviction, "Don't worry, John, I'm going to put their light bulbs out."

Buterakos

While I was in New York, Buterakos called from Flint, Michigan. His voice came thundering out of the receiver. "How are you, Big Man?" He said the upcoming game in Ann Arbor was causing considerable interest—not the least of it my participation—and though he was busy himself and would not be there, he knew many people who were going.

Had he seen Karras, I wanted to know.

Well, they'd had a kind of falling out, Buterakos said. The two of them didn't see eye to eye on the Karras Golf Classic anymore. Karras had assigned his authority to someone else. They weren't speaking. Buterakos seemed forlorn at the other end. It wasn't only the golf tournament. Things were changing. It wasn't like old times anymore. So few of the old Lions were left.

Well, that was all sad news, I said.

Oh, *he* was all right, he shouted cheerfully into the phone. He was the same. He wasn't going to let anyone change his life style. Nossir. He began telling me about a vacation that he had taken at a dude ranch near Tucson, Arizona. He told it to me like a play, performing all the parts. He had been picked up at the airport by a young college kid got up in the most immaculate sort of western duds, close-fitted, and his cowboy boots shone like teak. He was very unctuous and polite and he called Buterakos "sir" and he snapped his fingers in a most supercilious manner to arrange for Buterakos' baggage to be taken out to the station wagon. I could hear Buterakos snap his fingers over the phone. He described the station wagon as having the name of the dude ranch embossed in little gold letters on the front doors. The college kid drove.

About two miles out of town, Buterakos cleared his throat. He asked, "I wonder if you could tell me. Have my whips arrived?"

"I beg your pardon, sir."

"A small packing case of whips. They were supposed to have arrived by air freight to await my arrival."

The driver said no, he had not been made aware of such a package.

"Crap!" said Buterakos.

After a while the driver said pleasantly, "Sir, I think you'll find that the horses at the Bar-S Ranch are very well behaved, and that you'll not have any need for your whips."

"No need for my whips!" Buterakos exclaimed. "Hell, boy, why do you think I come to the Bar-S Ranch—to ride horses? Hell no. I come to *whip* them."

The driver sucked in his breath as Buterakos rambled on: "What sort of vacation have I let myself in for if my whips haven't arrived. Christ!" He struck his knee. "Goddamn mails. Can't trust anything in the country these days."

"You whip the horses . . ." the driver said weakly.

"As many as I can get at," Buterakos said.

To keep up the fiction Buterakos told me that after his arrival he had hurried into Tucson to purchase some whips, quite a variety, from the long circus whips with ten-foot thongs, to shorter, more businessman-like whips, like thin billy clubs, which he would unpack and lay out in rows so the maid would come in to clean his room and see him standing over them, gloating, and occasionally reaching down to touch one. He told me he carried a circus whip with him into the dining room at mealtimes, the long thong trailing behind, and the people would look up from their bowls of salad and watch him sit down alone at a far table and prop up the whip on the chair next to him. In the evening he kept the shades of his room up, so that guests walking back from their friendly games of bridge or canasta would glance in and see the alarming sight of Buterakos apparently practicing, rearing back and cracking his whip down on the bed. Occasionally he would open the door to his bunkhouse and shout out into the night, "Tomorrow I want a palomino—!" then slam the door so it sounded like a gunshot in the desert air.

All of it made a tremendous impression. People called him "The Whipper" and avoided him for fear that he would lash out at them. They thought that he was mad.

Once or twice, he told me, he would make an entrance at the saddling corral just as one of the riding tours was about to get under way into the desert—wearing enormous woolly chaps and a Mexican sombrero and a bright spangled shirt that looked as if it had been borrowed off the back of a Las Vegas croupier. A gasp would go up from the guests, now mounted, staring down at the small *ranchero*, and the whispers would go up: ". . . The Whipper, The Whipper, The Whipper."

Buterakos would light up a large cigar and eye the horse that had been brought out for him. "This horse doesn't look very fresh to me. He looks down in the ears. Have I ever *had* this horse before?"

"No, sir."

"Well, bring me another one. Bring me a brown one. And see that you bring me one that's bigger."

He wandered among the horses. He told me that one of the riders was a Bostonian lady who had been coming to the Bar-S Ranch for twenty-eight years. She was riding a large white horse. Buterakos looked up at her. "I like the frame on your horse, ma'am," he said politely. "I wonder if you'd let me *test* it tomorrow."

While such exchanges were going on, the contingent of guests would move toward one of the desert trails, looking back over their shoulders with long stares as if horrified by the smoking results of an Indian massacre. They returned from their rides to discover Buterakos sitting by the pool with his whip dangling in the water ("to keep the ends from drying out and flaking," as he put it), and he would look up and call out cheerfully, "Must have missed you folks. Took the West Fork Trail by mistake. Got my whip caught up in a tree."

"Did any of them ever catch on?" I asked.

"Oh, sure," Buterakos said. "They began to laugh after a while. But the woman from Boston and the snotty kid who drove the station wagon, they never did."

"That's quite a vacation," I said.

"I'm sorry to tell you about Karras," he said abruptly. "I mean, we had such great times together. But I think he's in trouble up there. It's the end of the game, don't you see? They tell me he's very quiet at the camp, and then suddenly he bad-mouths someone. He lashes out. He's not having fun anymore. There's no joking around. It's going to be very hard for him."

"I'm sure it will work out," I said lamely.

"It's a bad time for anyone when it's all closing out, but it's real hard on him. It's bad for me, too. You think I don't care?"

"I know you do."

"Damn right, Big Man."

Lions

August 17   At the first team meeting I went to after returning to training camp from New York, Coach McCafferty started off by asking for volunteers to play on the offensive team for my four plays at Ann Arbor against the Lions. A few hands went up—Tom Nowatzke's, Don Nottingham's, Bill Curry's, a few rookies', and Fred Miller put his hand up and said that he would like to volunteer for the Detroit *defense*. The laughter rose around the room, the chair legs complaining shrilly as players turned and began jeering and asking how much they would get paid and would I write about their contribution fulsomely—until finally there was so much racket that McCafferty banged the lectern and said to hell with a volunteer system, he was going to make up the team list *himself,* and he would guarantee that anyone who missed a bed check or dragged his ass down on the practice field would find himself on the Plimpton squad.

The movie screen was pulled down so we could watch films on the Lion defenses, and the mood of hilarity changed abruptly. The whir of the projector became a background for the coaches' comments on specific situations they wanted us to remember. In the semidarkness the players leaned forward and made notes in their books. When the lights came on again, John Idzik stepped up to the lectern and offered some additional comments.

"Now the Detroit tackles play loose off the ball; both of them are readers; all the front four do a lot of shifting in the line and jumping around. Mitchell out on the end likes to fake outside and come inside. He does that more than he should. Karras—well, he's terribly strong on top; he uses his hands well; he hops around and reads well, and he can throw you to either side. He'll do funky things to you. We don't know much about Haverdick, who may come in at the other tackle position, except that he plays high. Larry Hand at the other end position comes on you hard all day. We think we can run our running plays at Mike Lucci and Wayne Walker. The other Detroit linebacker, Paul Naumoff, is the best they've got. He's all over the field, and he'll go over the top of benches to hit you. He does the forty in four-point-seven. To get away from him, the Nineteen Straight would be a good play to run. In their defense secondary, Dick LeBeau, number forty-four, is at the corner and he likes to give you the outside. Lem Barney, at the other corner, likes to guess a lot, but it rarely gets him into trouble. His first step is always back, but he reacts so quickly that there's no point in trying to take advantage of it; in the films you saw his feet move in a blur. A good play against Barney is the Sixty-six Dig—five yards down and cut. Barney's feet take him backwards so quickly that the short cut just might work against him. The Lions have a great defensive secondary. All of them have great vision, and they help each other out. But they have such confidence in themselves that they stick to single coverage. They match you—your personnel against theirs. They dare you to beat them."

There was a sudden sharp explosion in the back of the room. Heads turned. Danny Sullivan had killed a fly with his playbook.

"Quiet it down," Idzik said.

"We're killing bugs back here," Sullivan said.

"Well, do it without making so much noise," Idzik said. He turned to a paper on his lectern. "The Lion defense is usually in a four-three," he continued. "Out of two hundred and twenty-two defensive formations, the Lions were in a four-three a hundred and twenty-two times. They blitzed thirty-two times on first down, fifty-two times on second down, and thirty-six times on third down. I'm telling you, their philosophy is quite simple: it's to get after you. Against Jim Hart, the Cardinal quarterback, they blitzed sixty-five percent of the time."

One of the quarterbacks in the front of the room whistled. It was odd to hear all this planning going on against my old teammates. Tom Nowatzke, also a former Lion, was sitting immediately in front of me, and occasionally he would raise a hand and offer a tip about his erstwhile teammates. At one point Idzik looked over Nowatzke's head, back to where I was leaning against the wall, and asked, "George, anything you'd like to tell us about the Lions?"

"There's nothing I can think of that you haven't pointed out," I said evenly. "You've covered everything very nicely."

Quarterback Meeting

August 18 We trooped into the coaches' meeting room and drew up chairs around a big table. The room was full of paraphernalia—movie projectors, screens, charts, a mimeograph

340

machine. Don McCafferty sat at the head of the table, flanked by his offensive coaches, Bobby Boyd and John Idzik; John Gordy sat at the foot of the table with me.

MC CAFFERTY: All right. Quarterback meeting. We've done four plays for you. We *think* the Lions will probably stay in a simple four-three defense. These plays are designed to work against the four-three.

BOYD: No checking off.

MC CAFFERTY: No automatics.

PLIMPTON: It's academic. I don't know how to check off a play.

MC CAFFERTY: All right. The first play is the Flank Right Ride Thirty-eight Sucker. We *were* going to have the Fourteen Sucker, in which the guard pulls towards you, but George, you're so slow coming out from under the center that he'll probably knock you down—which would be very embarrassing since he's your own man. With the Ride Thirty-eight, the guard pulls *away* from you and we've got to *hope* that Karras goes with him. That's the sucker. Then you hand the ball to the fullback coming through Karras' hole, in which we hope he will not be.

GORDY: I think Karras will sucker. He's very aggressive.

BOYD: That's the lollypop play.

IDZIK: One hopes.

MC CAFFERTY: Yeah. Nottingham's gonna be the fullback, and if Karras isn't influenced we might be minus one fullback. Okay, you got that one?

PLIMPTON: Yeah.

MC CAFFERTY: Let's hear you call it.

PLIMPTON: Ride thirty-eight sucker.

MC CAFFERTY: Wait a minute. You gotta do it right.

PLIMPTON: Sorry. Flank right; ride thirty-eight sucker.

MC CAFFERTY: On *what*, for Chrissakes?

PLIMPTON: On *one*.

MC CAFFERTY: Fine. Now here's the second one: Flank Right Split Thirty-four Wham, which is again a handoff. We put a surge on the defensive line, with the lead back coming through and hitting the defensive tackle, putting a wham on the guy, who will probably be Karras again. Now for Chrissake, give the ball to the *second* back coming by you, not to the first. In fact, open a bit more when you turn so's that first back will have more room to operate.

PLIMPTON: Right. Flank right split; thirty-four wham; on *two*.

MC CAFFERTY: Make all the snaps on *one* so you don't get your head cluttered up.

PLIMPTON: Okay.

MC CAFFERTY: Fine. All right, now your third play is the pass play, which we'll run out of the double wing. Double Wing Right Split.

PLIMPTON: Double wing right split.

MC CAFFERTY: Sixty-eight C.I. Now the "C" means a "close" pattern—which is the instruction for the halfback who should screen off the middle guard and bring the left side safety over. The "I" cut is just a three-step movement by the end, so in order to match him you're to take three steps back from the center and *fire*. Just remember what color jersey you have on. If it's blue, fire to that end in blue out there. Three steps and throw that gimpy duck you've been throwing in practice. We'll just have to hope it gets to him. Now Dick LeBeau of the Lions is over there. He's an excellent defender and he gets a little nosy once in a while, so he's the man you've got to worry about. But we hope our receiver can beat him and get in the slot between the middle guard and the weakside linebacker.

PLIMPTON: Are there secondary receivers on this play, in case the first one is covered?

MC CAFFERTY: Well, there *are* secondary receivers, but I'd stick to the first one. If you get in to big trouble, the fullback will be going out here in the flat (*jabs diagram with pencil*) and you can dump the pass out to him. But don't clutter up your mind. Just concentrate on the first receiver.

PLIMPTON: Right.

MC CAFFERTY: All right, now the fourth play. The thought here was that we'd best save it for last, since you're going to carry the ball *yourself*, and if we scheduled it as the *first* play we might not have the chance to see the other three. Haw haw haw haw. (*The men around the table lean back in their chairs and laugh uproariously.*)

PLIMPTON: Ahem.

MC CAFFERTY: Now, I know you've been talking about the possibility of running the bootleg, but after timing you in the forty-yard dash and seeing the way you run, there's no way you're gonna get around that end. Even if you fool him with your fake, he's gonna recover and catch up with you. So I think for the running play we'd better settle on the quarterback draw. Now here's how you call that: "Flank right split; quarterback fifty-two trap draw." The draw goes right up the middle through the number two hole. All our draws are in the fifty series, and when you designate it by "quarterback," it means to the people in the huddle that *you're* going to take it through. Right? Okay. Both the backs will flair out, the tight end will release, and to the defense it will look like a pass. Now the play action in front of you looks like this: the center and the left guard will step back one step, the center blocking left, and the left guard will pull and trap Karras.

GORDY: That is, if he's around after being belted on the first three plays.

MC CAFFERTY: Christ, he'll be around. Let's just hope he's up on the line enough so that he can be trapped. Now, George, the hole in front of you will only be open for a second. Normally our quarterbacks take three steps back before they turn and come up the middle, but considering your quickness . . .

PLIMPTON: Yeah?

MC CAFFERTY: . . . I think you'd better make it *two* steps. Now if you *do* make it through the hole, be on the lookout for your right tackle. He'll be coming in to block the middle guard, or the linebacker, Mike Lucci, and you should try to play off his block. Right? Right. And good luck to you. That's all, everybody.

GORDY: Coach, before we all go, I want to ask a question. Do you want George to stick to that exact order?

MC CAFFERTY: Well, I think it's best. We start out with the sucker, hoping Karras will be influenced, so that maybe Nottingham can slip by him. Then we're gonna put a little surge on him; the third one is a pass to test the arm, and the fourth one . . . Well . . .

GORDY: Suppose he scores a touchdown on the pass play?

MC CAFFERTY: Well, that means he won't have to call the quarterback sneak. Which may be a very good thing indeed. If he scores on *any* of these plays we'll all go out and have some champagne somewhere. Okay? Dismiss.

Airplane

August 21   At the entrance to the plane ramp a Baltimore fan named Hurst Loudenslager was standing beside a small phonograph, on which a record was emitting the tinny-sounding strains of "The Baltimore Colt Fight Song":

> *Let's go you Colts,*
> *Let's get the ball across the line*
> *For Bal-ti-more*
> *And Mar-y-land!*

Loudy, as everyone calls him, has been seeing the Colts off on their road trips since 1956, and has been on hand for their returns as well, often a lonely figure standing in the airport terminal at 5:00 A.M. In all these years he has apparently missed only one send-off, on an occasion when he was ill and under doctor's orders not to budge, but he sent a friend as a substitute bearing the phonograph (he has worn out two of them), the "Colt Fight Song" record (he has gone through six of these), and the small cards on which a special message in poetry is printed each time.

The exhortation on the card Loudy gave me as I walked up the ramp read, in part, as follows:

> *We're on our way to Lion land*
> *To get some Lion meat*
> *Sunday night we'll be a happy band*
> *'Cause the Lions we're gonna beat.*

For me the message was a mockery. A half-hour earlier Earl Morrall had come by in the airport lounge and said, "Hey, have you heard the news? The Lions don't want to play."

My heart jumped. "What's that?"

"They had a vote about your four plays, and they don't want to do it. I just heard from Mac."

It turned out that McCafferty had called Joe Schmidt in Detroit about some technical matters, and in the course of the conversation had remarked that he hoped that during my four plays the Lions' defensive unit would stay in a traditional 4-3 defense and not shift or stunt, since I had not learned any automatic calls to compensate. At the other end Schmidt cleared his throat and said that the whole matter was academic since the Lion team at its meeting the night before had decided to veto the project. Schmidt said there was nothing *he* could do about it; it was a team matter.

I found McCafferty, who was sitting in the airport cocktail lounge with the rest of the coaches. He shook his head disgustedly. "I know," he said. "Bush. It's real chicken-shit stuff."

"What am I going to do?" I asked. It was a frightening moment; a whole television show hung in the balance.

McCafferty said, "To hell with those Detroit people. I'll send you in anyway." He was visibly angered. "What's wrong with those guys screwing you up like that?"

"You mean . . . ?"

"Sure. For a series. What the hell difference does it make? There may be some paper work to do; we'd have to sign you to an official contract so that you'd be on the team roster."

Bobby Boyd interrupted. "That will give you a chance to renege," he said with a grin. "Insist that you won't sign unless they give you a big salary boost."

I felt great warmth toward McCafferty and the rest of them. I was a part of it all once more. Damn! And under conditions which would be completely realistic. I strode around the airport, almost weak-kneed with relief. I told Bill Curry about it. "Isn't that something for Mac to do?" I asked. "He's just going to stuff me in. I may be the starting quarterback."

"That's like him," Curry said. "Mac has mastered the art of living."

But then I was called over to a cocktail table by Carroll

Rosenbloom, the club owner. It was ten minutes to flight time. "What's this I hear?" he asked.

"The Lions balked at my participation in those extra plays," I explained. "But it doesn't make any difference. Mac's sending me in anyway."

"Wait a minute. He can't do that!" Rosenbloom said. "Not against the Lions. It won't wash."

"What?"

"The Commissioner established the rules."

Rosenbloom was adamant and went over to talk to McCafferty. The head coach shrugged his shoulders; there was nothing he could do. It had all collapsed again; so now the only hope was to get the Lion players to change their minds. I spent the flight to Detroit wondering why they had rebelled against my four plays. Once again, I was apart; staring out the window I felt remote from the team, who were joshing now with the stewardesses, and the gin rummy games picking up, and the slap and rustle of cards shuffling . . . as removed as if I were five miles down, where the tiny lights winked against the darkness, loosening my tie, yawning and getting ready to help clean the dinner plates before settling down in front of the TV set.

On the Bus

August 22   The dispute with the Lions was worked out somehow the next day. Gordy went and talked to them, and it turned out to be a question of emolument and insurance, and just what the ground rules were; apparently there had been a lack of communication. I had spent a restless night in the Ann Arbor motel; the news did not come through until just as we were getting on the bus to drive to the stadium.

I sat down next to Roy Hilton, the big end. "I hear it's all been straightened out. You're going in at half time," he said. "Well, now you've got something to think about."

"What's on *your* mind at the moment?" I asked.

"Rocky Frietas is the Lion playing opposite me," he said. "I'm thinking about him. He's a defender, a tremendous defender against a slap to the helmet. His arms come up like this." He made a violent motion in his seat.

"Do you do a lot of head-slapping?"

"I didn't used to," he replied. "In the New Orleans game in nineteen sixty-eight this fellow said, 'Hey, don't do that. My head hurts.' So I say, 'Okay.' "

I sat thinking of this odd compassion of Hilton's and watching the trees slide by the bus windows and the people on the streets moving on errands that I suddenly realized I envied. If I'd seen a man running frantically around a corner, his face pale and his eyes starting, I would have, accepted whatever he was running toward or away from in preference to my situation at that point. How odd that an hour earlier I had been despairing that perhaps I wouldn't be in this state of mental turmoil!

The Pre-Game Warm-Up

I remember walking with the team down a long tunnel with sunlight at the far end, and the distant band music coming through. The odd clash of our cleats reverberating in that hollow corridor and the grotesquery of men with wide high shoulder pads up around their ears gave me the sense of being part of an unlikely contingent from another environment—as if our intrusion into the sunlight at the end was like a progression of military tanks arriving on the periphery of a picnic. People stood and stared; a murmur went up. We trotted out onto the artificial surface, a huge metallic green carpet of fibers off which the heat shimmered, and I tried to lose myself in the anonymity of calisthenics, and then in the drills at our end of the field. I was wearing a large blue number one on my game jersey, the thoughtful gesture of someone who felt that I was due a rise in rating from the zero I had worn when I was with the Lions. The crowd continued to file in; over a hundred thousand were expected. At one end of the field stood a huge scoreboard—actionless now, though soon enough a finger would push a button and it would click on, ready to provide the statistics of our activity.

Locker Room

We returned to the locker room to wait. The place got quiet except for the low thump of Motown coming out of Bubba's cassette. He took it with him into the toilet stall. Outside we could hear the band music. Bob Vogel, the offensive tackle, gave a prayer before we went out. Everyone knelt, staring at the cement floor. As Vogel prayed he drew on a pair of hand-fit boxing gloves that fighters use on the light bags; his hands are delicate and bruise in the helmet-cracking. His prayer was a chatty monologue addressed to God; Vogel told Him that the team had worked hard and was prepared, and everyone hoped to do Him proud and play strong football. He asked Him to protect all the players from injury. I was interested that Vogel didn't ask for any special favors, such as a Colt victory; he was simply giving Him a report and letting Him know that everyone was going to do their best.

When it was over, I whispered to Jim Duncan on the next stool that I was surprised that no one had been praying for victory. He looked at me and blinked. "Why, Lem Barney over there in the Detroit Lion locker room, *he's* not praying for victory. Neither do I. If both teams pray for victory, why it's going to end up in a *tie*, and who wants that?"

Last Words

Mike Curtis was sitting next to me. He said, "You're sweating like a goat."

"I know. It's hot."

"Everybody's sweating. But not like a goat."

"Well, I'm nervous."

348

"Don't get nervous," he said. "Don't worry about it. If they get to you, just fall down. There's nothing you can do about it. Watcha going to do about it?"

The Grasshopper

About halfway through the first period, a grasshopper jumped up on my pants leg as I was sitting on the bench. He materialized on my knee and began rubbing his hind feet slowly back and forth. I became absolutely focused on him, as if such concentration would keep my mind from going awry with my commitment so close at hand. "Hey, Bill," I called to Kronick. He was crouched over one of his cameramen and pointing out to the center of the field. "Look at this."

He came over. "What?" He had to shout. The Lions' offense was moving against the Colts, and behind us the huge crowd was in an uproar.

"Down on my knee."

"What? What?"

"Look. It's a goddamn grasshopper."

He bent down and adjusted his glasses. "Yeah?"

"Look at its color. It's the same color as the fake grass— that sort of dusty metallic green. It just hopped up here, right up out of the TartanTurf."

"Yeah?"

"Isn't that the damnedest thing? Watcha think? What about getting a camera over here? Might be a great shot . . . I mean, sitting here with only a few minutes to go, staring at a grasshopper. Suspense," I said. "The audience might think I'd gone bonkers under the pressure."

The crowd rose to its feet, cheering a long pass completion.

"You all right?" Kronick asked. "Where's Gordy?"

They found him, and he came hurrying down the length of the bench. He was wearing a red shirt with a small blue alligator emblem and fancy trousers with wide colored stripes, an outfit I had stared at with envy ever since putting on the foreign-feeling accouterments of football. Another roar from the crowd went up, and then a groan. The Colts had taken over the ball. "What's up?" Gordy shouted. "Got a grasshopper here," I said. He bent over. "Grasshopper on my knee," I said into his ear. We looked. The grasshopper had gone. I bent off the bench and looked at the ground near my feet. "It was right here, John," I said.

He said, "Let's go and look at the Detroit defenses." I'm not sure he heard the business about the grasshopper; he never let on. We went and stood on the sidelines, the worst vantage point from which to see anything out on the field, especially anything of a technical nature. "Look," said Gordy. "That's an *over.* It's not a four-three. Christ! There's no telling what they're going to throw at you. You'll have to compensate if you see that formation." The Colts ran another play. "Look at that!" cried Gordy. "Another 'over.' See how that linebacker cheats way over, and the tackles move in?"

"John, it doesn't mean anything to me," I said. "I only know my four plays. It's too late. I want to sit down."

I returned to the bench. There were ten minutes left in the half. It seemed a long time. I kept thinking how nice it would be if those ten minutes, plus about thirty more, went by in a great gulp, and were now past, and whatever had happened could be looked back at in tranquillity. One wanted it long over with.

The First Play

When the first half ended, the referee picked up the ball and put it on the fifty yard line, and over the stadium loudspeaker it was announced that I was coming in for four plays.

I felt the vast attention focus with almost palpable weight, so that when I walked out toward the center of the field for my four plays I had the sense of being stooped, as if under a heavy bag of grain. Such a bedlam of gusty anticipation beat down from the sides of that bowl that the unexpected conceit came to mind that I was hearing the same sort of sound the

Christians of Nero's time must have heard when they stepped out to meet the lions of *their* day. There was nothing that seemed familiar or reassuring. My teammates' helmets were turned toward me, watching me, but they seemed strangers, and it was almost surprising to recognize someone behind the bars of the helmet—Bill Curry's friendly face and his voice, just barely audible in all that racket, saying, "Let's go get them, okay?"

The huddle formed and I called the first play, the Ride 38, which was supposed to sucker Karras. As I stepped up to the line my attention was abruptly caught by the Lions, already starting their defensive cries, jockeying their bodies, grim and keening in anticipation. Only then did I become aware of an almost tangible feeling of hatred—a chemical essence that seemed to be fomented by the confrontation of the two different-colored jerseys, almost as if the blue of the Lions and the white of the Colts created a mix of unbridled detestation. It was an astounding sensation to feel this so strongly. There was nothing in my experience to prepare me for it; the *scrimmaging* with both the Colts and the Lions had been violent and frightening enough, but it did not produce the raw hate. I had always remembered Vince Lombardi's line that "to play this game you must have fire in you, and there is nothing that stokes the fire like hate." Here it was, the embodiment of what he was talking about.

I stepped in behind Curry. I looked out into the Lion secondary, swallowed twice and, conscious that I was already beginning to flinch, I launched a high querulous voice into the count. The ball snapped back into my palm, but too far forward, so that it was on my fingertips and I barely had control of it. I withdrew it, gripping it at the back end, and shoveled it off, nose down, at Don Nottingham. The timing was inexorable. He had to stutter-step to control the handoff, and I heard the breath puff out of him as he was smacked down at the line of scrimmage. "Sorry," I called out. "Sorry."

I kicked at the ground in dismay. Then, as I turned away from the play, I was suddenly clouted hard across the helmet, a ringing concussive blow that popped my ears. I looked around astonished. It turned out that Jim Mitchell, the big

Detroit end, had seen me standing there and couldn't resist it: he was hot and furious and, as he said later, if I wanted to see NFL football at close hand he wanted to give me a taste of what it was *really* like. A whistle blew against the tumult of sound booming down from the sides of the bowl, and the referee threw down his yellow handkerchief. "Okay, that's unnecessary roughness," he called out. He picked up the ball and marched it smartly fifteen yards down to the thirty-five yard line.

The Lions took this with no grace whatsoever; they swore at him. Wayne Walker yelled, "Keep that goddamn thing in your pocket." As we walked to the new line of scrimmage, I was jostled and one of the Lions stepped on my foot.

I thought, My God, what's going on here? And I've got three more plays to go.

Two Plays

The second play was the 34 Wham. Karras was supposed to be whammed—whatever that meant—but just as I started the count out of the corner of my eye I saw him shift position, a big sideways hop like a monkey's at the bars of his cage to see something better, and he placed himself solidly in the four hole where Jack Maitland, who was to receive the handoff, was supposed to go. I had just cried "Blue!" to begin the count, and I remember feeling a fleeting touch of sympathy for Maitland, and then a more poignant sense of woe for myself; I was engineering a play that was utterly doomed.

Sure enough. The turn and handoff were crisp enough, and Maitland, the second back past, collected the ball properly, but his progress was short-lived, like someone running into the side of a hill. He burrowed for perhaps a yard. Whistles blew. "Sorry!" I called again.

Some sort of altercation began up at the line. Ferocious language; a shove or two. We stood panting in the heat, in that viscous soup of resentment and rage, and I gazed dumbly at the Colt and Lion players involved, too absorbed in my own problems to be concerned. I didn't know who they were, the jerseys and helmets providing shields of anonymity. The dispute was broken up by the referee. The storm of sound continued to drift down from the stands.

"Huddle!" I heard Curry shout. The players collected, and I called the pass play with its mysterious initials C.I. I flexed my thumb. Someone said, "Okay, good," and the huddle broke with a quick crack of hands, that inevitable procedure indicating discipline whatever the circumstances, and we walked up toward the line.

My pass traveled only fifteen feet before being smacked down by someone reaching up with an arm like a telephone pole. It turned out to be Jerry Rush, the Detroit lineman, who terminated my effort with such finality that it seemed as if I had taken careful aim and deliberately thrown the ball into his outstretched palm. I was jostled by someone rushing by and never saw the ball fall to the ground. Beyond Rush I could see Gordon Bowdell, the intended receiver, slowing up, his head down. "Where'd it go?" I called. "What happened to it?" Then I saw the referee pick up the ball and set it back down on the thirty-five. At least it had not been intercepted. "Sorry," I called out again.

The Quarterback Sneak

It turned out to be the perfect call. Mike Lucci of the Lions had called a blitz, and he came right up on the line to blow in and nail me in what he must have assumed was going to be another pass play. Beyond Curry, somewhat to my surprise, I could see an open area. At the signal the ball slapped into my hand. I took a step back, and then lurched forward as Lucci, overcommitted himself, rushed past me on my right. I found myself moving forward unencumbered—astonished, and with a twinge of fear that something had gone wrong, that this was not the proper state of things. Then Karras, appropriately enough, put everything to rights by getting me from behind at the ankles and dropping me clean. Mitchell came up and sat on me to make sure. The advance was about six yards. My eyes were grimaced almost shut throughout the play. If I had kept them ajar, and done some looking, and seen my right tackle coming across as McCafferty said he would, and used him properly and done some high stepping—well, perhaps I could have advanced deep into their secondary.

As it was, I was done, my nose bar resting on the Tartan-Turf. Someone called out, "Are you all right?" A gun went off somewhere, sending the players to the locker rooms. I trudged across the metallic grass. No one spoke to me. Just before the tunnel entrance I looked up at the great bank of faces—curious, staring down, a few hands clapping in support, friendly, some calling my name—to get me to look up at them and once again I sensed what I remembered about my stint with the Lions: that the onlookers enjoyed a certain relief watching my discomfiture out there, a reassurance that the professional world was not a place in which the amateur trafficked without being thumped badly. It was the correct state of things, and it was good to have it verified firsthand. They were sympathetic; I saw the hands going, and the smiles, and I felt a strong warmth toward them, knowing that soon enough I would be sitting up there with these people, wearing a straw hat against the sun and setting the soda pop under the seat to keep it cool.

The two teams walked into the tunnel together to the heavy crash of cleats against the wall. The darkness of the corridor contained no coolness; it was a furnace. Everyone stared straight ahead. Just as we got to the doors on either side of the tunnel that led to the two locker rooms, I caught Karras' eye and gave him a quick wan smile of greeting.

"Can't win 'em all, Georgie," he said. His voice had no humor in it; it was derisive. He disappeared through the door into the Lions' locker room.

Aftermath

I sat in the empty locker room with John Gordy. The team had left to start the second half. The water dripped in the shower stalls.

354

"I wanted you to do it so goddamn much," Gordy said. "I mean, really stick it to them."

"I'm sorry," I said.

"It was so goddamn close!"

"I know."

"It must have been goddamn hot out there."

"It was."

"Well, it's over, George."

"Yes. There are some things to be remembered, aren't there?"

"Christ, what a chance we had when they blitzed on the sneak."

"I know."

He picked up a roll of tape and began tossing it up and down in his palm. Outside there was a long sustained roar. "The Colts are in trouble," he said.

"John, what I remember now is not the good stuff but the hate. It was as thick as steam—really, I could hardly believe it out there. It just *poured* off everybody."

"One block could have sprung you," Gordy said. "You could have stepped into the end zone."

"John, why do you keep harping on that?"

"Because you worked so hard at it, and that's what it's all about, goddamn it. There's nothing else. *There is nothing else.*"

We sat looking at each other. "I've forgotten," Gordy said. "How many yards did you make when you played with the Lions?"

"I lost about twenty yards."

"Well, let's see, this time you picked up fifteen on the penalty, maybe a yard on the running plays, and six yards on the sneak—so that's *plus* twenty-two. You're improving." He began squeezing the tape between his hands. "It could have been a nice cool *fifty* yards," he said.

"I know," I said.

"God*damn* it was close."

"John, I don't see how you could have done it for all those years."

"What are you talking about?"

"That hate out there—all that preparation to get involved in something like that!"

"Look," he said. "If you don't want to remember that, there are other things to be remembered, right?"

"Sure," I said.

"Well, remember the other things for Chrissakes."

"Okay, John."

I took off my football shoes, worked my toes up and down, and I took a deep breath and thought how good the shower would feel.

So that was it. The journal ended there. Over a hundred pages
in the book were left blank, though perhaps that is in the nature
of most diaries—drying up on page ninety-three ("Weather fair
today"). The rest is blank surmise. I doubt I could have continued. Circumstances had changed so abruptly. Within a week
or so of my appearance in Ann Arbor I set off to Africa to do
another TV special, trying in this instance the profession of
wildlife photography, with my specific task to take a publishable
picture of an enormous elephant named Ahmed who lives on a
strange forested mountain rising out of the desert in northern
Kenya.

I left the Baltimore journal in New York, along with the
notes I had been keeping on Karras and Gordy for *their* book.
Football was closed out completely, as abruptly as the career of
a man not only fired from his profession but exiled from practicing it again, like a disbarred lawyer.

Occasionally I got snippets of news. Gordy sent a post card saying that he was going to marry his girl, the one whose father had the schooner. The scores of the exhibition games turned up in days-old copies of the Paris *Herald Tribune*. The Colts were not doing well, but I knew they were being brought along slowly. The Lions had won a couple of games. Then I read the stunning news that the Lions had let Karras go. I was sitting on the veranda of the Norfolk Hotel in Nairobi waiting to talk to an expert on elephants, and I was so startled by what I was reading that I called out in alarm and people sitting at nearby tables turned to see if someone was in need of medical aid. It was hard for me to believe. The story, only a half-column in length, offered few clues: a terse announcement from the front office; the expected outrage from Karras, blaming the action on his own outspokenness; a summary of his career.

Well, I thought, the three of us are done with it now. For them it was doubtless traumatic, but in my own case I could scarcely remember that I had played football at all. I tried a few notes while out on safari, sitting in the canvas camp chair in the shade of the acacia trees, but the associations were difficult. Even when I returned to New York and looked at the Baltimore journal with its strange big scrawl, neither the hand-writing nor what it described seemed personally relevant—as if I had come home to discover the manuscript of some lunatic third party lying in the drawer.

Still, a bond of devotion had been established with the Baltimore Colts, and as soon as I could, I took the train down to Baltimore to watch them play. The game was against the Miami Dolphins. For the first half I sat in the press box and strained against the opposition; the plywood desk creaked from the force as I leaned forward, staring at the distant field, jaw agape, applying a brand of body English that made the reporters on either side uncomfortable.

"Third and three is not an easy situation," I said to them.

"No," they said. "You've made us quite aware of that. It's fortunate the desks are bolted down."

They wanted to chat. "How's your friend Karras?"

"I'm told he's in Mexico somewhere—I haven't been able to reach him."

"What on earth is he doing down there? Mexican football? Haw haw haw."

"No," I said solemnly. "I'm told he's down there doing a film. He always toyed with the idea of getting into films."

"They shouldn't have let that cat go. No way."

"You're right," I said.

"Hey, what was it like down there?"

"What?"

"I mean when you played . . ."

"I don't know," I said truthfully. "It's not really very clear to me. I tried to keep some notes."

The reporters looked disappointed, but they were hopeful. They leaned in toward me, mouths slightly open, as if eventually, if they gave me enough time, it would all become clear and I would abruptly begin speaking to them in torrents about what it had been like.

The Colts were leading 14–0 at the half. I decided to watch the rest of the game with the Colt wives. They all sat together in the same section up in the third tier. I wondered if the management had set aside that lofty block of seats in order to spare them the concussion and heave of what their husbands were doing. The field of play was so far removed that one had the sense of watching from the gondola of a dirigible. Far below, tiny figures seemed to move in distant representation of some kind of precision drill: forming circles, then shifting into parallel lines, perfectly poised, Euclidean perfection, until they broke from the tension and scampered about creating confusion out of which, after a while, they would again form the circle, then the parallel lines—a steady succession of geometric patterns.

All of it was remote and quiet up where we sat. We were so close to the rim of the stadium that only about ten rows of people were behind us, so there was little of that great wave of sound ("the Baltimore Boom") that inundated those at ground level. From the sounds—an occasional shout of support from behind us—we might have been watching a high school baseball game in Vermont. There was considerable decorum. Everybody had been sitting in the same seats for season after season, and they all knew about the Colt wives, so if some outsider yelled out, "Bulaich, ya bum ya!" a person next to him was sure to point out that Bulaich's wife was the pretty one in the blue hat just four rows down, and he would look embarrassed and hope an opportunity would come later when he could shout something complimentary to make amends.

It was pleasant up there. The wives chatted amongst themselves and flattered each other on how they looked. Perhaps they were disguising enormous inner tensions, but they seemed to act with consummate aplomb. Keeping only half an eye on the game, they talked about their children, and schools, and who was going to make the dip for the get-together the Colt families were having the following week. Perhaps Joanie Karras was right: one had to develop a sense of detachment. If one of the Colts made an error across that infinitude of distance everyone would notice, but it was accepted as the most minor of accidents; if it was Jerry Logan, say, missing an easy interception, his wife would cry out, "Jerry, what are you *doing*?" as if he had spilled maple syrup on the new rug, and everyone would look down the line of seats at her and offer understanding grins.

By and large, they rooted with far less fervor than I did, seated amidst them, shouting and moaning, beer slopping over the rim of the cup, my knees drumming into the back of the person in front. Once, at a Harvard-Princeton game, I was pouring a shot of bourbon into a small silver cup just as a Harvard man intercepted the ball. I stood bolt-upright, unaware that in my excitement I was holding the whiskey bottle at the horizontal, the contents gurgling not into the cup but into the coonskin coat which encompassed the man sitting directly in front of me. A Princeton supporter, he was slumped in his seat watching the Harvard man run, until he felt the moisture on his back. He must have thought that behind him in my excitement I was urinating on him; what else could he have imagined? He shot to his feet, an eruption of coon fur, and turned. I realized what I was doing and apologized. I offered him a drink from what was left in the bottle. For the rest of the game we sat in the heavy reek of bourbon drifting from his coat.

The Colt wives were understanding of my excessive behavior. If the team was in difficulty down below, they would lean across and assure me that everything was "going to be okay."

They turned out to be right. The Colts kept their lead, and by the fourth quarter we began to relax. One of the wives asked, "Well, you've been down there. What was it like?"

"Well, I don't know really. I remember the hatred," I said vaguely, and smiled. I did not want to upset the wives.

Just then, someone shouted, "Hey, look!" Far below we noticed a fan jump out of his seat, vault a rail down onto the field and come running out across the cinder track onto the playing surface—heading for the line of scrimmage where the Dolphins were just breaking from their offensive huddle. A vast quick roar of anticipation went up from the huge crowd. There was a slapdash quality to the man's run, and some weave in it, so that he appeared either to be doing some preliminary dodging or affected by an excess of Baltimore booze.

Bubba Smith, who saw him coming, told me later in the locker room that the sight delighted him. The Colt defensive unit had been on the field a long time trying to contain the steady Miami drive, and his first thought was that he was probably going to get a rest; the police would scamper around after this cat, and if he were agile and had good moves it would be some time before they collared him, which would give Bubba a fine chance to rest his bones. He gave the guy a big encouraging smile.

It turned out that the interloper's intent was to make off with the ball, now lying uncontested in front of the Baltimore front four, with the Miami offense peeling from its huddle and moving up on it. He came down the line, running crouched with his hands cupped low, and almost surely would have gotten away with his souvenir, at least until the police caught him, had it not been for Mike Curtis waiting at his middle linebacker's position. Curtis' whole psyche as a defensive player is geared to removing the football from whoever is carrying it, and the sight of the ball being picked up must have triggered a perfectly normal and instinctive psychological response—an extreme example of the territorial imperative at work. Besides, the intruder was trafficking with the essential symbol of what the two teams were struggling over; if the *ball* was removed, what could it all mean? Curtis darted from his position, slicing between his linemen, and before his target could move more than a step or two, he hit him from behind with a ferocious shoulder block. Up rose the civilian as if launched from a trampoline; the ball sailed loose, and when he came down, two policemen were on the scene. They hustled him off between them, hurrying him along with his toes barely reaching the ground.

Behind me, a Baltimore fan leaned forward. "Hey," he said. "You see that? He learned in five seconds what you worked at for a month."

"What's that?" I asked.

"That if you stay around for more than six seconds in that pro football crowd you're sure to end up clobbered."

Everyone around nodded and laughed. I stared after the interloper, who was being carted through a distant gate.

I could not get the man out of my mind. I talked to Mike Curtis about him after the game. He had no sympathy for him whatever. "It was anarchy," he said. "That wise guy was exactly like some stranger climbing over my fence into my yard. He was interfering with the basic law that keeps people in their seats. He was like the one percent of the public that feels it can disrupt the majority with impunity. It's a weak permissive society that lets people get away with things like that."

I asked: "It had nothing to do with an instinctive move to knock down someone carrying the ball?"

Curtis smiled and said firmly, "Such people should not be allowed to disturb the tranquillity of society. In our society there are too many malcontents and too much hogwash."

The story was in the paper the next day, along with a photograph of the interloper in midair. He had come to Baltimore on an excursion bus from Rochester, New York. For the next week or so rumors drifted around: that he had been hospitalized; that he was suing the Balitmore Colts, as well as Mike Curtis, and, in what seemed an inspired nicety of law, also the Miami Dolphins, presumably for not coming to his aid.

I copied down his name, Donald Ennis, meaning to reach him at some point. Some months later I tried. His phone was listed in the Rochester directory, but I was told that the service had been suspended. His employer—the Kodak company—informed me that he was no longer on the payroll. I made inquiries, but Ennis seemed to have dropped completely from sight. Finally I tracked him to a small town in Kansas; a lead had come in that he was working as a bartender there. I was given a number which connected me with a boardinghouse, but his landlady said that he had left the previous week.

Eventually, over a year later, I reached him back in Rochester. When his voice came on, I was surprised. "Is this Mr. Ennis?"

"That's right," he said.

"Is this *the* Mr. Ennis who had the . . . er . . . difficulty in Baltimore last season?"

There was a distinct pause at the other end. "Who is this?" he asked finally.

I told him who I was and that there might even be a professional kinship between the two of us. I had seen his dash for the ball and wondered if he'd mind talking about it.

Again there was a long pause. "Well," he said. "I don't know."

His voice was soft and uncertain. I was poised for heavy heartiness, the kind that undercuts barroom conversation; it would say (as I moved the receiver back from my ear), "You saw it, eh? Wasn't that a *gas*, man! I mean have you ever seen such a thing—the way I got clobbered . . . Kee-*rist!*"

Instead, his manner was subdued. "Look," he said. "I don't take any pride in what I did. I wish I could forget the whole thing—that it had never happened."

He sighed and began to tell me something about himself. He was thirty-one, a strongly built man of over two hundred pounds. He had played football in high school, and in the armed services in which he had spent six years, most of it with the 82nd Airborne at Fort Bragg, North Carolina, interrupted by one tour in Korea and two in Vietnam.

I asked if he had ever volunteered for hazardous duty. "No," he said. "I know what you're getting at. I'm real normal, I swear. As a kid I challenged my friends—'I'll bet you won't dare do this,' that kind of thing—but that's typical when you're that age."

Ennis had worked as a lithograph plate inspector in the Kodak plant, and every year the management arranged a bus trip to Baltimore for a Colt football game. "There were about forty-five of us on the bus. We'd all signed up. The trip is a long one—seven hours from Rochester to Baltimore—and the guys play cards, shoot the breeze and drink a couple of beers. Not me—no, sir. I was nursing a hangover from the night before and I slept all the way to Harrisburg."

I interrupted to say that I marveled at the dedication of a group traveling so many hours to see a game. Ennis said it was easy—for him, at least; in the service he had learned to make time pass by turning his mind down so that it just barely ticked over. He could get days to speed by without realizing they'd gone.

"Well, we got to Baltimore at about one o'clock. We'd been on the road since six A.M. The game was scheduled to begin at four. It was starting late because it was going to be the second game of a television doubleheader. I had two beers before it started. We were all seated together. I was on the goal line, down in the front row, the railing directly in front of me."

A voice came on the telephone, faint but distinct: "Charlotte, what do you want me to do about the two cats?"

"Are you there?" I heard Ennis ask.

There was a distant clicking, and the circuit was re-established. "Go on," I said.

"Well, Baltimore got out ahead," he continued. "It was all sort of dull, so suddenly I turned to my friend sitting next to me and handed him my binoculars and football program. 'Eddie,' I said. 'How about holding these for a minute. I'll be right back.' It was completely spur-of-the-moment, I swear. Oh, perhaps before the game there was joking about souvenirs, and how the best of them would be the game ball, but that hadn't made any impression on me at the time. It just crossed my mind right *then,* and I decided to act on it. The first thing I knew, I was running out across the cinder track, and after four or five steps I was on the grass of the playing field. I'm sort of near-sighted, and I remember reaching up and touching the rims to be sure my glasses were in place on my nose."

"What did you see as you ran out?"

"When I got close, Bubba Smith was standing with his hands on his hips, and through the front of the helmet I could see that he was laughing. That was nice; I remember grinning back at him. I could hear the big roar from the crowd. I ran right down the line of Colts. The Dolphins were just breaking out of their huddle to my right. They were coming towards me, so that it was like being squeezed between those two lines. What was worrying me was that someone might stick out an arm as I went zipping by, so I ran sort of crouched, and I reached for the ball and got it good and clean. Just then Curtis got me from behind, slicing through the front four, I guess. I never knew he was coming; it was a complete shock. *Bam!* I don't remember hitting the ground, I swear. I was out on my feet."

"Well, what was the first thing—"

"I found myself being lifted off between two policemen. They had a grip on my belt, hoisting me up by my pants, so that I was being walked along on my tiptoes. I said, 'Hey, I'm not going anywhere.' One of the policeman was shaking his head. He said, 'How does it feel to be hit by Mad Dog Curtis?' I said, 'Wha?' He said, 'That's what hit you—The Mad Dog.'"

Ennis paused at the other end of the line. "I was the biggest yo-yo in the world for doing that," he said finally. "It was stupid; it cost me everything. But maybe Curtis was a pretty big yo-yo for hitting me like that. If I'd been a fourteen-year-old kid—hell, he'd have broken my back with that tackle. I lost my glasses and my hat. The police picked up my glasses, but I never got the hat back. Did you see the hat?"

"I beg your pardon?" I asked, startled.

"I mean, you were sitting up there in the stands watching. Did you happen to see my hat lying there on the ground? No? I suppose not. I guess a line judge, or somebody, picked it up and shoved it in his back pocket. It's gone."

"What was the result of all this?" I asked.

"Everything went bad after that. I was in jail until two-thirty in the morning. I was half-killed—black and blue from my knees to my shoulders, with a great bruise on my lower back. I passed out on my way to be fingerprinted. They took x-rays in the hospital; they stuck needles in my legs and feet and told me that I had a pinched nerve in my tailbone. My whole life changed. Just before running out there, I'd supposed that the worst that could happen to me was that I'd be thrown out of the game. Jesus Christ! I lost twenty pounds. I lost a good job. That's right, I was out for such a long time sick that I got dropped from my job. I don't know; maybe they did it because my picture was in the paper, but it was a good job and I lost it. And then my wife left me."

"What?"

"Well, she probably would have done that anyway; things weren't too good between us. But when she saw the pictures in the papers back in Rochester, she said, 'Well, that's the last straw,' and she was gone. She just threw up her hands."

"What about your friends?"

"Their reaction was mixed. The younger ones didn't mind too much. They're the ones I drink and pal around with, and they were surprised, but they thought it was sort of funny, like I'd become a real crazy drunk. But the older people— from forty to fifty—were shocked, and they couldn't get over it. One guy, who had been a friend, wouldn't even talk to me after that; he turned his back. Sometimes I'd see him across a room, glaring at me, and when he saw me looking at him he'd turn away.

"Then I began to get phone calls. People would track me down. Some of them were nice—a girl calling for a date and to exchange photographs—but most of them were cranks. One guy called and said he was going to *shoot* me. He said that I 'couldn't cut the mustard,' that I didn't deserve to live, and that he was going to gun me down. The phone rang all night long, especially in the early morning after the bars had closed and guys were still awake with nothing to do. What I did really *upset* people. A lot of them called up just to cuss me out and ask me how I dared disrupt something like a professional football game. Just who did I think I was? They were real mad; they could hardly speak over the phone they were so mad. They called from Georgia, from California. Sometimes they were more reasonable, but the first question they always asked was Why? and I never could give them an answer. Not ever."

"But then you traveled around . . ."

"And you know something? It follows me. I can't shed it. After I lost the job at Kodak I worked in bars around Rochester. Sure enough, sooner or later, the word would get around and someone would look behind the bar: 'Oh, it was you!' Some of them wanted to hear about it, but other guys cussed me out and said, 'Just who do you think you are, anyway?' "

"It will die away," I said.

"Jesus, I don't know," Ennis said mournfully. "A couple of weeks ago was the anniversary of the Colt-Miami game. The paper in town, the Rochester *Democrat-Chronicle*, managed to find me. This guy with a big cheery voice came on the phone and asked, "Hey, Ennis-babe, are you going down to watch the game in Baltimore this year?' Well, that was all right; the guy couldn't know what I'd gone through. So I said no, real abrupt-like, and the next morning the paper ran a story under a headline an inch high: NO GAME: STAYING HOME THIS YEAR."

We chatted a while longer. It was such a mournful tale. Once or twice Ennis laughed, a wincing self-deprecatory sound as if he could hardly believe what was happening to him. I kept thinking of Julian English in John O'Hara's novel *Appointment in Samarra*, and how one act—throwing a glass of whiskey in a friend's face at a country club dance—had shifted his life around and settled it in a downward groove. It was a spontaneous act, much like Ennis' dash for the football, and the consequences were appalling. What was it? English had finally finished himself off imbibing exhaust fumes in a closed garage. "You know something?" Ennis was saying. "Maybe *you* want to go down there again. But me? I couldn't do anything like that again in a million years . . . not *ever!*"

20

The Colts had a disappointing season that first year of my agonized support. They seemed to wilt at the end of the schedule.
The team's offense sagged badly, and though they reached the
play-offs with ease, an underdog Miami Dolphins team, the same
squad I had seen play when Donald Ennis ran out onto the field,
upset them 21–0. Pitched in gloom I watched the game on television at home. I wondered how my daughter could play on the
carpet in front of the set with so much pleasure, hammering
pegs into a board while scenes of such dismay were going on
behind her.

Then the following year, in 1972, the Colts went through
convulsive changes. Carroll Rosenbloom unloaded the team in
a complicated trade for the Los Angeles Rams, which had been
owned for a day or so by Robert Irsay, an air-conditioning mag-
nate from Chicago, who then became the Colt owner. As soon
as he took over, Irsay hired as his general manager Joe Thomas,

a genius by some accounts, who as a personnel manager was credited with the composition of two former expansion teams—the Minnesota Vikings and the Miami Dolphins—which in a remarkably short time had become Super Bowl contenders. Almost as soon as he was in control Thomas made a reassuring statement, in which he expressed satisfaction with the Colts as they stood. "The team is a good balanced mixture of veterans and youth," he said, "and not an old club as some make it out to be. John Unitas is as good a quarterback as there is in football. He's number one. The only problem is who will be number two."

As for Irsay, he announced, "Baltimore is Unitasville, U.S.A., in my book."

"Exactly," I thought at the time. "The club is in grand hands."

But the 1972 season started miserably. The team won only one of its first five starts, and suddenly Joe Thomas took a decisive step: he fired McCafferty, replacing him with John Sandusky, and he benched John Unitas in favor of Marty Domres, a young Columbia graduate who had toiled in the wings with the San Diego Chargers and had come to the Colts in a trade. All of this caused a tremendous stir. I found myself struck with a mounting sense of confusion and despair—as if the props had been knocked out from under one side of a structure as rock-ribbed and solid and familiar as one's own house, to which one had come home and found tilted alarmingly, the piano collapsed against the downside wall in a welter of wires and keys.

What caused the greatest impact was that the team's shattered state was so unexpected: perhaps what might happen to an expansion team—the Buffalo Bills, or a team perennially in the doldrums, like the Philadelphia Eagles—but not the Colts, who were a team composed of scores of people who every winter went to the Pro Bowl game.

When the Colts came to New York in early November with their 1–4 record to play against the Jets at Shea Stadium, I decided to go up and see my friends and what Joe Thomas had wrought. It had been announced in the paper that not only would Marty Domres start the game, but Unitas, representing the old guard that I had come to know, would not play unless his replacement was hurt. I found myself beset by a curious nagging hope that Domres *would* get hurt—just a small injury, like a blister on the heel—and Unitas would come in for the last quarter and save the day.

The game was a seesaw affair, full of shifts of fortune and drama, and Domres stayed in throughout. He had a bad first half, drilling passes into areas unoccupied by either friend or foe, but as if experience, even thirty minutes of it, was a true conditioner, he had a second half of considerable effectiveness. Unfortunately, there was an occasional lapse: on one play within range of a field goal which would have put Baltimore ahead, he spun back out of the protective pocket and began scampering around, mostly toward the midfield stripe, looking for someone to throw the ball to, until he was submerged for an enormous loss, well beyond field-goal range. "High school play!" the fan sitting next to me said. "Unitas must be cringing."

Domres' deep receivers were Havrilak and O'Brien: a makeshift pair. The Colts' lack of depth seemed symbolized by the latter's difficulty in his dual function as both wide receiver and field-goal kicker. When sudden decisions were made for a field-goal try, O'Brien—who uses a special kicking shoe in which he cannot run pass patterns without a considerable gimp, like a lady running for a bus with one heel gone—would rush to the sidelines to try to get the kicking shoe on before Domres, waiting for him desperately, had to call a time-out to keep the team from being penalized five yards for taking too much time. There was a fine lunacy to the situation—fifty-odd thousand people leaning forward on the edge of their seats watching O'Brien kneeling at the sidelines trying to beat the clock in a shoe change. He never made it; the heel always got stuck and the Colts would use up a time-out.

Every now and then during the game, I watched Unitas on the sidelines, his hands in the pockets of his blue windbreaker, standing alone, occasionally turning and restlessly stubbing at the ground with the toe of his shoe. He was not saddled with the job of talking on the phones linked to the spotters on the stadium rim, which is often the duty of a backup quarterback; every time I looked he was alone, behind the bench, gazing away from where Domres huddled with the offensive coaches on the sidelines. Later Domres said that he had used two plays Unitas had suggested in his last go-ahead touchdown drive, but Unitas denied having had anything to do with it.

That last Baltimore drive occurred with a minute and a half left in the game. The Colts scored on a thirteen-yard pass from Domres to Jim O'Brien, completely alone in the end zone, kneeling there to be sure and receiving the pass to his midsection like a supplicant, bowing over it in gratitude. With this play the Colts went ahead 20–17, but in his final series Joe Namath of the Jets reared back on third down, with long yardage to go, and pegged the ball as far as he could in the general direction of Eddie Bell, the diminutive Jet flanker. Jerry Logan of the Colts trotted back under it, much as an outfielder moves for a long drive that he has under control, but just as he was reaching for it he was run into by his teammate, Charlie Stukes, whose hands tipped the ball up into the air just long enough for Eddie Bell, whose eyes must have popped with surprise, to come onto the scene and collect the ball for a touchdown play that went eighty-three yards.

Up in the stands I stood stunned for a minute and then rushed for the locker room. I was let in by Ed Block. I watched quietly from a corner. No one looked at anyone else.

Following a defeat of this sort the locker room is not an easy place to visit. Football players can pull themselves together after a rout, rationalizing that no amount of personal effort would have had any discernible effect on the outcome. But after a *close* game—perhaps a block here, a tackle there, or a pass gathered in would have made the difference—the players sit on the stools in front of their cubicles and think about it. Keeping to the Colt tradition after a game, whatever the outcome, Bob Vogel, the big offensive tackle, offered a short prayer—short, personal and, as usual, very chatty, as if God were sitting atop a ladder placed in the middle of the room, chin in hand, like a character in a "meaningful" Broadway play. Vogel told Him that the team had let Him down, that they had messed up on various assignments and that they were going to have to knuckle down and work harder. He thanked Him for seeing to it that the Colts had gone through the game without serious injury, and he promised Him that the next time they would do better. Then the clubroom door was opened and the press was let in.

In Carroll Rosenbloom's day, the Colt locker room after a game was open to anyone who took the trouble to cadge an invitation, and the players had to pick their way through the crowds to get to the showers. Usually a number of youngsters in awe of where they were stood around, holding their blue woolen Colt caps in their hands. It was informal and friendly, and part of the tradition of the "Colt family." Joe Thomas had changed all of this, announcing that the locker room was off-limits to everyone except players, club officials and the press. The players were owed their privacy, and there were no exceptions, not even for young Jimmy Irsay, the owner's thirteen-year-old son. In Baltimore, I was told, Thomas had even cleared the corridor outside the locker room where the wives and girls had previously waited for their men to come out; now they were relegated to a lounge decorated by the Baltimore Oriole baseball club and somewhat ungallantly named The Bird Seed Room.

For one who remembered the cocktail-party atmosphere of the Rosenbloom era, the locker room seemed almost empty. I heard a murmur of voices from the coaches' room; I went and stood at the door. A circle of reporters was standing around John Sandusky, who had been appointed the new coach. He had on a beautifully tailored suit, as befits a head coach. He was shaking his head.

"Coach, it couldn't have been closer," one of the sportswriters said.

"There's only one game where 'close' counts—horseshoes," Sandusky replied.

I had never heard that maxim before, and I jotted it down on the back of my program. Back out in the main locker room I repeated it in admiration to a journalist friend. "Pretty good, eh? 'Horseshoes.' "

"Man, where have you been? Christ, that's standard phrase number one when a coach's lost a close one."

"Oh."

"The other standard one is that 'close' only counts in hand grenades. You've never heard that one either? Jesus."

I wandered off. The atmosphere was getting better. I looked into some of the wire-meshed cubicles and chatted with my former teammates. A considerable group of reporters stood around Domres' cubicle. I was seeing him for the first time. He has a lean, intelligent face, with light-blue eyes, and bears a startling, if youthful, resemblance to Prime Minister Trudeau of Canada—the same long-shaped head, high forehead and the hair thinning in front. He kept his voice low, the reporters leaning in on him, and it occurred to me that he might be doing this out of deference to John Unitas, just down the line, who, having not done anything more athletic on the sidelines than shrug his shoulders under his blue windbreaker, had taken a quick shower and was bent forward on his stool, lacing his shoes. No one was questioning him. Domres was saying softly, "I was really crushed when Eddie Bell scored on that last pass. We had the game won. It was like going from the penthouse to the out-house."

Well, I thought, not bad; there is a certain felicity of phrase being flung around here—first Sandusky's horseshoe re-mark, and now Domres! (At that very moment, if I had only known—it was reported in the press the next day—Joe Namath over in the Jets' locker room was describing the luck of that same tipped pass: ". . . down South, we call that 'spitting into a swinging crock.' ")

I leaned into Unitas' locker to shake his hand and say hello. It was hard to look him in the eye. A reporter came by. "Hey, John," he said. "I hear your kid's playing first-string safety for his team, and *third*-string quarterback. What's that about? Couldn't you teach him?"

"He prefers playing safety," Unitas said. "He puts it like this: 'I'd rather stick people than be stuck.' "

"Beautiful!" the reporter said.

I continued to wander around. One of the players pointed out Joe Thomas. A slight, thin figure, he was nattily dressed in a dark pin-striped suit, moving through the locker room somewhat nervously and with an abstracted air, as if he had put an expensive pair of cuff links down and could not remember exactly where. I introduced myself and asked if I could come down to Baltimore the following week and ask him what was going on. "Anytime," he said expansively.

I stopped by Bob Vogel's cubicle. He sat with a towel around the middle. We talked about birds. He told me that the most exciting moment of the previous year—this from a man who spends his autumn Sundays trying to remove the likes of Deacon Jones, Bob Lilly and Merlin Olsen from his path—was when a painted bunting came to feed at his bird-feeding station on the lawn in front of his house on the Chesapeake.

"Hey," he said. He did not want to talk about the football game at all. "Have you ever been to Hawk Mountain?"

"No," I said. "But I've heard of it."

"I read somewhere that during the fall migration thousands of hawks fly past there. It's in Pennsylvania. That's what I'd like to do when I quit football—take my kids down there and look at the hawks."

"Are your kids keen on birds?"

"They'd better be," he said firmly. He looked very determined.

"Which one's Irsay?" I asked. "Is he here?"

"The new owner?" Vogel squinted. Bird-watcher's eyes, I thought. "He's the one over there, beyond the towels—the florid one . . . reddish plumage and beak."

I grinned and went over to Irsay. He was staring at the floor. I introduced myself. I had heard that he was painfully shy. He shook hands. He has red hair, a big friendly face, red from the cold outside, with a flat nose on it, and he was wearing a red shirt and a red striped tie. Vogel was right; he *was* florid. I told him I was sorry about the Baltimore defeat.

"Let me tell you something," he said, and he gave me a quick look.

"What's that?"

"No one gets off this world alive."

"Oh?"

"That's right."

I did not bother putting this reflection down on the back of my program. I left the locker room knowing that it was hardly the place, especially after a Baltimore loss, to sit down with anyone and discuss aspects of the team's collapse. Surely it was such a complex matter. I knew enough to realize that the mechanism that constitutes a great team is in fact a fragile balance of skills and pride and attitude quite at variance with those words describing a team on the move as a "powerhouse" or "juggernaut"; the proper combination is so delicate that it does not take much jarring to throw the balance out of kilter.

One of the most acute observers of a phenomenon such as the Baltimore Colt decline would be Bill Curry, and I called him the next day. After he had talked about the practical reasons behind the team's difficulties ("We lost good players—John Williams, Norm Bulaich, Tom Matte, Eddie Hinton, Bubba Smith"), he began to talk about the team in more general terms. "What made the Colts different—and perhaps it's the special mark of championship teams—is that we'd cultivated a genuine atmosphere of respect, even love, for our fellow players. It was a tangible thing, a *force,* and you could actually see it work in a game. You could spot it in the films. In nineteen seventy, for example, we didn't line up the same backfield twice in a row for seventeen weeks. In theory it's impossible to function that way, and we'd fall behind in game after game. Yet invariably there'd be a tremendous surge: everybody would look at each other in the huddle, and you knew that *somebody* was going out to make a good play, and that somehow we'd do it in the end. It's a subtle quality, and I don't know how you hang onto it. But I do know when it begins to slip away. It starts with doubting. You begin to doubt each other. You doubt the front office and the changes it makes in policy and procedure. You get to spending too much time discussing such things, and wondering why you have a general manager and an owner who don't know your names; there are too many distractions; your concentration begins to slip away; you substitute it with complacency; you lose a game; you begin to blame others; you find that you're yelling at your teammates during a game, and they at you. Then, perhaps worst of all, you begin to realize that all the shouts of encouragement to get yourself and the others going again are phony and meaningless—'false chatter,' we call it—and that the reservoir that previously you could dip into for those qualities that won for you somehow has dried up."

Curry went on to say that when the team began to slide, many of the veterans were realistic about the need for change but without exception felt that it could have been done without players' prides being stepped on—that thoughtfulness and empathy should have been at a premium at that time. But there was none of this. By all accounts, McCafferty had no warning whatsoever that if he did not conform to front-office wishes he was going to be axed . . . and thus he had no opportunity to try to cope with a crisis situation. "That's just not the way you treat someone like that," Curry said. "John Unitas heard about his demotion on the clubhouse phone. He picked it up, listened for twenty seconds, then hung up the receiver and gestured at the floor. 'I'm benched,' he said. 'They hoped I wouldn't take it as a slap in the face.' "

"I understand that's the sort of thing that happened to Karras," I said.

"It was Thomas's *methods*," said Curry. "Do you want an example to show the difference? When the Colts decided to put Earl Morrall on waivers during the nineteen seventy off-season, Don McCafferty got on a plane and flew out to Detroit where Morrall lives, and he sat around with Earl and helped tide him over the news. It couldn't have been comfortable for either of them, but at least Mac made a considerable effort. Compare that to a twenty-second phone call."

In fact, the Colts did not take the front-office maneuvering complacently. When McCafferty was fired, Bill Curry was not only stunned, but so incensed about the blame for the team's poor showing being publically placed on the coach's shoulders that he called for a meeting of the players. Twenty-eight of them turned up in ex-Colt Ordelle Braese's restaurant, The Flaming Pit, where Curry read a strong, emotional statement in which he absolved the coach of blame, rebuked the team itself for its play, and the front office for its decision. Immediately there was criticism. "Too poetic," Mike Curtis said. Others felt it was too strong. Curry was astonished. "So many of them were scared," Tom Nowatzke, the big running back, told me later. "I kept comparing that meeting in my mind with the time that the Los Angeles Rams met and vowed to quit unless they got their coach, George Allen, back—and it *worked;* the stars stood up and were counted."

Finally, a watered-down statement was agreed on in which the team acknowledged its share of blame for its showing, but also placed its support behind John Sandusky, the new coach. McCafferty turned up to speak briefly to the team for the last time the next day, urging them to pull together. He said he was going to have a lot of free time now, and if anyone needed a fourth in a golf game—why, to call and let him know. In the absolute silence as he turned to walk out the door, Curry began to cry, perhaps as much as for what he was watching happen around him as for his old coach.

Two days after the Colt-Jet game, Joe Thomas called up from Baltimore and said that he had changed his mind and decided not to talk to me. It had all been hashed over, the changes had been made, and there was no point in going over them. It was a distracting matter, and what the Colt organization needed to do was forget the past and concentrate on football. "It's over and done with," he said. "I don't see any reason why that can of worms should be reopened. I'm not going to talk."

"Can of *worms*?"

"Who the hell cares anyhow?" he went on.

"But you've made some awesome changes," I pointed out. "Sacked McCafferty, benched Unitas . . ."

"Who cares? I'll tell you something: people don't care. They don't care who the coach is. No one has ever paid a dollar to see a coach on the sidelines. And they don't care who the quarterback is as long as he wins. They've got their own problems," he said. "Who the coach is that's walking up and down the sidelines doesn't mean a thing to them. I'm sorry; I'm not talking to you. I'm not going to reopen that can of worms."

I kept trying to persuade Thomas to change his mind, pointing out that I had talked to many of the Colts, and needed his side of things.

"I'm not going to reopen that can . . ." He sounded frantic.

"Yes, yes, I know," I said.

I decided to go down to Baltimore anyway. I took the Metroliner. When I got there I bought a copy of the Baltimore *Sun* to see if I could gauge the feelings of the citizenry about the changes Thomas was making.

The paper's letter column was full of references to the situation. "I'm so heartsick I could cry," wrote someone else about McCafferty's firing. "Joe Thomas is in Lizzie Borden's league." Another was even more direct about Thomas, threatening to "send him to the moon with a right cross." It was evident that the town was steaming.

I wondered which of the Colts to see. I knew that I would not get much out of either Unitas or McCafferty. Both of them had what are called "personal service" contracts, and being honored with these is contingent upon upholding Colt management policies. But there were others. I went to see Bubba Smith. Great Bubba! He moved gingerly through his new house with its purple chairs, chandeliers and the big bed with its ceiling mirror and foxtail spread. He was just off crutches, following his hospitalization after the most ironic of injuries: in an exhibition game in Tampa the kid holding the down marker froze while a play, with Bubba in it, moved helter-skelter toward him; instead of throwing the stick down, which is the required procedure, he backed away, wide-eyed, and Bubba hammered into the pole and drove it, by one estimate, two feet into the ground. Under the awful strain his legs wrapped grotesquely around the pole, and the innards of his right knee were torn askew—no one within yards of him.

Bubba was delighted to hear that Joe Thomas had refused to see me. "That's just like the man. At least he won't try to mess with your mind," he said. That was a phrase I had heard him use so often.

"Have they been messing with yours?" I asked.

Bubba snorted. "Just today I got a letter from the front office saying that I would be fined one hundred dollars for every day I missed therapy for my knee. Now what sort of a letter is that? I like to play football better than anyone. You think I'm going to miss therapy for my knee?" He glared at me. "Well?"

"No, Bubba," I said hastily.

"We are first-class," Bubba said. "You can't treat a team that's first-class like a gang of rookies. Why, when we played the Jets the first time I was fined a hundred dollars for being on the field, down by the sidelines, in my wheelchair."

"What on earth were you doing down there?" I asked. "Someone could have run into you."

"I'd seen something from the stands," Bubba said, "and I got myself wheeled down to the field to tell Billy Newsome that he was playing Winston Hill, the Jets' offensive tackle, all wrong. The consensus around the league is that Hill will hold you; he likes to get you close in, bulling at him, so that he can grab you without being caught at it. So the way to play him is to make sure that the official moves him up on the line where he belongs, and then hand-slap him and maneuver away from him so that if he tries to hold he's got to *reach* for you, and the official will see it. Well, Newsome was getting in too close—and I went down there in my wheelchair to the bench to advise him. A policeman came running up, holding onto this walkie-talkie. He apologized and said he could scarce believe it, but word had come down from Joe Thomas that if I didn't clear off the sidelines I was going to be fined a hundred dollars. I knew he was thinking that I could get hurt, but what a way to ask me to leave!"

Bubba shook his head. "Crazy," he said. "I wonder if Joe Thomas noticed that Winston Hill pushed my wheelchair off the field after the game." He laughed. "A great friend. He sent flowers to me in the hospital. You've always got to have a few friends. But I can't talk to the Man," he said. "When your ballplayers can't talk—well, it *infects* everything. It's all changed. The locker room of the Colts was always so *relaxed,* with the laughing and the carrying-on, and the cats who really would have retired came back for a couple of more years because it was so much fun. Now it sounds like a church in there."

I was going to spend the rest of the day with Bubba, but somewhat to my surprise, when I got back to the hotel for a lunch appointment, I learned that Joe Thomas had changed his mind—at least to the extent that he would see me and answer questions, though he said he would be "vague."

The Baltimore Colt office is in a depressed area of town; the stoop outside is often decorated by a collapsed drunk, his bottle in a paper bag beside him. Thomas was waiting for me in his office, sitting behind a desk that hemmed him in on three sides. The office was functional; the desk had two gray telephones and the only attempt at décor was a fake potted willow bush standing in a bucket of gravel in the corner.

Thomas began by talking about the anatomy of his decision-making. "What I've done has not been that difficult. I've always been involved in policy making. After all, people who don't want to make decisions never go any place. From the start, I could see something was wrong. Over the past eleven ball games, which includes pre-season, the Colts never played good *motivated* football. Look at last year's three final games: beaten by New England, only two touchdowns against Cleveland, none against Miami in the twenty-one–nothing play-off loss . . . Maybe the drop-off started back then. It begins to lodge in the back of your mind—it would in the mind of *any* general manager—that not only is something wrong, but something's got to be done about it. A rubber band begins to stretch. First, you try to find out what's wrong—where the weak spots are, so you can patch them up. But if there isn't any improvement, you really *have* to do something drastic. The rubber band snaps. It can't be as drastic as firing thirty-five players. You've got to blame the top man—just the way the country blames the President if things aren't going right, and gets rid of him in an election."

"McCafferty . . ."

"Out he goes. I'm not a vacillator. It's like marking a

true-and-false test: you can't compromise between one and the other. You make your decision and you *mark* it."

"It's the old adage, isn't it? If the bus keeps breaking down, you shoot the bus driver."

"Something like that. One thing is that you can always reckon on change to stir them up."

I asked about the methods which most of his team had found so upsetting. "What about that telephone call to Unitas?"

"There's no easy way to do that sort of thing," Thomas said. "Hell, I didn't have to call him at *all*. But I decided to tell him before he read it in the papers; after all, he's meant a lot to the franchise. Now it's done with. It's a new slate, a new season. I've got to find out if this other boy can play football. If Domres can't do it, we've got to find someone else."

I asked if his decisions had resulted in angry mail to the Colt front office.

"I thought there'd be much more flak," he said. "We got eight or nine letters, but even if we'd got eight hundred it would not have influenced me. I understand about sentiment." He looked very solemn. "But I also believe in statements like Branch Rickey's: that the greatest secret is to trade a player a year before he's through, no matter who he is. George Allen is coaching over in Washington with his retreads—well, he believes what *he* believes, and maybe he makes it work because he believes in it so strongly. But that's not my way."

"No, I can see." I said.

We looked at each other. Finally I asked, "What about the feeling that some of the Colts talk about—that what binds the team is love, respect—a sense of 'family.' "

"I think what you call 'family' is much more accurately described as a 'clique,' " Thomas said. "Those are the words that any clique would use to describe itself."

Well, I thought as I left him, a pragmatic, chilly, ruthless, possibly brilliant manipulator, and not a man I'd much like to work for. Of course, there were some Colts who were pleased with Thomas and who backed his unequivocal stand on such aspects as "sentiment." Mike Curtis was one of these. He had often told me that he thought of football as an "extension of childhood," and that those who practiced it should be treated with the authority and methods used to harness unruly children. He remembered Thomas' first meeting with the team with unabashed delight; he had appeared at the meeting quite nervous, sweating heavily, to announce: "I don't care if you guys like me or not. That's not what I'm interested in. I'm interested in winning."

"Surely McCafferty wouldn't have been out of character in saying exactly the same thing," I said to Curtis. I had called him on the phone. "Isn't the prime concern of all coaches to win?"

"McCafferty set what you might call a 'lenient posture,' " he answered. "That's all right if you're winning, but it's bad if you're losing. Ideally, ballplayers are supposed to be able to get themselves mentally prepared for a game, but in practice someone's got to beat their ass. You don't believe that?"

"But don't some players bridle under—"

"A lot of people don't like the sort of humiliation inflicted on them by a Don Shula or a Lombardi, but the point is that their system turns out better football players and stronger teams. I'm a great admirer of Shula's coaching. He just didn't *permit* mistakes. Mac's attitude seemed to be that mistakes were inevitable and should be kept to a minimum. Well, that's a difficult approach. It's true that Mac had two good years, but the first was a carry-over from Shula, and because we had an easy schedule, and even though that was the Super Bowl year we didn't exactly pound anybody. It's my feeling that with a club like McCafferty's, which doesn't function under the whiplash, there's not that intensity. You drop a ball—so what? No, give me the medieval approach."

"What about the function of management?" I asked.

"Well, at the moment the atmosphere is unsettling," Curtis admitted. "Everybody's suddenly an employee; many of them are concerned because they're not being pampered as they once were."

Certainly that was the one tremendous difference the players talked about: the change effected by the absence of

Carroll Rosenbloom, the former owner, who had put together the "Colt family." He *had* pampered them. Gregarious, easy in public, with a graceful way with words, he enjoyed the closest of relationships, both socially and professionally, with his players. For some of them he could actually be an inspiration; Bubba Smith once told me, "What there used to be in the Colt locker room was a good, sweet atmosphere, and I'd sit there before a game and know that the boss was going to be coming through and that he'd lean over me and say, 'Let's have a good game.' Not a pep talk, nothing like that, but he said it in a way that you knew you meant something to him, that you weren't just a carcass. That was something I waited for every Sunday. Not much, was it? But afterwards I felt like going out and ripping up the stadium for him."

The new owner, Irsay, was the antithesis of all this: a shy man, uncomfortable in public, who struggled through such public events as a press conference. At his first official appearance as the owner of the Colts, he announced into a battery of microphones that "we have transpired a deal." The players told me that against his hopes, he remained distant from them. He had an astonishingly difficult time with their names; rather than embarrass them by a mispronunciation or a clean miss he called everyone "Tiger," or occasionally "Big Fellow." It seemed almost a pathological difficulty; Bubba Smith, perhaps the most famous player on the team, he called "Bobo," and even his general manager, Joe Thomas, a man to whom he talked twice a day on the phone, and who possessed an ostensibly foolproof name, he referred to with the *th* pronounced: "Joe *Th*-omas."

Irsay had appeared only once before the team as a whole. It was planned that he address the team meeting in Kansas City. He arrived late; in fact, Don McCafferty went up to the hotel lobby to look for him, and while he was gone Irsay suddenly appeared and stepped up to say a few words. Obviously shy and awkward, he talked a little about himself. He said that he was a self-made man who had parlayed $800 into an empire. He had married a Polish girl. At this, John Idzik, the Polish-born assistant coach, gave a glad cry from the back of the room, which caused a ripple of merriment among the team. The outburst apparently startled Irsay. He finished quickly, wishing them luck in the game, and rushed out of the room. McCafferty reappeared, looking slightly bewildered, to say that he had looked around in the lobby and that Irsay was nowhere to be found.

"Well, he's come and gone," someone told him. "He talked. You missed it."

"Oh," said McCafferty.

Irsay lives up in Skokie, Illinois, just outside Chicago, and when I had the chance I went up there to see him. I was working on a story for *Sports Illustrated* on the demise of the Colts. In the large wood-paneled office of his air-conditioning plant, he seemed quite at home. Mementos were everywhere. Behind his desk were three mounted fish: a dolphin, a barracuda and a wall-eyed pike—all with jaws violently ajar, ready to snap.

"Let me tell you something," he said to me. "After watching the Colts play ten games and looking at the players, I knew I had to make changes. We had so much talent it wasn't funny, but they didn't give a damn. Everyone sulked. Nobody knew who they were playing next to. Why, they had people in the locker room talking *business* before a game. Don McCafferty is one of the greatest guys personality-wise there is, but *football-thinking*-wise . . . his method doesn't work. If you lose games, something's got to be wrong with the coaching."

He got up and began pacing swiftly around his office. He was wearing red again—tie, shirt and socks. His sentences came in sharp bursts. "I talked to Mac. I guess he didn't listen too carefully. I suggested that he start Marty Domres. Well, if had won with Unitas, he'd have looked good, right? But he didn't. So that was it. It's my club. I paid nineteen million dollars. It's *my* nineteen million." He glared at me.

I pointed out that despite the team's poor record, Unitas had been having a wonderful year—that statistically he was second among NFL quarterbacks at the time he was benched.

"Statistics don't always tell the truth," Irsay said. "They're misleading. A lot of those passes were little short ones

—short screens—and the quarterback gets credit for all the running the backs or ends do after they catch his pass. That's not right."

"What about the methods? The way Unitas was benched?"

"Why couldn't they have accepted it?" Irsay replied, almost plaintively. "Everybody can't be first-string. Why can't people like Tom Matte think back to the time when some veteran had to sit down on the bench for *him* to play? Why can't they accept it the way Bart Starr accepted being benched as the Green Bay quarterback? We're not trying to sideline anyone. It's very hard. Why can't they be . . . well, decent about it?"

There was something truly touching about Irsay. He talked about his dream of always owning a great team. Why? To win, of course. But what actually motivated him turned out to be a child's awe of the players themselves, a blatant hero-worship that literally tongue-tied him. "What I'd like to do," he said, "is invite some of them out on the *Mighty One III*, my boat, after the Miami game, which is the last game of the season. We could have a few beers and talk. I'd be proud to have dinner with them. I'm a Colt-lover. I saw Bobo Smith at a banquet in Cincinnati. What a guy! But maybe they won't come to the boat," he said sadly.

Living in Chicago, Irsay was rarely on the scene in Baltimore. He flew in for the games, and the players saw him in the locker room afterwards: "Hi, Tiger. Great game, Big Fellow." Joe Thomas, of course, they saw much more of. He came out to the practices, standing quietly, often next to the players, though rarely saying a word. The veterans, who evolved a number of nicknames for him—"The Piccolo Player" was one— seeing him come across the field, referred to him as "The Ominous Presence"; "Oh-oh, look sharp, here comes The Ominous Presence." "He stands and eyeballs you," Curry told me. "Frankly, it sort of takes the fun out of practice. He's like Poe's raven. He perches there, just a few feet away, peering at you, and you keep expecting him to cry out 'Nevermore!'"

The players were fond of Sandusky, and during these difficult times they worked hard for him at practice, though they were never quite able to forget how expendable they were. The rookies put tremendous effort into their drills when Thomas was around, exploding up and down in the push-ups of pre-practice calisthenics. The veterans laughed at them, but without any sense of superiority; everyone was unsure. The rumors continued to fly: no one who had played for over nine years would be back; Sam Havrilak, who at the age of twenty-four would be coming back for his fifth season the following year, told me that he wondered whether he was part of the "youth movement" or a veteran to be discarded. The most persistent rumor was that Thomas would make a clean sweep after the season and start afresh; subconsciously he could never accept a ready-made championship team.

I asked Curry if an atmosphere of this sort affected individual effort. He told me that he had been surprised; never having served on a losing team (first he'd been with the Green Bay Packers under Vince Lombardi, then with the great Colt teams), he had expected deterioration, whereas instead he felt that in the turmoil players found qualities in their fellows—indeed, perhaps in themselves—that they had not appreciated before. For instance, he had developed a true sense of awe about his line coach, Red Miller, for his determination and optimism. As for his own football skills, he couldn't speak for the others but he felt no diminution in them. He kept at what he had always done in contact drills, hurling himself full out against Mike Curtis, trying to perfect the blocking-down procedure that the center must attempt on the middle linebacker—which in this case must have seemed as if they were taking out their ideological differences on each other. In any case, however harassed and disturbed the players were, the humor, that saving condition which bolsters the football players' society to such a marked degree, was apparently always there, whatever the situation.

What were some instances of this, I asked.

Curry thought a bit and said that it wasn't easy—it never sounded as funny as it actually was—but, for example, one afternoon Dan Sullivan had suggested that Tom Matte, who was livid with fury at being sidelined and inactive, could be outfitted with a pair of leather handles on his rib cage, if he really wanted to contribute that much, so that the coaches could set him up around the field as a tackling dummy. It was that sort of joshing that made them laugh . . .

What about John Unitas?

Well, there hadn't been any of that sort of joking around him, Curry said, or about his situation. In fact, it was surprisingly quiet when Unitas was around, and painful, because of all the Colts, being the great legend, he was the only one suffering a *public* humiliation. The whole team felt the same sort of collective embarrassment for him that New England townspeople must have had when walking down the street and passing a popular friend stuck in the stocks for a minor indiscretion.

I told Curry that I had seen a game on television that fall in which the Colts had lost to San Francisco—a game in which Unitas substituted for Domres, who had been knocked temporarily silly, for one awful play in which, after receiving a standing ovation from the 49er crowd, he was not only thrown for a dozen yards on a pass attempt, but he had fumbled the ball away to the 49ers who quickly scored—a humiliation so appalling in Unitas' situation that damned if I didn't find myself comparing it to King Lear's on the hearth.

Yes, Curry agreed, there had been . . . well, *awkward* moments for Unitas that season for sure. But he wouldn't remember those. He'd remember Unitas in the Buffalo game at Baltimore, the last game of the season in their home park, perhaps the last time Unitas would ever play there if indeed he ever got into the game. For the players the first indication of drama came when a tremendous roar rose from the stands, such a sound that the players in the huddle could not hear Domres' signal calling. What the hell was it? Looking around, they could see no reason for it; no substitutes were coming in. Then one of them looked up in the sky, where there was an airplane towing a banner that read UNITAS WE STAND. The crowd had noticed—banks of people looking up, and then more, and then everyone standing—and the stadium had gone berserk. The cheering went on and on. Through this bedlam of noise Domres led the team to a touchdown against Buffalo, but in a quirk of fortune he pulled a muscle as he did so, pulling up lame as he ran the ball over for a score, and when he tested his leg on the sidelines he found that he had very little mobility.

On the next Baltimore offensive series Unitas came in to run the team. Curry said it was the goddamnedest sound he'd ever heard in Baltimore; he felt the earth was going to open up. When Unitas collected the huddle around him, he had to yell his plays. He called a couple of handoffs, and then came one of his patented passes, a wobbly thing that barely cleared a linebacker's fingertips. It reached Eddie Hinton just in front of a cornerback, that perfect timing, the ball thrown not with zing but with some propensity of slow motion as if to prolong an audience's pleasure in watching it, and Hinton collected it, moving at top speed, and broke a couple of tackles to run sixty-three yards for a touchdown.

"Then the earth *did* open up," Curry said. "And you know something? It's the only time in all my years at Baltimore that I ever saw John Unitas react to mass emotion. You know what he did? He held up both hands in a sort of shy salute."

"And the Colts?"

"Well, they went crazy. Along the sidelines a lot of them were crying. Sullivan ran back to the bench after the play, and he lifted up Unitas and set him down, and then he ran all the way back down the field to block for the extra point. The game ended a little later, and you wouldn't have believed the locker room—you'd have thought we'd won the Super Bowl, not beaten a team with one of the worst records in football. Everyone was yelling and carrying on. Fred Miller got up and made a noble speech, and as a last dramatic gesture he held up the game ball and offered it to Unitas. Everyone cried, 'Speech, speech, speech!' and finally it looked as though Unitas *was* going to say something. He'd never done that before. So everyone quieted down, smiling up at him in anticipation, and he looked at everyone and he said, 'Fuck you guys.' That's absolutely all he said—nothing else. But I'll tell you something: he tucked that game ball under his arm. I've seen him take

other game balls awarded him and toss them across the locker
room to somebody: 'Hey, Tom—or Rick, or Eddie, or Bubba—
you want this? You deserve it.' But this time he just tucked that
ball under his arm and it was *his!*"

John Gordy was philosophical about what was happening to Baltimore. "Things don't stay the same," he said. "It's really as simple as that."

"But this guy Thomas is really pushing it," I said. "It's the end of so many things."

"Well, that's no lie. It happens in football." He shrugged. "First it's me. Then Alex goes. Now it looks like the end of that Baltimore Colt team you knew."

Sure enough, Joe Thomas began to clean house. He got rid of Matte, Curry, Sullivan, Bulaich, Unitas and Logan, who were the stalwarts of the team, who hung around together, and who were vocal about what Thomas was doing. He also traded Billy Newsome, who hardly ever said a word about anything and was simply a fine football player, to the New Orleans Saints. Sandusky too, along with the entire staff. Others wanted to go. After the last game of the season, a loss to Miami, Ted

Hendricks, The Mad Stork, towered above Thomas, pinning him against the locker room wall, dripping water on him from the shower, ranting at him that he wanted out, that he couldn't stand what was going on. Bubba Smith begged to be traded. Thomas tried, but Bubba's knee, while he said it was eighty percent fully recovered and coming along strong, was too suspect for any team to take a chance on him. Bubba told me that the "Man" wouldn't even look at him, and that his one recurrent fantasy was to return to Baltimore with another team and "destroy" the Colts. Finally, just before the 1973 season, he was traded to Oakland. I often thought of the younger players, what they must have made of it all, sitting on the locker room benches and staring out at the drama speechless, like children at a dinner table whose parents are having a heated argument. Ultimately, it would depend on them—if following all the disruption they could recover and put together a team character.

During the turmoil of that last season Bob Vogel announced his retirement. This was easier for me to accept, because I remembered his telling me about Hawk Mountain and how he had always regretted that the football season was on during the fall bird migration and interfered with his going up to Pennsylvania to see the hawks floating in the thermals by the hundreds above the steep stands of pine.

It was rare that a football player found himself able to quit gracefully, and at the right time, like Bob Vogel. If a star just coming off his prime tried to retire, a chorus of criticism would rise and the front office would kick up a fuss about loyalty, amidst assurances that the player had four or five good years left, if not more. Under this sort of pressure, combined with the visceral reaction that came with the dog days of August and the memories of training camp (the early-morning sun steaming the dew off the practice field grass, the equipment waiting in rows on the gymnasium floor, the sensual pleasure of lemonade from ice-filled tubs after a hard practice, the guitars being strummed down the hall in the evening . . . all these providing associations that were too much to miss), the veteran would pack his suitcase and phone the front office to say that he had changed his mind and was coming in.

Gordy used to say that it was once a player gave up his choice of quitting to the front office that he compromised the end of his career, which was then bound to occur either because of an injury or because the coaches would finally become skeptical about his skills and let him go. In his own case the time had come at four o'clock on the sunny afternoon of July 31, 1968. All of it was indelibly in his mind. The Lions were preparing to play an exhibition game against Buffalo. Gordy had not been in training camp long because he had been working with the Players Association negotiators, and he had arrived in time to miss that part of the training schedule which includes rough scrimmage work; indeed, on this day he had left his shoulder pads in his locker. At the end of practice, Joe Schmidt ambled over and told Gordy that he felt Greg Barton needed to be tested by some live pass-rushing. Barton, who was the third-string quarterback, had been elevated temporarily because Greg Landry and Bill Munson, both ranked ahead of him, were out— Landry in the All-Star camp and Munson in the hospital having a cyst removed. "He needs the experience—just four or five red-dog plays," Schmidt said. Gordy answered, "Damn it, Joe, I thought the rough stuff was over." The assistant manager was sent running up the hill through the pine groves to get Gordy's shoulder pads out of his locker.

"It was the fourth play," Gordy said. "Nick Eddy blocked the weakside linebacker, but a rookie charged in and came down on the inside of my knee and blew open everything inside it. Technically, the two crisscrossing medial collateral ligaments came off the bone and rolled up into themselves—like a window shade snapping up. The meniscus cartilage, on which the knee joint rides, was torn, and so were the posterior and interior cruciates. Until that day I didn't know what any of these words meant, or indeed anything that went on under my kneecap. I started clawing at the ground, and I remember Joe standing over me, and Alex running over, and the looks on their faces, and the awful silence.

"They took me up to the training room in the back of a station wagon, lying between two tackling dummies so I'd be kept steady. Up there, the doctor touched my knee, and I could see him slide it back and forth as if there was nothing attached to it. I remember saying in this sort of resigned way, 'Well, if you ride the motorcycle long enough . . .'

"Oh, I thought about coming back," Gordy went on. "I ran for a couple of months after I got out of the cast—jogged around the empty stadium, always in the rain, it seemed—but the pain was constant, and when I tried to run *through* it I began reinjuring the tissue, and that's when I knew I was finished. I just wrapped myself up in the Players Association. Joe Schmidt called me on the phone a lot, and he told me that he'd use me at offensive tackle where there's less running; the temptation to give it at least a try was incredible, but what I did was just draw the shades down—like darkening a room so you don't see what's in it.

"I lost weight. I took off so much weight that I couldn't have pushed my way through a hedge. Mike Lucci saw me one day and said, 'My God, Gordy, you've got cancer.' He blurted it out very seriously. I lost so much weight—about forty pounds— that now I'm in awe of how truly *big* the people are who play in the line. I mean, they're goddamn *monsters*. The other day I ran into Merlin Olsen, who weighs about two eighty, and I couldn't believe I had once played against him. He looked at me, and I giggled at him and said, 'Boy, you'd have a ball now, wouldn't you?' Of course, he always did anyway."

And Karras. What a mockery! I was just about the last quarterback he would ever get his hands on. Most people felt that the decline for him began when he finally got seriously hurt—a knee injury sustained in a late-season game against Green Bay in 1969. I had gone up to Wisconsin to see the game. The hunting season was on and thousands of men with their rifles were off in the northern woods after deer. The night before the game the bars in Green Bay were full of their wives, out on the town, sitting in rows on the barstools. The Detroit football team had been warned about fooling around with them;

one could never be sure when the hunters would come back out of the woods, and it would be nothing for them to fire a shot through the kitchen window at a stranger in the house—and more's the delight if they then discovered they had pumped a bullet into a Detroit Lion. The people in the area really detested the Lions. At Lambeau Field the next day, a great rattling roar of hate went up at Detroit's appearance, with much of it reserved for Karras' individual introduction. He ran onto the field with his little choppy steps, turned and faced some distant television camera momentarily, and then trotted over to his teammates. The rage of the crowd had no humor in it.

I had asked Karras about it later. "It's undiluted," he said. "Just pure venom. They're honest in Green Bay—I mean, you *know* what's in their minds. They're not shifty people; they don't pussyfoot around in the darkness and stick a knife in your back. Nossir. What they do is wheel a howitzer as big as a locomotive right up to your front door, and they're so straightforward that they don't shoot it until you open up the door and say, 'Hello, who's there?' They're your straightforward people, Green Bay folk, and life in the National Football League would be beastly without them."

I was in the press box for the beginning of that game, in a glass-enclosed section with carpeting underfoot and long tables to sit at and write. The noise of the crowd barely came in through the glass, so that the game outside seemed to be at one remove, as if one were watching a distant touch-football game through a bus window.

I was not in there for long. Detroit kicked off and on the first defensive play Karras got into the Green Bay backfield and collected himself Bart Starr, the Green Bay quarterback. I let out a great involuntary whoop, drumming the table in front of me with my fists, and shouted his name, chortling in delight with my feet thumping up and down on the carpet. I quieted down rather quickly because I realized I was making the only noise in the room. The typewriters had stopped. People were staring. A Green Bay official in a club blazer came over. He bent down, his hands clasped behind his back like a deacon's, and *whispered* to me, as if to spare me the embarrassment of others overhearing his admonition, that outbursts of this sort were not allowed in press boxes and I would have to leave if I intended to continue them. I said I had not known; I was sorry. But after a while I left, walking out into the cold and into the quick life of all that shouting and cheering outside, not so much to find a place to let loose my own emotions as to escape such an antiseptic place.

Karras got hurt in the fourth quarter. Detroit had the game well in hand when he went down, his knee caught in a cross-check from Gale Gillingham, and a great bellow of delight went up from the Green Bay crowd. It was an odd cry, sustained, one almost of triumph, and it increased as more people noticed that Karras was not getting up; they rose up off their seats and shouted down at him, almost as if the force of their pleasure would keep him on the ground. I stared, speechless. Finally Karras rose and painfully hobbled, half hopping, for the sidelines under his own steam, waving off assistance from the converging Detroit players. If they had supported him or touched him, it would have cost Detroit a time-out. The crowd noise kept up, beating down on him from those banks of people.

I got into the locker room after the game to see him. He was sitting on a training table, his leg stuck out, with the knee in ice bags. He had a cigar in his mouth. In the showers next door we could hear the Lion players yelling over the roar of the water; victory over the Green Bay team was always sweet. Karras shifted heavily on the table.

"D'ja hear that crowd out there," someone said. "They just went crazy when you went down. Jesus!"

Karras said, "I'll tell you something. That was an ovation. That's the greatest ovation I ever got. They're so damn happy to see me go. I've tormented them all those years. It's a real ovation when you get something like that."

Subsequently, Karras was operated on—the cartilage had to be repaired—and that winter he was in a cast, sitting at home and wondering what sort of cane he was going to buy to ease him through his convalescence—an elegant number, with a silver head, for twirling purposes, or a knobby, utilitarian type. He reported to training camp that summer a somewhat changed figure; a relative quiet enveloped him, which bewildered even his teammates. Some felt his injury was bothering him, others reckoned that management had prevailed on him to contain his hi-jinks, and still others detected a mellowing process: that summer he had been elected to his neighborhood Parent-Teacher Association.

I went out to see him at training camp. He said that his injury, though improving daily, bothered him, and he spoke of retreating a bit because of it, "like a wounded dog." He was outraged by the mockery of not being a hundred percent fit when the Detroit Lions appeared to be a strong contender, and it was this that was the chief reason for his transformation: he had looked around and found himself on a team that had the potential to end up in the Super Bowl.

"In the years I've played for Detroit," he told me, "I've never felt this way before. In past years we've always said, 'Oh, if only we had an offensive line or a place-kicker or a quarterback or a punter.' We've always had an excuse. Now we don't have one. The coaches have put it together and they've presented it to us. They've said, 'Well, here you are. The gun is loaded. No more blanks. The live stuff's in there. It's up to you.'

"I felt this after the first exhibition game of the season —after we'd played the Kansas City Chiefs. We lost that game, but we'd only had about four days of practice, and I looked around and saw that we'd been given this very, very good machine. After the game I telephoned Buterakos who thought I was going to explode on him, which you usually do when you lose. He couldn't believe it, Knowing me, when I told him in this quiet voice that we were going a long way, that maybe we had a championship team. He kept saying, 'Hey, Alex, is that you, Big Man? You been hit on the head? You all right?' "

What had caused the change was that Joe Schmidt had managed to put together an offensive team in an organization which had always cherished its defense. In previous years the running backs would turn upfield to find their way barred by terrifying thickets of tacklers. Schmidt had concentrated on that most intricate of mechanisms, the offensive line, and it had finally begun to mesh.

"But the main thing," Karras said, "is that the team has depth. We have three good quarterbacks—Bill Munson, Greg Landry and Greg Barton—and a whole bunch of running backs —Mel Farr, Altie Taylor, Bill Triplett and Nick Eddy. They're all good. If a guy got hurt in the old days, the coaches would give this big gasp of horror and you'd see a rookie who looked like a stick give a little yell and come off the bench to take the guy's place. On the way out to the huddle his contact lenses would tumble out, and you'd see him put his hands out in front of him like a blind man, and he'd say, 'Well, if you just *point* me in the right direction, maybe . . .' I mean, they were *eager*, those cats we used to have, but they weren't very good. It's different now. If a guy gets hurt these days, the coaches give this little shrug of the shoulders and call out, 'Okay, next,' and off the bench comes a guy who's eight hundred feet tall, weighs as much as an apartment house and is quick enough to make your eyes pop, and he's got someone behind *him* who's just as good."

It was not only Karras. At every level of the Lion organization that autumn people found signs to suggest a great season. Friday Macklem, the equipment manager, told me that even *he* could tell because the players were being more careful about packing their gear for out-of-town games. "We have forty individual equipment bags that the players pack themselves," he said. "In a losing season—for example, the one we had a few years ago under Harry Gilmer—the players would forget to pack half their stuff. In the last game of the year against Green Bay, seven fellows didn't pack belts to hold up their football pants. Five of them forgot their thigh pads. Well, there've been no such lapses this year, and I'm telling you that's the mark of a winner."

The entire Detroit community had a sense of optimism about their team's chances. I was told that at a banquet Lem Barney, the brilliant cornerback, was asked what he thought the possibility was of the Lions getting to the Super Bowl, and before he could begin an answer the crowd was on its feet, yelling and stomping, banging glasses with forks and carrying on—an ovation that lasted for five minutes and was a tribute not only to Barney and the Lions but to the question, which in previous years would have been greeted with skeptical murmurs, if not raucous laughter. Detroit had not had a championship football team in thirteen years, and at the end of a season its citizens packed their snowballs ice-hard before lobbing them down on coaches and players to lend physical weight to their displeasure.

The Lions won the first four games of 1970, but then they began seesawing back and forth. Among others, they lost a game against New Orleans in which John Dempsey, who had a deformed foot, kicked an incredible record sixty-three-yard field goal in the final seconds to bring his team from behind. Karras used to say about that extraordinary feat that when he saw the Saints lining up in their field-goal formation, he laughed heartily and maneuvered himself in his defensive position so that when the play started he could stand up and get a good panoramic view of such idiotic proceedings. In fact, however, in the photographs of Dempsey's foot coming through the ball, the nearest Detroit player is Karras, an arm outstretched, his body half-suspended in air, as the ball starts beyond his fingertips on its long flight, going end over end very slowly, which is the mark of the long kick, and clearing the distant crossbar with space to spare.

But despite the New Orleans setback, and others, the Lions had a good enough record that year to reach the play-offs. Their first opponents were the Dallas Cowboys in a game scheduled for the day after Christmas. I talked to Karras a number of times over the phone; he was confident about the Detroit defense, but still worried about the offense, which was unpredictable and would have trouble with a stiff Dallas defensive unit, nicknamed "The Doomsday Defense." It would have been nice to have John Gordy with them still.

Christmas day, Gordy and I called him together out in Houston to wish him luck.

"We miss you, Bear," Karras said. "We could use you."

"Would I miss it?" Gordy asked on another extension.

"Your heart would bleed. The Lion organization gave us a little Christmas Eve party. Would you like to hear about it?"

"Not much," said Gordy. "I can imagine it."

"It was in this big room," Karras went on. "The chairs were taken out. We walked in there and stood up against the walls—a scene out of a high school dance with the girls on one side, the boys on the other, and a huge expanse of floor in between. We stood looking at each other for about twenty-five minutes. After a while, three or four people, probably from the front office, started singing Christmas songs. No one knew the words. Some people tried humming along, but it didn't work. The carols died away. Some hors d'oeuvre were brought in which were really bad. Then we had an eggnog apiece, which I thought was exciting. Mine had a little pepper floating around on the top. From there, we were led into the next room where they sat us down to a dinner of dry turkey and sweet potatoes. Nobody talked. Somebody tried to remember a grace, it being Christmas Eve and all, but after we'd bowed our heads and he said, 'God, we are thankful to Thee for . . . for . . .' he couldn't recall *what* we were thankful for, which killed off *that* grace. We had ice cream for dessert. Afterwards I went back to the hotel room and Bill Munson, my roomie, and I played a game of gin. I got beat and lost ten dollars. Then I turned out the light and went to sleep. That was my Christmas Eve."

"I'm glad to have heard about it," said Gordy. "Christ!"

"What's the Astrodome like?" I asked. The Lions were practicing in Houston's great covered structure which had an AstroTurf surface similar to the one they would be playing on in Dallas' Cotton Bowl.

"It's the most mammoth place," Karras replied. "It's eerie. Since it's enclosed, it's hard to get out of your mind that you're not there to play basketball."

"What about the AstroTurf?" I asked. "What's it like to run on? Does it squeak?"

"It kind of squishes," Karras said. "When there's no crowd in the Astrodome, and the place is quiet like a tomb, all you can hear is this squishing as the players run. The Texans are very proud of it; they think of it as a fancy Persian rug. Just before we go out to practice, this tall Texan dressed like an old-time preacher in a high-crowned beaver hat appears at the door of the locker room and calls out, 'Brethern, I am aware that your habit on your home fields—in places like Detroit and Cleveland, and even Atlanta in the heart of the South—is to spit and urinate on the ground when the urge is upon you. Here, we hain't got that habit.' He raises a long finger. 'There is to be no spitting and urinating on the AstroTurf. Offenders will be prosecuted to the fullest extent of the Texas law, which means they will be either lynched or shot, depending on whether the citizens or the constabulary get to them fustest.' "

"Fustest?" said Gordy.

"That's right, fustest," said Karras. "That's what the guy said."

"Can you kick a football up against the roof of the Astrodome?" I asked, trying to get things back on an even keel.

"It's impossible," Karras said. "No one can do it. I tried it myself. My first kick of the year. It went up and came down on the helmet of a player standing about fifteen feet away. He hadn't seen me kick it and didn't know what had happened. I called to him, 'Jesus, the roof's caving in.' He made a couple of quick, darting moves and turned a pale gray inside his helmet. I could see it."

The next day the Lions lost. The Detroit offense was stopped completely, and the game ended with Dallas ahead by the odd baseball score of 5–0. I watched it on television, and when it was over I called Gordy. He said, "That goddamn game destroyed my mind."

We couldn't think of anything to say to each other. The silence was so long that I wondered if he had gone off the line. I listened for his breathing and finally said, "Hey, are you there?"

"Yeh."

"How do you think Alex is?"

"I don't know."

"How did he play?"

"Five points against the Lion defense! *Three,* really, because two of those points came from a safety. That's great defense."

"How do you think *he's* taking it?"

"It'll be hard. That's a long way to come to lose like that. It'll take a lot of the juice out of him. I'll tell you something: I hope he quits."

Karras did not quit, of course. He came back the next summer, the same time that I was training down in Westminster with the Colts. The reports about him were varied. His knee was said to be completely recovered; he remained withdrawn from the others at camp, I was told, and he was taking his own time about getting himself ready. One word was that his lateral movement had slowed down—he could no longer "play the piano," as football players said. I kept hearing rumors that the front office wanted him out.

Just after the exhibition game against the Colts, Coach Schmidt called him in. "How do you feel?" he asked.

"Fine. I hope you're not getting nervous. I'm going to be coming on strong in the last two weeks. I'll be ready."

That was the last time they spoke.

Against Miami, the penultimate game of the exhibition season, at Karras' tackle position, the coaches played Dick Evey, who was embarrassed, and Karras was sent in to relieve him. Against Philadelphia, the last exhibition game, Karras started and had what was considered a fine game. Mark Nordquist, the Eagle guard who played against him, said that he'd had a rough time with him all afternoon. He said, "He came at me harder than anyone has all summer. I knew it was time for the season to start."

After the game Schmidt came around to the lockers, leaning in to congratulate his players, touching them lightly on the shoulder and offering a word or so, and Karras remembered being "sort of overlooked." He said to Joe, "We're going to go get 'em on Monday," referring to the preparations for the opening season game, which was against the Dolphins. "Joe seemed surprised," he recalled later.

That evening Karras flew to New York to appear on the Johnny Carson show. He had no inkling of what was to come. There was one player listed to be cut, and he worried vaguely that it might be Joe Robb, a veteran who played alongside him on the line and whose company he enjoyed. Karras appeared on the show, taped at 6:00 P.M. for broadcasting to the country later in the evening, and then took a cab out to La Guardia to catch a plane back to Detroit. At 8:30 he was paged at the airport, and to his surprise he discovered Joe Schmidt on the other end of the line. Once again, hearing his coach's voice his first thought was that he was going to be told that Joe Robb was to be cut.

"Joe? What do you want?"

"I hate to tell you this, Alex, but I had to put you on waivers today."

Karras found himself giggling. "What did you say?"

"I don't think you can do the job anymore."

"Come on, Joe. Do you really think those other men playing defensive tackle can do the job better than I can? You're kidding. Aw, come on."

Schmidt began to say something, but the connection was poor and Karras couldn't understand him, so he said, "Joe, you've been mumbling at me for five years," and hung up.

His prime concern at this point was how to break the news to his family. When he got home to Bloomfield Hills he decided to wait to tell Joanie until after they had watched his performance on the Carson show. Then he said, "Listen, I've got some good news and I've got some bad news. Which do you want to hear first?"

"The bad news."

"I got cut from the Lions tonight."

"That's not even funny," she said. It took him quite a long time to convince her. He never looked at her, but kept staring into the TV set. The late night movie was on; the Dead End Kids were chasing somebody, or being chased—it was hard to tell, the sound being off. An advertisement showing a kitchen scene came on in which Karras could tell by the expression on the man's face that he was gagging over his wife's coffee.

After a while Joanie remembered to ask him what the good news was.

"The good news?" said her husband. "Well, my plane didn't crash coming in."

Karras' next worry was how the news of his being cut would affect his two sons, the older one especially, whose best friend was Joe Schmidt's oldest boy. He got up early, before they took the bus to school, called them back as they started out the door and told them about it.

Peter said, "Good. I wasn't a Lion fan anyway. I'm a Ram fan."

The other son, Alex Jr. said, "Oh, that's good—you won't have to mess with that stuff anymore."

The two of them looked at their father briefly, and then went out to catch the bus.

Karras told me later, "I thought about those two kids' behavior, and how easy they made it for me. Maybe Joanie prepared them early that morning and told them to play it cool. But their reaction was natural and decent—though I never knew till then that Peter was a *Ram* fan. Christ! He liked the Los Angeles *Rams?*"

When I returned from Africa, I had read the news clippings about Karras' release. Bill Wallace, the football writer for the New York *Times*, who is not especially known for the acidity of his views, had written that any coaching staff which decided that Dick Evey (a lineman let go by both the Los Angeles Rams and the Chicago Bears) was a better tackle than Alex Karras should restart their college education, specifically in Psychology 1616, Clinical Diagnostic Evaluation of Children.

I kept thinking, whatever the reason, how hard it must have been not only on Karras, but also on Joe Schmidt for dropping him. The two had been the closest of friends in the old days, not only sharing the decade of a personal relationship, but also enjoying the bond of being defensive players on a team that rejoiced in its defense.

I happened to be in Detroit that fall for a visit. I called Schmidt and asked if I could see him. Though he must have known I wanted to ask him about Alex, he told me to come around to the Lion offices on Michigan Avenue. He always seemed out of place indoors, especially in an office—bursting in suits that scarcely seemed able to contain a body as solid and drumhead hard as a giant tuna's. He came right to the point. "If you want to ask me about Karras, I didn't feel he could run anymore. I wanted to tell him face to face, but he was in New York. I didn't feel he could do it anymore."

He paused, and we looked at each other. "It's as simple as that, is it?" I asked.

"I think so," he replied. "It was a judgment. Mine. I said at the time that it was the toughest decision I'd probably ever have to make."

"It's the great horror of coaching, isn't it?" I asked. "Letting someone go . . ."

"The greatest horror of coaching is losing," he said firmly.

I found myself staring at a framed document entitled *The Penalty of Leadership,* which hung on one wall. Schmidt was saying, "I remember telling myself when Harry Gilmer, my predecessor, was being snowballed—hell, *ice*balled at the end of his last season—that no such a thing would ever happen to me. As a ballplayer I'd never heard boos. Now I have."

His hands were flat on the desk, and he worked a piece of gum rapidly in his jaw. "The worst thing about coaching is that kind of thing—everything that's connected with losing. There's nothing worse than walking across a field towards a locker room if you've lost, and nothing better if you've won. It's bad enough if you're a player, though it's not as severe as it is for the coach. The player can walk away from losing, but the coach—well, he has to face the responsibility of losing. He has no other choice. If he could somehow condition himself to *accept* losing—well, then he should get out of football; he's in the wrong profession. What the good coach has to be able to do is disperse those pressures: he has to accept the abuse, but never let any of it influence his actions; he must never let the pressure get to him to the extent he throws up his hands. And he's got to build up enough self-discipline so that he doesn't

lean forward over his desk and use these hands to pop a reporter."

"Oh?"

The blue of the stone in his championship ring twinkled
as he turned his big hands over.

"Do you think it's changed you, Joe?" I asked.

"I don't enjoy myself as much as I used to. I still have a
sense of humor, but I don't show it as much as I used to. People
say that coaching has made me uptight, but it's not that. I want
to win, and in football a coach only has fourteen chances during
the season to do it. A baseball coach has a hundred and sixty-
two games on his schedule. In football, you *cannot* lose."

"What about the fans? The boos, and those snowballs
you vowed that—"

"I hear them," he said. "But you have to watch out for
rabbit ears. I remember that during the first season I came out
on the front steps and found the Monday trash spread all over
my front lawn, and the garbage cans overturned. We'd lost a
game that weekend, and I was paranoid enough to think that
some fans were responsible—that this was their way of being
critical. I stomped around, wanting to pop someone. Then I
found out that it was our dogs.

"But the stuff comes in," he went on. He rang his secretary and asked her to bring in some fan letters. He leafed
through the pile. "Quite a lot of them start out 'You big ass-
hole,' " he said. "Most of it is second-guessing." He read from
a few. " 'Why didn't you start Landry?' 'Why don't you use a
prevent defense?' 'Don't you understand that the name of the
game is pass!' I have bales of it. The real kooky ones are in a
file about a foot high. I suppose it's good for people to get this
sort of thing off their minds. It wouldn't be good for a guy to
walk around all choked up with something as important as
wanting to tell an NFL coach that 'the name of the game is
pass.' "

"No," I said.

"The pressure of not being able to get that off his mind
might cripple him with a stroke. Right?"

"Absolutely."

Suddenly Schmidt looked around his office as if he had never seen it before, and then leaned forward with a smile. "Hey, how's The Bear? He gave me that *Penalty of Leadership* plaque you've been looking at."

"Gordy? Oh, he's fine. He's very much interested in a girl who's got him interested in tennis and skiing and sailing. They're going to get married."

"He's into yachts, is he?"

"And listen, he's lost forty pounds."

"Goddamn. I'll tell you something: I miss him. I miss Karras. I miss all of them."

That day I had lunch with Wayne Walker, who had played alongside Schmidt through the sixties, and was still at it, now in his twelfth year. He had been across the line from me at Ann Arbor, crouched and waiting in that distinctive posture of his, with arms up and palms down, as if to fend off something coming up at him from the ground. He had been one of the most vociferous in not wanting the Lions to participate in my series of plays with the Colts.

"Hey, what was that about?" I asked him. "You damn near scotched that whole television show."

"Well, there was always the chance of someone getting hurt. Also, there was the chance that you might complete a pass to someone and make us look bad."

"No kidding," I said, enormously pleased. "You mean you were scared that I was going to embarrass you?"

"I'm not sure 'scared' is the right word."

"But damn, that's something." I really *was* pleased. "Was that why Mitchell slugged me? To intimidate me so I wouldn't embarrass you?"

Walker laughed. "Well, that wasn't right, what Mitchell did to you. I got angry with him for that. I mean, he didn't *have* to do that. I think we could have contained you without that sort of measure."

"The quarterback sneak worked," I said.

"Great call," he said.

"It was the only one left in my repertoire."

He laughed. "Well, I'll tell you something. I really tried to get to you. Your line was fired up."

"What about the pass play?"

"The ball was coming right for me. I would have intercepted if Jerry Rush hadn't knocked it down."

"Come on," I said. "Gordon Bowdell was coming across on a slant. He was cutting right in front of you."

"An interception," Walker said firmly.

"Well, you wouldn't have gone far," I said. "I would have cut you down at the knees."

We ordered lunch. "Did you see Joe?" Walker asked.

"I just came from there. I wanted to ask him about Alex. Joe seemed just about the same—maybe a little pressured."

"I don't think he's changed inwardly," Walker said. "Maybe outwardly. All those years when he was playing, everyone really liked him, so when he became a coach the early comments and vibrations of discontent affected him bad. He wasn't used to displeasing anyone. Then the boos came, and nothing like *that* had ever happened before. What he really missed was *playing*, that simple act of knocking someone down —such an easy and basic activity compared to the mental pressures and woes of coaching. In the early days he'd sometimes knock on the door at training camp, and come in and close the door and have a few laughs. But it happened less and less as he began to refuse to expose himself to as many people. It's too bad. He could still keep up with his old friends. It might help him. It's so simple; you just knock on someone's door. Of course, there aren't many of us around anymore."

"So you never see him—to relax and have a few laughs?"

"Who, Joe? Never. But maybe that's my fault, too. When he took over as coach, I began to stay away from him; I didn't want our friendship to compromise him. Well, that was too bad, because that's what football is really all about—being with a bunch of guys, laughing. You're only on the field about one one-hundredth of the time you devote to football, so it's the rest of it that's so important. I still have some good laughs."

"Was Alex still having laughs when he was cut?" I asked.

409

"Aw hell, I don't think Alex really wanted it that last year," Walker said. "I don't think he was enjoying it."

"How could you tell?"

"He'd lie on his bunk a lot. Nothing seemed to excite him. He said he was thinking of getting a clam for a pet—it sort of suited his mood. He didn't talk much. He just wasn't enjoying it the way he used to."

"Did it surprise you that he was cut?"

"It was in the cards, I think. I remember walking with Schmidt down to the practice field during training camp, and off in a far corner of the field was Alex and a whole gang of people shooting a TV commercial. I said, 'Joe, Alex is really doing good.' And Joe said, 'Let's hope he's doing good enough to make the team.'

"I miss him. I truly miss him. Too few of us are left. Dick LeBeau had the locker next to mine. Alex's was across the room. When the rookies began swearing and carrying on and snapping towels and acting big, there was always Alex to look for to give them the big superior shrug. Now, with Alex gone, who do I really *know*? They've all gone. I think many too many players leave before their time. They talk themselves into believing they're too old, when in fact physically they can do it. It really depends on their frame of mind. They should think of themselves as being indestructible." He looked at me. "Did I tell you about Dick LeBeau's knee?"

I shook my head.

"Well, he had a knee injury that needed off-season surgery. I came to the Ford Hospital to see him through it. Outside in the corridors the place was chaos—a number of girls were there, including his ex-wife, all of them on hand to offer comfort, and none of them knowing the others would be there. LeBeau is a helluva ladies' man. Well, he asked me to be with him in the operating room. He'd insisted on a spinal anesthetic so he could chat with the doctors, though they put a canvas shield at his waist so he couldn't see what they were doing to his knee. When I got there the doctors were about to start, and Dick motioned me over. 'Hey, King,' he says to me. 'Stick around, will you?'

"'I'm here.'

"'I've got to find out something. They've put up this shield so I can't see. But you're a football player. You'll know.'

"'Know what?'

"'When the doc lifts up my kneecap,' LeBeau whispers, 'take a peek under there and, man, tell me what it is that makes me so fucking quick!'"

Walker roared with laughter. "We've been in it twelve years, the two of us, great goddamn times."

There was a silence for a moment, and Walker stared down at the tablecloth and began turning a water tumbler slowly in his hand. "I don't know," he said. "Maybe the longer you stay, the more you begin to wonder."

"What do you mean?"

Abruptly he began talking about Chuck Hughes, the young reserve Lion tight end who had gone into a game in the final minutes against the Chicago Bears and three plays after making a spectacular catch had suddenly pitched forward to the ground with such abruptness that his teammates on the sidelines, Walker among them, thought he was faking an injury to stop the clock. But then Dick Butkus, the Chicago middle linebacker, started waving desperately at the sidelines, standing over Hughes, looking down. The medical people ran out, and the big crowd started quieting down. It got so quiet that the players standing by the Lion bench, half the field away, could hear the thumps of the doctors beating on Hughes's chest to try to get his heart going again. He was carried off the field on a stretcher, no one sure what had happened. The game started up again but ended in a few minutes. The Lion drive collapsed and Chicago won the game. It didn't seem important, one way or the other. In the locker room Doc Thompson was crying; "I think we've lost him," he said. "To hell with the ball game," Joe Schmidt said to the team. "Let's pray for the kid." Charlie Sanders, who played first string at Hughes' tight end position, was so distraught that when he was finally able to get into his street clothes, he had to be carried home from the locker room.

"Lombardi, or maybe it was Paul Brown, used to say

that winning wasn't everything; it was the *only* thing," Walker said. "Well, I can't buy that anymore—not after that game and Hughes's dying." He told me that two weeks later when he got up to give a talk at a banquet, the scene—the quiet of the crowd, the sound of the hollow thumps coming across the field, the kneeling doctors—had flooded in on him, and in mid-sentence he had stopped and been unable to continue. "I guess I suddenly realized that the thing that had been giving me all that laughter, all those good times . . . well, it wasn't the same anymore. It won't be so hard to leave it now."

23

I saw Gordy and Karras from time to time during the next year. Gordy was in New York, so I ran into him more often. He was continuing to have his difficulties with yachting. Newly married, he told me he had been invited to crew aboard his father-in-law's seventy-foot schooner in October for the Mayor's Cup Race, which is for pre-1935 yachts over a course running from the Battery at the foot of Manhattan out to Sandy Hook and back.

"His boat is called the *So Fong*," Gordy said, "which means 'Pure Fragrance' in goddamn Mandarin. The day of the race was screaming windy, and it was raining so hard that I said to my wife Bitsy, and her father, that they were crazy, that even a *football* game would be called off in such weather. They were not impressed. So I told them to set me down somewhere in the *So Fong* where I couldn't get in the way, and they promised. What a day it was! The rain was moving absolutely horizontally; it was like buckets of water were being thrown at us. When we left the car, I had to carry Bitsy across puddles so big that I swear they had whitecaps, to get to where the *So Fong* was docked. We moved out into the East River just by the Fulton Fish Market. The sails were up, and I was standing in the stern, trying to pull a parka they'd found for me over my head, when the boom, or whatever you call that thing, came sweeping along and caught me just like a clothesline tackle and knocked me cartwheeling into the East River. Jeezus!

"The parka was over my head, so I couldn't see and couldn't breathe. I began to rage! I thought, *No!* I wasn't going to end up finished in the East River, not after all those years colliding around in football. Finally I got the parka off my head and floated up, and first I saw the World Trade Center towers on the skyline, and then bobbing alongside I saw Bitsy's head. She had this big grin. She'd been sitting in the cockpit and had looked back and seen me there on the stern with my arms up, blind, trying to worm my way into the goddamn foul-weather parka, and the boom coming across, watching it come quite slowly but inevitably, like a funny movie scene, and when I went over, *nudged* really, she stepped up and did a nice little dive, absolutely classic, over the rail to join me. I bobbed up and saw her. I said, 'What the hell are you doing here?' She said, 'You know you always take me everywhere you go.'"

"What was going on back on the *So . . . So . . . ?*"

"The *So Fong*. Did I tell you that meant 'Pure Fragrance' in goddamn Mandarin?" I nodded. "Well, Bitsy's father was coming up the stairs—I guess they call it the 'companionway'—with some maps under his arm, and as he got to deck level he caught a quick glimpse of his daughter going over the side, just a sight of her ankles and the heels of her deck shoes, and he was very surprised; he knew that something odd was going on. He rushed to the stern, but they couldn't turn the *So Fong* around in the big wind, at least not quickly enough, so she just went sailing off into the distance like she was well rid of us. We were picked up by the Coast Guard. The people on board pulled Bitsy out of the water with a boat hook—she only weighs ninety pounds—but a whole mess of them hauled away at me, like heaving a big fish into a little boat—a dinghy, isn't it?"

414

I nodded again. "What did they say when you were delivered back on board her father's boat?" I asked.

"Well, the *So Fong* people were all terribly embarrassed —partly because they hadn't been able to turn the boat around before the Coast Guard reached us, and also because no one had thought to throw us a life preserver. But mainly they were embarrassed for *us*.

"No one spoke to us. We sat together in the cockpit, and held hands, and looked at the rain. The waves in the East River were standing up straight and we could hardly believe we had both been in there. Eventually, the race was called off. A couple of other people had been tumbled in too and had been pulled out by the Coast Guard. I went home with Bitsy to Englewood, mixed myself a very large drink, and sat and stared into a big log fire. I did that for a long time."

Karras, on quite a different tack, was trying to remain very much in the public eye. Every time I tried to reach him, he was off somewhere—a movie in Mexico, a script conference in Hollywood (was he pressing his Ace Zerblonski character on some startled producer?). He had been doing some television commercials. I saw one of them, a credit-card commercial, in which he appeared as a gas station attendant dealing with a customer whose gas tank he'd filled but who had discovered no cash in his wallet and could not produce a credit card—a situation resolved by Karras' picking up the car, a small sports model, and tilting it up to drain the gas back into a big bucket, shaking the car to get the last drops out.

He was often a guest on television talk shows—not so much for his expertise on football as for the individualism and humor he brought to the television screen. I saw him two or three times on the Carson show. His entrances were very slow and shy; he was always voluminously attired in over-modish clothes, usually tentlike Hawaiian beach shirts. Sometimes he had a cigar. On one occasion he was carrying a knitting bag. He reached in, slowly removed a jockstrap with an orange rose stitched on it. He talked solemnly about the need for hemstitching colorful designs to brighten up what has traditionally been such a bland item of apparel. "We have done some very fancy work," he said. "A clipper ship under sail is probably our fanciest."

"A clipper ship under sail," said Carson, rocking back and forth behind his desk and looking enormously pleased.

On the surface, at least, Karras seemed to be doing well. For a while he had his own television show in Chicago. It was an interview program, and usually his guests were athletes from the Chicago teams. They sat down somewhat nervously on black leather revolving chairs. Karras had no compunction about hinting at a guest's personal peccadilloes or needling him about athletic letdowns he might have experienced. After setting Bobby Douglass, the Chicago Bear quarterback, on edge by asking him if he "messed around," Karras began carping on the fact that Douglass had gained only six yards passing in the previous game. "Six *yards*," he kept saying. Finally he offered the suggestion that if those six yards were broken down into *inches*, it would appear less humiliating; why, let's see, that would be 216 inches, which certainly sounded better.

The producer of the show was a harried man, by all accounts, who was rarely put at ease by the sort of hi-jinks and innovation that Karras injected into the program. On one occasion Karras arrived with an elderly gentleman he had found on the street outside the studio, who was not only in an advanced stage of drunkenness but dressed in what appeared to be worn-out Napoleonic attire—a cloak with one epaulet hanging askew. Karras placed him in one of the black leather chairs, where he promptly fell asleep, his head collapsed to one side, his mouth ajar, his chest rising and falling rhythmically. Though he was on camera, he was never mentioned throughout the program; the guests came on, stared briefly at him and then at Karras, who would lean forward with great sincerity to provide the most traditional of sports interview questions: "Now tell me, Dick, what went wrong? Why couldn't the Bears put any points up on the scoreboard last Sunday?"—and all the time the station switchboard was heavy with calls: "Who's that old geezer, anyway? What's he . . ."

416

But I had heard that despite his apparent success, his bitterness about his dismissal was deep. I was told that when he left home on trips, he always had someone with him—usually Tom Vance, his peppery friend from the Players Association who had become his agent—to keep him entertained and his mind off what had happened. I had not seen Karras since he had been dropped. Perhaps I had written him a letter; I don't remember. It was an awkward business. Being in Africa when I heard the news, and not having done something about it then, it was almost too late—it would bring something up that presumably he was trying to forget. I missed having done it, and I kept being reminded when I caught a glimpse of him on television.

Then one day Karras telephoned me in New York. "You've got to come to Boston," he said.

"Is that you, Alex?" I asked, recognizing his voice.

"Yeah. You've got to get on the next plane."

"It's great to hear from you. Are you all right?"

"I'm doing a TV show up here, a pilot. It's different. It's going to knock them dead. I want you to be in it."

"Oh?"

He would tell me little about what he wanted me to do, other than that he wanted me to perform with him in a wrestling skit. "We don't really work with a script," he said. "It's spontaneous—a lot of freewheeling."

"I can imagine," I said.

The television studio was an hour by car from the airport. Karras was waiting on the sound stage where a boxing ring was set up. His torso was wrapped in a lion's pelt that looked more like a cobbler's apron. Under his arm he held a large cardboard apparatus fashioned to resemble a lion's head. When he put it on, the outfit made him look enormous.

"How are you, Al?" I asked. "Everything okay?"

"Isn't this great?" Inside the lion's head his voice was muffled.

"What are we supposed to do?"

He took off the head and explained that when the

417

cameras were set up, I would join him in the ring wearing a sweat suit, and he was to teach me a few simple wrestling holds so that I could take on a lady wrestler.

"Oh yes," I said.

The switcheroo was that when the lady wrestler entered the ring, she would go not for me but for Karras, and toss him over her shoulder and slam him down to the mat. Then the camera would move in for a close-up of his face, just off the canvas, and catch what was referred to in comedic repertoire as a "slow burn."

I did what was asked of me, and afterwards we went over to a small set of wooden bleachers set along one side of the sound stage. Karras was carrying his lion's head. He put it down beside him. "The show opens with a shot of these bleachers filled with weird people," he explained. "Then these cheerleaders come out wearing letters on their sweaters, so that when they stand in a line it spells out my name. The girls weigh well over two hundred pounds apiece. They kick up their legs, and they cry out through megaphones to the crowd, 'All right, let's give it a *K*. An *A*. All right, now an *R*.' And the crowd yells back on command. The girls are *huge*, the fattest ones we could find in Boston. Elephants."

The stagehands set up the next scene. I told Karras that I was sorry I hadn't been in touch with him about his being dropped from the Lions. I had been out of the country, and time had slipped away . . .

He touched the lion's head. "It was the front office," he said. "They never could stand that I said what was on my mind. Perhaps there's no place in sports for an athlete who has strong opinions. I have opinions; I have a family; I do what other people do—pay taxes and bills—and I bang at the plumbing with my foot when it doesn't work. I've always thought that I've got as much right as anyone to express myself on topics other than playing defensive tackle. The Lion front office could never stand that, so they let me go."

He smoothed the fur on his costume. "What the hell," he said. "I'm happy now. When I played football in the beginning, there was that pseudo-ego thing—the pleasure of smacking somebody and hearing the crowd go 'Oh.' But after a while football became a job. It's simply a better form of life than being in the mills of Gary, Indiana. Sure, football took me out of those doldrums. I don't wear a blue shirt. But to say I loved it, that it always gave me a big thrill, is crazy: how can you love it when you have coaches blowing whistles at you and your knees are being ripped up? It's a nasty-ass way to make a buck. That always horrifies people; they say, 'Well, if you don't like it, get out of it.' The point is that once you're in it, you *can't* get out of it easily, any more than a dentist or a doctor can throw his profession aside and get out of it. Hell, no; you're stuck."

He looked down at his shoes. They had been painted baby-blue to contrast with his lion costume. "Those sons of bitches in Detroit," he said. "What did they *mean* taking that thing away from me."

We had a little place on the northern shore of Long Island that summer, on the curve of the bay across from Gardiner's Island, a little yacht club next door which had a small marina, where often two or three big sloops and a yawl were tied up to the pilings. Terns hovered above the slip through which the boats entered the marina. The lanyards of the yacht club flagstaff slapped against the metal of the pole in the slightest breeze, a constant distant click that one heard above the sound of the waves sifting at the beach, the wind bending the saw grass and the cries of the children playing on the yacht club beach on the far side of the dunes. I sat in the living room in front of the typewriter and gazed out at the blue sweep of the bay. It was difficult to concentrate on football. A disparate and confused montage came to mind: I remembered the Baltimore Colts and the July heat at camp; and the deaf-mutes semaphoring to each other on the campus walks; and the slap of a screen door in the distance, the shrill squeak of chairs in the cellar classroom, with the sound of the rock records from upstairs drifting in; and how the slight wind caught the frisbees sailing in the evening and held them almost motionless; and Bubba's pink Continental and how he rocked it to the beat of the music; and the time The Crocodile threw the beer; and the tinny music of the little phonograph outside the plane that took us all to Ann Arbor; and watching Bob Vogel draw on his boxing gloves as he prayed before the game; and the sound of spikes in the long tunnel, and then the overpowering suffusion of hatred, the steam of it, and Mitchell's eyes above his helmet bar. Then I thought about the collapse of the team, and The Piccolo Player watching them do their calisthenics. Most of them had gone now, the contexts had changed; new teams for some, and retirement and mowing the lawn on Sunday after-noons for others.

It had happened to Karras and Gordy too, and my pic-ture of them was less in the football arena with the white num-bers 71 and 75 against the blue jerseys, and the mud and how Gordy looked with his front teeth out. Football had gone from their lives, just as it surely had from mine. It was not clear how I *did* see them now. But then, looking out at the bay, I imagined a schooner coming in, the big sails luffing as she came up into the wind. A big crowd was aboard—some of them in deck chairs, a mixture of Colts and Lions, some still wearing helmets with either the horseshoe or the blue lion rampant on the sides, but a few of them with their helmets off so that I could recognize them across the water: Unitas and Curry and Tom Matte and Dick LeBeau and Puffer of the Bloomfield Hills Jets. The midgets were there too, scurrying about among the snapping lines, and sitting in the stern I saw Buterakos, a whip trailing in the water as if he were fishing.

Up in the bow was Karras, wearing a T-shirt and his "Jewish Open" golf hat. He seemed to be struggling with a mammoth mushroom anchor, though it was not clear what he wanted to do with it. It was easier to picture Gordy; after all, he was a fledgling yachtsman. He was standing at the tiller, an unlit pipe upside down in his mouth—a suave yachtsman's affectation—and I would walk out on the dunes and wave. He would see me and wave back, and as behind him the crew scurried about the deck, the lines whipping in the wind, he would take the pipe out of his mouth and call, "Hey there, baby, ahoy! Ahoy! We're going up the coast. You coming? Ahoy there! Ahoy!"

ABOUT THE AUTHOR

George Plimpton is a graduate of Harvard University and King's College, Cambridge University. In 1953, in Paris, he became the editor of *The Paris Review*, a literary quarterly which in 1973 celebrated its twentieth anniversary, and he has since edited the four volumes of interviews with famous literary figures entitled *Writers at Work* that first appeared in the magazine. His books include *Out of My League, Paper Lion, The Bogey Man* and a juvenile entitled *The Rabbit's Umbrella;* he is also the co-author (with Jean Stein) of an oral-history volume, *American Journey: The Times of Robert F. Kennedy.*

A special contributor to *Sports Illustrated* and an associate editor of *Harper's Magazine,* Mr. Plimpton lives in New York City with his wife, Freddy, and a small daughter, Medora Ames.